THE HARMONIA SACRA

THE HARMONIA SACRA,

A COMPILATION OF

GENUINE CHURCH MUSIC.

COMPRISING A GREAT VARIETY OF METRES,

𝔥𝔞𝔯𝔪𝔬𝔫𝔦𝔷𝔢𝔡 𝔣𝔬𝔯 𝔣𝔬𝔲𝔯 𝔙𝔬𝔦𝔠𝔢𝔰:

TOGETHER WITH A COPIOUS EXPLICATION OF

THE PRINCIPLES OF VOCAL MUSIC.

EXEMPLIFIED AND ILLUSTRATED WITH TABLES,

IN A PLAIN AND COMPREHENSIVE MANNER.

BY JOSEPH FUNK AND SONS.

"And the ransomed of the Lord shall return and come to Zion with songs and everlasting joy upon their heads; they shall obtain joy and gladness, and sorrow and sighing shall flee away."—ISAIAH

TWENTY-FIFTH EDITION

CONTAINING A SELECTION OF THREE-PART TUNES FROM THE FIRST AND SECOND EDITIONS OF
A COMPILATION OF GENUINE CHURCH MUSIC

Good Books®

Intercourse, PA 17534

in cooperation with
Eastern Mennonite College and Seminary, Harrisonburg, Virginia

Design by Dawn J. Ranck

THE HARMONIA SACRA
Copyright © 1993 by Good Books, Intercourse, Pennsylvania 17534
International Standard Book Number: 1-56148-104-1
Library of Congress Catalog Card Number: 93-44361

Library of Congress Cataloging-in-Publication Data

The Harmonia sacra : a compilation of genuine church music : comprising a great variety of metres, harmonized
for four voices : together with a copious explication of the principles of vocal music . . . / by Joseph Funk and sons.
-- 25th ed.
    1 score.
    For 3-4 voices, principally unacc.
    Shape-note notation.
    ISBN 1-56148-104-1 : $19.95
    1. Hymns, English. 2. Choruses, Sacred (Mixed voices)
3. Anthems. 4. Shape note hymnals. 5. Music--Theory, Elementary.
6. Mennonites--Hymns. I. Funk, Joseph, 1777-1862.
M2131.M4H37 1993

                                                                 93-44361
                                                                 CIP
                                                                 M

ACKNOWLEDGEMENTS

In bringing this twenty-fifth edition to completion, I owe a debt of gratitude to:

- Mary K. Oyer, for her constant encouragement. Mary's love for and knowledge of hymnody have been a rich resource.

- Matthew Lind, faithful fellow shape-note enthusiast, who made late-night paste-up sessions endurable and who kept me ever vigilant in the quest for clean copy.

- Kenneth Nafziger, for his helpful editorial counsel and for selecting and supplying three-part songs from early editions for inclusion in Part III of this edition.

- Lillie M. Burkholder, Mary Ellen Meyer, Lancaster Mennonite Historical Society, and Eastern Mennonite College Historical Library, for making available for reproduction old editions of *Genuine Church Music* and *The Harmonia Sacra*.

- Daniel B. Suter, for his warm support for this project.

- James Powell, for research assistance, and Mennonite Historical Library at Goshen College, for use of the J. D. Hartzler hymnal collection.

- Eastern Mennonite College and Seminary for its grant to encourage this project.

- Merle Good and Good Books, whose decision to publish this new edition came as a major assist to our efforts to get *The Harmonia Sacra* back in print and to revitalize this spirited old singing tradition.

> *"Ooh may I see thy tribes rejoice,*
> *And aid their triumphs with my voice!*
> *This is my glory, Lord, to be*
> *Join'd to thy saints, and near to thee."*
> (Isaac Watts, Psalm 106)

—James Nelson Gingerich
Goshen, Indiana
Fall, 1993

INTRODUCTION

In 1832 a Mennonite named Joseph Funk published a remarkable songbook that would have a profound influence on Mennonite singing for the following four or five generations. Its name, *Genuine Church Music,* indicated the compiler's intention that the contents be songs that, in his words, "have stood the test of time and survived the changes of fashion."

Its oblong, horizontal format, as well as its distinctive shape notes of the *fasola* system, linked it with dozens of songbooks published in America at the time to encourage musical literacy. The variety of musical content, ranging from simple psalm tunes and American folk melodies to complex early American anthems, offered ideal materials for singing schools. To reach his educational goals, Funk introduced his music with a lengthy "Elucidation of the Science of Vocal Music" (later called "Rudiments of Music"). Here he taught note reading of pitches by the *fasola* system: *mi, fa, sol,* and *la* each had a unique shape to help the learner hear pitch relationships. In addition, he described in detail the reading and conducting of rhythm.

The book's organization by poetic meter—L.M. (long meter: 8.8.8.8. syllables per line), C.M. (common meter: 8.6.8.6.), and S.M. (short meter: 6.6.8.6.), for example—made it a useful complement to books of hymn texts. In 1847 it was the tune book chosen for the first Mennonite book of hymn texts in English, *A Selection of Psalms, Hymns, and Spiritual Songs.* Each text was assigned one of the tunes from *Genuine Church Music.*

Funk's book was accepted immediately. Within fifteen years, four editions had been published and 28,000 copies sold, and by the seventeenth edition in 1878, 80,000 copies had been printed. The twenty-four editions over 161 years stayed close to Funk's original vision, with a few dramatic changes:

- By the fifth edition (1851), Funk and his sons decided to expand the shape-note system to include all seven notes of the octave. They added distinctive shapes for *do, re,* and *ti* to the *fasola* system. They also changed the name of the book to *Harmonia Sacra.*
- In the twelfth edition (1867), the three voices with melody in the middle expanded to four, with the melody in the tenor voice.
- Various editions introduced new pieces and removed others. The fifteenth edition (1876), for example, introduced an early nineteenth-century anthem, "Praise God from whom all blessings flow," known to users of *The Mennonite Hymnal* (1969) as "606."
- After the seventeenth edition (1878), the material on the rudiments of music was omitted.

- The twenty-fourth edition (1980) changed the entire format, from a horizontal to a vertical, hymnal-type book. Even more striking was the exchanging of soprano and tenor voices, making the notation match the practice of *Harmonia Sacra* singers in Virginia's Shenandoah Valley, where sopranos sing the tenor melody and tenors take the accompanying soprano line. This "Legacy Edition" made it easier for people to read and hear the songs because they look and sound much more like hymns in standard hymnals of today.

The present edition, the twenty-fifth, restores the format of the twenty-third and previous editions. It brings back the full "Rudiments of Music" section. The music begins on page 53, with Part I, "Containing the most appropriate tunes of the different metres, for public worship." Part II, "Containing the longer tunes of different metres, set pieces, and anthems" begins on page 249. The current edition's compilers have included at the end of this section twenty-six pieces (pages 355-80) that had moved in and out of earlier editions. Finally, Part III (pages 381-98) offers twenty-seven three-voice hymns from the first and second editions. These permit singers to try the *fasola* method of reading notes and thus to hear the textures that were important to Joseph Funk in 1832.

We hope this new edition will help perpetuate community music-making among Mennonites by reinvigorating traditional *Harmonia Sacra* singing.

—Mary K. Oyer
Goshen, Indiana
Fall, 1993

PREFACE.

WHEREVER man inhabits the earth the power of music is felt and acknowledged. This influence of sweet sounds, like most other gifts of our bountiful Creator, may be so used as to be the instrument of much good, or perverted to the purposes of deep and extensive evil.*

As it would be a most pernicious error to imagine that the love of music is the same thing with Christian piety, so it would be a mistake of no trifling magnitude, to deny the utility of music in awakening and strengthening our devotional affections. That utility has been demonstrated in every age by the happy experience of those who have aspired to hold communion with the Father of mercies. And it is a fact as consolatory as it is remarkable, that while Christians are lamentably divided in many articles of their faith and practice, they all agree that God should be praised in musical strains; and that, when the heart goes with the voice, this is one of the most delightful and edifying parts of His worship. Hence, in addition to those divine songs with which it has pleased the Holy Spirit himself to fill many a page of the Inspired Volume, and in imitation of them, a great number of the servants of God have employed the talent He has given them, in furnishing materials for this branch of worship, adapted to the manifold situations and emotions of the pious mind. And similar exertions have been made to supply a large and variegated treasure of music, suited in union with those poetic materials, to express and to heighten our religious desires, hopes and enjoyments. By these COMBINED MEANS, we feel more intensely and more profitably, that in God we live, move, and have our being; that all our blessings

---

* "MUSIC, though consecrated to the service of the sanctuary, and capable of good improvement in subserviency to devotion, has been, and is often, wretchedly abused to the vilest purposes. It should, therefore, be used in religious ordinances with jealousy and caution, lest it should produce a false fervor, and subserve the cause of vice, delusion, superstition, or enthusiasm"—DR. SCOTT.

are bestowed by his paternal kindness, and that our everlasting welfare results from his redeeming love towards us in Christ Jesus our Lord.

Since the first Edition of the " GENUINE CHURCH MUSIC" was brought before the public, some changes in music have taken place; among which, the practice of applying seven different syllables to the seven original sounds or notes of the scale has gained considerable ascendency, and is worthy of notice. And as this mode of solmization has become so prevalent, we think it advisable to adopt it.

But as we are well aware that the patent note system is far preferable, and has many advantages over the round, we have had the three notes, to which the three syllables Do, RE, and SI, are applied, also characterized in a uniform styl with the others, so that the singers are enabled to apply the syllables to them on sight, with the same ease as they do to the four characters. By this method the repetition of FAW, SOL, and LAW, in the scale—which has been objectionable to some—is avoided, and may be deemed an improvement.

Moreover, as the principal motive and intention in bringing out this work is to promote the cause of religion and devotion, and a solemn, dignified, and expressive style of singing in the Church of God, we have, for the greater convenience of worshiping assemblies, divided it into two parts. The FIRST PART containing a variety of the most appropriate tunes and hymns of the various kinds of metres to be sung in the time of public worship. And these are arranged in metrical order, forming a series of metres from Long Metre, or Metre First, throughout all the different kinds of poetic measures up to Metre Eighty. This order and arrangement of the metres will be found very convenient for the chorister, in selecting suitable tunes for the psalms and hymns which are to be sung by the congregated worshipers.

The SECOND PART is composed mostly of longer tunes, set pieces, and anthems, whose rhythmical construction is somewhat more intricate and difficult to perform. These are more particularly adapted to be sung in Singing-schools and Societies, though they all abound with solemn and devotional matter, not unbecoming a worshiping assembly in the house of God.

But notwithstanding the different changes and the new arrangement of matter as now presented, the great mass of the musical and poetical compositions are identical with those in former Editions, to which a number of tunes and hymns of a later date have been added, which we trust will be found of equal merit with those dignified, solemn, and heart-affecting productions of musical genius which have stood the test of time, and survived the changes of fashion. Such music, with its sublime, flowing, melodious style and pathetic expression, will never become obsolete IN THE HOUSE OF GOD; it cannot even lose a particle of its interest, while human nature remains unaltered. No frequency of use can wear out these venerable airs with the Zion traveler; no fondness for novelty can make us insensible to their sterling merit. Other pieces which are added, will be found, we doubt not, to possess much attractive beauty, and have been selected with a view to the singing of "Psalms and hymns and spiritual songs," constructed in a vast variety of poetic measures.

The Rudiments and elucidation of the science of Vocal Music, which succeed this preface, have cost us much research and labor; and for the acquisition of which, many standard works on music, both German and English, have been consulted, together with our own knowledge and experience, gained from teaching for a long series of years. And no pains have been spared to lay before our readers, in a plain, familiar, and comprehensive style—illustrated by examples and tables—every thing that is necessary in acquiring a practical knowledge of the science of Vocal Music.*

In conclusion, that this work may be instrumental in promoting, in some degree, the praises of Him, the Triune God and everlasting Father, whom angels adore, and to whom all the redeemed incessantly sing high hallelujahs, is the fervent wish of

THE COMPILERS.

* Although this work is principally intended for vocal performance, as the notes are formed in a different figurate manner, to facilitate the learner in applying the syllables to them; yet its elementary principles are equally applicable to instrumental performance, as they go hand in hand. The pitch of a note is the same whether it proceed from the vocal organs, or from the pipe or string of an instrument or any other sounding body. The scales of vocal and instrumental music—their tones and semitones, with all their intervals, both major and minor, and the letters which represent them are the same; as also the common chord with its inversions, and the inversion of all the intervals of the diatonic scale.

TO TEACHERS.

—:o:—

The position of a teacher of sacred church music is an important and highly responsible one. He should be prepared and qualified to teach and instruct his class in the elements of music, with correctness and facility, both in theory and practice, and to do this he should make it his object to become as familiar as possible with the method of instruction, and of imparting knowledge in an easy and familiar manner. He should be deeply imbued with the desire of doing good, and of refining the taste and elevating the affections. Music should be with him not merely an entertainment, a pastime, or a *means of support ;* but as a talent to be used for the service of Him to whom angels sing their high hallelujahs, and who gave it to man therewith to praise Him who is worthy of all honor and praise. Hence singing-schools of sacred Psalmody should be conducted in such a manner as to prepare its members to engage in praising God acceptably in song ; and although it is not a direct place of worship, it certainly is a place where its members should be trained and prepared for the service and participation of that holy place.

A school of sacred vocal music has so far a resemblance to the house of God, that it is a scene from which all levity should be banished far away. During a great part of the time spent in our employment, we are singing words of the most solemn and devotional import. And is such an avocation to be contemplated as a mere unmeaning form, or to be trifled with as a despicable jest ! It is impossible, if the heart possess any reverence for God and religion. All decent people admit that a light carriage in the church deserves severe rebuke : and for our part we cannot see that much less reprehension is due to the same carriage in a school of Psalmody. To have no ear, no relish for the beauties of harmony, is a defect which those who labor under it should certainly not be forward to betray. We can at best only think of it with compassion. But when a stupid contempt of music obtrudes itself into a school, with the additional deformity of injustice, bad breeding, and the scorn of sacred things, it deserves the utmost severity of censure.

It is an obvious principle in every department of religious worship, that emotions should be unfeigned. They should not be suffered to rise merely through gratified taste, but be made to spring up in the mind while it is employed in the contemplation of holy things. This important distinction will not be preserved in the hours of devotion, where it has been neglected in the seasons of practice. It requires specific religious training in schools and family circles : and will not be maintained in any other way. Habit has its influence in devotion as in other things. The deportment of singers and teachers during the hours of practice, therefore, becomes a matter of great moment. To cultivate the praises of the highest God, is a solemn work, and should ever be so regarded. Volumes would fail to show the importance of this principle. How, then, can any teacher of devotional music dare to treat it with neglect ! Yet this neglect seems to be almost universal. No wonder that the friends and cultivators of the art have so many difficulties to encounter. Let their efforts be fully Christianized, and the difficulties will be seen to vanish.

OF

VOCAL MUSIC.

COME youth, and with profundity explore
This sacred science; ponder and adore
The beauties which in Harmony abound,

And the exalted rapture of sweeet souud:
Direct your thoughts to those harmonic lays,
And in poetic numbers your CREATOR praise.

CHAPTER I.
—

OF MUSIC AND MUSICAL SOUNDS.

Section 1.—Music is composed of sounds producd by the human voice or by different kinds of musical instruments.

These sounds vary in pitch according to certain fixed and determinate degrees.

The pitch and gradation of these sounds from the lowest or most grave to the highest or most acute, form the whole scale of musical sounds.

A combination and succession of these sounds, sweetly tuned and performed in rhythmical order, have, by their rich, mellifluent, melodious, and harmonious progression—their sweetly moving accents and flowing numbers, a benign, winning, and powerful influence over the human mind.

Sec. 2.—The *Natural Scale* of musical sounds, though its extent is unlimited, consists of only *seven primary notes*. For it is found that after singing or playing these seven notes, if we continue the series, we repeat another scale similar to the first, and so on, as far as the extent of the voice or the instruments will go.

The voice in producing these sounds naturally passes from the first sound taken, a *step* to the second; from the second a *step* to the third; from the third a *half-step* to the fourth; from the fourth a *step* to the fifth; from the fifth a *step* to the sixth; from the sixth a *step* to the seventh; and from the seventh a *half-step* to the eighth, which completes the Octave, and is the first note of a succeeding scale.

NOTE.—The whole range of human hearing comprised between the lowest note of the organ, and the highest cry of know insects, seems to include about NINE OCTAVES, which will extend to sixty-four diatonic intervals.

Sec. 3.—There are three distinctions made in musical sounds; 1st, they may be *high or low;* 2nd, they may be *long or short;* 3rd, they may be *loud or soft.*

These three distinctions of sound embrace PITCH, LENGTH, and POWER.

Pitch regards a sound as *high or low;* Length, as *long or short;* and Power, as *loud or soft;* and these three distinctions form the essential property and peculiar qualification of good musical sounds.

On these three distinctions are founded three departments, namely, MELODY, RHYTHM, and DYNAMICS or Musical Elocution, which departments will be noticed and treated of in their proper places.

Sec. 4.—The doctrine of music may be arranged under six different heads: 1. Notation; 2. Rhythm; 3. Intonation; 4. Melody; 5. Harmony; and 6. Dynamics or Musical Elocution. But such is the nature of music, that the different heads or departments cannot be treated separately and apart; but by their close connection, they will be intermingled in theory and practice, though in the main they may be considered separately.

NOTE 1.—By NOTATION are given or represented all the marks and characters appropriate for the purpose of writing music, with their signification and use.

2. RHYTHM is the division of time into short portions, by a regular succession of motion, impulses and sounds, with regard to measure, accent, emphasis, and cadence; and flowing numbers, in the union of music and poetry.

3. INTONATION is practising the notes of the scale with the voice, or playing them on an instrument, according to fixed degrees of sound, and giving a correct sound to all the diatonic intervals, the triads and their inversions, and all the disjoint intervals in the whole scale.

4. MELODY is an agreeable succession of single sounds in a piece arranged according to the laws of Intonation and Rhythm, so as to be musical and pleasing to the ear. Melody and intonation are closely connected.

5. HARMONY is an agreeable succession of chords, or concordant notes, in two, three or four parts, moving together according to the rules of progression, which produce a diversity of flowing sounds highly pleasing, attractive, inviting and delightful.

6. DYNAMICS or MUSICAL ELOCUTION consists in giving each tone or note that sound, stress, and modulation of voice which the subject of the poetry requires, in relation to loud or soft, strong or mild, and the swelling or diminishing of the sounds or notes.

QUESTIONS.

Of what is music composed?—How do these sounds vary?—What forms the whole scale of musical sounds?—Has the scale of musical sounds any limitation?—Of how many primary sounds does the scale consist?—If there are only seven primary sounds, how can the scale be unlimited?—What is the order in which the voice produces these sounds?—How many distinctions are made in musical sounds?—What is the first distinction?—The second?—The third?—What forms the essential property of good musical sounds?—What departments are founded on these three distinctions?—Under how many heads is the doctrine of music treated?—What are those six heads?

——:0:——

CHAPTER II.

NOTATION.

OF THE STAFF, CLEFS, LETTERS, &C.

Sec. 5.—The pitch of musical sounds or tones is represented by a character called a staff. The scale and music are written on the staff with notes. The *position* which the notes occupy on the staff represents the *pitch*, and the notes, by their relative value, the *length* of sounds.

The staff consists of five lines and four spaces. Each line and each space is called a degree of sound; thus there are nine degrees of sound on the staff. When more than nine degrees are wanted, the spaces below and above the staff are used; and if a still greater compass is wanted, additional lines are used, called leger or added lines.

THE STAFF WITH ADDED LINES.

Sec. 6.—Each part of music has a separate staff, and these differ in pitch. Hence to adjust their pitch, and to distinguish them, characters are used called Clefs. There are two clefs in common use, the F clef and the G clef.

The F clef represents F, the fourth line of the Base Staff, and the seventh sound of the General Scale of music.

The G clef represents G, the second line of the Tenor staff, and the eighth sound of the General Scale. It is also used on the second line of the Treble and alto staffs, representing G also, and the fifteenth sound of the General Scale when sung by female voices.

EXAMPLES OF THE STAFFS AND CLEFS.

Base Staff and Clef.	Tenor Staff and Clef.	Treble Staff and Clef.
F-Clef-7	G-Clef-8.	G-Clef-15.

NOTE.—It is ascertained that the interval between the male voice and the female is exactly an octave, which is the most perfect chord in the scale of music. Hence, as the Treble is principally assigned to female voices, it is placed an octave higher in the General Scale than the Tenor. From this we learn that the ALL-WISE CREATOR has implanted harmony between the sexes of the human race. [How happy would all those be who stand together in matrimonial relation, if they would observe, by a pious life, and a holy conversation, in Christian love, to fill up the interval of life with sweet harmonious chords, so that no dissonant or jarring string might vibrate between them!]

Sec. 7.—BRACE.—When music is written on these staffs, and performed simultaneously, they are united by a character callen a *Brace*, and form a Score. The score may, however, consist of *two, three* or *four* parts. When two parts only are united, it is called a *Duet ;* when three parts, a *Trio ;* and when four parts, a *Quartet.*

EXAMPLE :

Score of TRIO.

Sec. 8.—NUMERALS.—Numerals are used to point out the different degrees of sound in the scale of music. They will also be exclusively used in this work, in a fractional position, to indicate the different measures in the movements of Common, Triple, and Compound time.

Sec. 9.—LETTERS.—To represent the seven original sounds of music, the first seven letters of the alphabet are used, namely, A, B, C, D, E, F, G. These letters are placed on the staffs in alphabetical order, counting upwards from the lowest. The natural diatonic scale of the minor key commencing with A, and that of the major key commencing with C, in the following manner :

A　B　C　D　E　F　G　A　B
1　2　3　4　5　6　7　Numerals of the Minor Scale.
Numerals of Major Scale.　1　2　3　4　5　6　7

Sec. 10.—But as letters are not calculated to show forth and adjust the *length* of sounds, the proper length is indicated by the form of certain characters called Notes. And besides the rhythmical representation of these notes, they have also a distinct figurate form whereby the syllables *do, re, me, faw, sol, law,* and *si* are applied to them in solmization individually, on sight—their form indicating the syllable which is applied to them.

And as these syllables are always used in the scale in the same relation and invariable position to the key, they form a strong and inseparable association with the proper pitch of the intervals of the scale which they individually and invariably occupy. And as they have thus the proper pitch of the intervals of the scale associated with their names, it is of great service to the vocal performer, to have them communicated to the mind on sight, as thereby he will be enabled to strike the proper interval of the scale *on sight* of the note, and be relieved of the irksome task of finding the name by calculation, in every change of key. See those notes with their corresponding *Rests*, exemplified by the following Table. [See table next page.]

As these notes, by their names—as a whole note, a half note, &c., indicate to the *mind*, their proper relation of sound ; and by their heads, stems, hooks or dashes, represent to the *eye*, the same relative length, it is almost superfluous to state, that *one* semibreve is equal in duration of time, to *two* minims, or *four* crotchets, or *eight* quavers, or *sixteen* semiquavers. For it is evident that as many parts as the whole note is divided into, so many of these parts it will take to amount to the same whole note again. And if we allow four seconds of time to sound out the whole note, we must allow but two seconds for the half note, one for the quater note, half a second for the eighth note, and a quarter of a second for the sixteenth. This is the invariable proportion and comparative relation in which these notes stand to each other ; a strict observance of which is of the highest importance, both to the vocal and to the instrumental performer.

EXAMPLES :

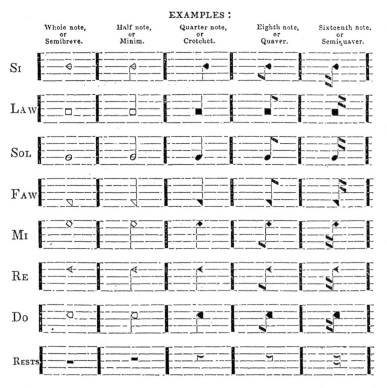

| | Whole note, or Semibreve. | Half note, or Minim. | Quarter note, or Crotchet. | Eighth note, or Quaver. | Sixteenth note, or Semiquaver. |

SI

LAW

SOL

FAW

MI

RE

DO

RESTS

RESTS are marks of silence, and are named after the notes which they represent.

NOTE 1.—Other notes are sometimes used, as a thirty-second and sixty-fourth ; these notes are, however, too quick and short for sacred music, and can easily be dispensed with.

A note called a BREVE, from which the semibreve derived its name—was also formerly used : but this note is too long and heavy a sound for any musical expression.

NOTE 2.—Nothing can be more certain than the fact that there is a true and inseparable union and association formed between these syllables which are applied to the notes and the proper pitch or sound of the intervals which they respectively and invariably occupy in the scale. For on this fact is founded the whole doctrine of transposition, and of transposing with the keys, the syllables with the notes, in their relative position to the keys. And it is evident that when the diatonic scale, which consists of tones and semitones, is sung to a series of notes and syllables always applied in the same order and relation to those tones and semitones, as they stand in their fixed position in the scale, that such an association will unavoidably be formed between them.

And hence arises the utility of having the notes characterized and formed in such a manner as to communicate by their different forms, the syllable which is applied to them, individually, so as to enable the singers to strike the proper pitch of the sound on sight of the note. And is it not strange that any should deny the usefulness of the character notes by which the syllables are known by the forms of the notes, when common sense and sound reason dictate that it opens and paves a highway for the student of vocal music to travel on, and to pursue his course with pleasure till he has acquired a complete knowledge of the science of music. And is this in any wise degrading to the science—diminishing its value—or robbing it of its intrinsic merit ? By no means. It is adorning it with the vesture of simplicity, the richest dress in which it and its sister sciences can be arrayed. And in proof of this, let us cast our eyes to other arts and sciences, and see what has been done by the use of different characters, to pave the way for instruction, and to communicate to the mind correct ideas of what is to be inculcated and taught, and we will find an almost endless variety of characters, figures, cuts, drawings and delineations used to facilitate the learner in his progress in gaining scientific knowledge.

Do not the Lexicographers, WALKER and WEBSTER, in their famed Dictionaries—which are taken as standard works—use many different characters, to convey to the mind on sight a correct pronunciation of the words and the proper sounds of the letters,—all of which might be acquired by a reference to grammar rules ? And is there less propriety for the singer to have the correct sound of the notes conveyed to the mind on sight, by characters which might otherwise be acquired by having reference to the rules laid down in the science ; which is, by making a calculation from the key ?

NOTE 3.—Rests are essential to music, in order to keep the accent in its proper place in the measure; and if sparingly used and skilfully observed, give variety, beauty, and expression both to music and poetry. When long intervals of silence occur in any part of the score, let those on the silent part, for their own improvement, notice the parts which others are singing, and mark the time with them, till they arrive at the place where their own parts unite again. This is far preferable to poring over their own staff and measures of silence, by which is gained but little improvement.

Sec. 11.—Notes become subject to some variation by having additional characters annexed or added.

A dot or point (.) placed after any note, adds one-half to its original length. Thus a dotted whole note is equal in length to three half notes: a dotted half note to three quarters, and so on.

Four dots between the lines of the staff, mark the place from whence a strain or piece of music is repeated.

EXAMPLES:

Sec. 12.—A Pause (⌢) placed over or under a note protracts or lengthens it out about one third longer than its original time: though this protraction may be longer or shorter according to the expression of the poetry, and the taste of the judicious performer.

A soft, graceful swell given to a paused note, followed by a momentary rest, is highly ornamental.

The pause is frequently used on the note of the last syllable in a line of poetry, and agrees with its final pause, which, in reading is marked with a suspension of the voice.

The pause is also used over *Rests* which need lengthening out; as also over *Bars*, where it is thought proper to have a momentary pause between two measures. Some of the most striking effects depend upon this character, and when well performed, it adds strength and beauty to music and poetry.

EXAMPLES:

Sec. 13.—Notes are frequently tied together by a circular line called a Tie: or grouped together by hooks or dashes. All the notes thus tied or grouped, are sung or warbled to one syllable of verse.

If three notes are thus tied or grouped together, with the figure 3 above or below them, they are performed in the time of two notes of the same kind without the figure, and are called Triplets. Triplets, when smoothly and skilfully performed, are ornamental to music.

EXAMPLES:

Tie.   Group.   Triplets.

QUESTIONS.

What character represents the pitch of musical sounds?---On what character is the scale and music written?---With what characters is music written on the staff?---What does the position of the notes represent?---How many degrees of sound can be written on the staff?---What is done when more than nine degrees of sound are wanted?---If a still greater compass is needed?---How many clefs are in common use?---Why are they called the F clef and the G clef?---How many sounds does the octave contain?---What is a score?---How many letters of the alphabet are used to represent musical sounds ?—How many original sounds are there in music ?—How many notes are in common use ?—How are the notes named ?—What is the form of the whole note ?—Ans. An open note without a stem.—The half note ? A. An open note with a stem.—The quarter note ? A. A black note with a stem.—The eighth note ? A. A black note with a stem and one hook.—The sixteenth note ? A. A black note with a stem and two hooks.—What is the use of rests ?—Has each note a corresponding rest ?—How much does a dot add to a note ? —What do dots indicate when placed on the staff?—What is the use of the pause ? —On what note is the pause most frequently used ?—What is a tie ?—A group ?— A Triplet ?

———:o:———

CHAPTER III.

—

NOTATION.

—

OF SHARPS, FLATS, NATURALS, &c.

Sec. 14.—The diatonic scale consists of five tones and two semitones. These are sometimes called *steps* and *half-step*, because the voice steps along through the scale from one interval to the other ; but the interval of a semitone is only half the distance of the interval of a tone. And to adjust the semitones and always keep them in their fixed position in the scale, throughout the course of transposition three characters are used —a *Sharp* (♯), a *Flat* (♭), and a *Natural* (♮). A sharp *raises* a letter or note a semitone ; a flat *depresses* a letter or note a semitone ; and a natural *restores* a letter or note thus sharped or flatted, to its original sound. When these characters occur, in the course of a piece of music, they are called *Accidentals*, and operate only on the notes before which they are placed.

When sharps or flats are placed at the commencement of a tune, they operate on all the notes of the letters which are thus sharped or flatted, throughout the tune. Thus they prepare and adjust the tones and the semitones for the new key, and become the signature (or sign for the key note) to the tune. And when accidentals occur throughout the tune, on the letters thus sharped or flatted, they are raised or depressed, as the case may require, by a natural.

EXAMPLES :

Signature by sharps.   Signature by flats.
F Sharp.   F and C Sharp.   B Flat.   B and E Flat.

ACCIDENTALS.

Sharps.   Flats.   Naturals.

Sec. 15.—BARS.—When music is written on the staff, it is divided into measures by a character called a Bar.

There are three bars in use on the staff—the common bar, the broad bar, and the double bar. When a short bar is added to the broad bar, it forms a close.

EXAMPLES :

Common Bar.   Broad Bar.   Double Bar.   Close.

The common bar is used to divide the staff into equal timed measures according to the measure note or notes, of either Common, Triple or Compound measures.

The broad bar is used, by some authors, at the close of each line in poetry. But as that frequently falls in the middle of the regular measures of the staff, it is omitted by others. However as the last syllable of each line of poetry is distinguished by the *final pause*, which marks the bounds of the metre by a suspension of the voice, there can be no impropriety in using it to point out that important syllable or word.

The double bar is used at the end of a strain which is to be repeated from the mark of repetition. (*Example Sec.* 11.) It is also used at a change of measure from Common to Triple, or Compound time, or the reverse. Also at a change of mode from major to minor, or the reverse. Likewise at the commencement of a chorus.

The close is used at the end of a tune or any piece of music.

Sec. 16.—SYNCOPATED AND DRIVING NOTES.—A syncopated note is the blending of two notes into one,—an unaccented with an accented in the middle of a measure, with the previous accented note of the same measure tied with it. As this note is struck on the unaccented part, while the hand, in marking the time, is at rest, and its sound continued over the accented part, while the hand is in motion, the regular movement in that measure is thereby thwarted, or broken in upon, which produces a fluttering effect on the note, or on the syllable or word applied.

When a longer note is wanted in a measure than the measure will contain, the long note is cut through, and one part is put in the next measure, and both parts tied together across the bar: these two notes compose the *driving note*. Thus *two half notes sung across a bar* produce the same sound with *a whole note in a measure;* a half and a fourth note across the bar, the same sound with a dotted minim in a measure. The same remarks apply to two fourth notes driven across a bar, and a half note in a measure.

The driving note is sometimes called a *syncope*—a synonymous term with syncopation—both signifying the division, or cutting through a note by a bar, or accent expressed or understood. Hence the driving note may also be termed a syncope, as it is cut through by a bar, and commences on the unaccented part of the measure, and extends to the accented.

APPOGIATURA.—The appogiatura is a note of embellishment. It is a diminutive note, prefixed to a principal note, and is always on the accented part of the measure. It borrows its time from the principal note that follows and to which it is tied. As this note produces a fluttering sound similar to that of a syncope, it may be brought in at this place, and classed with the syncopated notes.

PASSING OR TRANSIENT NOTES.—These are also called *ornamental and grace notes.* They, too, are diminutive notes, and are used between the essential notes, where they become intermediate steps on the unaccented parts of the measure, in passing from one disjoint interval to another, and thus connect, embellish, and soften those intervals, diminish the roughness of the leap, and direct an easy and graceful movement.

They borrow their time from the preceding note to which they are tied.

CHOOSING NOTES.—Choosing notes are set perpendicularly one above the other, either of which may be sung: and as there is always a concordant interval between them, both may be sung at the same time by different voices.

EXAMLLES :

Syncopated notes.   Driving notes.   Appogiatures.

EXAMPLES:

Passing or Grace Notes.   Choosing Notes.

NOTE.—Since the diminutive notes in the preceding section are merely orna-mental, and not taken in the account in the harmony; and since other graces—*so called*—are frequently introduced, in many works, such as the Acciacatu-ra, Cadenza, Grupetto, Mordento, Portemento di voce, Transient Shake, Contin-ued Shake, Stracino, and the Turn; the only disign of the most of which is, to display the dexterity and facility of execution of the performer; and when skil-fully performed, they *may* be tolerated; but they have no place in music designed to exhibit and call forth the emotions of the heart. They have no soul in them. And when they are reserved for the flight of some fanciful, injudicious perform-er, they too often prove the empty wanderings of ignorance and folly. And rather than simplicity should be so offended, it would be better to dispense with them altogether. They are rather ornamental than graceful, designed to give brilliancy, and not to excite emotions. The imagination may indeed be amused, but the heart remains uninterested. Such an attempt at display exhibits not only want of taste and judgment, but also want of science. The fact is, that music resembles every other art; the farther a person advances in the study of it, the more does he delight in the simplicity of manner, and the less is he at-tracted by superficial ornament.—*Porter's Mus. Cyc.*

QUESTIONS.

Of what does the diatonic scale consist?---What are these tones and semitones sometimes called?---How many tones and semitones are contained in the scale?---What characters are used to regulate these tones and semitones?---What effect has a sharp on a letter or note?---A flat?---A natural?---What effect have flats and sharps when placed at the beginning of a tune?---How is the staff divided?---By what character is the staff divided into measures?---What, then, is the use of the common bar?---The broad bar?---The double bar?---The close?---What is a synco-pated note?---A Driving note?---Appogiatures?---Passing or grace notes?---Choos-ing notes?

CHAPTER IV.

NOTATION.

OF RHYTHMICAL MEASURES IN COMMON, TRIPLE, AND COMPOUND TIME

Sec. 17.—Among the different writers on music, no less than twenty-six different measures of time have been brought out, all of which are marked or expressed by numerals placed in a fractional position. Those of Common or even time are expressed by the fractions $\frac{2}{1}, \frac{2}{2}, \frac{2}{4}, \frac{2}{8}, \frac{4}{4}, \frac{4}{4}, \frac{4}{8}, \frac{4}{16}$. Those of Triple or uneven time are expressed by the fractions $\frac{3}{2}, \frac{3}{4}, \frac{3}{8}, \frac{3}{16}, \frac{9}{4}, \frac{9}{8}, \frac{9}{16}$. And those of compound time—which is also an even time, by the fractions, $\frac{6}{2}, \frac{6}{4}, \frac{6}{8}, \frac{12}{8}, \frac{12}{16}, \frac{12}{32}, \frac{18}{8}, \frac{18}{16}, \frac{18}{32}, \frac{24}{16}, \frac{24}{32}$. Many of the fore-going measures have, however, gone out of use; but some are still re-tained by some authors, which, when dispensed with, will simplify and improve the science. If we retain seven different measures of the twen-ty-six above-mentioned, it will be an ample supply for all the purposes of music, no matter how intricate the rhythmical construction may be.

Of the seven different measures which will be retained and used in this work, three will be in Common time, two in Triple, and two in Compound.

The numerals used for all these different measures will be placed in a fractional position, to which fractions the whole note will be the in-teger. Thus the fractions will at once express the contents of the dif-ferent measures to which they are invariably used.

Sec. 18.—COMMON OR EVER TIME.—To Common or even time will be assigned three distinct measures; the first will be marked with the figures $\frac{2}{2}$; the second $\frac{4}{4}$; and the third $\frac{2}{4}$. Of these three meas-ures, it will, however, be found that the first and second, by their close

connection and commingling, are identical, save that to the first may
be assigned a slower movement, as it is mostly employed to the most
solemn, devotional, and dignified music for the church of God.   These
measures are called *even*, because they naturally divided into even parts
—two and four—and have feet of equal or even measured verse applied
to them ; and in their primitive state will admit of no other feet of poetry ; though they may be so arranged and varied in their derivatives,
that they will admit all the various metres that are contained in poetry,
to be sung to them.

Measures are in their primitive state when they are filled with the
notes which the fraction, by which they are marked, expresses.   The
upper figure, or numerator of the fraction, giving the number of notes
which a primitive measure contains ; and the lower figure, or denominator of the fraction, points out into how many parts the whole note is
divided, and thus specifies whether they be half, fourth, or eighth
notes.

Sec. 19.—The three foregoing measures will be illustrated in their
primitive state, with a number of derivatives, by the following

EXAMPLES :

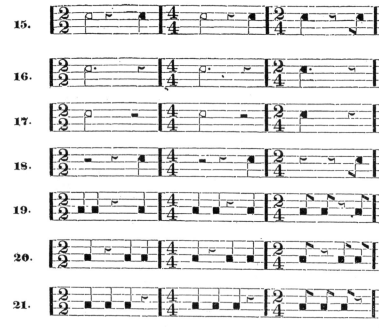

minim for its measure note, whereas the others have a semibreve; and consequently its rhythmical movement is faster.

Sec. 20.—Triple or Uneven Time.—To Triple or uneven time will be assigned two distinct measures. The first is marked by the fraction $\frac{3}{2}$; and the second by $\frac{3}{4}$. These two measures are identical in their rhythmical construction, and only differ in the length of their measure notes; the first containing three minims in its primitive measure, and the second three crotchets; in consequence of which, the second flows along more quickly in its rhythmical movement than the first.

These measures are all uneven, because they naturally divide into *three* equal parts; and thus having an uneven number of notes in their primitive measures, none other than uneven measured verse can readily be applied to them in their primitive state. But they may be so varied and arranged in their derivatives, that verse composed of all the various kinds of feet and metres may be applied to them.

As in Common or even time, so in Triple or uneven time, the fractions point out or mark the contents of the primitive measures. The improper fraction $\frac{3}{2}$ designates by its upper figure or numerator, 3, that three notes fill the measure; and the lower figure or denominator, 2, designates that the whole note is divided into two parts, and consequently, those three notes which fill the measure are half notes. In like manner the fraction $\frac{3}{4}$ designates that three fourth notes constitute its primitive measure.

Sec. 21.—These two measures of Triple time will be illustrated in their primitive form, and with a number of their derivatives, by the following

Note.—In the foregoing examples of the three measures of Common or even time, their primitives and their derivatives, the learner will readily discover that these measures are alike in nature, and that the first and second are identical. For, in the third example of derivatives, the derivative of the first is the primitive of the second, and the derivative of the second is the primitive of the first; and in all the subsequent derivatives their measures are alike. They are also the same in their accents, for in many tunes they intermix, having, in some measures, two minims and one accent; and in others four crotchets, with two accents. The third measure differs from the first and second only in that it has a

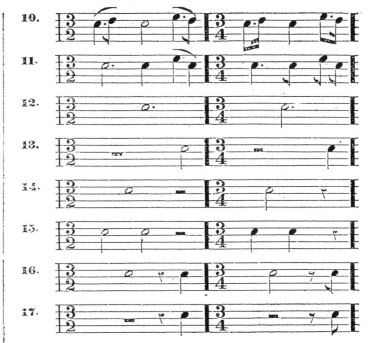

NOTE.—In the foregoing examples of the two measures of Triple time, it may readily be discovered, that in their primitives and in their derivatives their rhythmical construction is the same, save that the first measure is slower in its movement than the second—the first having three minims in its primitive measure, and the second three crotchets. These measures may be so constructed and varied, as to take one, two or three accents to the measure, according to the requisition of the poetry which is applied. This will be noticed and illustrated in its proper place.

Sec. 22.—COMPOUND OR DOUBLE TRIPLE MEASURES.—The Com

pound measure is an even measure; as two uneven numbers added together make an even.—Two distinct measures will be assigned to Compound time; the first of which will be designated by the fraction $\frac{6}{4}$, and the second by $\frac{6}{8}$. These two measures, like the former, are identical in their rhythmical construction, and only differ in the duration of their time; as the fourth notes are longer than the eighths.

These measures are even, because they naturally divide into two equal parts, and have two accents in each measure.

As in Common and Triple time, so in Compound, the fractions point out the contents of the primitive measures. The improper fraction $\frac{6}{4}$, designates that six fourth notes constitute the primitive measure; and the fraction $\frac{6}{8}$, that six eighth notes are contained in the primitive measure.

Sec. 23.—See the measures of Compound time—in their primitives, with many of their derivatives—illustrated by the following

EXAMPLES:

15.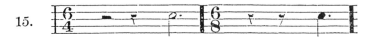

NOTE.—In the foregoing examples of the two measures of Compound time, it will readily be seen that they are the same in their primitive construction, and in their derivatives, save that the first contains two pointed minims in a measure, and the second two pointed crotchets, and, consequently, the second is performed faster than the first. These measures may be so constructed and varied as to take two feet of dactylic verse, or two feet of trochaic.

In all the foregoing examples of the primitive and derivative measures, in Common, Triple, and Compound time, it will be found, that by the various constructions and rhythmical arrangements of the different notes and ties, in the various measures, all the different feet of poetry may be applied to them, and agree with them in time, accent, emphasis and cadence.

QUESTIONS.

How many varieties of measure are used in this work ?—What are the different kinds of time and movement of these seven measures? Ans. Common or even time; Triple, or uneven time; and Compound time.—How many varieties has Common time ?--Triple ?--Compound ?—By what fraction is the first measure of Common time marked ?—The second ?—The third ?—The first measure of Triple ?—The second ? —The first measure of Compound ?—The second ?—Is the Compound measure an even or an uneven measure?—Ans. It is an even measure, because two uneven numbers added together make an even.—Can these seven different measures be so arranged and constructed in their notes that all the different feet of poetic measures may be applied to, and agree with them, in all their rhythmical construction relative to time, accent, emphasis, and cadence ?

——:o:——

CHAPTER V.
——
RHYTHM.
—
OF TIME, ACCENT, EMPHASIS, AND CADENCE.

Sec. 24.—Nothing is more essential to the due performance of music than adjusting the *time* to the intention and meaning of the poetry.

Some of the most striking effects of music are produced by the change of time.

The *slow* naturally has a solemn, grave, and serious tendency, and the *lively* tends to joy and cheerfulness.

Destroy the time, or thwart the measure, and you rob the strain of its interest and charm.

The less we are made sensible of anything mechanical in giving or keeping the time, the more fully will the effect of the melody and harmony be allowed to operate, and the more deeply will the mind be penetrated with the feeling to be awakened.

But as notes are used in different rhythmical measures and movements, as also have different measures of poetry applied, they have not a positive length, but only a relative; yet it is proper that some definite time should be fixed for all the different measures, in the movements of Common, Triple, and Compound time, as a standard to guide the chorister to a consistent movement in all those measures; from which, however, it may be allowed to vary according to the requirement of the poetry.

Perhaps the most appropriate time which can be assigned to all the foregoing varieties of measure, is *three seconds* to the first and second measures of Common, and to the first of Triple and Compound time; and the third of Common, and second of Triple and Compound, about one-third faster.

Thus we have six measures— the first and second of Common time being blended into one—all of various rhythmical movements; this being an ample supply for all the poetic measures that can be written.

All the measures of Common time have *two* beats in the measure; a *down* beat on the first part of the measure, and an up beat on the second; and when two feet of trochaic verse are applied to them, they have two accents, but when only one foot of verse is applied, they have but one accent.

NOTE.—Some authors and teachers recommend four beats—down—left—right —up—to be given to the measures of 4-4 time; there may be some advantage in this arrangement, and the judicious teacher will decide for himself between two or four beats.

The measures of Triple time have *three* beats to each measure, two *down* and one *up*. In their primitive state they have but one accent, and one dactylic foot of verse applied to them; but each measure may be so varied as to take two, and even three accents to the measure, with two or three feet of trochaic verse.

The Compound measures have two accents in the measure, whether the verse be even or uneven—trochaic or dactylic, and *two* beats to each measure, a *down* beat on the first part, and an *up* beat on the fourth.

Each of the foregoing measures, in their different movements, may be so arranged, as to take as many accents as it has beats performed to it : but no accented syllable can properly be sung to a note on which the hand is not in motion, when marking the time. (See chap. 6.)

The first and second measures of Common time are identical in their rhythmical construction, as is evidently seen in the examples of the derivatives in chap. 4, sec. 19. But still it may be of some advantage to music to retain them both, and use the first to those pieces, the most of whose measures contain but one foot of verse and one accent; and the second to those pieces whose measures mostly contain two feet of verse, and two accents.

Note.—To measure musical time with accuracy and precision, a vibratory pendulum may be used, which may be regulated by the length of its cord, to swing or vibrate to any given time.

A pendulum is a heavy body, such as a piece of brass or lead, suspended by a wire or cord, so as to swing backward and forward. And when it swings, it is said to vibrate; and that part of a circle through which it vibrates is called its arc. The vibrations are nearly equal whether it pass through a less or greater space of its arc; so that there will be no material difference in its vibrations or oscillations, whether it pass *six feet* through its arc, or only *six inches*. Hence,

A ball of some heavy metal of about one inch in diameter, suspended by a fine dense cord of 39.2 inches in length from the centre of the ball to the centre of its motion, or the pin from which it is suspended, will vibrate once every second. The length of this pendulum will vibrate to the beats of the measures of the third movement of Common time, and to the first of Triple, and the second of Compound : each of these movements having one second allowed to each part of their measures, and consequently to each beat.

For the first and second movements of Common time, and the first of Compound, the cord of the pendulum must be 88.2 inches long: this makes one vibration in one and a half seconds, and vibrates in accordance with those measures which have two beats to the measure, and are performed in three seconds.

The second movement of Triple time has no equivalent in its measure, as it has three beats, performed in two seconds; whereas the third movement of Common time has but two in the same space of time; and, consequently, this requires a cord whose length is but 17 inches, to vibrate in accordance with the beating of its time.

There is now an instrument constructed called a Metronome, which by a short pendulum, with a sliding weight, and set in motion by clock-work, serves to measure time in music.

Sec. 25.—Accent and emphasis form the essence of versification and music. It is from this source that poetry and music derive their dignity, variety, expression, and significancy. Without these requisites music and poetry would be heavy and lifeless : they would fail to animate our feelings : and the meaning of the verse would be ambiguous and unintelligible. Consequently, as the accent of the music must exactly and invariably agree with the accent and emphasis of the poetry, when united, it makes it indispensably necessary for the learner to acquire some knowledge of the nature and propriety of accent and emphasis, and the rules for applying them, both to music and poetry.

Accent is the laying of a peculiar stress of the voice on a certain syllable in a word, or on a note in music, that they may be better heard than the rest, or distinguished from them. Every word of more than one syllable, has one or more syllables accented. For example: the words *music*, *musical* and *musically* have the first syllables accented ;

the words *become, becoming,* and *becomingly* have the second syllable accented ; and the words *contravene, contravener,* and *contravention,* have the third syllable accented. Now, when monosyllables, which, properly speaking, have no accent, are combined with other syllables, and form a phrase, the stress which is laid on one syllable, in preference to another, is called emphasis: and thus emphasis, in monosyllables, supplies the place of accent, and is the same with it in dissyllables and polysyllables.

Sec. 26.—Time in music and poetry is the quantity or length by which is assigned to every particular note and syllable its due measure, without making it either longer or shorter than it ought to be There are two kinds of time in music, namely, *Common or equal time,* and, *Triple or unequal time.* These TIMES are regulated by the accent, which is laid on particular parts of the measure, the regulation of which must agree with the measures of poetry into feet, where the accent is laid on particular syllables, by means of which the voice steps along through the verse in a regularly measured pace, which is delightful, musical, and pleasing.

Poetry is measured by feet. All feet in poetry consist either of two or of three syllables. Feet of two syllables are equal, and feet of three syllables are unequal. Consequently, poetry may be divided into two parts, namely, *equal measured verse* and *unequal measured verse.* Verse of equal measure consists of feet of two syllables, and verse of unequal measure consists of feet of three syllables. Each of these measures may be subdivided into two parts ; the first or equal measure into TROCHAIC and IAMBIC, and the second or unequal measure into DACTYLIC and ANAPAESTIC measure.

Verses of Trochaic measure consist of feet of two syllables, having the first syllable of each foot accented, and the last unaccented.

Verses of Iambic measure consist also of feet of two syllables, having the first syllable of each foot unaccented, and the second accented.

Verses of Dactylic measure consist of feet of three syllables, having the first syllable of each foot accented, and the last two unaccented.

Verses of Anapaestic measure consist also of feet of three syllables, having the first two syllables unaccented, and the last accented.

EXAMPLES :
TROCHAIC FEET OF POETRY WITH MEASURES OF MUSIC.

IAMBIC FEET OF POETRY WITH MEASURES OF MUSIC.

In the foregoing representations, where the poetic measures are divided into their respective feet of two and three syllables, the words used at the head of each of their divisions represent by their accent, the respective feet of poetry and measures of music to which they belong. Thus the Trochaic foot is represented by the dissyllables, beauty, bounty, kindness, &c.; the Iambic by befriend, become, attend, compose, &c.; the Dactylic by the trissyllables cherubim, paradise, meditate, gravitate, &c.; and the Anapaestic by appertain, intervene, importune, overflow, &c.

In the example of trochaic feet, it will readily be seen, that the accent of the poetry, in each division, agrees with the accent of the music.

But as the first part of the musical measure is invariably accented, and the last part unaccented, it will be discovered, that,

In the example of Iambic measure the feet must be divided by the common bar, and the first syllable of each foot put in the last part of the measure, and the last syllable in the first part, as may readily be seen in the example. And thus the accent of the poetic feet and of the musical measures will agree and be retained in their proper places.

In the example of the Dactylic feet, it will be seen that the poetic feet agree with the measures of music; they both having the accent on the first part; but,

In the example of Anapaestic feet it will be discovered that the foot of poetry must be divided by the bar, and the first two syllables of each foot put in the last part of one measure, and the last syllable in the first part of the next ; so that the two unaccented syllables possess the unaccented part of the musical measure, and the accented syllable the accented part.

The preceding are the principal feet and measures, of which all species of English verse wholly or chiefly consist. These measures, however, are capable of many variations, by their intermixture with each other, and by the admission of secondary feet. From this intermixture it is, that we have such a variety of metres

NOTE.—The *Secondary* feet of poetry are—

1. A SPONDEE, having both the words or syllables accented, as in the words A̅-men, pa̅le mo̅on.

2. A PYRRHIC, having both the words or syllables unaccented, as ŏn thĕ hĭgh rŏck.

3. AN AMPHIBRACH, having the first and last syllables unaccented, and the middle one accented, as in the words, dĕ-lī̅ght-fŭl, ă-me̅nd-mĕnt.

4. A TRIBRACH, having all its syllables unaccented, as in the words, nŭ-mĕ-ră-blĕ, vă-rĭ-ă-blĕ, cŏn-quĕr-ă-blĕ.

The Spondee and Pyrrhic are both feet of two syllables, the one having both syllables accented, and the other both unaccented; and the Amphibrach and Tribrach are both feet of three syllables, the one having all its syllables unaccented, and the other the first and third unaccented, and the middle accented. Hence,

No piece of poetry can be formed by the secondary feet alone, which is evident from the fact that the Spondee has both its syllables accented ; and the Pyrrhic and the Tribrach have all their syllables unaccented; consequently the Spondaic measure would form a line in succession of all *accented* syllables ; and the measure of the Pyrrhic and Tribrach would each form a line in succession of all *unaccented* syllables. The Amphibrach measure, as it has the first and third syllables unaccented, and the second accented, would, by a regular suc-

cession of its feet, form a line of one accented syllable and two unaccented ones, and thus lose itself in the Dactylic or Anapaestic measure. Hence, it is evident that there can be no poetry formed of the four secondary feet alone ; but that they only tend to improve, enrich, beautify, and diversify the poetry of the four principal feet.

QUESTIONS.

Have notes a positive or only a relative length ?—May not some positive length of time be assigned to them and to the different measures ?—What is the most appropriate length of the first two measures of Common time, and the first measure of Triple and Compound ?—How much faster should the last measures of their movements be sung ?—How many accents have the measures of Common time?—The measures of Triple ?—Of Compound?—Have their measures more or less accents according to their rhythmical construction ?—How many accents can each measure take ? Ans. As many as it has beats.—How many beats are given to the measures of Common time ?—To Triple ?—To Compound ?—What is accent ?—What is time in music and poetry ?—How is poetry measured ?—How many different feet of poetry are there in music ?

——:o:——

CHAPTER VI.

RHYTHM.

ON MARKING OR BEATING TIME.

Sec. 27.—For the purpose of performing music in its proper time, as it steps forth with its flowing numbers through the various rhythmical movements, it is necessary to mersure the time as it flows along. This measurement is performed by the singers with a motion of the hand down and up, in regular process of time, principally on the accented part or parts of the measure. For this marking of the time, the right hand should be used, and the motion of it should be so quick as to allow the rest to be equal with the motion. The first part of every measure, in all the various movements, has a down beat. In the measures of Common time which contain four fourth notes, there is a down beat on the first, a rest on the second, an up beat on the third, and a rest on the fourth ; and when these measures have but two notes, the rest of the hand should likewise be equal to the motion.

In the measures of Triple time, where there are three beats in the measure, two down and one up, the rest of the hand should likewise be equal with its motion. And in the measures of Compound time, the rest of the hand should be double to that of its motion ; for where there are six quarter notes in a measure, there is a down beat on the first, a rest on the second and third, an up beat on the fourth, and a rest on the fifth and sixth ; and in all the various forms of the measure, the rest should be double to the motion. And as there is a down beat on the first part of every measure in all the movements of time ; so all the measures in the various movements and rhythmical constructions, have the first part accented ; and thus the hand and accent of the voice move together.

When the measures of Common time contain but two parts, with one foot of Trochaic verse, they have but one accent, which is on the first part ; but when they contain four parts, with two Trochaic feet of verse, they have two accents, which are on the first and third parts of the measure, being the same parts on which the hand is in motion. And thus the hand and the accent of the voice still move together.

The measures of Triple time, when in their primitive state, have but one accent, which is on the first part ; and in that state they take *one* foot of Dactylic verse. But they may be so constructed as to take *two* and *three* accents and two and three feet of Trochaic verse. For where the measure contains two crotchets and two minims, and has two feet of Trochaic verse applied, it has two accents, one on the first part, which falls on the first crotchet, and the other on the second part, which falls on the first minim ; and when it has six crotchets, and three feet of Trochaic verse applied, it has three accents—one on each part of the measure, which is on the same part the beat is performed in marking the time. In marking this measure we have a down beat on the first crotchet and rest on the second—down, on the third and rest on the

fourth,—up on the fifth, and rest on the sixth ; thus it has an accent to every beat, and the hand and the accent still move together.

The measures of Compound time have two accents and also two beats, which fall on the first and fourth parts. They contain either two feet of Dactylic verse, or two feet of Trochaic, according to their construction.

Sec. 28.—The Compound measure is an even measure ; it can take *two thees*—or two feet of unequal measured verse ; but cannot, like Triple measure, take *three twos*, or three feet of equal measured verse. And notwithstanding the equal quantity of notes which fill their measures, they differ widely in their rhythmical movements,— the one taking *two threes*, with *two* accents and *two* beats ; and the other *three twos*, with *three* accents and *three* beats, as in the following

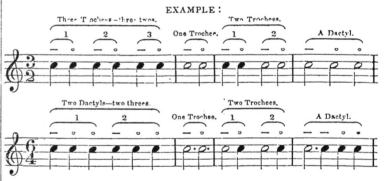

EXAMPLE :

In the above example, the *first* Triple measure contains six quarter notes, and has *three Trochees*—six syllables—applied to it ; and the first Compound measure has the same number of quarter notes and *two Dactyls* applied to it—also six syllables ; but in their rhythmical movements there is a wide difference in *this* and the following measures, as indicated by the abbreviatures.

Sec. 29.—Since a practical knowledge of time and accent, and of beating time with accuracy, according to the movements of the various measures, lies at the foundation of correct performance, and is the most important requisite we will illustrate it more clearly by the following examples.

In these examples will be used the following abbreviatures, viz.: *d* will stand for *down beat;* *u* for *up beat;* and *r* for *rest.* The dash (—) marks the accented note, and the semi-circle (◡) the unaccented. The numerals point out the parts of the measure according to their divisions. For the poetic feet written in each measure, and their respective accents, see sec. 26, with examples.

EXAMPLES OF COMMON OR EVEN TIME. (See Sec. 30.)

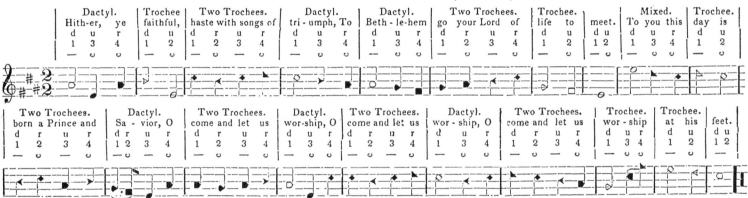

Sec. 30.—In the foregoing example of common time, the movement is marked for two half notes to the primitive measure; and yet there are six measures with four quarter notes. Now the measures which contain two half notes have one accent, and one foot of trochaic verse; and those which contain four quarter notes have two accents, and two feet of trochaic verse, and yet they move smoothly and sweetly together throughout the whole tune. Each of these measures has two beats— one *down* and one *up.* There is an accented down beat on the first part of every measure, in all the movements of time; and when the measure contains two half notes, there is an unaccented up beat, as in

that state it has but one accent, and one foot of trochaic verse; but when it consists of four quarter notes, it has an accent on the up beat also, and contains two feet of trochaic verse. All the measures can take as many accents as they have *regular* beats; and no measure should have more beats than it can take accents.

Throughout this example are found measures containing *one, two, three,* and *four* syllables of verse—all combined in one piece of music, moving in succession. Moreover, some of these measures have but one accent, and embrace one foot of trochaic verse, and others one foot of dactylic. Other measures have two accents, and two feet of trochaic verse. Hence we see how various the measures, in the self-same tune may be formed, in their rhythmical construction, to answer the purposes of the various kinds of poetic numbers, and still retain a uniform movement and regular beat on all the accented parts of the measures. Hence also the propriety of giving only *two* beats to the measures of *all* the movements of Common time, which are nothing more than primitives and derivatives to each other, and should, in all cases, be treated as such. (See examples, Sec. 19.)

Note.—It is proper here to observe, that when a measure in $\frac{2}{4}$ time has a pointed crotchet in the first part of the measure, the point is swelled out, as it falls on the second part of the measure, which is frequently accented; but when in $\frac{4}{4}$ time there are pointed crotchets in the first or second part of the

measure, they are not swelled, but smoothly lengthened out, because they fall on such parts of the measure as cannot be accented.

In poetry and music the greatest attention is due to accent: for it is by a due observance of the accent that the poet is led and guided through the measures of his poetic numbers and sweetly flowing lays: and the musician, in the construction of his musical measures and rhythmical progression.

Sec. 31.—In the *first example* the movement is in Triple time, where the measure has *one accent*, and three beats, two down and one up. Some of the measures are primitive, and take one foot of dactylic verse; others have a slight variation of notes, but the same verse and rhythmical numbers; and others have one foot of trochaic verse, by uniting the two crotchets of the first and second parts of the measure into one minim.

EXAMPLES OF TRIPLE OR UNEVEN TIME. (See Sec. 31.)

EXAMPLE FIRST.

EXAMPLE SECOND.

EXAMPLE THIRD.

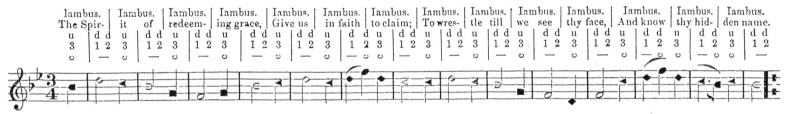

EXAMPLE FOURTH.

In the *Second example* the movement is also in Triple time, where save that the measures vary in their rhythmical construction; some of the measure has two accents, and two feet of trochaic verse applied which have three accents and three feet of trochaic verse; and others to it. By the *abbreviatures* the pupil will see that one foot of verse is one accent, and one foot of the same verse contained in them: all of sung to two crotchets, and another to the two minims which are in which is clearly seen by the abbreviatures in the examples. (Sec. 29.) a measure; and thus the first crotchet, which occupies the first part of In the *fourth example,* we have the same Triple movement and the measure is accented, and the second unaccented; and the first measure as in the first, except that in these measures the first and minim, which occupies the second part of the measure is accented, and second parts of the measure are united in one note and sung to or the second which occupies the third part is unaccented. In this meas- syllable; thus including one trochaic foot, whereas in the first exam ure there is a down beat on the first crotchet, and a rest on the second, ple the measure is in its primitive state, and embraces one foot of dac- and again a down beat on the first minim, and an up beat on the tylic verse. Both these measures are, however, subject to the same second. When the hand beats on a minim, its rest should be equal accentuation. Hence we see that the Triple measures are subject to with its motion. three varieties of accent, and to which may be applied various feet of

In the *Third example* we have the same movement as in the second poetic measures.

EXAMPLES OF COMPOUND OR DOUBLE-TRIPLE TIME. (See Sec. 32.)

EXAMPLE FIRST.

Two Dactyls.	Trochee.	Two Dactyls.	Trochee.	Two Dactyls.	Trochee	Two Dactyls.
How te - dious and taste - less the	hours, When	Je - sus no lon - ger I	see ; }	The mid-sum-mer sun shines but	dim, The	fields strive in vain to look gay.
Sweet prospects, sweet birds and sweet	flow'rs, Have	all lost their sweetness to	me ; }			

```
u         d   r    u   r   r   r  d    u          d   r   u  r    r   r  d    u       d   r   u   r   r   r   d   u    d   r     u   r   r   d
2         1   2    3   4   5   6  1    2          1   2   3  4    5   6  1    2       1   2   3   4   5   6   1   2    1   2     3   4   5   6   1
```

EXAMPLE SECOND.

Two Trochees.	Mixed.	Two Trochees.	Mixed.	Two Trochees	Mixed.	Two Trochees.	Mixed.
An - gels, roll the	rock a - way	Death! yield up the	might - y Prey ;	See! he ri - ses	from the tomb,	Glow - ing with im-	mor - tal bloom.

```
d   r  r   u   r  r    d   r    r   u    d   r  r    r   u  r    d   r  r    u     d   r    u   r    d   r   r    u     d   r   r   u   r   r   d   r   r   u
1   2  3   4   5  6    1   2    3   4-6   1   2  3    4 - 6    1   2  3   4 - 6    1 - 3    4 - 6    1   2   3    4-6   1   2   3   4   5   6   1   2   3   4-6
```

Sec. 32.—In the *first example* is given the first movement of Compound time. This measure has two accents, and always two beats; a down beat on the first note of the primitive measure, and an up beat on the fourth, and in its primitive state, has two feet of dactylic verse applied to it, as in the examples. When this measure contains two pointed minims, and one foot of trochaic verse, it has *in that form,* but one accent, which is frequently the case at the close of one line of poetry, and the commencement of another. The pupil will readily discover by the abbreviatures, (Sec. 29,) that the rest of the hand, in marking this measure, is double to that of its motion, which should be duly observed and practiced.

In the *second example,* the movement is also in compound time, with the measures varied and constructed with notes and ties, in such a manner as to apply two feet of trochaic verse to some, and one foot and a half to others. The motion of the hand, in beating time, should be as quick on a long note as it is on a short one, so that a regular and uniform motion and rest be sustained throughout all the measures of a whole piece of music.

NOTE.—From the foregoing examples and definitions, it is evident, that accent and emphasis adjust and regulate the time of the measures in music and of the feet in poetry, and also the motion of the hand in marking the time of the various measures, in all the different movements. And from this fact, as well as the fact that the two movements of Common time are identical, as shown in the examples, Sec. 19, we can find no use for four beats in any measure of Common time. And it is strange to us how the idea should ever have occurred, of introducing six beats to the measure of Compound time,

Sec. 33.—The motion of the hand, in beating time, should accompany the accent. And although the hand must in some measures, beat on an unaccented part, yet in other measures, in the same tune, that part may be accented: and thus the hand is always in motion on the accented part of the measure, and should rest on the unaccented. To have a continual motion of the hand, in marking the time, shackles the singers, and produces heavy and lifeless performance. The more natural and easy the singers can move along, in marking the time, the more charming and powerful will the effect of the melody and harmony prove, and operate on the minds of the performers and the audience.

Sec. 34.—Decency and order should characterize the marking of the time. The hand should be kept open, and move perpendicularly up and down, with a quick motion, but not too high. The rest of the hand should always be equal to its motion, and in slow movements about double. In triple time, the hand has two down beats and one up; in all the other movements the motion of the hand is simply up and down. All contortion, closing, twisting, or irregular motion of the hand should be carefully guarded against, and avoided, and an easy motion and rest sustained throughout.

NOTE.—Some authors arrange the measures of the different movements into four divisions, namely; Double, Triple, Quadruple, and Sextuple, and give two beats to the first, three to the second, four to the third and six to the fourth. This arrangement seems to have, at first sight, a good deal of consistency; since the first has two parts to the measure, the second three, the third four, and the fourth six, in their primitive form. But when we take into consideration the accentuation of the different measures of those movements (Sec. 26)—the commingling of the measures of the first and third, (Sec. 30)—the different rhythmical constructions and movements of the measures of the second and fourth, (Sec. 28)—and besides this, the four and six beats which those authors direct—the propriety of this arrangement vanishes away.

The mode of beating the triple measure with the second beat horizontally seems to have gained some practice: though we decidedly prefer two down beats and one up. This mode is more uniform with all the other beats in the different movements, and less subject to lead singers to a disorderly habit in the motion of the hand.

QUESTIONS.

How many beats are in the measures of Common time?—How are they performed?—Which part of the measure has invariably a down beat?—What part of the measure is invariably accented?—Has the measure but one accent?—If the measure has four notes and two accents, on what parts of the measure do the accents fall?—Are the beats then performed on the accented parts of the measure?—How many beats has the measure of Triple time?—How are the beats performed?—How many accents are in it when in its primitive form?—Can it take more than one accent in its derivative measures?—How many beats has the measure of Compound time?—How many accents?—On what parts of the measure do the accents fall?—Are the beats performed on the accented parts of the measure?—Must the accents of the measures of music and the feet of poetry always agree?—If the measure of Triple time contains six quarter notes, and the measure of Compound time contains the same number, will they agree in their movement?—Why not?

———:o:———

CHAPTER VII.

INTONATION.

MELODY—MUSICAL INTERVALS, SCALES, &c.

Sec. 35.—As letters represent the seven original sounds on the staff of music, (Sec. 9,) it is of great importance that the student be well acquainted with their situation, and commit them to memory, as on the following,

SCALES.

BASE STAFF.

B	Space above	10
A	Fifth line	9
G	Fourth space	8
F	Fourth line	7
E	Third space	6
D	Third line	5
C	Second space	4
B	Second line	3
A	First space	2
G	First line	1

TENOR AND TREBLE STAFF.

G	Space above	15
F	Fifth line	14
E	Fourth space	13
D	Fourth line	12
C	Third space	11
B	Third line	10
A	Second space	9
G	Second line	8
F	First space	7
E	First line	6

Sec. 36.—As musical sounds may be high or low, (Sec. 3,) a scale is used to represent them in their different pitch.

In the following scales of the major and minor modes, is represented the gradual succession of the tones and the semitones, rising by steps and half-steps, counting from the lowest upwards, and thus forming the diatonic scale in both keys.

DIATONIC SCALE—MAJOR AND MINOR.

MAJOR SCALE.

MINOR SCALE

Each of the above scales is made up of seven sounds, (Sec. 2,) with the inversion of the first, which becomes an eighth, and thus completes the octave, and commences a second scale.

These scales consist of five tones and two semitones—or five steps and two half-steps—which are distinguished on this scale, by the lines and spaces, the spaces of the semitones being only half as wide as those of the tones. By this the pupil will discover, that the semitones lie between B and C, and E and F; they also lie *invariably*, between the syllables Si and Do, and Mi and Faw. The letters and notes are placed on the lines, in the above scale, in the same order in which they are placed in their natural position on the lines and in the spaces of the staff.

Sec. 37.—By comparing the sounds C, D, E, F, of the major scale above, with G, A, B, C, we find that the distance of each of these

fourths consists of three tones and a semitone; therefore any tune formed by one will be similar to that of the other.

These four sounds are termed a *Tetrachord*; they composed the Ancient Greek Scales, and the enumeration of all the sounds of their system; though it appears from Gardiner's "Music of Nature," that their music was all written in the minor scale. The two Tetrachords, taken in succession, form the diatonic scale; the chief sound or key of which is taken from C; *it* being the letter from which the natural major key proceeds.

TETRACHORDS OF THE MAJOR SCALE.
First Tetrachord.   Second Tetrachord.

In both these Tetrachords the semitones or half steps lie between the third and fourth intervals; and thus they are alike in all their sounds, except that the first commences on C, and the second on G.

TETRACHORDS OF THE MINOR SCALE.
First Tetrachord.   Second Tetrachord.

The Tetrachords of the minor scale are unlike in the location of the semitones, the first of which has the half step between the second and third; and the second has it between the first and second of the scale. They also differ with the Tetrachords of the major, owing to the fact, that those of the major proceed from C and G, and the minor from A and E. Both the major and the minor, however, have the semitones between B and C, and E and F; as also between Si and Do, and Mi and Faw.

NOTE.—In counting intervals *in this work*, both the extremes will be counted and taken into the number. Thus, C, D, E, F, form four intervals of the scale, reckoning from grave to acute; though there are only three *intervals*, or *spaces between* them. The term INTERVAL is applied both to the distance between the notes, and to the notes themselves. Thus E is not only said to be at the distance of a third above C, but is *itself* called the *third* above C; G is not only said to be at the distance of a *fifth* above C; but is itself called a fifth above C; in both which cases the extremes are taken into the number. So when the voice gradually ascending or descending by intervals, is compared to steps and half steps, the first sound will of course, be its first step, the second sound its second, the third, its third, &c.; and as the scale is unlimited, whatever sound or letter the voice or the instrument may strike. there are still intervals below it or above, from which that step proceeds. In the scale of music, the half steps are taken into the number of intervals as well as those of the steps.

Sec. 38.—Two disjoint Tetrachords, one arranged above the other, form the diatonic scale. Those two Tetrachords, the first of which proceeds from C, and the second from G, form the major scale; and those two, the first of which proceeds from A, and the second from E, form the minor scale.

NATURAL MAJOR SCALE.

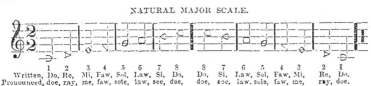

NATURAL MINOR SCALE.

NOTE.—It is very desirable that singers pronounce the syllables clearly and distinctly in solmization: it adds greatly to the beauty of music, and will lead to a correct pronunciation of the poetry, when applied to music, which is of the greatest importance.

Sec. 39.—The following rhythmical exercises should be practiced in a school, with a full accent, and a regular marking of the time, until the pupils have acquired a ready motion of the hand, and a command of voice, in striking the accented notes with strength and firmness, and with a clear voice; and the unaccented in a soft, smooth, and easy manner. In training a school, no pains should be spared in the intonation of the voice, and in a regular marking of the time, as thereon depends *wholly*, all future success in bringing out music in rhythmical order, and with taste and elegance.

EXERCISES IN RHYTHM.

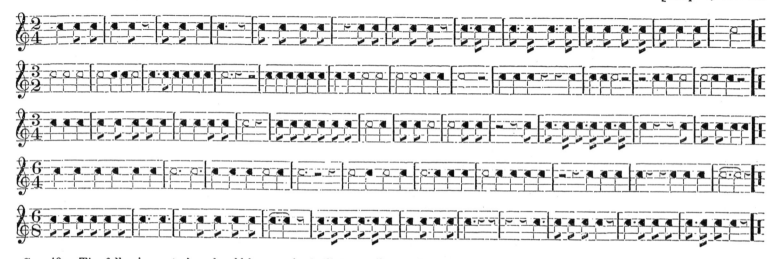

Sec. 40.—The following exercises should be practiced till the pupils have acquired firmness in sounding, with precision, and with a smooth and clear voice, every interval in the diatonic scale, ascending and de- scending, both in the major and the minor keys : also till they have gained a thorough knowledge of the location of the semitones in their different positions, in both keys.

EXERCISES IN MELODY.

Sec. 41.—As the Tonic or key note is the most important interval in the musical scale, and the chord based on it the principal one in every piece of music, it will be proper, in this place, to give exercises on the intervals of this chord, and on the various positions and changes in which these intervals may be sung, having the tonic of either the major or the minor scale for their fundamental note.

Exercises on the Intervals of the Common Chord.
INTERVALS PROCEEDING FROM THE MAJOR TONIC.

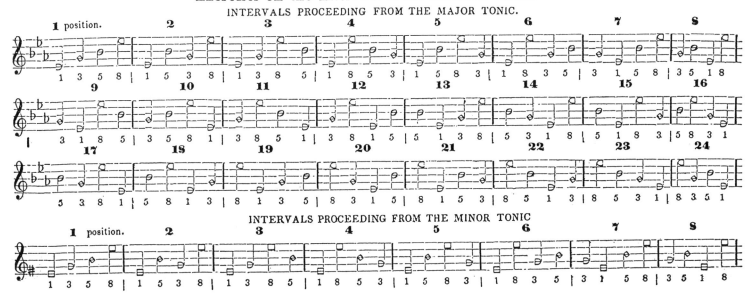

INTERVALS PROCEEDING FROM THE MINOR TONIC

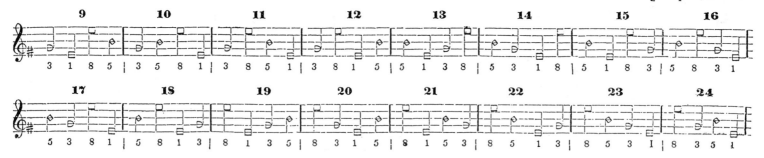

QUESTIONS.

How many letters of the alphabet are used to represent musical sounds?—How are these letters placed on the Base staff?—How on the Tenor and Treble?—Are the Tenor and Treble alike in pitch?—How many tones are in the scale of music? —How many semitones?—Between which letters do the semitones lie?—Between which notes do the semitones lie?—How many modes are there in music? Ans. Two, the major and the minor.—Wherein do these modes differ? Ans. In the location of the semitones.—How many sounds form a Tetrachord?—How many Tetrachords compose the diatonic scale?—How many notes are applied to the diatonic scale?—What syllables are applied to these notes?—In how many different positions can the intervals of the common chord be sung?

——:o:——

CHAPTER VIII.

___

MELODY.

—

OF INTERVALS, CHORDS, AND THEIR INVERSION.

Sec. 42.—The intervals of the scale are seven, (Sec. 2,) the first of which is called—

The *Tonic*, which is the key note or principal sound, and which governs all the rest.

The second is called the *Supertonic*, because it is next above the Tonic. (*Super*—above.)

The third is called the *Mediant*, as it is half way between the Tonic and Dominant. It varies with the mode, being the greater third in the major, and the lesser third in the minor.

The fourth is called the *Subdominant*, being next below the Dominant. But the term arises from its being a fifth below the Tonic, the same degree that the dominant is above. (*Sub*—under.—)

The fifth is called the *Dominant*, from its importance in the scale, and from its immediate connection with the Tonic; and as it is heard in the Base immediately before the final perfect cadence, it is said to govern the Tonic in both the major and the minor scales.

The sixth is called the *Submediant*, from its being half way between the Tonic and the Subdominant descending. Like the Mediant, it varies with the mode, being the greater sixth in the major mode, and the lesser sixth in the minor.

She seventh is called the *Leading note*, from its leading to the Tonic. It is also called the *Subsemitone*, from its being a semitone below the Tonic. Moreover it is called the *sharp seventh*, from its being of a sharp sound in the major scale, and is frequently sharped in the minor.

The eighth is the inversion of the Tonic and is the same note with it though it is an octave higher in the general Scale.

Sec. 43.—In the following scale is exhibited the connection of the three parts of music, Base, Tenor, and Treble ; with the degrees of sound of all the letters expressed by numerals, on the staffs, as they rise in acuteness, on the scale. The Treble staff is the same with the Tenor, except that it rises an octave higher in the scale ; owing to the fact, that the female voice is more acute by one octave, than that of the male. Hence there are represented on the scale 22 musical sounds, from G, the first line of the base staff, to G, the space above the fifth line of the Treble staff ; this being the ordinary compass of the human voice, including male and female : though the ordinary compass of either sex is only fifteen sounds. (See note on Sec. 6.)

The two natural keys, major and minor, with their intervals, as represented above, should be well understood. Of the seven intervals, of either key, five are steps or tones, and two are half-steps or semitones. In the major key the semitones always lie between the third and fourth and the seventh and eigth intervals of the scale ; and in the minor key they lie between the second and third and fifth and sixth intervals. (See on this, Sec. 36, with scale.)

THE GENERAL SCALE OF MUSIC.

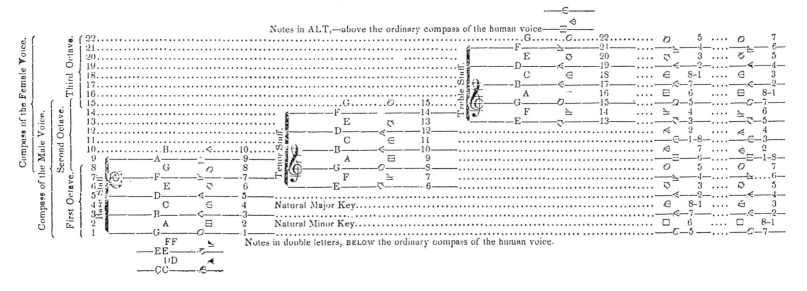

From the fact that there are but seven original sounds in the scale of music, and that it takes eight sounds to complete the scale, some difficulty seems to arise, in finding out the eighth sound. But when it is taken into consideration that the key note of either the major or the minor scale is always taken as *one*, and is the first interval in the diatonic scale; and that it occurs or comes round again every eighth interval, [like the Sabbath, which is the first day of the week, and comes round every eighth day; though there are but seven days in the week,] it is easily perceived, that the eighth is nothing more than an inversion of the first; and with the same sound that commences a succeeding scale, the preceding is completed: thus the Tonic is the first sound in the scale, and is also the last.

By the three braces which include the octaves in the above scale, it will be seen that the first brace includes the first note and the eighth; the second brace includes the eighth and the fifteenth; and the third includes the fifteenth and the twenty-second. Thus it is manifest that the last note of a preceding octave, is the first note of a succeeding one. The same method is perceivable in the braces of the double octaves; the first of which includes the first and the fifteenth, for the compass of the male voice; and the second includes the eighth and the twenty-second, for the compass of the female voice; thus still including in the braces, the last note and the first of each octave.

Although the ordinary compass of the human voice is limited to three octaves, comprising twenty-two musical sounds; yet there are some voices which can surpass this limitation;—the instruments have yet a much wider range; and the musical scale knows no bounds. Hence we see in the scale, notes in double letters below; also notes in Alt above; these might form new octaves above and below; and be continued octave upon octave, without finding to them any limitation.

NOTE.—It is found by a mathematical calculation, based upon the number of vibrations to a second of time, that the five intervals of the diatonic scale termed *steps* are not exactly equal to each other, while the two *half-steps* are each of them a little more than half-steps, and the one between 7 and 8 is greater than the one between 3 and 4.

Dr. Calcott, in his musical Grammar, divides the scale into tones of 9 commas and tones of 8 commas; and the two diatonic or natural semitones into 5 commas, and the chromatic or artificial semitones into three or four, according to the magnitude of the tone.

Thus the scale is divided into major tones of 9 commas, and into minor tones of 8; and into natural or major semitones of 5 commas, and into artificial or minor semitones of 3 or 4 commas.

According to this theory, if we suppose a string on an instrument which sounds out one or Do of the scale, to have 24 vibrations in a second of time, then one-half of its length, vibrating at the same tension, will sound eight of the scale, and will vibrate just twice as fast, or 48 times to the second. Preserving this ratio, the relative number of vibrations to every sound of the present scale will be as follows:

C	D	E	F	G	A	B	C
1	2	3	4	5	6	7	8
24	27	30	32	36	40	45	48

Now, in order to give the length of a string which will make the proper number of vibrations to each of the intervals of the scale, we must take 24, the number of vibrations for the fundamental or 1, for a numerator, and the other numbers, which give the vibrations of the other intervals for denominators, and the fractions will stand thus:

$$1. \quad \frac{24}{24}=\frac{1}{1}; \quad 2. \quad \frac{24}{27}=\frac{8}{9}; \quad 3. \quad \frac{24}{30}=\frac{4}{5}; \quad 4. \quad \frac{24}{32}=\frac{3}{4}; \quad 5. \quad \frac{24}{36}=\frac{2}{3}; \quad 6. \quad \frac{24}{40}=\frac{3}{5}; \quad 7. \quad \frac{24}{45}=\frac{8}{15}; \quad 8. \quad \frac{24}{48}=\frac{1}{2}.$$

These fractions express what part of the length of the whole or fundamental string is required to give the proper number of vibrations to each interval of the scale. And here we find that the Octave takes one-half of the string, the fifth two-thirds, the third four-fifths, &c. See the following

EXAMPLES OF VIBRATIONS.

Unison......	. . . .	1
Fundamental .	. . . .	1
Octave......	. . . .	2
Fundamental .	. . . .	1

Fifth........　. 3
Fundamental　. 2
Third........　. 5
Fundamental　. 4

The foregoing examples of the unison, octave, fifth and third will suffice as specimens of all the rest of the intervals of the diatonic scale, which are the second, fourth, sixth and seventh, the length of whose strings is expressed above.

From the foregoing examples, we see that the proportion of the vibrations for each interval of the scale is fixed. And according to this theory, if we suppose the distance from 1 to 2 of the natural scale, or from C to D, to be 22, then the scale will stand as follows :

From 1 to 2,　2 to 3,　3 to 4,　4 to 5,　5 to 6,　6 to 7,　7 to 8,

22 ;　　20 ;　　12 ;　　22 ;　　20 ;　　22 ;　　13.

Thus when we take 22, the distance from 1 to 2, as the standard of a step, then from 2 to 3 will be a step of 20, and so on, as in the above diagram.

Now if the intervals of the scale could be performed according to this mathematical standard, which is based on the number of vibrations of a string to each interval as represented above, it would produce the most perfect harmony. But as the scale in this arrangement could not be transposed to other letters of the scale, it would in this fixed position, like the purest honey, soon cloy. Hence,

In order to adjust the scale to an equal temperament, all the distances, as just given in the mathematical diagram, are added together, the aggregate of which is 131 ; this number divided by 12, the number of semitones in the scale, will produce $10\frac{11}{12}$ as the distance of each half-step ; and making each step twice as great, will give $21\frac{10}{12}$ as the distance of a step. Thus all the tones of the scale are equalized, and so are the semitones also, and made just half the distance of a tone ; and in this equal temperament it is transposed to all the letters of the scale, and to all the chromatic semitones.

Sec. 44.—The intervals of the scale are used both in a conjoint and in a disjoint manner. They are used conjointly, when they follow each other in the order of the scale ; and disjointly when they are separated, and form longer intervals or skips, such as the third, fourth, fifth, sixth, seventh and eighth. (See exercises, sec. 41.) These skips may also include their octaves, as the tenth, twelfth, fifteenth, &c.

Disjoint intervals are consonant or dissonant, according to the degrees of sound they are distant from each other. The combination of sound produced by the *first, third, fifth* and *eighth* intervals of the scale, major or minor, called the Common Chord or harmonic triad, (exercises, sec. 41,) are consonant intervals, and when sounded together, form a delightful chord, producing the most sublime and pleasant harmony ; but the second and seventh are discords. (See table, sec. 50.)

A Common Chord or harmonic triad, consists of a fundamental note, and its third and fifth, and usually its octave : and notwithstanding the chord which proceeds from the key note is the most perfect, yet every letter of the scale may be made the fundamental note of a common chord, major, minor, or imperfect.

Every consonant triad must have a perfect, or major fifth. A major triad has a major third from the *first* to the *third*, and a minor third from the *third* to the *fifth* ; and a minor triad has a minor third from the *first* to the *third*, and a major third from the *third* to the *fifth*. (Examine the scale.)

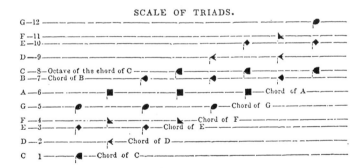

SCALE OF TRIADS.

In the foregoing scale are exhibited six consonant triads and one dissonant. Three of the consonant triads are major, and three are minor. In the dissonant triad, both the thirds are minor, and so is the fifth, in consequence of which, the chord is dissonant.

Sec. 45.—INVERSION OF INTERVALS.—When the lower note of any interval is placed an octave higher, or the higher note an octave lower, the change thereby produced is called *inversion.* Any interval and its inversion complete the octave. Thus let C and D form a major second, then invert C by placing it an octave higher, and it will produce, from D to C, a minor seventh, which, with the major second, completes the octave. Moreover, let B and C form a minor second, then invert B, by removing it an octave above, and it will produce from C to B, a major seventh, which, with the minor second, completes the octave.

INTERVALS AND THEIR INVERSION.

A Minor 2nd becomes a Major 7th;

A Major 2nd becomes a Minor 7th.

A Major 3rd becomes a Major 6th;

A Major 3rd becomes a Minor 6th.

A Minor 4th becomes a Major 5th;

A Major 4th becomes a Minor 5th.

A Minor 5th becomes a Major 4th;

A Major 5th becomes a Minor 4th.

A Minor 6th becomes a Major 3rd;

A Major 6th becomes a Minor 3rd.

A Minor 7th becomes a Major 2nd;

A Major 7th becomes a Minor 2nd.

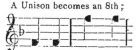

A Unison becomes an 8th;   An 8th becomes a Unison.

In the foregoing inversion of Major and Minor intervals, are exhibited fourteen, namely minor and major seconds, minor and major thirds, &c., with unison and octave. These will be farther noticed in treating on Harmony, Chap. 10.

QUESTIONS.

How many intervals are in the diatonic scale?—How are they called as they ascend?—How many sounds does the general scale contain?—How many octaves?—Is the musical scale limited to 22 sounds?—What is the difference between the pitch of the Tenor and the Treble staff?—Between the major and the minor keys?—Between which of the intervals are the semitones located in the major scale?—In the minor?—What different effects do the different locations of the semitones in those keys produce?—What is to be understood by conjoint intervals?—What by disjoint?—What is a common chord or Harmonic Triad?—What is a Major Triad?—A Minor?—A dissonant?—Are the major and the minor Triads both consonant?—Why are they consonant?—What is meant by inversion?—How many different intervals are produced by inversion?

—:o:—

CHAPTER IX

MELODY.

TRANSPOSITION OF THE SCALE.

Sec. 46.—There are two modes of keys in music, the major and the minor, (Sec. 36 and 43.) In their natural state, the major has C for its fundamental note or key, and the minor has A. But were the keys confined to these two letters alone, their bounds would be too limited. Consequently, there is a much wider range provided for them by transposition. For this purpose flats and sharps are used as signs, to modulate the sounds, by means of which not only every musical letter, but every chromatic semitone may be made the tonic or key note both major and minor. Hence there are twenty-four keys in the scale of music, twelve of which are major and twelve are minor.

In the scale of the major and minor modes, (Sec. 36,) the half-steps or semitones lie between B and C, and E and F; and in the major scale they lie between the third and fourth, and seventh and eighth intervals; and in the minor they lie between the second and third and fifth and sixth intervals; and in both scales they lie between the syllables Mi and Faw, and Si and Do. Now in this their natural position the tones and semitones of the letters and of the notes of the major and minor scales agree; but as the letters are immovably fixed in the scale—and the intervals of the scale, when transposed, also keep their fixed position in relation to the tonic or key note, there is a disunion produced by their removal, between the fixed scale of the letters, and the moving scale of the keys, which must be adjusted and modulated by the use of flats and sharps on the letters, so that they yield to the new key according to its requirement.

In order to make each one of the twelve semitones in the chromatic scale the key-note of a major scale, and also of a minor, it is requisite to use five sharps and six flats, or six sharps and five flats, as follows:

In the natural scale the major key is on C and the minor on A; but when the signature is—

	Major key is		Minor
F sharp,....................	G	......	E
F, C sharp,.................	" " D	......	B
F, C, G sharp,.............	" " A	......	F♯
F, C, G, D sharp,.........	" " E	......	C♯
F, C, G, D, A sharp,......	" " B	......	G♯
F, C, G, D, A, E sharp,..	" " F♯	......	D♯
B flat,.....................	" " F	......	D
B, E flat,..................	" " B♭	......	G
B, E, A flat,...............	" " E♭	......	C
B, E, A, D flat,...........	" " A♭	......	F
B, E, A, D, G flat,........	" " D♭	......	B♭
B, E, A, D, G, C flat,.....	" " G♭	......	E♭

When the keys are transposed by sharps, they rise a fifth in the scale, and the dominant of the former scale becomes the key note of a new scale; and when they are transposed by flats they are lowered a fifth and the subdominant of the former scale becomes the key-note of a new scale. Thus every additional sharp or flat removes the scale in like manner next to the dominant or subdominant.

In the remove of the scale, there should never more than six sharps or six flats be used. For either six sharps or six flats will remove the key to the same interval, as in the above scale, six sharps remove the major key to F♯, and six flats to G♭: which is the intermediate semitone between F and G, and the self-same interval of the scale.

It is a very singular fact,—which evidently arises from the division of the scale into twelve semitones,—that if we take any number of sharps to transpose the key, the complement to twelve of flats will transpose it to the same interval. For instance, seven sharps bring the major key on C♯, and five flats—the complement to twelve—bring it on D♭, the same chromatic interval. Seven flats transpose the key on C♭; and five sharps—the complement to twelve—transpose it on B, which is the same chromatic interval of C♭. This will hold good with any number of sharps and the complement of flats to twelve; or of flats, and the complement of sharps to twelve. But in such cases double flats and double sharps would have to be used, which for the facility of execution, should be avoided in all cases.

The two keys stand in relation to each other. The relative minor is a third below or a sixth above the major, on the scale; and the relative major is a third above or a sixth below the minor, on the scale. When the scale is changed, and the keys removed to other letters, higher or lower, they always stand in the same relation: and thus we have the fundamental notes of both keys, in every scale. (See Table, page 44, 45.)

Sec. 47.—Besides the diatonic scale, which is composed of tones and semitones, there is another called the *Chromatic Scale*, which is composed of semitones alone. The chromatic scale is, however, nothing more than a subdivision of the diatonic into semitones; which is effected by the use of flats and sharps. This scale ascends by sharps and descends by flats, as seen in the following scale:

CHROMATIC SCALE.

Ascending by sharps.

Do,   do, Re,   re, Mi, Faw, faw, Sol,   sol, Law,   law, Si,   Do.

Descending by flats.

Do, Si,   si,   Law,   law, Sol,   sol, Faw, Mi,   mi,   Re,   re,   Do.

NOTE.—The doctrine which holds forth that the semitones are produced by a change of the vowel sounds of the syllables applied to the notes seems to be somewhat doubtful and uncertain; for if the slender sound of a vowel in the syllable applied to a note would raise a note a semitone; and if the broad sound would depress it, what would be the consequence where words or syllables of both broad and slender sounds are sung to the same letter and sound of the scale?—Which is evidently the case in many tunes, and for the proof of which it will only be necessary to refer to the following tunes, namely, Sterling, Miles' Lane, Martyn, Bozrah, Tavoy, &c. Now by giving proper attention to the above named tunes, it will be found when the poetry is applied to the notes, that in many measures there will be broad and slender vowel sounds applied to consecutive notes of the same sound—of the same letter; and yet no deviation from the self-same sound heard or discovered, by the application of the different vowel sounds. And even when vocal and instrumental music are performed together, there is no discordance of sound discoverable on these notes; but all the sounds, both from the vocal organs, and from the strings and pipes, mingle and flow together, in sweetest unison and harmony.

From the foregoing remarks, it is evident, that if the different sounds of the vowels by their broad and slender sounds, have the power to change the pitch of a note a semitone higher or lower, in one instance, they have the same power also in other instances; and if such be the case, will it not be best to guard against their changing the sound of the notes in every case; and to get the proper pitch of the accidental semitones by a change of sound, and not by a change of syllable? as by far the greater number of notes that would be affected by that change, would thereby become discordant and unharmonious.

A proper knowledge of the Chromatic scale will lead to a more full and extensive knowledge of the Diatonic, in its different positions when transposed. For by the flats and sharps used in the Chromatic scale, the keys of the diatonic are modulated, and the tones and semitones fixed in the proper intervals in the new keys, in every change of key, and it will be obvious to the student that the Chromatic scale is nothing more than a subdivision of the Diatonic into semitones; where the lower letter of a tone is sharped, or the upper flatted to produce the intermediate semitone, and thus form a scale of semitones alone.

Sec. 48.—It should be well understood that the letter of the key note or tonic is *always* taken as ONE, and that the tonic may assume *any letter or chromatic semitone* as the key note, either of the major or of the minor key, and that in the major scale the order of intervals must always be from 1 to 2 a tone; from 2 to 3 a tone; from 3 to 4 a semitone; from 4 to 5 a tone; from 5 to 6 a tone; from 6 to 7 a tone; from 7 to 8 a semitone. And in the minor scale, from 1 to 2 a tone; from 2 to 3 a semitone; from 3 to 4 a tone; from 4 to 5 a tone; from 5 to 6 a semitone; from 6 to 7 a tone, and from 7 to 8 a tone. To this order, in the minor scale, there may be some exception: for wherever the seventh leads to the key, it is sharped, and thus produces a semitone between the seventh and eighth.

This is the order of the keys, in their intervals, *in every position*, which is manifested in the scales of Table of the Transposition. In the first scales, major and minor, the intervals are natural, as the keys are in their natural position—the major key on C, and the minor key on A. But so soon as the scales are transposed to other letters, more or less flats or sharps must be used, to modulate the sounds in their new position. For instance—

Let G, the dominant of the natural major scale be taken as the key-note or tonic of a new major scale, according to the scale of G, in the following Table : then from G to A is a tone, from 1 to 2 a tone ; from 2 to 3 a tone, from A to B a tone ; from B to C a semitone, from 3 to 4 a semitone ; from 4 to 5 a tone, from C to D a tone ; from D to E a tone, from 5 to 6 a tone ; from 6 to 7 a tone, from E to F naturally a semitone, which must here be a tone, and consequently F must be sharped, then from F sharp to G a semitone, and from 7 to 8 a semitone. Thus we find that in the major key of G, F must be sharped.

In like manner as sharps raise the keys a fifth to the dominant, so flats lower them a fifth, (Sec. 46,) to the subdominant. For by making F sharp, the major key will be transposed from C to G, the dominant, a fifth higher ; and by making B flat, the major key will be transposed from C to F, the subdominant, a fifth lower.

NOTE.—By inversion the fifth above will become a fourth below ; and the fifth below will become a fourth above.

As the major and the minor scales stand in relation together, and invariably keep their relative position, in every remove, the minor being a relative to the major, a third below or a sixth above ; and the major being a relative to the minor, a third above or a sixth below ; and as they are alike in the intervals of the dominant and subdominant, they are subject to the same order, when transposed, also in the inversion of the intervals.

Let D, the subdominant of the natural minor scale, be taken as the key-note or tonic of a new minor scale ; then from D to E is a tone, and from 1 to 2 is a tone ; from 2 to 3 is a semitone, and from E to F a semitone ; from F to G a tone, and from 3 to 4 a tone ; from 4 to 5 a tone, and from G to A a tone ; from A to B a tone, but from 5 to 6 only a semitone, therefore B must be made flat ; then from B♭ to C is a tone, and from 6 to 7 a tone ; from 7 to 8 a tone, and from C to D a tone. Hence we see the necessity of making B flat, in the key of D minor or F major.

NOTE.—In all the foregoing changes of key by flats and sharps, the vocal performer has no difficulty in making the flat and sharp sounds of the letters, seeing that the syllables of the scale have the proper sounds of the scale associated with their names ; and the natural rise and fall of the voice is the same in every change of key ; and thus the singer performs them without being aware of it, except when accidentals occur. But the case is different with the instrumental performer, where on keyed instruments, the keys of the chromatic semitones are short keys, constructed between the long keys of the natural scale ; thus between the long keys of A and B, is a short key to strike the semitone A sharp or B flat ; and as there is naturally but a semitone between B and C, also between E and F, there are no short keys between B and C, and E and F, because they are the natural semitones in the diatonic scale ; but between C and D, D and E, F and G, G and A, there are also short keys to strike the semitones of C sharp or D flat ; D sharp or E flat ; F sharp or G flat ; and G sharp or A flat. Hence the player on an instrument must observe to strike the short keys on all the letters that are sharped or flatted in the signature, throughout the whole piece of music. From this fact it follows, that the less number of sharps and flats that can be used in the signature, the easier will be the execution to the instrumental performer.

The necessity and use of the Chromatic Scale, at the front of the following Table of Transposition, is because the *keys* are movable and changeable in their position, and the *letters* of the scale are permanent and fixed. Here the student will see at a glance, how the semitones run out from the chromatic scale, through all the movable scales—which are represented in this table in the form of a ladder—preparing and adjusting the intervals of the new scales for their assumed key, both major and minor. But,

For want of room on this table, we have given only two examples of the minor scale in connection with its relative major, which, if due attention be given to this, it will be amply sufficient to give the learner a due knowledge of the minor scale in connection with the major ; as the relative minor is *always* a third below or a sixth above its relative major : and the relative major a third above or a sixth below its relative minor.

The minor scale has of late been too much neglected and set aside, and we think every effort should be made to revive it again. We have the minor key, as those in former ages. (See more on minor scale, as much need now to express our sorrow, humility, and penitence by page 43.)

TABLE OF TRANSPOSITION.

SCALES WITH SHARPS.

CHROMATIC SCALE.	Scales of C Maj. and A Min. NATURAL.	Scale of G. ONE SHARP.	Scale of D. TWO SHARPS.	Scale of A. THREE SHARPS.	Scale of E. FOUR SHARPS.	Scale of B. FIVE SHARPS.	Scale of F♯. SIX SHARPS.
C natural							
B natural						B—8—Do	
A sharp or B flat						A♯—7—Si	
A natural	A—8—Law			A—8—Do			
G sharp or A flat				G♯—7—Si		G♯—6—Law	
G natural	G—7—Sol	G—8—Do					
F sharp or G flat		F♯—7—Si		F♯—6—Law		F♯—5—Sol	F♯—8—Do
F natural	F—6—Faw						E♯—7—Si
E natural	E—5—Mi	E—6—Law		E—5—Sol	E—8—Do	E—4—Faw	
D sharp or E flat					D♯—7—Si	D♯—3—Mi	D♯—6—Law
D natural	D—4—Re	D—5—Sol	D—8—Do	D—4—Faw			
C sharp or D flat			C♯—7—Si	C♯—3—Mi	C♯—6—Law	C♯—2—Re	C♯—5—Sol
C natural	C—8—Do; C—3—Do	C—4—Faw					
B natural	B—7—Si; B—2—Si	B—3—Mi	B—6—Law		B—5—Sol	B—1—Do	B—4—Faw
A sharp or B flat							A♯—3—Mi
A natural	A—6—Law; A—1—Law	A—2—Re	A—5—Sol	A—1—Do	A—4—Faw		
G sharp or A flat					G♯—3—Mi		G♯—2—Re
G natural	G—5—Sol	G—1—Do	G—4—Faw				
F sharp or G flat			F♯—3—Mi		F♯—2—Re		F♯—1—Do
F natural	F—4—Faw						
E natural	E—3—Mi		E—2—Re		E—1—Do		
D sharp or E flat							
D natural	D—2—Re		D—1—Do				
C sharp or D flat							
C natural	C—1—Do						

In these Tables, it will be observed, that we have ascended in each successive scale a *fifth*, or descended a *fourth*—according to the order of inversion,—and that in the ascending scales by sharps, one additional sharp was required in each successive transposition; and in the descending scales by flats, one additional flat was required. This is the regular order of transposition, both by sharps and flats.

SCALES WITH FLATS.

Chromatic Scale.	Scale of C. NATURAL.	Scales of F Maj. & D Min. ONE FLAT.	Scale of B♭. TWO FLATS.	Scale of E♭. THREE FLATS.	Scale of A♭. FOUR FLATS.	Scale of D♭. FIVE FLATS.	Scale of G♭. SIX FLATS.
C natural							
B natural							
B flat or A sharp			B♭—8—Do				
A natural			A—7—Si				
A flat or G sharp					A♭—8—Do		
G natural			G—6—Law.		G—7—Si		
G flat or F sharp							G♭—8—Do
F natural		F—8—Do.	F—5—Sol.		F—6—Law.		F—7—Si
E natural		E—7—Si					
E flat or D sharp			E♭—4—Faw.	E♭—8—Do	E♭—5—Sol		E♭—6—Law.
D natural		D—6—Law. D—8—Law	D—3—Mi	D—7—Si			
D flat or C sharp					D♭—4—Faw	D♭—8—Do	D♭—5—Sol
C natural	C—8—Do.	C—5—Sol C—7—Sol	C—2—Re	C—6—Law	C—3—Mi	C—7—Si	
B natural	B—7—Si						C♭—4—Faw.
B flat or A sharp		B♭—4—Faw B♭—6—Faw	B♭—1—Do	B♭—5—Sol	B♭—2—Re	B♭—6—Law	B♭—3—Mi
A natural	A—6—Law	A—3—Mi A—5—Mi					
A flat or G sharp				A♭—4—Faw	A♭—1—Do	A♭—5—Sol	A♭—2—Re
G natural	G—5—Sol	G—2—Re G—4—Re		G—3—Mi			
G flat or F sharp						G♭—4—Faw	G♭—1—Do
F natural	F—4—Faw	F—1—Do F—3—Do		F—2—Re		F—3—Mi	
E natural	E—3—Mi	E—2—Si					
E flat or D sharp				E♭—1—Do		E♭—2—Re	
D natural	D—2—Re	D—1—Law					
D flat or C sharp						D♭—1—Do	
C natural	C—1—Do.						

MINOR SCALE.

"We hardly know why it is, but tunes written in the minor scale have been exceedingly rare in some of the singing-books that have been published for a few years past. Our fathers, we know, used this scale much more extensively than we have been accustomed to do. Have we become degenerate plants of a strange vine? Has the very decided predominance given to the major scale been owing to the fact that we have come to be a very joyful and happy people; and that we have no occasion for sorrow, humiliation, penitence, sadness and grief? Many of the psalms, if the sentiment contained in them, and the feelings expressed therein, be a criterion of judgment, were sung in the minor strain. This is the natural expression of emotions of sadness, penitence and grief. And certainly our Creator hath established the laws of the minor scale as really as he has the major scale. He has adapted that to our natures, and our natures to that as really as he has our natures and the major scale, the one to the other. And in a world like ours there is certainly a demand for tunes written in the minor scale. As long as we live in a world of sorrow—as long as we are sinful beings—have transgressions to confess, and mercies for which to supplicate, we shall have need to do it in strains, and in a manner corresponding to the feelings of the heart. But so little has this key been used of late, that many choirs know not how to perform a minor tune creditably; and many singers are highly prejudiced against it. And the reason is not that their natures do not, at proper times, require it; but because they have been educated to execute major music solely, and have no taste for anything else; so that education and taste here do not answer at all to the demands of nature. Seldom do we hear a tune sung anywhere in that key, on the Sabbath at public worship, or in the social circle: and when such tunes have been selected, it has been a somewhat difficult thing to execute them, so little has the voice been accustomed to sing in this scale,"

The following exercises are designed to illustrate the subject of Transposition still farther. Each scale is here written out in full. The teacher should exercise his class in these scales, and instruct them in the same, until they become familiar with each key.

KEY OF C.

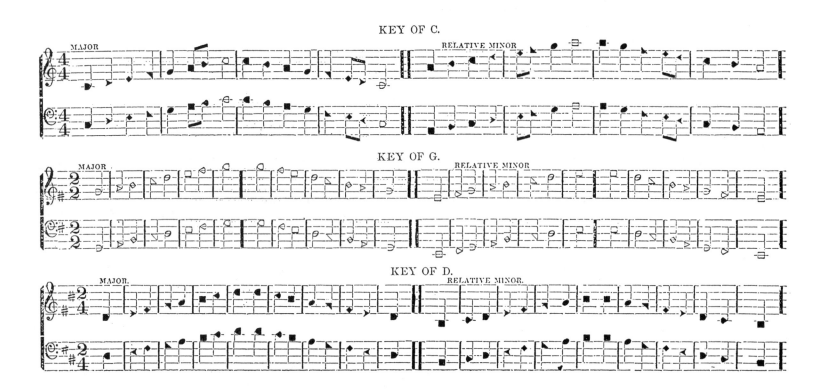

KEY OF G.

KEY OF D.

KEY OF A.

KEY OF E.

KEY OF F.

KEY OF B FLAT.

KEY OF E FLAT.

KEY OF A FLAT.

QUESTIONS.

What do we understand by the word mode? Ans. A certain disposition of the tones and semitones of the scale, with respect to the tonic or key note.—How many modes are there in music?—What are these two modes called?—Wherein does the major mode differ from the minor?—How many different keys can be had in the scale of music?—How many major?—How many minor?—What characters are used in transposing the keys?—What effect does a sharp, placed on a letter, produce?—A flat?—When we have one sharp as the signature, where is the tonic or key note?—When two sharps?—When three sharps?—When four sharps?—When one flat?—When two flats?—When three flats?—When four flats?—Of what does the Chromatic scale consist?—How many semitones does the Chromatic scale contain?—In what intervals do the major and the minor scales differ?—What is the position of the relative minor key to any major?—The relative major to any minor?—Do the major and minor keys always stand in the same relative position?

CHAPTER X.

HARMONY.

OF CHORDS, THEIR INVERSION, &c.

Sec. 49.—For the purpose of music sounds must be agreeable in themselves; they must have that clearness which distinguishes them from mere noise, and that sweetness which distinguishes them from harsh and disagreeable sounds. A succession of single musical sounds forms MELODY ; and a succession of combined melodical sounds forms HARMONY. In other words, melody consists in the agreeable succession of single sounds ; and harmony consits in the succession of a combination and accordance of different sounds.

Not only may single intervals be inverted and changed, (Sec. 45,) but also the combined intervals of chords may be inverted. The common Chord or Harmonic Triad, which is based on each letter of the scale as its fundamental note, (see Scale, Sec. 44,) may, by inversion, assume *three* different positions on each letter ; the first of each being a *direct* chord, and the other two *inverted* chords.

These Triads or Common Chords, in the following scale, are close chords ; as no chord can be formed closer together than a third. Every chord is known by its *fundamental sound ;* thus the first chord presented in the following scale, is called the chord of C, because it has C for its fundamental sound. The chord of D has D for its fundamental sound : the Chord of E has E, &c.

The first position of each of the following chords has its *fundamental sound* the lowest, the *third* in the middle, and the *fifth* the highest.

The *second* position has the *third* the lowest, the *fifth* in the middle, and the *fundamental* the highest ; because the fundamental is *inverted.*

The *third* position has the *fifth* the lowest, the *fundamental* in the middle, and the *third* the highest, because the third is *inverted.*

Thus every letter has a direct chord, and two inverted chords. The *fundamental note* of each letter is taken as *one,* from which the degrees of pitch of all the others are counted. Thus when the first or fundamental note is inverted, it becomes an eighth ; and when the third is inverted, it of course becomes a tenth from the fundamental note ; but as the fundamental note by inversion, becomes *one of a new octave,* so the tenth may in like manner, become a *third* in the new octave. (See keys on General Scale, Sec. 43.)

In the following scale, the triads which are based on C, F, and G—being the tonic, subdominant and dominant intervals of the scale—are major triads ; and those which are based on D, E, and A—being the supertonic, mediant, and submediant intervals—are minor triads. The triad based on B, the sharp seventh, is a dissonant triad, and its inversions produce major fourths and minor thirds.

INVERSION OF THE HARMONIC TRIAD OR COMMON CHORD.

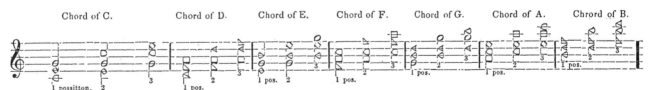

Chords of disjoint intervals may be dispersed into greater degrees or leaps, and passing in different ways, over many intermediate intervals in proceeding from one note of the chord to the other, as in the following examples of

DISPERSED CHORDS.

Sec. 50.—As intervals or chords are *consonant* or *dissonant*, according to the degrees of sound of which they are composed; and as there are fourteen intervals in the diatonic scale, (Sec. 45,) it will be expedient to give a representation of them, and of the number of semitones of which each of them is composed, as manifested in the following.

TABLE OF CONCORDS AND DISCORDS.

No. of Intervals.	No. of Semitones.	Intervals.	Concords and Discords.
14	13	An octave	A perfect chord.
13	12	Maj. seventh	A discord.
12	11	Min. seventh	A discord.
11	10	Maj. sixth	An imperfect chord.
10	9	Min. sixth	An imperfect chord.
9	8	Maj. fifth	A perfect chord.
8	7	Min. fifth	A discord.
7	7	Maj. fourth	A discord.
6	6	Min. fourth	A concinnous sound.
5	5	Maj. third	An imperfect chord.
4	4	Min. third	An imperfect chord.
3	3	Maj. second	A discord.
2	2	Min. second	A discord.
1	1	A Unison	The most perfect chord.

The UNISON, or the same identical sound, although it cannot properly be reckoned an *interval*, is always considered as such when employed in harmony. And as the scale of music is unlimited, we cannot see that it could be otherwise; for there are always intervals or steps below and above, from which every interval must proceed or step, no matter where it is found in the scale. (See note on Sec. 37.) And when the voices of the different parts of music, throughout a piece, sweetly harmonize, on the different chords, and close on a unison, must they not close on an interval of the scale?

The unison is an accordance or coincidence of sound proceeding from an equal number of vibrations of sounding bodies in a given time, and is the most perfect of all the musical sounds in the whole scale of music. (See note on vibrations, page 36.)

Next to the unison is the octave, which consists in a double number of vibrations in a given time, and is so sweet a chord with the unison, that they are scarcely distinguishable from being the self-same sound.

Next to the eighth is the perfect or major fifth, which in its vibrations is as three to two, and is a perfect chord of a sweet and charming sound; and next to the fifth in sweetness, is the major third, which in its vibrations is as five to four.

These four sounds, the unison, eighth, fifth and third, form the common chord, being the most essential sounds in every piece of music.

The minor third is also a consonant interval, and is the third of a minor triad in the minor scale; in its vibrations it is as six to five.

The minor fifth and the major fourth—each containing seven semitones are discords; and so are the major and minor seconds; and also the major and minor sevenths.

The minor fourth is termed a concinnous sound; it is not a very disagreeable discord; neither is it, by *itself*, a concord: one and four are rather dissonant, but when six is added they become consonant.—Also five and eight do not perfectly accord; but when three is introduced, they become concordant.

The major and minor sixths—the one containing ten semitones and the other nine, are both imperfect chords, though they are frequently used in harmony.

The foregoing order of consonant and dissonant intervals, in the diatonic scale, is applicable to all the octaves in the scale of music, no matter to how many octaves the General scale may ascend or descend. For in like manner as 1, 3, 5, 8, in the first octave, harmonize, so will 8, 10, 12, 15, harmonize in the second; 15, 17, 19, 22, in the third, &c. All the octaves are the same, except as they differ in gravity and acuteness. If 1, 8, 15 and 22, the fundamental notes of four octaves rising in acuteness, were sounded together by musical voices, it would produce a volume of sound which could not easily be distinguished from being the self-same sound proceeding from one voice. The same effect will be produced by striking four keys of the same letter at once, on a well-tuned instrument.

Sec. 51.—The chief excellence of harmony, or music performed in different parts, consists in a proper succession of the fundamental chords of the scale; a due order of the different notes in their inversions; and the enchaining and binding together the chords in their harmonical progression.

The tonic or key note is the most important, and the chord based on it is the principal one in every piece of music, both in the major and minor keys. Regularly every tune both begins and ends with the tonic chord.

Next to the key note, the dominant or fifth of the scale takes rank. It occurs more frequently in a piece of music than any other note, as by far the greater number of chords in ordinary tunes contain it. For this reason, and because it is the base note which regularly leads to a final close, it is called the *dominant*. The chord based on this note is also called the dominant chord, which occurs more frequently than any other except the chord of the tonic. In modulation by sharps, the dominant is also the key note of the nearest relative key.

The subdominant is the next note of importance in the scale, because its chord has the *tonic* for its *fifth*. In modulation by flats, it is the key note of the second relative key, having the original key note for its dominant.

NOTE.—As the dominant is a fifth above the tonic, and is the nearest relative key in the ascending scale, and to which the tonic is transposed by sharps; so the subdominant is a fifth below the tonic, and is the nearest relative key in the descending scale, and to which the key is transposed by flats. Hence the name *sub*-dominant.

The submediant is the third in relative importance, as its chord has two notes in common with the tonic chord, and must hence intimately blend, as also enchain with the other chords. This note is also the principal chord or tonic of the relative minor key. (See inversion of the Harmonic Triad, &c., Sec. 49.)

In the minor key, the third of the scale, or the tonic of the relative major key, frequently occurs. These chords have likewise two notes in common, which sweetly blend together in harmonical progression.

QUESTIONS.

What is the quality of good musical sounds?—In what does melody consist?—In what harmony?—How many positions can the common chord assume by inversion?—can each letter of the scale be made the fundamental note of the common chord?—What is the first position of the chord of each letter called?—What are the inverted positions called?—What is the difference between the major and the minor triads?—What is a close chord?—A dispersed chord?—Is the unison an interval in the scale of music?—How can it be an interval when it is identical? Ans. Because wherever it is found in the scale there is an interval below or above from which it takes its step.—Which are the intervals in the scale that compose the common chord?—Are the minor fifth and major fourth concords or discords? How many semitones does each of them contain?—How many intervals does the diatonic scale contain?—If there are but eight intervals in the octave, how can you get fourteen?—Are the major and the minor sixths consonant or dissonant intervals?—Will the consonant intervals in one octave be consonant throughout all the octaves in the General Scale?—What is the chief excellence of harmony?—Which is the most important chord?—The next of importance to the tonic?—The next of importance to the dominant?—The next to the subdominant?

CHAPTER XI.

DYNAMICS.

MUSICAL ELOCUTION.

Sec. 52.—A good quality of tone is an essential property to dynamic expression; and that quality consists in *purity, fulness* and *firmness.*

A tone is PURE when it is clear and smooth, having no extraneous sounds mixed with it, such as hissing, screaming, or mumbling sounds. Impurity of sound is often produced by an improper position of the parts of the mouth.

A tone is FULL when it is delivered in a free and unconstrained use of the appropriate organs of sound, and with a good volume of voice. Faintness of sound is often produced by a careless or negligent use of the vocal organs.

A tone is FIRM which is correctly given, and held steadily, without change during the whole length of the note; being perfectly under the control of the performer.

Hence, striking below the proper sound and sliding up to it, as from *five* to *eight*, &c. A wavering or trembling of the voice, and a change just at the close of a tone, produced by a careless relaxation of the organs, which should always be held firm and immovable in their proper position until the sound ceases, should be carefully guarded against and avoided. Moreover, the voice may be rendered disagreeable by being too *nasal, labial, dental* or *guttural:* that is, it may be forced too much through the nose, the lips, the teeth, or be formed too deeply in the throat. All these disagreeable sounds should be carefully corrected.

The most effectual way to correct these errors in producing sounds, is to let the pupil sound on the syllable *awe*, frequently, by marking the position of the vocal organs while sounding, and then proceed sounding the syllables which are applied to the notes, keeping the vocal organs, as much as possible, in the same position while sounding them. By this process the voice will acquire both strength and sweetness, and free itself from every disagreeable impediment. Care, however, should be taken that the voice be not made too guttural by this process.

A blending of the words when applied to music is an injury to good performance, and impairs and lessens the power of music. And, as many who read with a clear and distinct articulation, are apt to slide into this error when singing, it is deemed expedient to give a few examples, to show where the blending of words not only debases the sentence, but, in some instances, perverts the meaning of the phrase. For instance:

Example 1.　A storm that last..still morning, }
For......A storm that lasts till morning. }

Ex. 2.　He is content in..neither place, }
For......He is content in either place. }

Ex. 3.　Over waste..sand deserts, }
For......Over wastes and deserts. }

Ex. 4.　Who ever heard of such a..notion, }
For......Who ever heard of such an ocean. }

Ex. 5.　Swee..tis the da..yof sacre..drest, }
For......Sweet is the day of sacred rest. }

Ex. 6.　O com..man..dlet..tus worship, }
For......O come and let us worship. }

Ex. 7.　My bear..tshall trium..phin the Lord, }
For......My heart shall triumph in the Lord. }

Ex. 8.　Call whil..e may be foun..doh see..kim whil..e's near, }
For......Call while he may be found, Oh seek him while he's near. }

Ex. 9.　Ser..vim wi..thall thy art,.tan min..Dan..dworshi..pim with fear, }
For...Serve him with all thy heart and mind, And worship him with fear. }

Ex. 10.　He by hi..zown almighty wor..Dwill all your fear..sremove, }
For....He by his own almighty word Will all your fears remove. }

Besides this, we sometimes hear the words *when, where, while,* &c., pronounced in singing, as if they were written whe..en, whe..are, whe..ile, &c. All such incorrect and corrupt pronunciation and articulation have a tendency to obscure the expression and destroy the beauty of the sentence.

NOTE.—Whenever the teacher discovers a fault, let him first point it out and imitate it himself, and afterwards give the true style of performance; then let him require the pupils to imitate both the correct and incorrect examples. It is not enough for the teacher to say that a fault exists; he must actually point it out, and exhibit it by his own performance, and this over and over again, until the pupils obtain a clear perception of it, and know both how to produce it, and how to correct and avoid it.

Sec. 53.—One of the greatest excellencies of sacred vocal music, is that strict union which should ever subsist between the words and the music. Hence the first object of the chorister is, to choose a tune to which the words are suited or ally themselves, both in sentiment and quality. Much of the beauty and strength of sacred music depend upon this. For psalms and hymns of prayer and supplication a minor key should generally be chosen, because it is of a plaintive, soft and melting quality; and for those of praise and thanksgiving, a major key, because it is of a cheerful, lively, and animating quality. This may be considered a general rule, yet there may be some exceptions, as some tunes of the major key partake, in some measure, of the soft, gentle, and subduing qualities of the minor, and some of the minor key, in some degree, partake of the enlivening and cheering qualities of the major. Hence, as there are psalms and hymns which contain devotional matter, of both prayer and praise intermingled, so there are tunes suited for all those poetical productions which are adapted to the emotions of the pious mind. Now, when the poetry is truly expressive, and thus adapted to music, there is something grand and subduing in the harmonious progression of full chords, which brings a calm over the soul, rivets the attention, and enraptures the feelings in view of the sentiment, and thus produces a frame of mind, in the Zion traveler, which is highly devotional.

Sec. 54.—In the connection of words with musical sounds, good elocution is necessary, as well for the vocal musician as for the orator. Every word to which music is applied, should be pronounced distinctly and grammatically. The sound should be prolonged entirely on the vowel, and the mouth kept open in one fixed position from the beginning to the end of the sound, and the consonants before and after the vowels forcibly and quickly, yet distinctly articulated. Without this, little expression can be given to vocal music; and for good and dignified performance it is indispensably necessary that it be strictly observed.

Every word and every sentence should be pronounced, in singing, with a clear voice, and with the same distinctness as when spoken or read; so that the sentiment of the poetry when united with the sound of music, be well understood. For to "sing with the Spirit and to sing with the understanding also," those heaven inspiring words in unison with the sweet strains of music, with their soft and soothing accents, is what has such a benign and powerful influence over the human mind. And when singers can realize the subject, and enter into the proper feeling and spirit of the poet, there is but little danger of not producing dynamic expression and musical elocution. And nothing can compensate for a want of feeling, and the realization of the expression of the poetry, because in the performance, the tone, the graces in the modulation of the voice, and sound, should all be suited to the subject which the poetry expresses, which is the *only true guide* to dynamical expression and musical elocution.

NOTE.—"Writers have attempted with great ingenuity, to lay down rules for the varieties of expression; but whoever undertakes to follow rules in giving expression, presents us with a mere skeleton, without life and animation. Every appearance of effort disgusts us . . . . True expression clothes her song in characteristic display of grace, majesty and pathos; not a single note will be breathed in vain. She wisely considers that ornament should ever be subordinate to the sentiment, and that the grand end of the composition is to speak to the judgment as well as the hearing. The most common mistake with composers and church choirs is, in attempting to express words and not ideas.—Singing the word *small* with such softness as scarcely to be heard, or exerting all the powers of the lungs on the word *large*, is punning, not expressing; trifling with the words and neglecting the sentiment. Instead of considering how this or that word should be executed, the first object should be to study the true meaning and character of the subject, so that effect may not only be given to a word here and a word there, but the sense of the whole sentence expressed, so as to be understood and *felt*. It is true the expression of the whole is conveyed by appropriate emphasis on particular words, but it is not simply the words which demand emphasis, but their connection with the sentence.

Religious feeling is full of dignified and placid joy, of which the gentle swelling of the emphatic words gives the most appropriate idea.

"Many terms are prefixed, by composers, to the several strains, as directions for the performer. These terms are usually Italian, such as *Andante, Affetuoso, &c.* In following such directions there is danger in attempting to express what the performer does not actually feel. In such a case the effect will often be ludicrous; and at best can but astonish us with the art and dexterity manifested. In true expression, the composer and performer are lost sight of; the attention is rivited, and the feelings enraptured in view of the sentiment.

[Porter's Musical Cyclopedia.

In all vocal performance of sacred music, singers should enter into those emotions which are expressed by the poetry. They should avoid a dull, heavy, unfeeling style of performance, and cultivate that which comes from the heart, which has some soul, some meaning, and which is appropriate to the words and music. There is something in the nature of musical tones, when combined with sacred poetry, which is heavenly and divine; and in the pious mind produces that lowly prostration of soul, and those pure affections with which we ought to approach the throne of the Deity.

——:o:——

ORIGIN AND UTILITY OF MUSIC.

"The capacity of the human mind for poetry and music has been common to every age and nation; and though too generally perverted to evil and sinful purposes, it was doubtless originally implanted by the CREATOR, for wise and holy reasons, and should be consecrated to His service and glory. Accordingly hymns or songs or praise form a considerable portion of the Sacred Scriptures, some of which were composed on particular occasions, and sung as a part of solemn worship at the time or afterwards, in commemoration of the transactions celebrated in them."—Ex. 15; 1 Sam. 2; 2 Sam. 22.

But it was not with man that this heavenly science originated. It claims to have descended from the skies. For when the Lord "laid the foundations of the earth, ... the morning stars sang together, and all the sons of God shouted for joy." Job 38: 4–7. And at the nativity of CHRIST, there appeared to the shepherds a "multitude of the heavenly host praising God, and saying, Glory to God in the highest, and on earth peace, good will towards men." From

this we may readily infer that these heavenly songsters were no strangers in Eden, in that day when the Creator himself walked and talked with his earth-born children in Paradise, and that the sound was prolonged by them in that blissful and happy place.

Hence sacred song is coeval with the creation; and the first music of the human voice must have been a holy exercise of a joyous ascription of praise to the bountiful Lord and Creator. And how consoling and heart-cheering has this heavenly science ever since proven to the people of God, both under the Old and the New Testament dispensation, in awakening and strengthening their devotional affections, when holding communion with the Father of Mercies!

What a high rank did music obtain under king David, that sweet singer of Israel, and his son Solomon, who not only cultivated it to a high extent, but by the inspiration of the Spirit of God, furnished material for the devotional exercises, which are highly valued by the people of God, and have been added to the inspired volume. How great must their influence have been, in promoting this heavenly science, when, at the dedication of the Temple, there were about four thousand singers and players on instruments, (according to 1 Chron. 23: 5,) who performed together with so much accuracy, that their sounds were as ONE SOUND to be heard in praising the Lord. And when they lifted up their voices, with the trumpets and cymbals, and instruments of music, and praised the Lord, the house was filled with a cloud, even the house of the Lord: so that the priests could not stand to minister by reason of the cloud: for the glory of the Lord had filled the house of the Lord. 2 Chron. 5: 7—14.

"We can scarcely enlarge our thoughts to conceive the effects which these high praises of God, sung by so vast a multitude, with harmonious elevation of heart and voice, on these joyful occasions, must have produced. It naturally leads us to consider the songs of the redeemed of the Lord in glory: and perhaps we are not, in this world, capable of more just and spiritual ideas of them, than are suggested by these subjects, though we may be sure that they are unspeakably more sublime, enlarged and refined.

"Hear I, or dream I hear their distant strains,
Sweet to the soul, and tasting strong of heaven."

"How holy, how glorious is the God we worship! How wonderful are his perfections! 'It is good to sing praises unto his name,' from the affections of an overflowing heart. What can be more delightful than songs of joy issuing from lips that taste the love of God! Such were the Psalms of David, and such the songs of the primitive Christians, the martyrs, and the reformers. Such are the songs we should cultivate. They will prove a rich foretaste of joys unseen and eternal."

HARMONIA SACRA.

"A Poet he, and touched with heav'n's own fire, | Breathes a gay rapture through your thrilling breast,
Who with bold rage or solemn pomp of sounds, | Or melts the heart with airs divinely sad:
Inflames, exalts, and ravishes the soul: | Or wakes to horror the tremendous strings.
Now tender, plaintive, sweet almost to pain | Such was the Bard, whose heavenly strains of old,
In love dissolves you; now in sprightly strains | Appeased the fiend of melancholy Saul,"—ARMSTRONG.

PART I.

CONTAINING THE MOST APPROPRIATE TUNES OF THE DIFFERENT METRES, FOR PUBLIC WORSHIP.

Metre 1.   OLD HUNDRED. L. M.

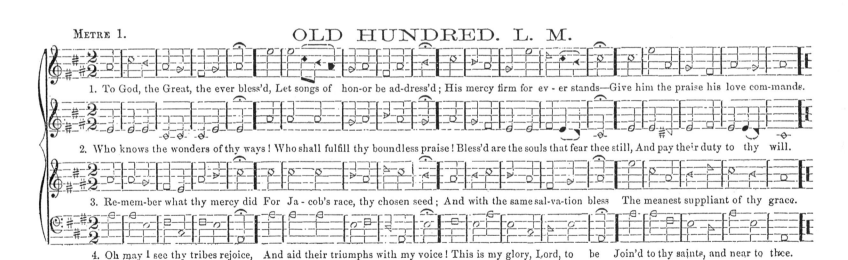

1. To God, the Great, the ever bless'd, Let songs of hon-or be ad-dress'd; His mercy firm for ev - er stands—Give him the praise his love com-mands.

2. Who knows the wonders of thy ways! Who shall fulfill thy boundless praise! Bless'd are the souls that fear thee still, And pay their duty to thy will.

3. Re-mem-ber what thy mercy did For Ja - cob's race, thy chosen seed; And with the same sal-va-tion bless The meanest suppliant of thy grace.

4. Oh may I see thy tribes rejoice, And aid their triumphs with my voice! This is my glory, Lord, to be Join'd to thy saints, and near to thee.

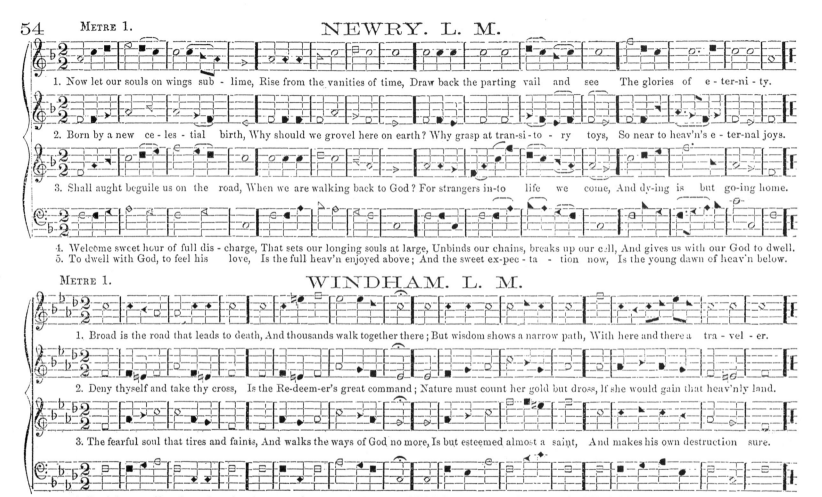

54 METRE 1.

NEWRY. L. M.

1. Now let our souls on wings sub - lime, Rise from the vanities of time, Draw back the parting vail and see The glories of e - ter-ni - ty.

2. Born by a new ce - les - tial birth, Why should we grovel here on earth? Why grasp at tran-si - to - ry toys, So near to heav'n's e - ter-nal joys.

3. Shall aught beguile us on the road, When we are walking back to God? For strangers in-to life we come, And dy-ing is but go-ing home.

4. Welcome sweet hour of full dis - charge, That sets our longing souls at large, Unbinds our chains, breaks up our cell, And gives us with our God to dwell.
5. To dwell with God, to feel his love, Is the full heav'n enjoyed above; And the sweet ex-pec - ta - tion now, Is the young dawn of heav'n below.

METRE 1.

WINDHAM. L. M.

1. Broad is the road that leads to death, And thousands walk together there; But wisdom shows a narrow path, With here and there a tra - vel - er.

2. Deny thyself and take thy cross, Is the Re-deem-er's great command; Nature must count her gold but dross, If she would gain that heav'nly land.

3. The fearful soul that tires and faints, And walks the ways of God no more, Is but esteemed almost a saint, And makes his own destruction sure.

4. Lord, let not all my hopes be vain, Create my heart en-tire-ly new, Which hypocrites could ne'er attain, Which false a-pos - tates nev-er knew.

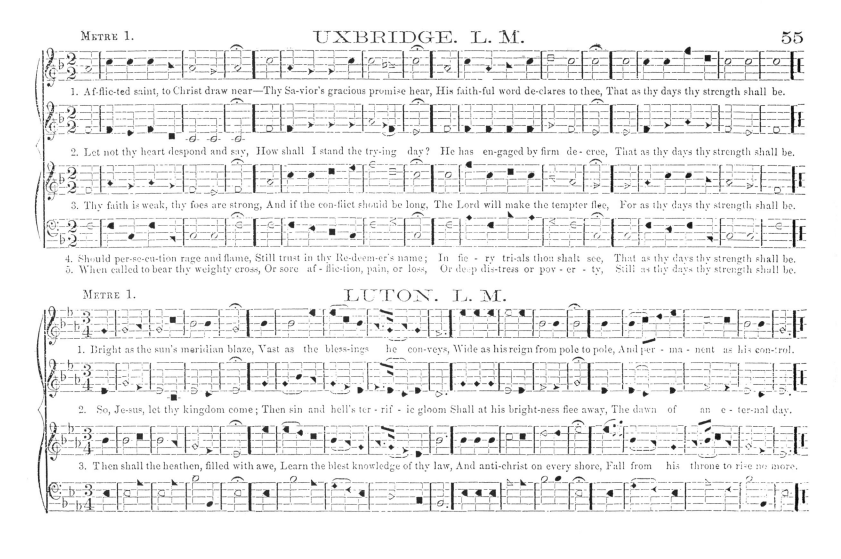

Metre 1.

UXBRIDGE. L. M.

55

1. Af-flic-ted saint, to Christ draw near—Thy Sa-vior's gracious promise hear, His faith-ful word de-clares to thee, That as thy days thy strength shall be.

2. Let not thy heart despond and say, How shall I stand the try-ing day? He has en-gaged by firm de-cree, That as thy days thy strength shall be.

3. Thy faith is weak, thy foes are strong, And if the con-flict should be long, The Lord will make the tempter flee, For as thy days thy strength shall be.

4. Should per-se-cu-tion rage and flame, Still trust in thy Re-deem-er's name; In fie-ry tri-als thou shalt see, That as thy days thy strength shall be.
5. When called to bear thy weighty cross, Or sore af-flic-tion, pain, or loss, Or deep dis-tress or pov-er-ty, Still as thy days thy strength shall be.

Metre 1.

LUTON. L. M.

1. Bright as the sun's meridian blaze, Vast as the bless-ings he con-veys, Wide as his reign from pole to pole, And per-ma-nent as his con-trol.

2. So, Je-sus, let thy kingdom come; Then sin and hell's ter-rif-ic gloom Shall at his bright-ness flee away, The dawn of an e-ter-nal day.

3. Then shall the heathen, filled with awe, Learn the blest knowledge of thy law, And anti-christ on every shore, Fall from his throne to rise no more.

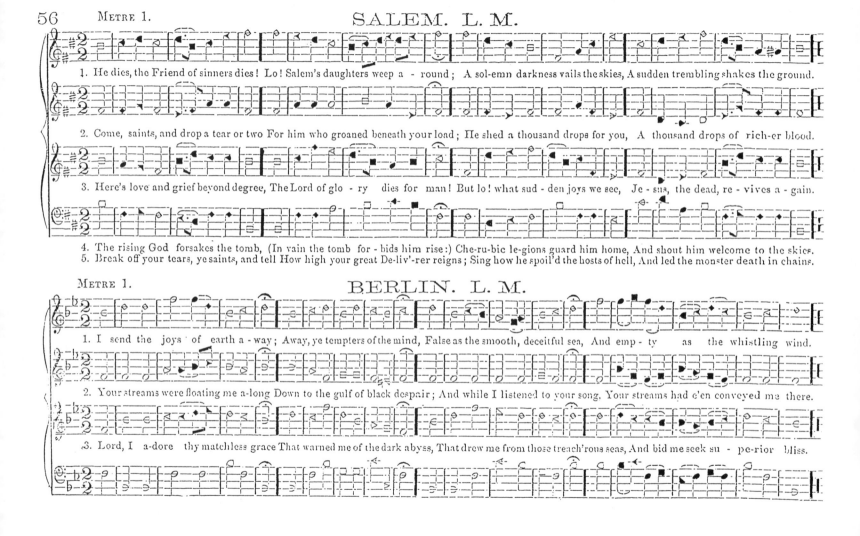

56   Metre 1.   SALEM. L. M.

1. He dies, the Friend of sinners dies! Lo! Salem's daughters weep a - round; A sol-emn darkness vails the skies, A sudden trembling shakes the ground.

2. Come, saints, and drop a tear or two For him who groaned beneath your load; He shed a thousand drops for you, A thousand drops of rich-er blood.

3. Here's love and grief beyond degree, The Lord of glo - ry dies for man! But lo! what sud - den joys we see, Je - sus, the dead, re - vives a - gain.

4. The rising God forsakes the tomb, (In vain the tomb for - bids him rise:) Che-ru-bic le-gions guard him home, And shout him welcome to the skies.
5. Break off your tears, ye saints, and tell How high your great De-liv'-rer reigns; Sing how he spoil'd the hosts of hell, And led the monster death in chains.

Metre 1.   BERLIN. L. M.

1. I send the joys of earth a - way; Away, ye tempters of the mind, False as the smooth, deceitful sea, And emp - ty as the whistling wind.

2. Your streams were floating me a-long Down to the gulf of black despair; And while I listened to your song, Your streams had e'en conveyed me there.

3. Lord, I a-dore thy matchless grace That warned me of the dark abyss, That drew me from those treach'rous seas, And bid me seek su - pe-rior bliss.

METRE. 1.

HEAVENLY FLIGHT. L. M.

1 While on the verge of life I stand, And view the scene on ei - ther hand, My spir - it struggles with my clay, And longs to wing its flight a - way.

2 Where Jesus dwells my soul would be, And faints my much loved Lord to see; Earth, twine no more about my heart, For 'tis far bet - ter to de - part.

3 Come, ye an-gel - ic en-voys, come, And lead the will-ing pil-grim home! Ye know the way to Je-sus' throne,—Source of my joys and of your own.

4 That blissful in-ter-view, how sweet, To fall trans-port-ed at his feet: Raised in his arms to view his face, Thro' the full beam-ings of his grace.

METRE 1.

SOLEMNITY. L. M.

1 'Twas on that dark, that dole-ful night, When powers of earth and hell arose, Against the Son of God's de-light, And friends be-trayed him to his foes.

2 Be - fore the mournful scene began, He took the bread and bless'd and brake ; What love thro' all his actions ran ! What wondrous words of grace he spake !

3 "This is my bo - dy broke for sin, Re-ceive and eat the living food ;" Then took the cup and blessed the wine; "'Tis the new cov'nant in my blood."

4 For us his flesh with nails was torn, He bore the scourge, he felt the thorn ; And justice pour'd up-on his head Its heav - y ven-geance in our stead.

METRE 1.

GRAVITY. L. M.

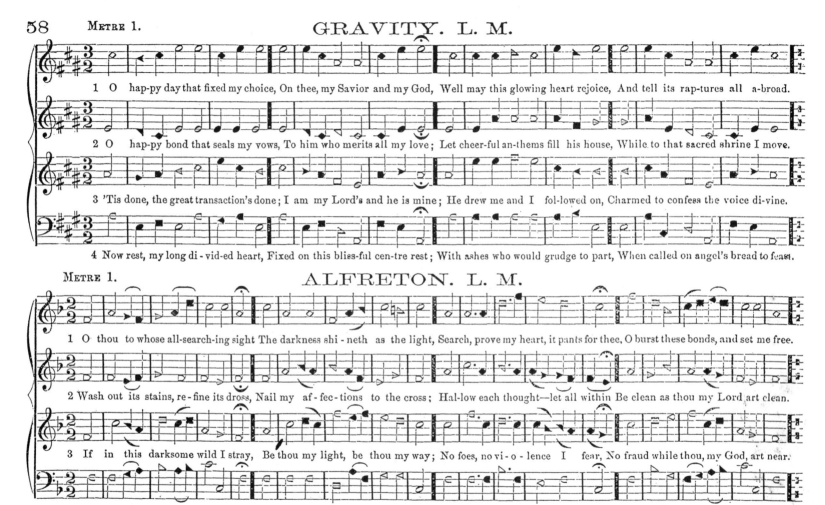

1 O hap-py day that fixed my choice, On thee, my Savior and my God, Well may this glowing heart rejoice, And tell its rap-tures all a-broad.

2 O hap-py bond that seals my vows, To him who merits all my love; Let cheer-ful an-thems fill his house, While to that sacred shrine I move.

3 'Tis done, the great transaction's done; I am my Lord's and he is mine; He drew me and I fol-lowed on, Charmed to confess the voice di-vine.

4 Now rest, my long di - vid-ed heart, Fixed on this bliss-ful cen-tre rest; With ashes who would grudge to part, When called on angel's bread to feast.

METRE 1.

ALFRETON. L. M.

1 O thou to whose all-search-ing sight The darkness shi - neth as the light, Search, prove my heart, it pants for thee, O burst these bonds, and set me free.

2 Wash out its stains, re-fine its dross, Nail my af-fec-tions to the cross; Hal-low each thought—let all within Be clean as thou my Lord art clean.

3 If in this darksome wild I stray, Be thou my light, be thou my way; No foes, no vi - o - lence I fear, No fraud while thou, my God, art near.

4 When ri-sing floods my soul o'er-flow, When sinks my heart in waves of woe. Je - sus, thy time-ly aid im - part, And raise my head, and cheer my heart.

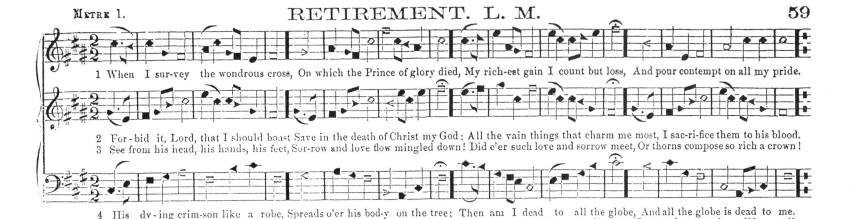

1 When I sur-vey the wondrous cross, On which the Prince of glory died, My rich-est gain I count but loss, And pour contempt on all my pride.

2 For-bid it, Lord, that I should boast Save in the death of Christ my God; All the vain things that charm me most, I sac-ri-fice them to his blood.
3 See from his head, his hands, his feet, Sor-row and love flow mingled down! Did e'er such love and sorrow meet, Or thorns compose so rich a crown!

4 His dy-ing crim-son like a robe, Spreads o'er his bod-y on the tree; Then am I dead to all the globe, And all the globe is dead to me.
5 Were the whole realm of nature mine, That were a pres-ent far too small; Love so a-maz-ing, so di-vine, De-mands my soul, my life, my all.

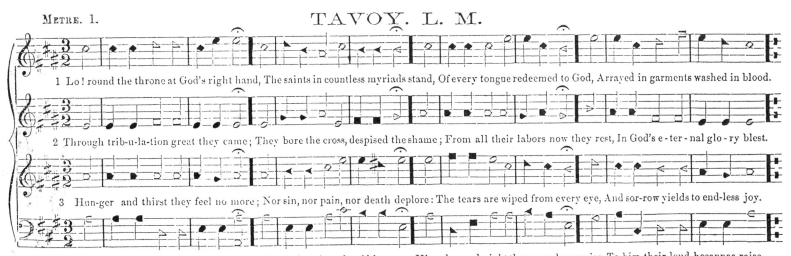

1 Lo! round the throne at God's right hand, The saints in countless myriads stand, Of every tongue redeemed to God, Arrayed in garments washed in blood.

2 Through trib-u-la-tion great they came; They bore the cross, despised the shame; From all their labors now they rest, In God's e-ter-nal glo-ry blest.

3 Hun-ger and thirst they feel no more; Nor sin, nor pain, nor death deplore: The tears are wiped from every eye, And sor-row yields to end-less joy.

4 They see their Sa-vior face to face, And sing the triumphs of his grace; Him, day and night they ceaseless praise, To him their loud hosannas raise.
5 Wor-thy the Lamb for sinners slain, Thro' endless years to live and reign; Thou hast redeemed us by thy blood, And made us kings and priests to God.

METRE 1.

WELLS. L. M.

1 Ye na-tions round the earth, rejoice Before the Lord your sov'reign King; Serve him with cheerful heart and voice, With all your tongues his glory sing.

2 The Lord is God, 'tis he a-lone Doth life, and breath, and being give; We are his work and not our own—The sheep that on his pas-tures live.

3 En-ter his gates with songs of joy— With praises to his courts re-pair, And make it your di-vine em-ploy To pay your thanks and hon-ors there.

4 The Lord is good, the Lord is kind, Great is his grace, his mer-cy sure; And the whole race of man shall find, His truth from age to age en-dure.

METRE 1.

BOURBON. L. M.

1 From deep dis-tress and troubled thoughts, To thee, my God, I raise my cries; If thou se-vere-ly mark our faults, No flesh can stand be-fore thine eyes.

2 But thou hast built thy throne of grace, Free to dispense thy pardons there, That sinners may approach thy face, And hope and love, as well as fear.
3 As the be-night-ed pilgrims wait, And long and wish for breaking day, So waits my soul be-fore thy gate; When will my God his face dis-play.

4 My trust is fixed up-on thy word, Nor shall I trust thy word in vain, Let mourning souls address the Lord, And find re-lief from all their pain.
5 Great is his love and large his grace, Thro' the re-demp-tion of his Son; He turns our feet from sinful ways, And par-dons what our hands have done.

HEALING BALM. L. M

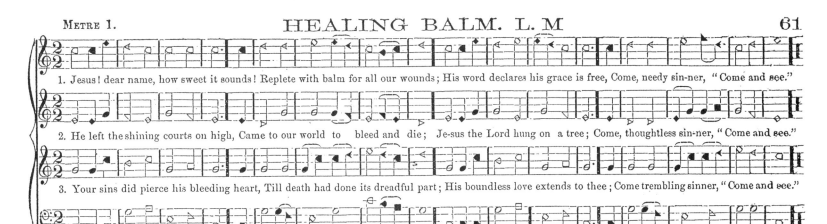

1. Jesus! dear name, how sweet it sounds! Replete with balm for all our wounds; His word declares his grace is free, Come, needy sin-ner, "Come and see."

2. He left the shining courts on high, Came to our world to bleed and die; Je-sus the Lord hung on a tree; Come, thoughtless sin-ner, "Come and see."

3. Your sins did pierce his bleeding heart, Till death had done its dreadful part; His boundless love extends to thee; Come trembling sinner, "Come and see."

3. His blood can cleanse the foulest stain, Can make the vilest sin - ner clean; This fountain open stands for thee; Come, guilty sin - ner, "Come and see."

MAGDEBURG. L. M.

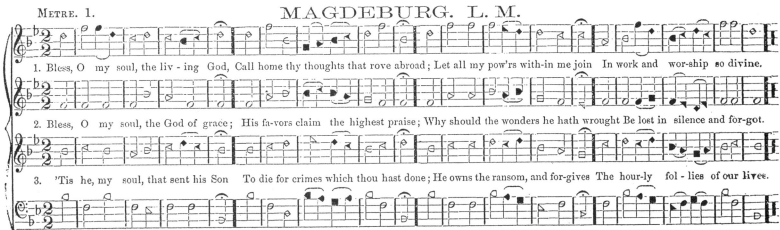

1. Bless, O my soul, the liv - ing God, Call home thy thoughts that rove abroad; Let all my pow'rs with-in me join In work and wor-ship so divine.

2. Bless, O my soul, the God of grace; His fa-vors claim the highest praise; Why should the wonders he hath wrought Be lost in silence and for-got.

3. 'Tis he, my soul, that sent his Son To die for crimes which thou hast done; He owns the ransom, and for-gives The hour-ly fol - lies of our lives.

4. The vi-ces of the mind he heals; And cures the pain which nature feels; Redeems the soul from hell, and saves Our wasting lives from threat'ning graves.

62

Metre 1.

KEDRON. L. M.

1. Ye that pass by, be-hold the Man,   The Man of grief condemned for you; The Lamb of God for sinners slain, Weep-ing to Cal - va - ry pur-sue.

2. His sa-cred limbs, they stretch, they tear, With nails they fasten to the wood—His sa-cred limbs exposed and bare, Or only   cov - ered with his blood.

3. See there! His temples crowned with thorns, His bleeding hands extended wide; His streaming feet transfixed and torn, The fountain gushing from his side.

4. Thou dear, thou suff'ring Son of God, How doth thy heart to sinners move? Sprinkle on us thy precious blood, And melt us with thy dy - ing love.

Meter 1.

HEBRON. L. M.

1. Stand up, my soul, shake off thy fears, And gird the gos-pel ar-mor on; March to the gate of end-less joys, Where thy great Captain Savior's gone.

2. Hell and thy sins re-sist thy course, But hell and sin are vanquished foes; Thy Je-sus nail'd them to the cross, And sung the tri-umph when he rose.

3. What tho' the prince of darkness rage, And waste the fu-ry of his spite, E - ter-nal chains con-fine him down To fie - ry deeps and endless night.

4. Then let my soul march bold-ly on, Press for-ward to the heaven-ly gate; There peace and joy e - ter-nal reign, And glitt'ring robes for conq'rors wait.

Metre 1.

STERLING. L. M.

1 Give to our God im-mor-tal praise; Mer-cy and truth are all his ways; Won-ders of praise to God be-long, Re-peat his mer-cies in your song.

2 Give to the Lord of lords re-nown; The King of kings with glo-ry crown; His mer-cies ev-er shall en-dure, When lords and kings are known no more.

3 He built the earth, he spread the sky, And fixed the star-ry lights on high; Won-ders of grace to God be-long, Re-peat his mer-cies in your song.

4 He fills the sun with morning light, He bids the moon di-rect the night; His mer-cies ev-er shall endure, When suns and moons shall shine no more.

Metre 1.

TENDER THOUGHT. L. M.

1 A - rise, my tend'rest thoughts, a-rise, To tor-rents melt my streaming eyes; And thou, my heart, with anguish feel, those evils which thou canst not heal.

2 See hu-man na-ture sunk in shame! See scan-dals pour'd on Je-sus' name! The Father wounded thro' the Son; The world abus'd, the soul undone!

3 See the short course of vain de-light, Clo - sing in ev - er - last-ing night;— In flames that no abatement know, Tho' briny tears for-ev-er flow.

4 My God, I feel the mournful scene! My bow-els yearn o'er dy-ing men! And fain my pity would reclaim, And snatch the firebrands from the flame.

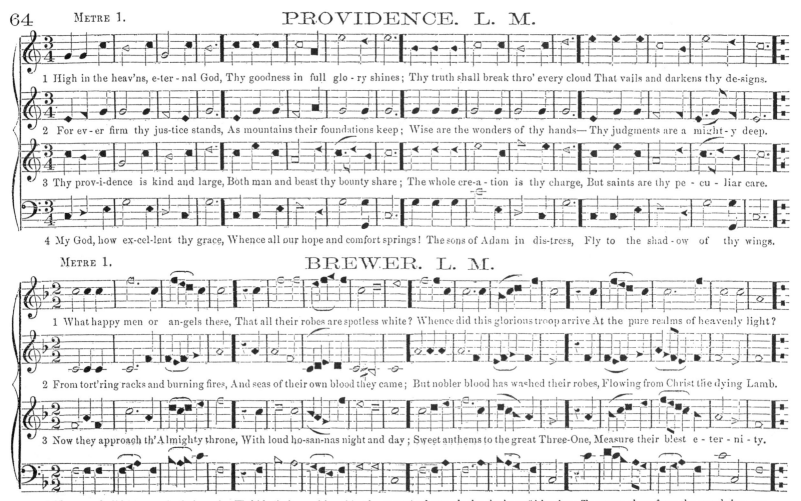

64   METRE 1.   PROVIDENCE. L. M.

1 High in the heav'ns, e-ter-nal God, Thy goodness in full glo-ry shines; Thy truth shall break thro' every cloud That vails and darkens thy de-signs.

2 For ev-er firm thy jus-tice stands, As mountains their foundations keep; Wise are the wonders of thy hands— Thy judgments are a might-y deep.

3 Thy prov-i-dence is kind and large, Both man and beast thy bounty share; The whole cre-a-tion is thy charge, But saints are thy pe-cu-liar care.

4 My God, how ex-cel-lent thy grace, Whence all our hope and comfort springs! The sons of Adam in dis-tress, Fly to the shad-ow of thy wings.

METRE 1.   BREWER. L. M.

1 What happy men or an-gels these, That all their robes are spotless white? Whence did this glorious troop arrive At the pure realms of heavenly light?

2 From tort'ring racks and burning fires, And seas of their own blood they came; But nobler blood has washed their robes, Flowing from Christ the dying Lamb.

3 Now they approach th'Almighty throne, With loud ho-san-nas night and day; Sweet anthems to the great Three-One, Measure their blest e-ter-ni-ty.

4 No more shall hunger pain their souls; He bids their parching thirst be gone, And spreads the shadow of his wings To screen them from the parch-ing sun.

Metre 1.

DEVOTION. L. M.

1 Oh for a sweet, in-spir-ing ray, To an - i - mate our fee-ble strains, From the bright realms of endless day, The blissful realms where Jesus reigns.

2 There low before the glorious throne, A-dor-ing saints and an-gels fall! And with de-light-ful wor-ship own, His smile their bliss, their heav'n, their all.

3 Im - mor-tal glo-ries crown his head, While tune-ful hal-le-lu-jahs rise, And love, and joy, and triumph spread, Thro' all th' as-sem-blies of the skies.

4 He smiles, and seraphs tune their songs, to boundless rapture while they gaze ; Ten thousand thousand joyful tongues Re-sound his ev - er - last - ing praise.

Metre 1.

WINCHESTER. L. M.

1 No more, dear Savior, will I boast Of beauty, wealth, or loud applause, The world has all its glories lost, A - - mid the tri-umphs of the cross.

2 In eve-ry fea-ture of thy face Beauty her fairest charms displays ; Truth, wisdom, majesty and grace Shine thence in sweet-ly mingled rays.

3 Thy wealth the pow'r of thought transcends, 'Tis vast, immense, and all divine : Thy empire, Lord, o'er worlds extends—The sun, the moon, the stars are thine.

4 Yet (Oh how mar-vel-ous the sight !) I see thee on a cross ex-pire ; Thy God-head veil'd in sable night, And an - gels from the scene re - tire.

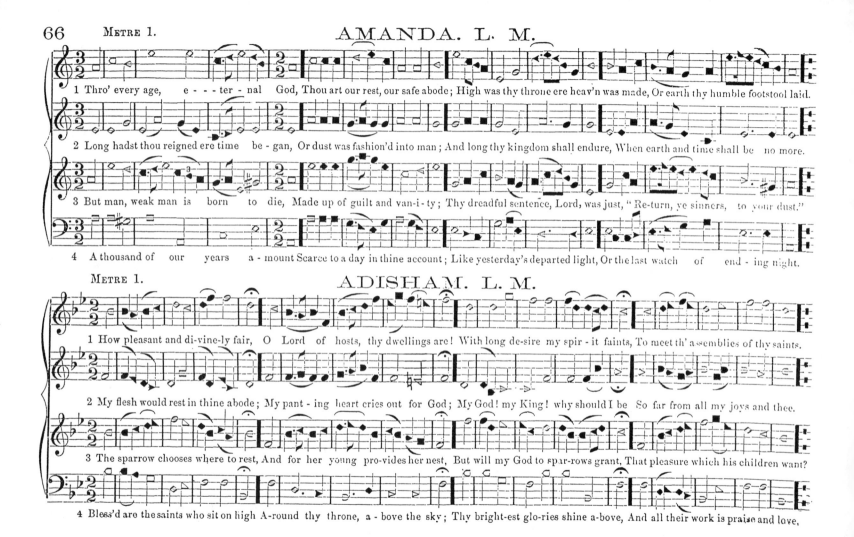

Metre 1.

AMANDA. L. M.

1 Thro' every age, e - - - ter - nal God, Thou art our rest, our safe abode; High was thy throne ere heav'n was made, Or earth thy humble footstool laid.

2 Long hadst thou reigned ere time be - gan, Or dust was fashion'd into man; And long thy kingdom shall endure, When earth and time shall be no more.

3 But man, weak man is born to die, Made up of guilt and van-i-ty; Thy dreadful sentence, Lord, was just, "Re-turn, ye sinners, to your dust."

4 A thousand of our years a - mount Scarce to a day in thine account; Like yesterday's departed light, Or the last watch of end - ing night.

Metre 1.

ADISHAM. L. M.

1 How pleasant and di-vine-ly fair, O Lord of hosts, thy dwellings are! With long de-sire my spir - it faints, To meet th' assemblies of thy saints.

2 My flesh would rest in thine abode; My pant - ing heart cries out for God; My God! my King! why should I be So far from all my joys and thee.

3 The sparrow chooses where to rest, And for her young pro-vides her nest, But will my God to spar-rows grant, That pleasure which his children want?

4 Bless'd are the saints who sit on high A-round thy throne, a - bove the sky; Thy bright-est glo-ries shine a-bove, And all their work is praise and love.

METRE 1.

WESTON. L. M.

1. Sinners, oh, why so thoughtless grown? Why in such dreadful haste to die? Daring to leap to worlds unknown! Heedless a - gainst thy God to fly.

2. Wilt thou despise e - ter-nal fate, Urged on by sin's de-lu-sive dreams? Madly at the in - fer-nal gate, And force thy pas - sage to the flames?

3. Stay, sin-ner, on the gospel plains, And hear the Lord of life unfold The glo-ries of his dy - ing pains!— For-ev-er tell - ing yet un - told!

METRE 1.

ROCKBRIDGE. L. M.

1. Sweet is the work, my God, my King, To praise thy name, give thanks and sing, To show thy love by morning light, And talk of all thy truths at night.

2. Sweet is the day of sac-red rest, No mor-tal care shall seize my breast, O may my heart in tune be found, Like Da-vid's harp of solemn sound.

3. My heart shall triumph in my Lord, And bless his works, and bless his word; Thy works of grace, how bright they shine, How deep thy counsels! how divine!

4. Fools never raise their thoughts so high; Like brutes they live like brutes they die; Like grass they flourish, till thy breath Blasts them in ev-er-last - ing death.

68 METRE 1. SHOEL. L. M.

1 Who is this fair One in dis-tress, That travels through the wilderness? And press'd with sorrows and with sins, On her be-lov-ed Lord she leans.

2 This is the spouse of Christ our God, Bought with the treasures of his blood; And her request, and her complaint, Is but the voice of eve-ry saint.

3 O let my name en-gra-ven stand Both on thy heart and on thy hand; Seal me upon thine arm and wear, The pledge of love for-ev-er there.

4 Stronger than death thy love is known, Which floods of wrath could never drown; And hell and earth in vain combine, To quench a fire so much di-vine.

METRE 1. SUPPLICATION. L. M.

1 Show pit-y, Lord, O Lord, for-give, Let a re-pent-ing reb-el live; Are not thy mercies large and free? May not a sin-ner trust in thee?

2 My crimes are great, but can't sur-pass The pow'r and glory of thy grace; Great God, thy nature hath no bound, So let thy pard'ning love be found.

3 O wash my soul from ev-ry sin, And make my guilty conscience clean; Here on my heart the bur-den lies, And past of-fenc-es pain my eyes.

4 My lips with shame my sins con-fess A-gainst thy law, against thy grace; Lord, should thy judgments grow severe, I am condemned but thou art clear.

METRE 1. MIGDOL. L. M.

1 Soon may the last glad song a-rise, Thro' all the mil-lions of the skies, That song of triumph which records That all the earth is now the Lord's.

2 Let thrones, and pow'rs, and kingdoms be O-be-dient, might-y God, to thee! And over land, and stream and main, Now wave the scepter of thy reign.

3 Oh let that glo-rious anthem swell, Let host to host the tri-umph tell, That not one rebel heart remains, But o-ver all the Sa-vior reigns.

METRE 1. RETREAT. L. M.

1 From eve-ry storm-y wind that blows, From every swell-ing tide of woes, There is a calm, a sure re-treat; 'Tis found be-fore the mer-cy seat.

2 There is a place where Je-sus sheds The oil of glad-ness on our heads—A place of all on earth most sweet; It is the blood-bought mercy seat.

3 There is a scene where spirits blend, Where friend holds fellowship with friend; Tho' sunder'd far, by faith they meet Around one common mer-cy seat.

4 There, there on ea-gle wings we soar, And sin and sense mo-lest no more: And heav'n comes down our souls to greet, And glory crowns the mercy seat.

70

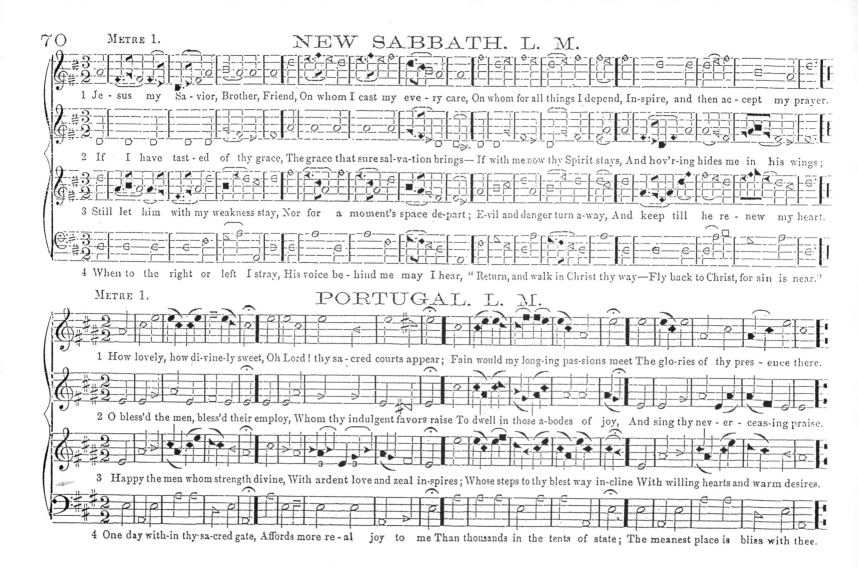

NEW SABBATH. L. M.

METRE 1.

1 Je - sus my Sa - vior, Brother, Friend, On whom I cast my eve - ry care, On whom for all things I depend, In-spire, and then ac - cept my prayer.

2 If I have tast - ed of thy grace, The grace that sure sal-va-tion brings— If with me now thy Spirit stays, And hov'r-ing hides me in his wings;

3 Still let him with my weakness stay, Nor for a moment's space de-part; E-vil and danger turn a-way, And keep till he re - new my heart.

4 When to the right or left I stray, His voice be - hind me may I hear, "Return, and walk in Christ thy way—Fly back to Christ, for sin is near."

PORTUGAL. L. M.

METRE 1.

1 How lovely, how di-vine-ly sweet, Oh Lord! thy sa - cred courts appear; Fain would my long-ing pas-sions meet The glo-ries of thy pres - ence there.

2 O bless'd the men, bless'd their employ, Whom thy indulgent favors raise To dwell in those a-bodes of joy, And sing thy nev - er - ceas-ing praise.

3 Happy the men whom strength divine, With ardent love and zeal in-spires; Whose steps to thy blest way in-cline With willing hearts and warm desires.

4 One day with-in thy sa-cred gate, Affords more re - al joy to me Than thousands in the tents of state; The meanest place is bliss with thee.

METRE 1.

REST. L. M.

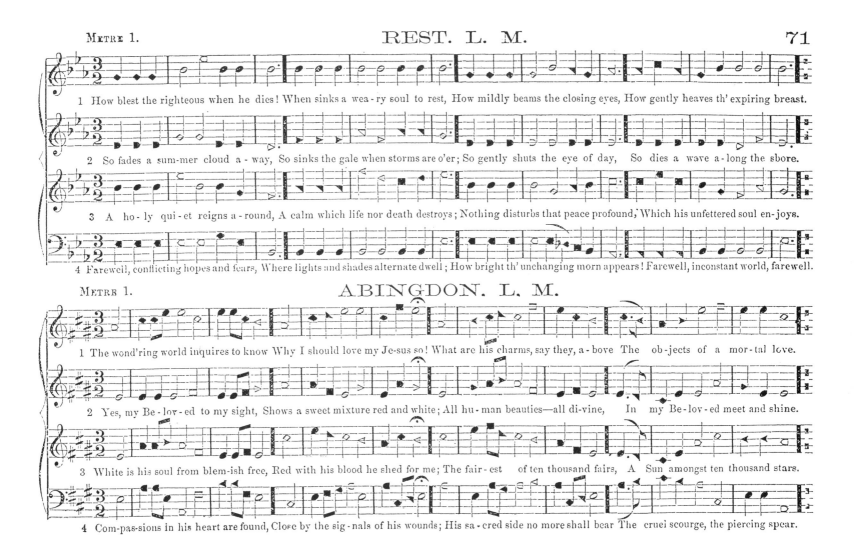

1 How blest the righteous when he dies! When sinks a wea-ry soul to rest, How mildly beams the closing eyes, How gently heaves th' expiring breast.

2 So fades a sum-mer cloud a-way, So sinks the gale when storms are o'er; So gently shuts the eye of day, So dies a wave a-long the shore.

3 A ho-ly qui-et reigns a-round, A calm which life nor death destroys; Nothing disturbs that peace profound, Which his unfettered soul en-joys.

4 Farewell, conflicting hopes and fears, Where lights and shades alternate dwell; How bright th' unchanging morn appears! Farewell, inconstant world, farewell.

METRE 1.

ABINGDON. L. M.

1 The wond'ring world inquires to know Why I should love my Je-sus so! What are his charms, say they, a-bove The ob-jects of a mor-tal love.

2 Yes, my Be-lov-ed to my sight, Shows a sweet mixture red and white; All hu-man beauties—all di-vine, In my Be-lov-ed meet and shine.

3 White is his soul from blem-ish free, Red with his blood he shed for me; The fair-est of ten thousand fairs, A Sun amongst ten thousand stars.

4 Com-pas-sions in his heart are found, Close by the sig-nals of his wounds; His sa-cred side no more shall bear The cruel scourge, the piercing spear.

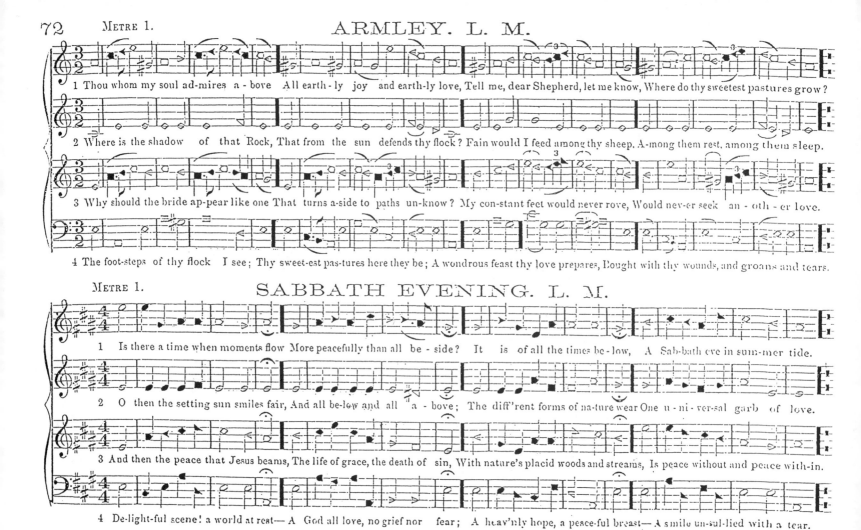

72

METRE 1.

ARMLEY. L. M.

1 Thou whom my soul ad-mires a-bove All earth-ly joy and earth-ly love, Tell me, dear Shepherd, let me know, Where do thy sweetest pastures grow?

2 Where is the shadow of that Rock, That from the sun defends thy flock? Fain would I feed among thy sheep, A-mong them rest, among them sleep.

3 Why should the bride ap-pear like one That turns a-side to paths un-know? My con-stant feet would never rove, Would nev-er seek an-oth-er love.

4 The foot-steps of thy flock I see; Thy sweet-est pas-tures here they be; A wondrous feast thy love prepares, Bought with thy wounds, and groans and tears.

METRE 1.

SABBATH EVENING. L. M.

1 Is there a time when moments flow More peacefully than all be-side? It is of all the times be-low, A Sab-bath eve in sum-mer tide.

2 O then the setting sun smiles fair, And all be-low and all a-bove; The diff'rent forms of na-ture wear One u-ni-ver-sal garb of love.

3 And then the peace that Jesus beams, The life of grace, the death of sin, With nature's placid woods and streams, Is peace without and peace with-in.

4 De-light-ful scene! a world at rest— A God all love, no grief nor fear; A heav'nly hope, a peace-ful breast— A smile un-sul-lied with a tear.

METRE 1.

WEBER. L. M.

1 Oh! that I could for - ev - er dwell, De-light-ed, at the Sa-vior's feet, Be-hold the form I love so well, And all his ten-der words re-peat.

2 The world shut out from all my soul, And heav'n brought in with all its bliss :—Oh! is there aught from pole to pole, One moment to compare with this !

3 This is the hid-den life I prize,— A life of pen-i-ten-tial love: When most my follies I de-spise, And raise my highest thoughts above.

METRE 1.

ORLAND. L. M.

1 A-wake, Je-ru-sa-lem, a-wake! No lon-ger in thy sins lie down; The garment of sal-va-tion take, Thy beau-ty and thy strength put on.

2 Shake off the dust that blinds thy sight, And hides the promise from thine eyes; A-rise and struggle in-to light— Thy great De-liv'r-er calls, A-rise.

3 Shake off the bands of sad despair, Si-on, as-sert thy lib-er-ty! Look up, thy broken heart pre-pare; And God shall set the cap-tive free.

4 Ves-sels of mer-cy, sons of grace! Be purged from every sin-ful stain! Be like your Lord, his word embrace, Nor bear his hal-low'd name in vain.

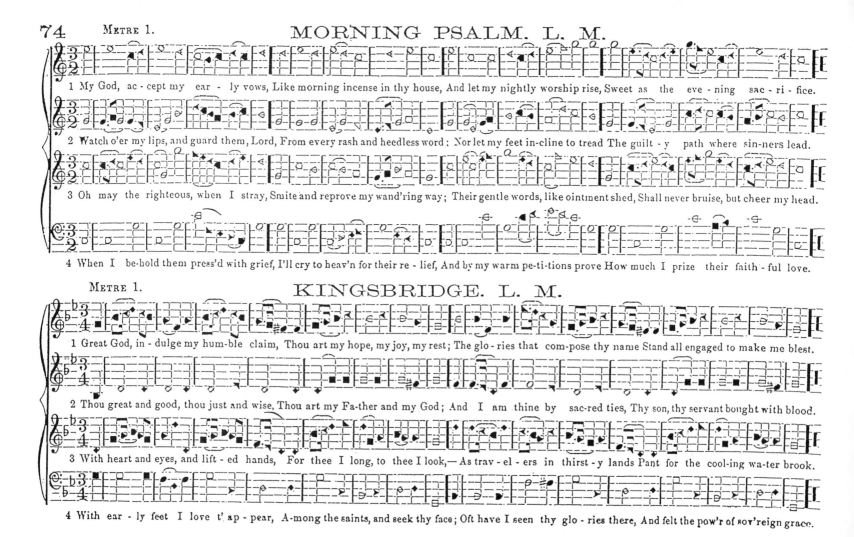

74   METRE 1.

MORNING PSALM. L. M.

1 My God, ac-cept my ear-ly vows, Like morning incense in thy house, And let my nightly worship rise, Sweet as the eve-ning sac-ri-fice.

2 Watch o'er my lips, and guard them, Lord, From every rash and heedless word; Nor let my feet in-cline to tread The guilt-y path where sin-ners lead.

3 Oh may the righteous, when I stray, Smite and reprove my wand'ring way; Their gentle words, like ointment shed, Shall never bruise, but cheer my head.

4 When I be-hold them press'd with grief, I'll cry to heav'n for their re-lief, And by my warm pe-ti-tions prove How much I prize their faith-ful love.

METRE 1.

KINGSBRIDGE. L. M.

1 Great God, in-dulge my hum-ble claim, Thou art my hope, my joy, my rest; The glo-ries that com-pose thy name Stand all engaged to make me blest.

2 Thou great and good, thou just and wise, Thou art my Fa-ther and my God; And I am thine by sac-red ties, Thy son, thy servant bought with blood.

3 With heart and eyes, and lift-ed hands, For thee I long, to thee I look,—As trav-el-ers in thirst-y lands Pant for the cool-ing wa-ter brook.

4 With ear-ly feet I love t' ap-pear, A-mong the saints, and seek thy face; Oft have I seen thy glo-ries there, And felt the pow'r of sov'reign grace.

1 Come gra-cious Spirit, heavenly Dove, With light and comfort from above;   Be thou our guardian, thou our guide, O'er

1 Come gra-cious Spirit, heavenly Dove, With light and comfort from above;   Be thou our guardian,

1 Come gra-cious Spirit, heavenly Dove, With light and comfort from above;   Be thou our guardian, thou our guide, O'er every thought and

1 Come gracious Spirit, heavenly Dove, With light and comfort from above;   Be thou our guardian, thou our guide, O'er every thought and step preside, O'er

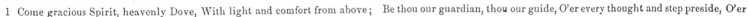

eve - - ry   thought   and step pre - side.

thou our guide, O'er eve-ry thought and step pre - side.

step pre - side, O'er eve-ry thought and step pre - side.

eve - - ry   thought   and step pre - side.

2 Conduct us safe, conduct us far,
  From every sin and hurtful snare;
  Lead to thy word that rules must give,
  And teach us lessons how to live.

3 The light of truth to us display,
  And make us know and choose thy way;
  Plant holy fear in every heart,
  That we from God may ne'er depart.

4 Lead us to holiness, the road
  That we must take to dwell with God;
  Lead us to Christ the living way,
  Nor let us from his pastures stray.

5 Lead us to God our final rest,
  In his enjoyment to be bless'd;
  Lead us to heaven the seat of bliss,
  Where pleasure in perfection is.

76

LOUELLA. L. M.

METRE 1.

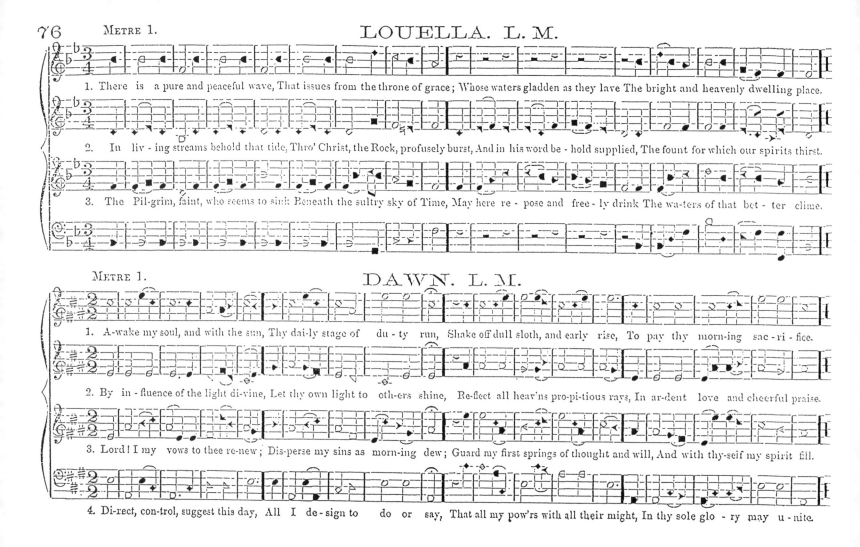

1. There is a pure and peaceful wave, That issues from the throne of grace; Whose waters gladden as they lave The bright and heavenly dwelling place.

2. In liv-ing streams behold that tide, Thro' Christ, the Rock, profusely burst, And in his word be-hold supplied, The fount for which our spirits thirst.

3. The Pil-grim, faint, who seems to sink Beneath the sultry sky of Time, May here re-pose and free-ly drink The wa-ters of that bet-ter clime.

DAWN. L. M.

METRE 1.

1. A-wake my soul, and with the sun, Thy dai-ly stage of du-ty run, Shake off dull sloth, and early rise, To pay thy morn-ing sac-ri-fice.

2. By in-fluence of the light di-vine, Let thy own light to oth-ers shine, Re-flect all heav'ns pro-pi-tious rays, In ar-dent love and cheerful praise.

3. Lord! I my vows to thee re-new; Dis-perse my sins as morn-ing dew; Guard my first springs of thought and will, And with thy-self my spirit fill.

4. Di-rect, con-trol, suggest this day, All I de-sign to do or say, That all my pow'rs with all their might, In thy sole glo-ry may u-nite.

Metre 1.

PARK STREET. L. M.

1. A-rise! a - rise, with joy sur-vey The glo-ry of the la - ter day; Already is the dawn be-gun, Which marks at hand a rising sun, Which marks at hand a rising sun.

2. "Behold the way!" ye heralds cry: Spare not—but lift your voices high: Convey the sound from pole to pole, "Glad tidings" to the captive soul, "Glad tidings" to the captive soul!

3. "Behold the way to Zion's hill: Where Israel's God delights to dwell! He fixes there his lofty throne, And calls the sacred place his own, And calls the sacred place his own."

4. The north gives up—the south no more Keeps back her consecrated store; From east to west the message runs, And either India yields her sons, And either India yields her sons.

Metre 1.

EFFINGHAM. L. M.

1. When shall thy love-ly face be seen? When shall our eyes behold our God! What lengths of distance lie between, And hills of guilt, a heav - y load.

2. Our months are a - ges of de - lay, And slow-ly eve-ry moment wears: Fly, winged time, and roll a - way These te - dious rounds of slug-gish years.

3. Ye heav'n-ly gates, loose all your chains, Let the e - ter-nal pillars bow; Bless'd Savior, cleave the starry plains, And make the crys - tal mountains flow.

4. Hark! how thy saints u-nite their cries! And pray and wait the gen-'ral doom; Come thou, the soul of all our joys, Thou, the DESIRE OF NATIONS, COME.

METRE 1.

GRATITUDE. L. M.

1. My God, how end-less is thy love! Thy gifts are eve-ry eve-ning new; And morning mer-cies from a-bove Gent-ly dis-til like ear-ly dew.

2. Thou spreadst the curtain of the night, Great Guardian of my sleeping hours; Thy sovereign word restores the light, And quickens all my drowsy pow'rs.

3. I yield my pow'rs to thy command, To thee I con-se-crate my days; Per-pet-ual blessings from thy hand De-mand per-pet-ual songs of praise.

METRE. 1.

VESTAL. L. M.

1. Blest Je-sus, source of grace divine, What soul-refreshing streams are thine, O bring these heal-ing wa-ters nigh, Or we must droop, and fall, and die.

2. No trav-el-ler thro' desert lands, 'Midst scorching suns and burning sands, More needs the current to ob-tain, Or to en-joy re-fresh-ing rain.

3. Our long-ing souls a-loud would sing, Spring up, ce-les-tial foun-tain, spring; To an a-bun-dant riv-er flow, And cheer this thirst-y land be-low.

4. May this blest riv-er near my side Through all the des-ert gent-ly glide; Then in Im-man-uel's land a-bove, Spread to a sea of joy and love.

METRE 1.

DANVERS. L. M.

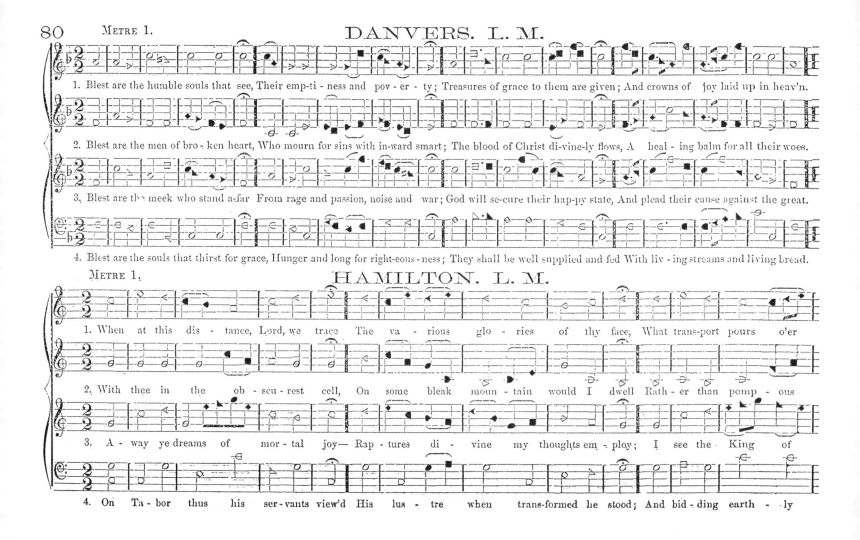

1. Blest are the humble souls that see, Their emp-ti-ness and pov-er-ty; Treasures of grace to them are given; And crowns of joy laid up in heav'n.

2. Blest are the men of bro-ken heart, Who mourn for sins with in-ward smart; The blood of Christ di-vine-ly flows, A heal-ing balm for all their woes.

3. Blest are the meek who stand a-far From rage and passion, noise and war; God will se-cure their hap-py state, And plead their cause against the great.

4. Blest are the souls that thirst for grace, Hunger and long for right-eous-ness; They shall be well supplied and fed With liv-ing streams and living bread.

METRE 1.

HAMILTON. L. M.

1. When at this dis-tance, Lord, we trace The va-rious glo-ries of thy face, What trans-port pours o'er

2. With thee in the ob-scu-rest cell, On some bleak moun-tain would I dwell Rath-er than pomp-ous

3. A-way ye dreams of mor-tal joy— Rap-tures di-vine my thoughts em-ploy; I see the King of

4. On Ta-bor thus his ser-vants view'd His lus-tre when trans-formed he stood; And bid-ding earth-ly

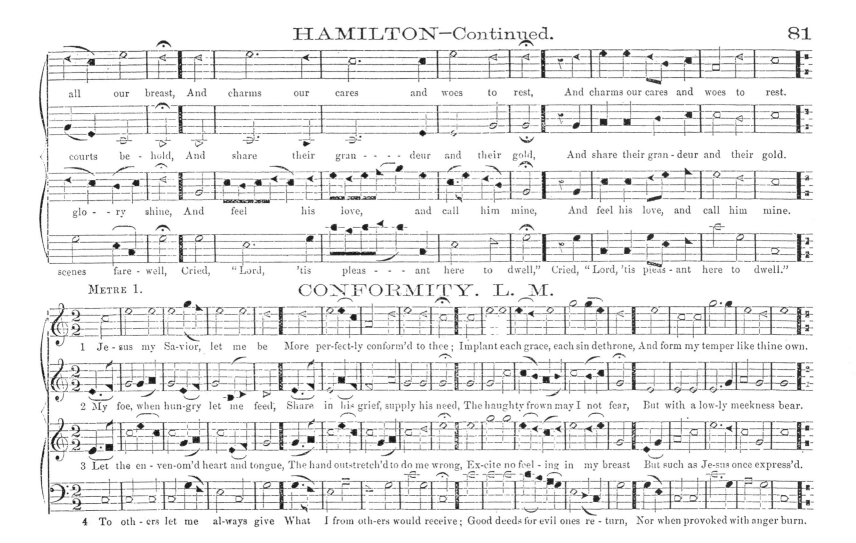

all our breast, And charms our cares and woes to rest, And charms our cares and woes to rest.

courts be-hold, And share their gran - - - deur and their gold, And share their gran-deur and their gold.

glo - ry shine, And feel his love, and call him mine, And feel his love, and call him mine.

scenes fare-well, Cried, "Lord, 'tis pleas - - - ant here to dwell," Cried, "Lord, 'tis pleas-ant here to dwell."

METRE 1.

CONFORMITY. L. M.

1 Je-sus my Sa-vior, let me be   More per-fect-ly conform'd to thee; Implant each grace, each sin dethrone, And form my temper like thine own.

2 My foe, when hun-gry let me feed; Share in his grief, supply his need, The haughty frown may I not fear,   But with a low-ly meekness bear.

3 Let the en-ven-om'd heart and tongue, The hand outstretch'd to do me wrong, Ex-cite no feel-ing in my breast   But such as Je-sus once express'd.

4 To oth-ers let me al-ways give What I from oth-ers would receive; Good deeds for evil ones re-turn, Nor when provoked with anger burn.

Metre 1.

GILGAL. L. M.

1 My dear Re-deem-er and my Lord, I read my du - ty in thy word; But in thy life the law ap - pears Drawn out in liv - ing char-ac-ters.

2 Such was thy truth and such thy zeal, Such deff'rence to thy Fa-ther's will, Such love, and meekness so di - vine, I would transcribe and make them mine.

3 Cold mountains and the midnight air Witness'd the fer - vor of thy pray'r; The desert thy temp-ta-tions knew, Thy con-flict and thy vict'ry too.

4 Be thou my pat-tern; make me bear More of thy gra-cious im-age here; Then God the Judge shall own my name Among the fol-low'rs of the Lamb.

Metre 1.

REPOSE. L. M.

1 Thou on-ly Sov'reign of my heart, My ref-uge, my Al-might-y Friend— And can my soul from thee depart, On whom a - lone my hopes de-pend.

2 Whith-er, ah whith-er shall I go, A wretched wand'rer from my Lord! Can this dark world of sin and woe One glimpse of hap-pi - ness af-ford!

3 E - ter-nal life thy words im-part; On these my fainting spir-it lives; Here sweeter comforts cheer my heart Than all the round of na-ture gives.

4 Let earth's al-lur-ing joys com-bine, While thou art near in vain they call; One smile, one blissful smile of thine, My dearest Lord, outweighs them all.

MEAR. C. M.

1 Sing to the Lord ye dis-tant lands, Ye tribes of eve-ry tongue; His new dis-cov-ered grace de-mands, A new and no-bler song.

2 Say to the na-tions, Je-sus reigns, God's own Al-might-y Son; His pow'r the sink-ing world sus-tains, And grace sur-rounds his throne.

3 Let heav'n pro-claim the joy-ful day, Joy through the earth be seen; Let cit-ies shine in bright ar-ray, And fields in cheer-ful green.

4 The joy-ous earth, the bend-ing skies, His glo-rious train dis-play; Ye mountains sink, ye val-leys rise, Pre-pare the Lord his way.

METRE 2.

BARBY. C. M.

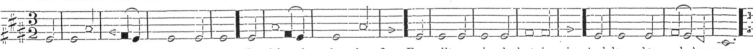

1 The Savior! O what end-less charms, Dwell in the bliss-ful sound! Its in-fluence eve-ry fear dis-arms, And spreads sweet comforts round.

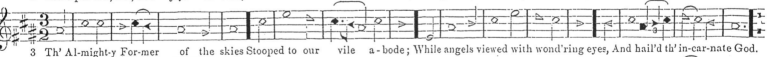

2 Here par-don, life, and joys di-vine, In rich ef-fu-sion flow, For guilt-y reb-els, lost in sin, And doomed to end-less woe.

3 Th' Al-might-y For-mer of the skies Stooped to our vile a-bode; While angels viewed with wond'ring eyes, And hail'd th' in-car-nate God.

4 Oh, the rich depths of love di-vine, Of bliss, a bound-less store! Dear Sa-vior, let me call thee mine—I can-not wish for more.

84

METRE 2.

DUBLIN. C. M.

1 Out of the deeps of long dis-tress, The bor-ders of de-spair, I send my cries to seek thy grace, My groans to move thine ear.

2 Great God! should thy se-ver-er eye, And thine im-par-tial hand, Mark and re-venge in-i-qui-ty, No mor-tal flesh could stand.

3 But there are par-dons with our God, For crimes of high de-gree; Thy Son has bought them with his blood, To draw us near to thee.

4 I wait for thy sal-va-tion, Lord, With strong de-sires I wait; My soul in-vi-ted by thy word Stands watch-ing at thy gate.

METRE 2.

BALERMA. C. M.

1 Shep-herd di-vine, our wants re-lieve, In this our e-vil day; To all thy tempt-ed fol-low'rs give The pow'r to watch and pray.

2 Long as our fie-ry tri-als last, Long as the cross we bear; O let our souls on thee be cast In nev-er-ceas-ing prayer!

3 The Spir-it of re-deem-ing grace, Give us in faith to claim; To wres-tle till we see thy face, And know thy hid-den name.

4 Till Thou thy per-fect love im-part, Till Thou thy-self be-stow; Be this the cry of eve-ry heart— "I will not let thee go."

Metre 2.   DUNDEE. C. M.

1 Ye lit - tle flock whom Je - sus feeds, Dis - miss your anx-ious cares, Look to the Shep - herd of your souls, And smile a - way your fears.

2 Though wolves and li-ons prowl a - round, His staff is your de-fense ; 'Midst sands and rocks, your Shepherd's voice, Calls streams and pastures thence.

3 Your Fa-ther will a king-dom give, And give it with de - light ; His fee - blest child his love shall call, To tri - umph in his sight.

4 Ten thousand prais - es, Lord, we bring, For sure supports like these ; And o'er the pi - ous dead we sing, Thy liv - ing prom - is - es.

Metre 2.   CROWLE. C. M.

1 God of my life, look gent - ly down, Be - hold the pains I feel ; But I am dumb be - fore thy throne, Nor dare dis - pute thy will.

2 Dis - eas - es are thy ser-vants, Lord, They come at thy com-mand ; I'll not at-tempt a murm'r-ing word A - gainst thy chast'ning hand.

3 Yet I may plead with humble cries, Re - move thy sharp re - bukes ; My strength consumes, my spir - it dies, Through thy re - peat - ed strokes.

4 Crush'd as a moth be - neath thy hand, We mold - er to the dust ; Our fee - ble pow'rs can ne'er with-stand, And all our beau - ty's lost.

METRE 2.

ARLINGTON. C. M.

1 Am I a sol-dier of the cross, A fol-low'r of the Lamb, And shall I fear to own his cause, Or blush to speak his name?

2 Must I be car-ried to the skies On flow'-ry beds of ease, While oth-ers fought to win the prize, And sailed thro' bloody seas?

3 Are there no foes for me to face? Must I not stem the flood? Is this vile world a friend to grace To help me on to God?

4 Sure I must fight if I would reing, In-crease my courage Lord; I'll bear the toil, en-dure the pain, Sup-port-ed by thy Word.

METRE 2.

DIVINITY. C. M.

1 A-wake, a-wake the sa-cred song, To our In-car-nate Lord; Let eve-ry heart and eve-ry tongue A-dore th' E-ter-nal Word.

2 That aw-ful Word, that sov'reign Pow'r By whom the worlds were made, (O hap-py morn, il-lus-trious hour,) Was once in flesh ar-rayed.

3 Then shone Al-might-y pow'r and love, In all their glo-rious forms, When Je-sus left his throne a-bove, To dwell with sin-ful worms.

4 To dwell with mis-er-y be-low, The Sa-vior left the skies, And sunk to wretch-ed-ness and woe, That worthless man might rise.

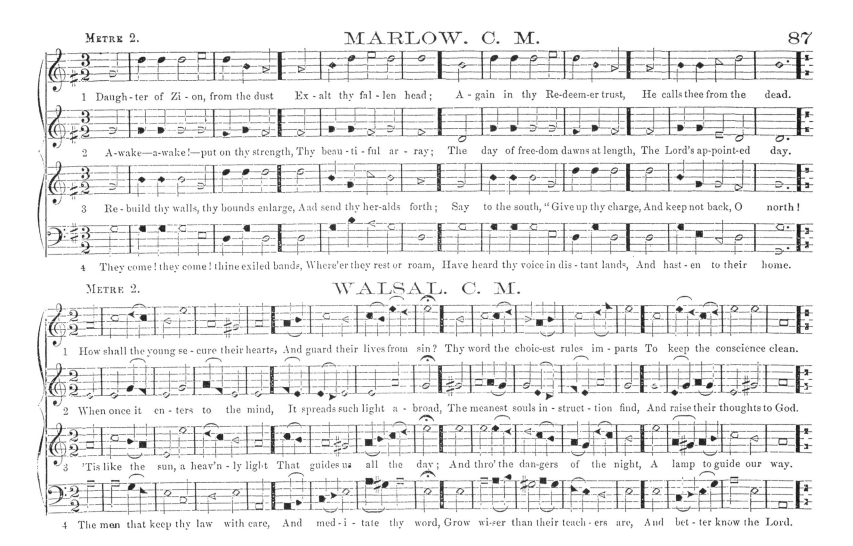

1 Daugh-ter of Zi-on, from the dust   Ex-alt thy fal-len head;   A-gain in thy Re-deem-er trust,   He calls thee from the   dead.

2 A-wake—a-wake!—put on thy strength, Thy beau-ti-ful ar-ray;   The   day of free-dom dawns at length, The Lord's ap-point-ed   day.

3 Re-build thy walls, thy bounds enlarge, And send thy her-alds   forth;   Say   to the south, "Give up thy charge, And keep not back, O   north!

4   They come! they come! thine exiled bands, Where'er they rest or roam, Have heard thy voice in dis-tant lands, And hast-en to their   home.

METRE 2.   WALSAL. C. M.

1 How shall the young se-cure their hearts, And guard their lives from sin? Thy word the choic-est rules im-parts To keep the conscience clean.

2 When once it en-ters to the mind,   It spreads such light a-broad, The meanest souls in-struct-tion find, And raise their thoughts to God.

3 'Tis like the sun, a heav'n-ly light That guides us all the day; And thro' the dan-gers of the night, A lamp to guide our way.

4 The men that keep thy law with care, And med-i-tate thy word, Grow wi-ser than their teach-ers are, And bet-ter know the Lord.

METRE 2.

WARWICK. C. M.

1 How sweet the name of Je-sus sounds In a be-liev-er's ear! It soothes his sorrows, heals his wounds, And drives a-way his fear.

2 It makes the wound-ed spir-it whole, And calms the troubled breast; 'Tis man-na to the hun-gry soul, And to the wea-ry rest.

3 Dear name, the Rock on which I build, My shield and hi-ding place; My nev-er-fail-ing treas-'ry filled With boundless stores of grace.

4 Je-sus! my Shep-herd, Hus-band, Friend, My Proph-et, Priest and King,—My Lord, my life, my Way, my End, Ac-cept the praise I bring.

METRE 2.

WINTER. C. M.

1 Hap-py the soul that lives on high, While men lie grov'ling here, His hopes are fixed a-bove the sky, and faith for-bids his fear.

2 His conscience knows no secret stings, While grace and joy combine To form a life whose ho-ly springs Are hid-den and di-vine.

3 He waits in se-cret on his God, His God in se-cret sees; Let earth be all in arms a-broad, He dwells in heavenly peace.

4 His pleasures rise from things un-seen, Be-yond this world and time, Where neith-er eyes nor ears have been, Nor thoughts of mortals climb.

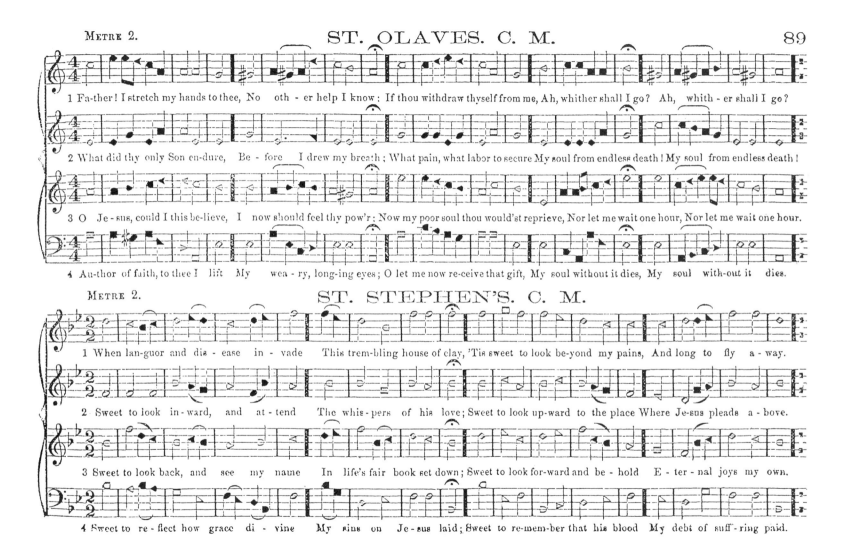

METRE 2.

ST. OLAVES. C. M.

89

1 Fa-ther! I stretch my hands to thee, No oth - er help I know: If thou withdraw thyself from me, Ah, whither shall I go? Ah, whith - er shall I go?

2 What did thy only Son en-dure, Be - fore I drew my breath; What pain, what labor to secure My soul from endless death! My soul from endless death!

3 O Je - sus, could I this be-lieve, I now should feel thy pow'r: Now my poor soul thou would'st reprieve, Nor let me wait one hour, Nor let me wait one hour.

4 Au-thor of faith, to thee I lift My wea - ry, long-ing eyes; O let me now re-ceive that gift, My soul without it dies, My soul with-out it dies.

METRE 2.

ST. STEPHEN'S. C. M.

1 When lan-guor and dis - ease in - vade This trem-bling house of clay, 'Tis sweet to look be-yond my pains, And long to fly a - way.

2 Sweet to look in - ward, and at - tend The whis-pers of his love; Sweet to look up-ward to the place Where Je-sus pleads a - bove.

3 Sweet to look back, and see my name In life's fair book set down; Sweet to look for-ward and be - hold E - ter - nal joys my own.

4 Sweet to re - flect how grace di - vine My sins on Je-sus laid; Sweet to re-mem-ber that his blood My debt of suff'-ring paid.

METRE 2.

ST. MARTIN'S. C. M.

1 Be - hold the glo - ries of the Lamb, A-midst his Father's throne! Prepare new hon - ors for his name, And songs be-fore un-known.

2 Let el - ders wor - ship at his feet, The church a-dore a-round, With vi - als full of o-dors sweet, And harps of sweet-er sound.

3 Those are the pray'rs of all the saints, And these the hymns they raise; Je-sus is kind to our complaints, He loves to hear our praise.

4 E - ter - nal Fa - ther, who shall look In - to thy se - cret will? Who but the Son shall take that book, And o - pen eve - ry seal!

METRE 2.

WINDSOR. C. M.

1 That aw - ful day will sure - ly come, Th'ap-point-ed hour makes haste, When I must stand be - fore my Judge, And pass the sol - emn test.

2 Thou love-ly Chief of all my joys, Thou Sov'reign of my heart, How could I bear to hear thy voice, Pro-nounce the sound "de-part!"

3 The thun-der of that dis - mal word Would so tor-ment my ear, 'Twould tear my soul a - sun - der, Lord, With most tor - ment - ing fear.

4 What, to be ban-ished for my life, And yet for - bid to die! To lin - ger in e - ter - nal pain, Yet death for - ev - er fly!

HEAVENLY JERUSALEM. C. M.

1 Je - ru - sa - lem! my hap - - - - - py home, Name ev - er dear to me! When shall my

2 When shall these eyes thy heav'n - built walls, And pear - ly gates be - hold? Thy bul - warks

3 O when, thou cit - y of my God, Shall I thy courts as - cend? Where con - gre

4 There hap-pier bow'rs than E - den's bloom, Nor sin, nor sor - row know; Bless'd seats! through

la - bors have an end In joy, and peace, and thee?

with sal - - - - va - tion strong, And streets of shi - ning gold?

ga - tions ne'er break up, And Sab - baths nev - er end.

rude and stor - my scenes, I on - - - ward press to you.

5 Why should I shrink at pain and woe,
Or feel at death dismay?
I've Canaan's goodly land in view,
And realms of endless day.

6 Apostles, prophets, martyrs there
Around my Savior stand;
And soon my friends in Christ below
Will join the glorious band.

7 Jerusalem, my happy home—
My soul still pants for thee;
Then shall my labors have an end,
When I thy joys shall see.

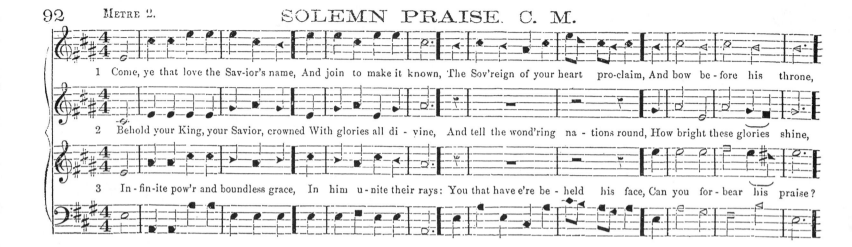

1 Come, ye that love the Sav-ior's name, And join to make it known, The Sov'reign of your heart pro-claim, And bow be - fore his throne,

2 Behold your King, your Savior, crowned With glories all di - vine, And tell the wond'ring na - tions round, How bright these glories shine,

3 In - fin-ite pow'r and boundless grace, In him u - nite their rays: You that have e're be - held his face, Can you for - bear his praise?

The Sov'reign of your heart pro - claim, And bow be - - - fore his throne.

And tell the wond'ring na - tions round, How bright these glo - - - ries shine.

You that have e'er be - held his face, Can you for - - bear his praise?

4 When in his earthly courts we view
    The glories of our King,
We long to love as angels do,
    And wish like them to sing.

5 And shall we long and wish in vain?
    Lord, teach our songs to rise!
Thy love can animate the strain,
    And bid it reach the skies.

METRE 2.

SWANWICH. C. M.

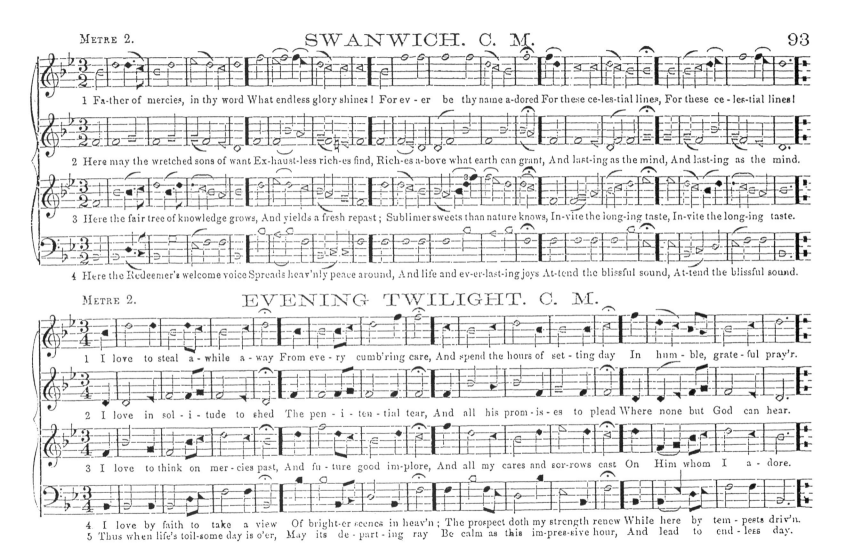

1 Fa-ther of mercies, in thy word What endless glory shines! For ev - er be thy name a-dored For these ce-les-tial lines, For these ce - les-tial lines!

2 Here may the wretched sons of want Ex-haust-less rich-es find, Rich-es a-bove what earth can grant, And last-ing as the mind, And last-ing as the mind.

3 Here the fair tree of knowledge grows, And yields a fresh repast; Sublimer sweets than nature knows, In-vite the long-ing taste, In-vite the long-ing taste.

4 Here the Redeemer's welcome voice Spreads heav'nly peace around, And life and ev-er-last-ing joys At-tend the blissful sound, At-tend the blissful sound.

METRE 2.

EVENING TWILIGHT. C. M.

1 I love to steal a - while a - way From eve - ry cumb'ring care, And spend the hours of set - ting day In hum - ble, grate-ful pray'r.

2 I love in sol - i - tude to shed The pen - i - ten - tial tear, And all his prom - is - es to plead Where none but God can hear.

3 I love to think on mer - cies past, And fu - ture good im-plore, And all my cares and sor-rows cast On Him whom I a - dore.

4 I love by faith to take a view Of bright-er scenes in heav'n; The prospect doth my strength renew While here by tem - pests driv'n.

5 Thus when life's toil-some day is o'er, May its de - part - ing ray Be calm as this im-pres-sive hour, And lead to end - less day.

94

IRISH. C. M.

1 I'll bless the Lord from day to day; How good are all his ways; Ye hum - ble souls that used to pray, Come help my lips to praise.

2 Sing to the hon - ors of his name, How a poor suff'r - er cried, Nor was his hope ex - posed to shame, Nor was his suit de - nied.

3 When threat'ning sorrows round me stood, And endless fears a - rose, Like the loud bil-lows of a flood, Re - doub - ling all my woes;

4 I told the Lord my sore dis-tress, With heav-y groans and tears— He gave my sharp-est tor - ments ease, And si - lenced all my fears.

METRE 2.

ISLE OF WIGHT. C. M.

1 My God, con - sid - er my dis-tress, Let mer - cy plead my cause; Tho' I have sinn'd a-gainst thy grace, I can't for - get thy laws.

2 For - bid, for - bid the sharp re-proach Which I so just - ly fear; Up - hold my life,— up-hold my hope, Nor let my shame ap - pear.

3 Be thou a sure - ty, Lord, for me, Nor let the proud op-press; But make thy wait-ing ser - vant see The shi-nings of thy face.

4 My eyes with ex - pec - ta - tion fail; My heart with - in me cries, When will the Lord his truth ful - fil, And bid my com-forts rise?

Metre 2.

PETERBOROUGH. C. M.

95

1 What wis-dom, maj-es-ty, and grace Thro' all the gos-pel shine! Tis God that speaks, and we con-fess The doc-trine most di-vine.

2 Down from his star-ry throne on high, Th' Almighty Sa-vior comes; Lays his bright robes of glory by, And fee-ble flesh as-sumes.

3 The might-y debt that sin-ners owed, Up-on the cross he pays; Then thro' the clouds ascends to God, 'Midst shouts of loft-iest praise.

4 There He our great High Priest appears, Before his Father's throne; Min-gles his merits with our tears; And pours sal-va-tion down.

Metre 2.

MEDFIELD. C. M.

1 My Shepherd will sup-ply my need, Je-ho-vah is his name; In pas-tures fresh he makes me feed, Be-side the liv-ing stream.

2 He brings my wand'ring spirit back When I for-sake his ways, And leads me for his mer-cy's sake, In paths of truth and grace.

3 When I walk thro' the shades of death, Thy pres-ence is my stay; One word of thy sup-port-ing breath Drives all my fears a-way.

4 Thy hand, in sight of all my foes Doth still my table spread; My cup with bless-ings o-ver-flows, Thine oil a-noints my head.

METRE 2. <h1>GENEVA. C. M.</h1>

When all thy mer-cies, O my God, My ris-ing soul sur-veys, Trans-

When all thy mer-cies, O my God, My ris-ing soul sur-veys, Trans-port--ed

1 When all thy mer-cies, O my God, My ris-ing soul sur-veys, Trans-port--ed

When all thy mer-cies, O my God, My ris-ing soul sur-veys, Trans-

port-ed with the view I'm lost In won--der, love, and praise.

with the view I'm lost In won--der, love, and praise.

with the view I'm lost In won-der, love, and praise.

port-ed with the view I'm lost In won--der, love, and praise.

2 Unnumber'd comforts on my soul
   Thy tender care bestow'd,
 Before my infant heart conceived
   From whom these comforts flow'd.

3 When in the slippery paths of youth
   With heedless steps I ran,
 Thy arm unseen convey'd me safe,
   And led me up to man.

4 Ten thousand thousand precious gifts
   My daily thanks employ;
 Nor is the least a cheerful heart
   That tastes those gifts with joy.

5 Through every period of my life,
   Thy goodness I'll pursue;
 And after death, in distant worlds,
   The glorious theme renew.

ANTIOCH C. M.

1 Joy to the world, the Lord is come, Let earth re-ceive her King; Let eve-ry heart pre-pare him

2 Joy to the earth, the Sa-vior reigns, Let men their songs em-ploy, While fields and floods and rocks and

3 No more let sins and sor-rows grow, Nor thorns in-fest the ground; He comes to make his bless-ings

4 Blest be the Lord who sent his Son To take our flesh and blood; He for our lives gave up his

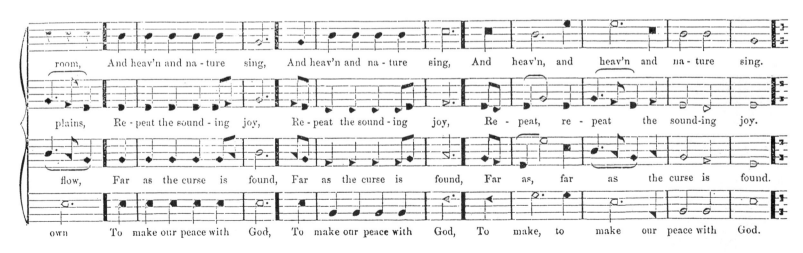

room, And heav'n and na-ture sing, And heav'n and na-ture sing, And heav'n, and heav'n and na-ture sing.

plains, Re-peat the sound-ing joy, Re-peat the sound-ing joy, Re-peat, re-peat the sound-ing joy.

flow, Far as the curse is found, Far as the curse is found, Far as, far as the curse is found.

own To make our peace with God, To make our peace with God, To make, to make our peace with God.

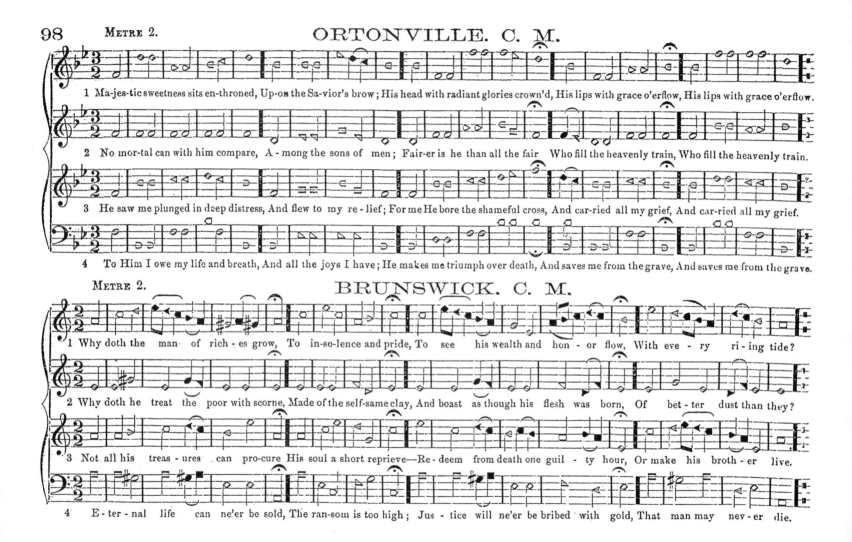

Metre 2.

ORTONVILLE. C. M.

1 Ma-jes-tic sweetness sits en-throned, Up-on the Sa-vior's brow; His head with radiant glories crown'd, His lips with grace o'erflow, His lips with grace o'erflow.

2 No mor-tal can with him compare, A - mong the sons of men; Fair-er is he than all the fair Who fill the heavenly train, Who fill the heavenly train.

3 He saw me plunged in deep distress, And flew to my re - lief; For me He bore the shameful cross, And car-ried all my grief, And car-ried all my grief.

4 To Him I owe my life and breath, And all the joys I have; He makes me triumph over death, And saves me from the grave, And saves me from the grave.

Metre 2.

BRUNSWICK. C. M.

1 Why doth the man of rich-es grow, To in-so-lence and pride, To see his wealth and hon-or flow, With eve-ry ri-ing tide?

2 Why doth he treat the poor with scorne, Made of the self-same clay, And boast as though his flesh was born, Of bet-ter dust than they?

3 Not all his treas-ures can pro-cure His soul a short reprieve—Re-deem from death one guil-ty hour, Or make his broth-er live.

4 E-ter-nal life can ne'er be sold, The ran-som is too high; Jus-tice will ne'er be bribed with gold, That man may nev-er die.

UNION. C. M.

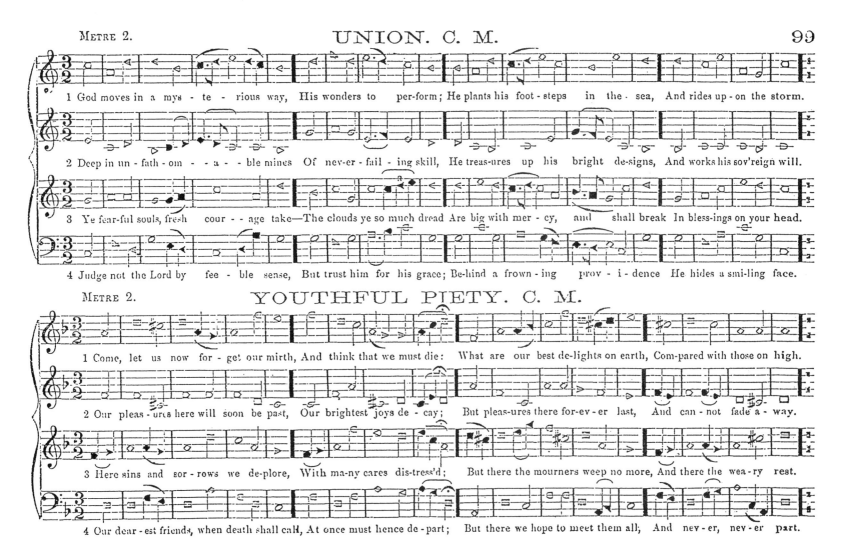

1 God moves in a mys-te-rious way, His wonders to per-form; He plants his foot-steps in the sea, And rides up-on the storm.

2 Deep in un-fath-om-a-ble mines Of nev-er-fail-ing skill, He treas-ures up his bright de-signs, And works his sov'reign will.

3 Ye fear-ful souls, fresh cour-age take—The clouds ye so much dread Are big with mer-cy, and shall break In bless-ings on your head.

4 Judge not the Lord by fee-ble sense, But trust him for his grace; Be-hind a frown-ing prov-i-dence He hides a smi-ling face.

METRE 2. YOUTHFUL PIETY. C. M.

1 Come, let us now for-get our mirth, And think that we must die: What are our best de-lights on earth, Com-pared with those on high.

2 Our pleas-ures here will soon be past, Our brightest joys de-cay; But pleas-ures there for-ev-er last, And can-not fade a-way.

3 Here sins and sor-rows we de-plore, With ma-ny cares dis-tress'd; But there the mourners weep no more, And there the wea-ry rest.

4 Our dear-est friends, when death shall call, At once must hence de-part; But there we hope to meet them all, And nev-er, nev-er part.

METRE 2.

AWFUL MAJESTY. C. M.

1 Sing to the Lord, ye heavenly hosts, And thou, O earth, a - dore; Let death and hell throughout their coasts, Stand trembling at his power.

2 His sound-ing cha-riot shakes the sky, He makes the clouds his throne; There all his stores of light - ning lie, Till vengeance darts them down.

3 His nos-trils breathe out fie-ry streams, And from his aw-ful tongue, A sovereign voice di-vides the flames, And thunders roar a - long.

4 Think, O my soul, that dread-ful day, When this in - cens - ed God, Shall rend the skies and burn the seas, And fling his wrath a - broad!

METRE 2.

DEVIZES. C. M.

1 Thrice happy souls, who, born from heaven, While yet they sojourn here, Humbly begin their days with God, And spend them in his fear, And spend them in his fear.

2 So may our eyes with ho-ly zeal, Pre-vent the dawn-ing day, And turn the sacred pa-ges o'er, And praise thy name and pray, And praise thy name and pray.

3 Midst hourly cares my love presents Its incense to thy throne; And while the world our hands employs, Our hearts be thine a-lone, Our hearts be thine a - lone.

4 As sanc-ti-fied to no - bler ends, By each re-fresh-ment sought, And by each various provi - dence, Some wise instruction brought, Some wise instruction brought.

PARADISE. C. M.

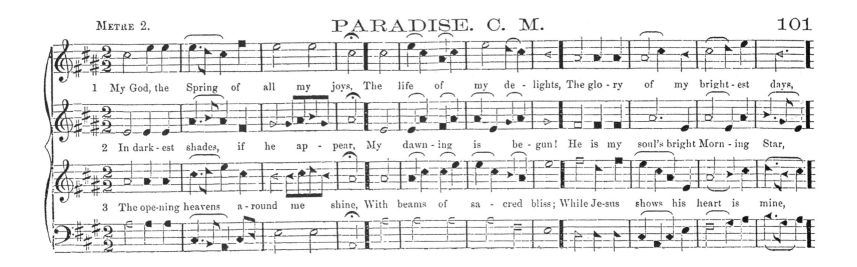

1 My God, the Spring of all my joys, The life of my de - lights, The glo - ry of my bright - est days,

2 In dark - est shades, if he ap - pear, My dawn - ing is be - gun! He is my soul's bright Morn - ing Star,

3 The ope-ning heavens a - round me shine, With beams of sa - cred bliss; While Je-sus shows his heart is mine,

And com - fort of my nights, And com - fort of my nights.

And He my Ri - sing Sun, And He my Ri - sing Sun.

And whis - pers, I am His, And whis - pers, I am His.

4 My soul would leave this heavy clay,
   At that transporting word!
Run up with joy the shining way,
   T' embrace my dearest Lord,
   T' embrace my dearest Lord.

5 Fearless of hell and ghastly death,
   I'd break through every foe;
The wings of love and arms of faith,
   Should bear me conq'ror through,
   Should bear me conq'ror through.

METRE 2.

AUGUSTA. C. M.

1 While thee I seek, protect-ing Pow'r, Be my vain wishes still'd; And may this con-se-cra-ted hour With bet-ter hopes be filled.

2 Thy love the pow'r of thought bestowed—To thee my thoughts would soar; Thy mer-cy o'er my life has flow'd, That mer-cy I a-dore.

3 In each e-vent of life how clear Thy ru-ling hand I see! Each bless-ing to my soul more dear, Be-cause con-ferred by thee.

4 In eve-ry joy that crowns my days, In eve-ry pain I bear, My heart shall find de-light in praise, Or seek re-lief in pray'r.

METRE 2.

ASBURY. C. M.

1 Behold the Savior of man-kind, Nail'd to the shameful tree! How vast the love that him in-clin'd To bleed and die for me! To bleed and die for me!

2 "My God!" he cries, all nature shakes, And earth's strong pillars bend! The temple's vail in sunder breaks—The solid marbles rend, The solid marbles rend!

3 "'Tis finish'd—now the ransom's paid—Receive my soul," he cries, Behold he bows his sacred head—He bows his head—and dies! He bows his head—and dies.

4 But soon he'll break death's envious chain, And in full glory shine: O Lamb of God, was ever pain, Was ev-er love like thine, Was ev-er love like thine!

1 Blest Je - sus, when my soar - ing thoughts O'er all thy gra - ces rove, O'er all thy gra - ces rove,

2 Not soft - est strains can charm mine ears Like thy be - lov - ed name, Like thy be - lov - ed name!

3 Wher-e'er I look, my wond'r - ing eyes Un - num-bered bless - ings see! Un - num-bered bless-ings see!

4 Hast thou a ri - val in my breast?—Search, Lord, for thou canst tell, Search, Lord, for thou canst tell,

How is my soul in trans - port lost— How is my soul in trans - port lost— In won - der, joy, and love.

Nor aught be-neath the skies in - spire, Nor aught be - neath the skies in - spire, My heart with e - qual flame.

But what is life with all its bliss! But what is life with all its bliss! If once com-pared with thee!

If aught can raise my pas - sions thus, If aught can raise my pas - sions thus, Or please my soul so well.

METRE 2.

BETHEL. C. M.

1. Let Zi - on and her sons re - joice, Be - hold the prom-ised hour; Her God hath heard her mourning voice, And comes t' ex-alt his power.

2. Her dust and ru - ins that re - main, Are pre - cious in our eyes; Those ru - ins shall be built a - gain, And all that dust shall rise.

3. The Lord will raise Je-ru - sa - lem, And stand in glo - ry there; Na - tions shall bow be - fore his name, And kings at-tend with fear.

4. He sits a Sov'reign on his throne, With pi - ty in his eyes; He hears the dy - ing pris-'ners groan, And sees their sighs a - rise.

METRE 2.

FAIRFIELD. C. M.

1. With rev'rence let the saints appear, And bow before the Lord; His high command with rev'rence hear, And tremble at his word, His high command with rev'rence hear, And, &c.

2. How terrible thy glories rise. How bright thine armies shine! Where is the pow'r with thee that vies, Or truth compared with thine? Where is the pow'r with thee that vies, Or, &c.

3. The northern pole and southern rest, On thy supporting hand; Darkness and day from east to west, Move round at thy command, Darkness and day from east to west, Move, &c.

4. Thy words the raging winds control, And rule the boisterous deep; Thou mak'st the sleeping billows roll, The rolling billows sleep, Thou mak'st the sleeping billows roll, The, &c.

METRE 2.

CAMBRIDGE. C. M.

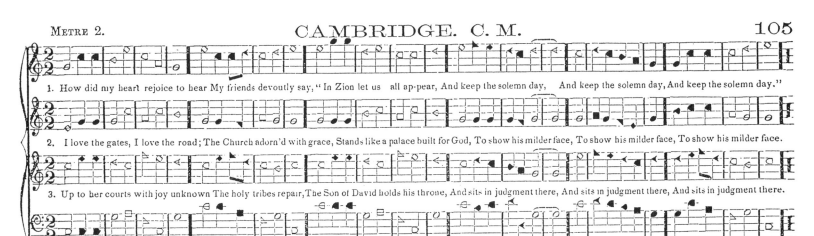

1. How did my heart rejoice to hear My friends devoutly say, "In Zion let us all ap-pear, And keep the solemn day, And keep the solemn day, And keep the solemn day."

2. I love the gates, I love the road; The Church adorn'd with grace, Stands like a palace built for God, To show his milder face, To show his milder face, To show his milder face.

3. Up to her courts with joy unknown The holy tribes repair, The Son of David holds his throne, And sits in judgment there, And sits in judgment there, And sits in judgment there.

3. He hears our praises and complaints; And While his awful voice, Divides the sinners from the saints, We tremble and rejoice, We tremble and rejoice, We tremble and rejoice.

METRE 2.

CONDESCENSION. C. M.

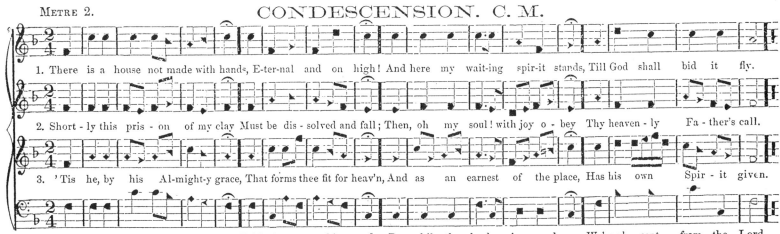

1. There is a house not made with hands, E-ter-nal and on high! And here my wait-ing spir-it stands, Till God shall bid it fly.

2. Short-ly this pris-on of my clay Must be dis-solved and fall; Then, oh my soul! with joy o-bey Thy heaven-ly Fa-ther's call.

3. 'Tis he, by his Al-might-y grace, That forms thee fit for heav'n, And as an earnest of the place, Has his own Spir-it given.

4. We walk by faith of joys to come, Faith lives up-on his word; But while the bo-dy is our home, We're ab-sent from the Lord.

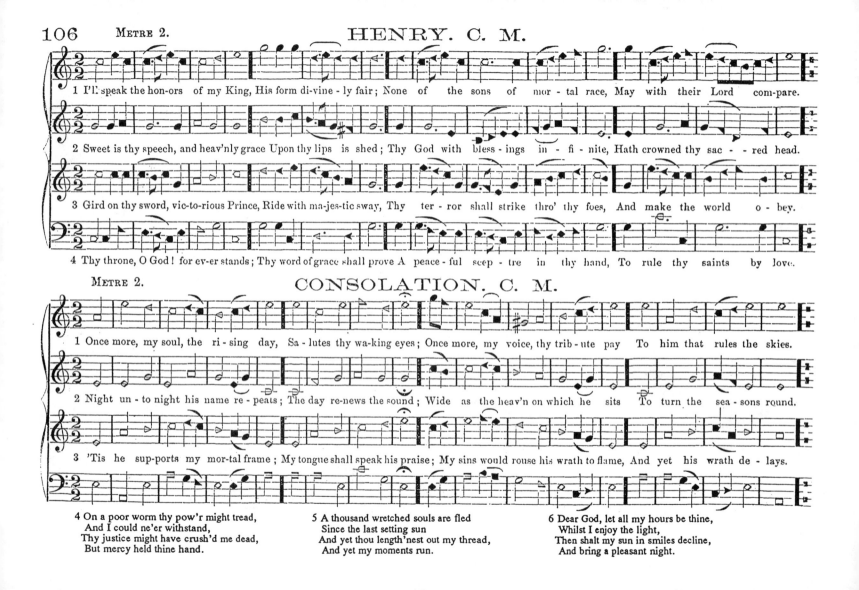

106

METRE 2.

HENRY. C. M.

1 I'll speak the hon-ors of my King, His form di-vine-ly fair; None of the sons of mor-tal race, May with their Lord com-pare.

2 Sweet is thy speech, and heav'nly grace Upon thy lips is shed; Thy God with bless-ings in-fi-nite, Hath crowned thy sac---red head.

3 Gird on thy sword, vic-to-rious Prince, Ride with ma-jes-tic sway, Thy ter-ror shall strike thro' thy foes, And make the world o-bey.

4 Thy throne, O God! for ev-er stands; Thy word of grace shall prove A peace-ful scep-tre in thy hand, To rule thy saints by love.

METRE 2.

CONSOLATION. C. M.

1 Once more, my soul, the ri-sing day, Sa-lutes thy wa-king eyes; Once more, my voice, thy trib-ute pay To him that rules the skies.

2 Night un-to night his name re-peats; The day re-news the sound; Wide as the heav'n on which he sits To turn the sea-sons round.

3 'Tis he sup-ports my mor-tal frame; My tongue shall speak his praise; My sins would rouse his wrath to flame, And yet his wrath de-lays.

4 On a poor worm thy pow'r might tread,
 And I could ne'er withstand,
Thy justice might have crush'd me dead,
 But mercy held thine hand.

5 A thousand wretched souls are fled
 Since the last setting sun
And yet thou length'nest out my thread,
 And yet my moments run.

6 Dear God, let all my hours be thine,
 Whilst I enjoy the light,
Then shalt my sun in smiles decline,
 And bring a pleasant night.

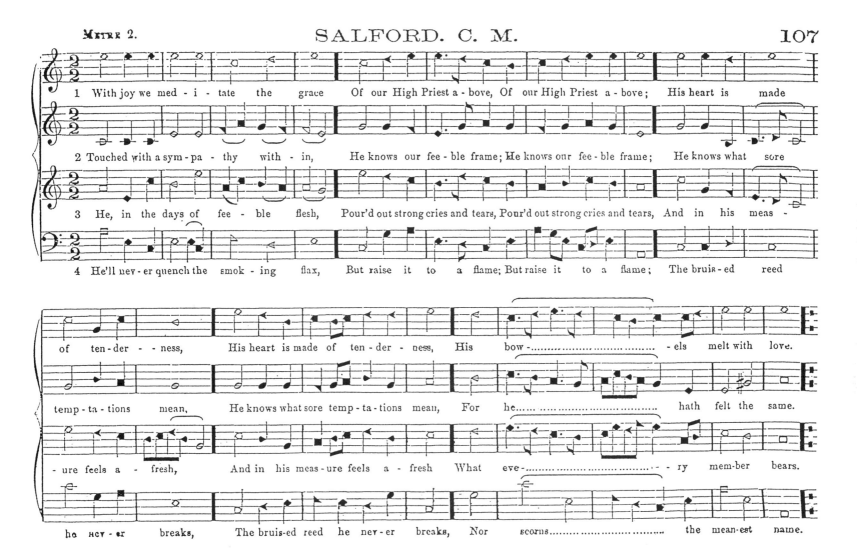

METRE 2.

PRIMROSE. C. M.

1. Ho - san-na to the Prince of light, That clothed him-self in clay, En-tered the i - ron gates of Death, And tore the bars a - way.

2. Death is no more the king of dread, Since our Im-man - uel rose; He took the ty - rant's sting a - way, And spoiled our hellish foes.

3. See how the Conq'ror mounts a-loft, And to his Fa - ther flies, With scars of hon - or in his flesh, And tri-umph in his eyes.

4. There our ex - alt - ed Sa-vior reigns, And scat-ters bless - ings down; Our Je - sus fills the mid - dle seat Of the ce - les-tial throne.

METRE 2.

MILES' LANE. C. M.

1. All hail the pow'r of Je-sus' name! Let an - gels prostrate fall, Bring forth the roy-al di - a - dem, And crown him, crown him, crown him, crown him Lord of all.

2. Crown him, ye martyrs of our God, Who from his al-tar call; Ex - tol the Stem of Jes-se's rod, And crown him, crown him, crown him, crown him Lord of all.

3. Ye cho-sen seed of Is - rael's race; A remnant weak and small, Hail him who saves you by his grace, And crown him, crown him, crown him, crown him Lord of all.

4. Ye Gentile sinners, ne'er for-get The wormwood and the gall; Go spread your trophies at his feet, And crown him, crown him, crown him, crown him Lord of all.

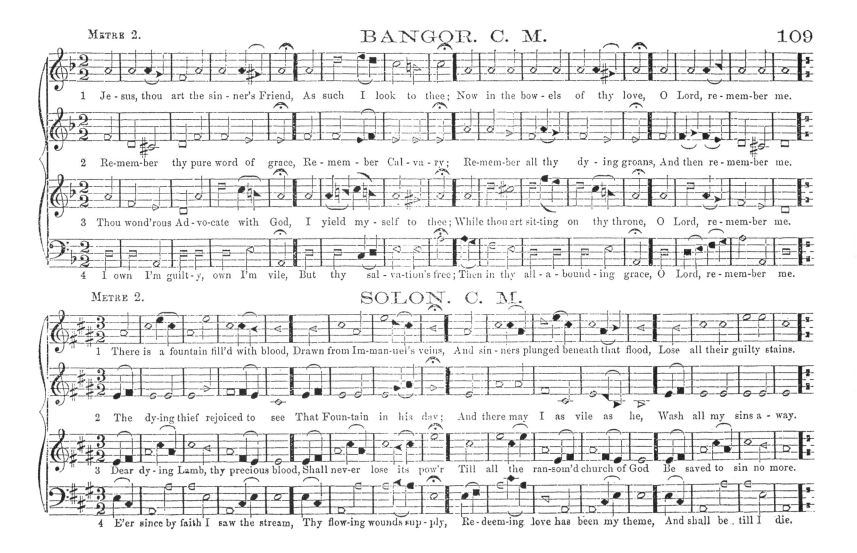

Metre 2. BANGOR. C. M.

1 Je-sus, thou art the sin-ner's Friend, As such I look to thee; Now in the bow-els of thy love, O Lord, re-mem-ber me.

2 Re-mem-ber thy pure word of grace, Re-mem-ber Cal-va-ry; Re-mem-ber all thy dy-ing groans, And then re-mem-ber me.

3 Thou wond'rous Ad-vo-cate with God, I yield my-self to thee; While thou art sit-ting on thy throne, O Lord, re-mem-ber me.

4 I own I'm guilt-y, own I'm vile, But thy sal-va-tion's free; Then in thy all-a-bound-ing grace, O Lord, re-mem-ber me.

Metre 2. SOLON. C. M.

1 There is a fountain fill'd with blood, Drawn from Im-man-uel's veins, And sin-ners plunged beneath that flood, Lose all their guilty stains.

2 The dy-ing thief rejoiced to see That Foun-tain in his day; And there may I as vile as he, Wash all my sins a-way.

3 Dear dy-ing Lamb, thy precious blood, Shall nev-er lose its pow'r Till all the ran-som'd church of God Be saved to sin no more.

4 E'er since by faith I saw the stream, Thy flow-ing wounds sup-ply, Re-deem-ing love has been my theme, And shall be till I die.

METRE 2.
Slow and solemn.
FUNERAL THOUGHT. C. M.

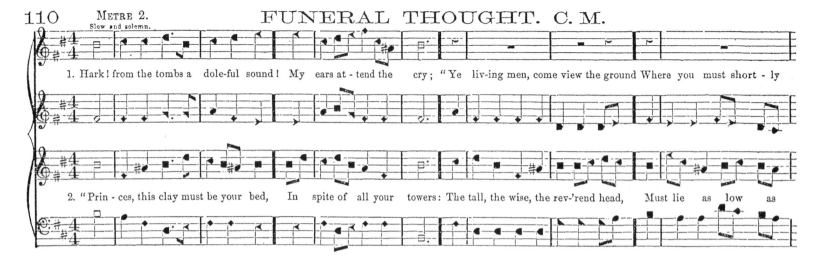

1. Hark! from the tombs a dole-ful sound! My ears at-tend the cry; "Ye liv-ing men, come view the ground Where you must short-ly

2. "Prin-ces, this clay must be your bed, In spite of all your towers: The tall, the wise, the rev-'rend head, Must lie as low as

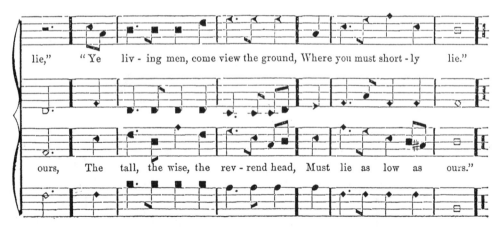

lie," "Ye liv-ing men, come view the ground, Where you must short-ly lie."

ours, The tall, the wise, the rev-rend head, Must lie as low as ours."

3. Great God, is this our certain doom?
   And are we still secure?
   Still walking downward to the tomb,
   And yet prepare no more?

4. Grant us the power of quickening grace,
   To fit our souls to fly;
   Then when we drop this dying flesh,
   We'll rise above the sky.

METRE 2.

YOUTHFUL GLORY. C. M.

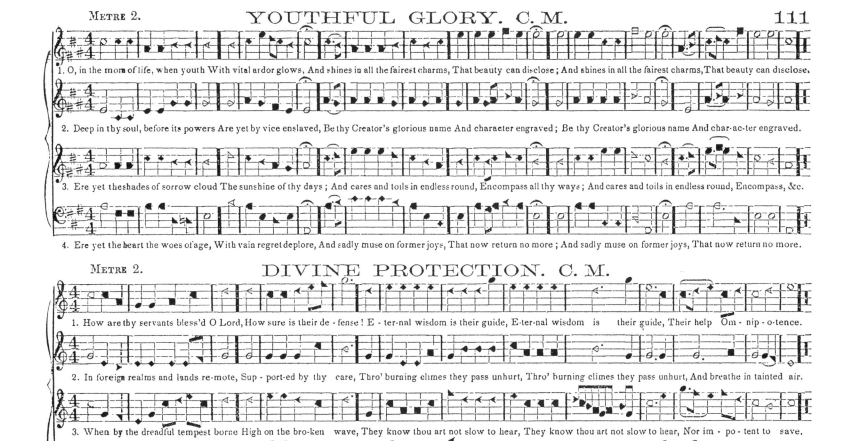

1. O, in the morn of life, when youth With vital ardor glows, And shines in all the fairest charms, That beauty can disclose; And shines in all the fairest charms, That beauty can disclose.

2. Deep in thy soul, before its powers Are yet by vice enslaved, Be thy Creator's glorious name And character engraved; Be thy Creator's glorious name And char-ac-ter engraved.

3. Ere yet the shades of sorrow cloud The sunshine of thy days; And cares and toils in endless round, Encompass all thy ways; And cares and toils in endless round, Encompass, &c.

4. Ere yet the heart the woes of age, With vain regret deplore, And sadly muse on former joys, That now return no more; And sadly muse on former joys, That now return no more.

METRE 2.

DIVINE PROTECTION. C. M.

1. How are thy servants bless'd O Lord, How sure is their de - fense! E - ter-nal wisdom is their guide, E-ter-nal wisdom is their guide, Their help Om - nip - o-tence.

2. In foreign realms and lands re-mote, Sup - port-ed by thy care, Thro' burning climes they pass unhurt, Thro' burning climes they pass unhurt, And breathe in tainted air.

3. When by the dreadful tempest borne High on the bro-ken wave, They know thou art not slow to hear, They know thou art not slow to hear, Nor im - po-tent to save.

4. The storm is laid; the winds re-tire, O - be-dient to thy will; The sea that roars at thy command, The sea that roars at thy command, At thy com-mand is still.

METRE 2.

EVAN. C. M.

1. In mer-cy, Lord, re-mem-ber me, Through all the hours of night, And grant to me most gra-cious-ly The safe-guard of thy might.

2. With cheer-ful heart I close my eyes, Since thou wilt not re - move, Oh, in the morning let me rise, Re - joic-ing in thy love!

3. Or, if this night should prove the last, And end my transient days; Oh! take me to thy promised rest, Where I may sing thy praise.

METRE 2.

ELIZABETHTOWN. C. M.

1. O! for a clo - ser walk with God, A calm and heavenly frame; A light to shine up - on the road, That leads me to the Lamb.

2. Where is the bles-sed - ness I knew, When first I saw the Lord? Where is the soul re - fresh-ing view Of Je - sus and his word?

3. What peace-ful hours I once en - joy'd! How sweet their mem'ry still! But they have left an ach-ing void The world can nev - er fill.

4 Re-turn, O ho - ly Dove! re - turn, Sweet mes - sen-ger of rest! I hate the sins that made thee mourn, And drove thee from my breast.
5. The dear-est i - dol I have known,—What-e'er that i - dol be,—Help me to tear it from thy throne, And wor-ship on - ly thee.

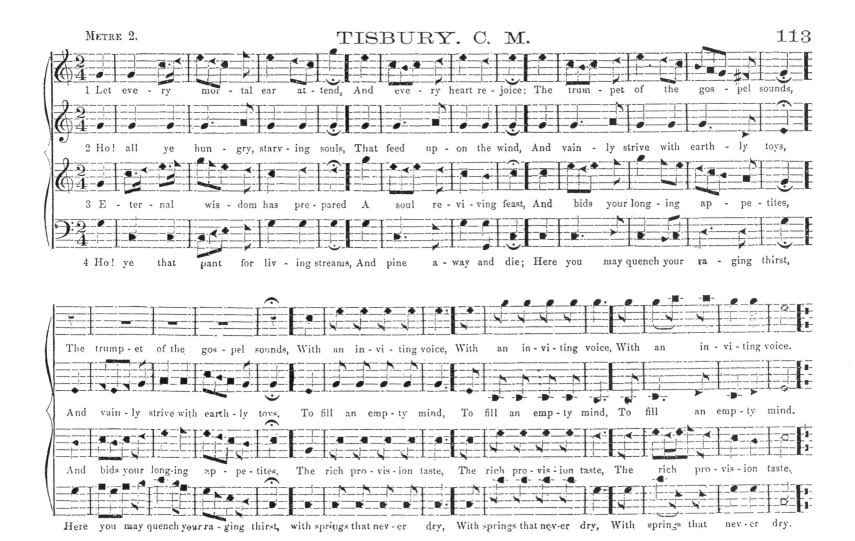

1 Let eve - ry mor - tal ear at - tend, And eve - ry heart re - joice: The trum - pet of the gos - pel sounds,

2 Ho! all ye hun - gry, starv - ing souls, That feed up - on the wind, And vain - ly strive with earth - ly toys,

3 E - ter - nal wis - dom has pre - pared A soul re - vi - ving feast, And bids your long - ing ap - pe - tites,

4 Ho! ye that pant for liv - ing streams, And pine a - way and die; Here you may quench your ra - ging thirst,

The trump - et of the gos - pel sounds, With an in - vi - ting voice, With an in - vi - ting voice, With an in - vi - ting voice.

And vain - ly strive with earth - ly toys, To fill an emp - ty mind, To fill an emp - ty mind, To fill an emp - ty mind.

And bids your long - ing ap - pe - tites, The rich pro - vis - ion taste, The rich pro - vis - ion taste, The rich pro - vis - ion taste.

Here you may quench your ra - ging thirst, with springs that nev - er dry, With springs that nev - er dry, With springs that nev - er dry.

114 Metre 2.

LIBERTY HALL. C. M.

1 A - las! and did my Sa - vior bleed, And did my Sov - reign die? Would he de - vote that sac - red head For such a worm as I?

2 Thy bod - y slain, sweet Je - sus, thine, And bathed in its own blood, While all ex - posed to wrath di - vine, The glo - rious Suff'r-er stood.

3 Was it for crimes that I had done, He groan'd up - on the tree: A - maz-ing pit - y! Grace un-known! And love be-yond de-gree!

4 Well might the sun in dark - ness hide, And shut his glo - ries in, When God the might-y Ma - ker died For man, the crea-ture's sin.

Metre 2.

NINETY-FIFTH C. M.

1 This is the day the Lord hath made, He calls the hours his own; Let heav'n rejoice, let earth be glad, Let heav'n rejoice, let earth be glad, And praise surround the throne.

2 To-day he rose and left the dead, And Sa-tan's empire fell: To-day the saints his triumph spread, To-day the saints his triumph spread, And all his won-ders tell.

3 Ho - san-na to th' a-nointed King, To Da-vid's Ho-ly Son; Help us, O Lord, descend and bring, Help us, O Lord, descend and bring Sal - va - tion from thy throne.

4 Blest is the Lord who comes to men With messages of grace, Who comes in God his Father's name, Who comes in God his Father's name, To save our sinful race.

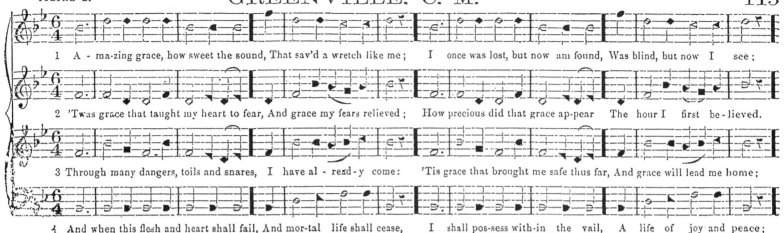

1 A - ma-zing grace, how sweet the sound, That sav'd a wretch like me;　I once was lost, but now am found, Was blind, but now I see;

2 'Twas grace that taught my heart to fear, And grace my fears relieved;　How precious did that grace ap-pear　The hour I first be-lieved.

3 Through many dangers, toils and snares, I have al - read-y come:　'Tis grace that brought me safe thus far, And grace will lead me home;

4 And when this flesh and heart shall fail, And mor-tal life shall cease,　I shall pos-sess with-in the vail, A life of joy and peace;

Was blind, but now I see, Was blind, but now I see,　I once was lost, but now am found— Was blind, but now I see.

The hour I first be - lieved! The hour I first be - lieved!　How pre-cious did that grace ap-pear, The hour I first be - lieved!

And grace will lead me home, And grace will lead me home,　'Tis grace that brought me safe thus far, And grace will lead me home.

A life of joy and peace, A life of joy and peace;　I shall pos-sess with-in the vail A life of joy and peace.

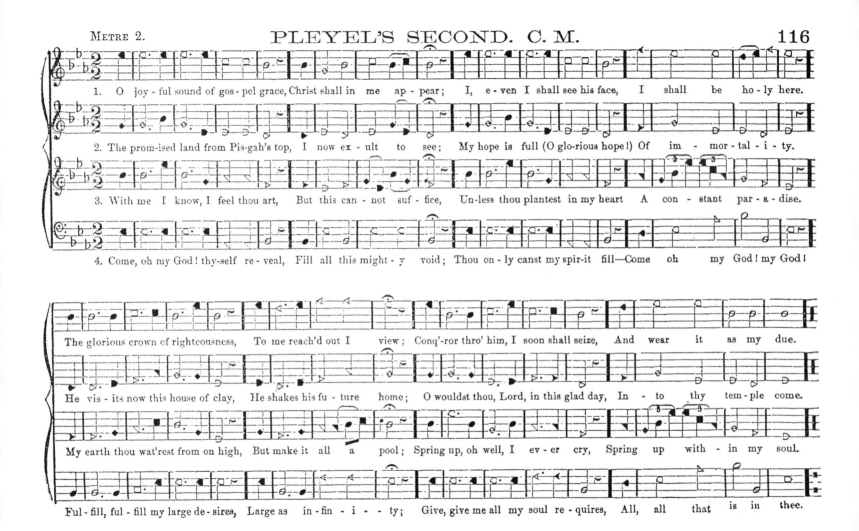

1. O joy-ful sound of gos-pel grace, Christ shall in me ap-pear; I, e-ven I shall see his face, I shall be ho-ly here.

2. The prom-ised land from Pis-gah's top, I now ex-ult to see; My hope is full (O glo-rious hope!) Of im - mor-tal - i - ty.

3. With me I know, I feel thou art, But this can-not suf-fice, Un-less thou plantest in my heart A con - stant par-a-dise.

4. Come, oh my God! thy-self re-veal, Fill all this might-y void; Thou on-ly canst my spir-it fill—Come oh my God! my God!

The glorious crown of righteousness, To me reach'd out I view; Conq'-ror thro' him, I soon shall seize, And wear it as my due.

He vis-its now this house of clay, He shakes his fu-ture home; O wouldst thou, Lord, in this glad day, In - to thy tem-ple come.

My earth thou wat'rest from on high, But make it all a pool; Spring up, oh well, I ev-er cry, Spring up with-in my soul.

Ful-fill, ful-fill my large de-sires, Large as in-fin-i - ty; Give, give me all my soul re-quires, All, all that is in thee.

METRE 2.

WILTSHIRE. C. M.

1 From thee, my God, my joys shall rise, And run eternal rounds, Beyond the limits of the skies, beyond the limits of the skies, And all created bounds, And all created bounds.

2 The holy triumphs of my soul Shall death itself outbrave, Leave dull mortality behind, Leave dull mortality behind. And fly beyond the grave, And fly beyond the grave.

3 There, where my blessed Jesus reigns In heaven's unmeasured space, I'll spend a long eternity, I'll spend a long eternity, In plea - - ure and in praise, In pleasure and in praise.

4 Millions of years my wand'ring eyes shall o'er thy beauties rove, And endless ages I'll adore, And endless ages I'll adore, The glo - - ries of thy love, The glories of thy love.

METRE 2.

ROCHESTER. C. M.

1 Come chil-dren, learn to fear the Lord; And that your days be long, Let not a false or spite-ful word, Be found up - on your tongue.

2 De - part from mischief, practice love, Pur - sue the works of peace; So shall the Lord your ways ap-prove, And set your souls at ease.

3 His eyes a-wake to guard the just, His ears at-tend their cry:—When broken spir-its dwell in dust, The God of grace is nigh.

4 What though the sor-rows here they taste, Are sharp and te-dious too, The Lord who saves them all at last, Is their sup-port - er now.

METRE 2. MISSIONARY'S ADIEU. C. M.

1 My dear-est, love-ly, na-tive land, Where peace and pleasure grow, Where joy with fair-est, soft-est hand, Wipes off the tears of woe—

2 O sac-red home, how sweet thou art, And all thy scenes how dear! Thou dost with chords entwine my heart, And seem'st to say, "stay here!"

3 My pa-rents, broth-ers, sis-ters, friends, My warm af-fec-tion know, And love from each my path at-tends, And can I from them go?

4 No sighs of grief my bo-som heave, No tears of an-guish roll; My friends, my *all* I *glad-ly* leave, For Je-sus cheers my soul.

Thy Sab-baths, laws, and hap-py shores, And names, I love them well, And look-ing o'er those rich-est stores, How can I say, Fare-well!

Thou al-ways didst an an-gel prove, My youth-ful fears to quell, Thou still art clad with smiles of love, And can I say, Fare-well!

The thoughts of days that now are past, No pen nor tongue can tell; Though to my heart they cling so fast, Yet I *must* say, Fare-well!

Ye winds, then waft me far a-way, The tale of love to tell; To coun-try, home, and friends I say, Fare-well! O yes! Fare-well!

FARNHAM. C. M.

1 Ye glitt'ring toys of earth, a-dieu, A no-bler choice be mine; A re-al prize at-tracts my view, A treas-ure all di-vine:

2 Je-sus, to mul-ti-tudes un-known,— O name di-vine-ly sweet! Je-sus, in thee, in thee a-lone, Wealth, hon-or, pleas-ure meet!

3 Should earth's vain treasures all depart, Of this dear gift pos-sess'd, I'd clasp it to my joy-ful heart, And be for-ev-er bless'd:

Be-gone un-wor-thy of my cares, Ye spe-cious baits of sense; In-es-ti-ma-ble worth ap-pears The pearl of price im-mense.

Should both the In-dies at my call Their boast-ed stores re-sign; With joy I would re-nounce them all, For leave to call thee mine.

Dear Sov'reign of my soul's de-sire, Thy love is bliss di-vine! Ac-cept the wish that love in-spires, And bid me call thee mine.

Metre 2.

ST. NICHOLAS. C. M.

REV. WM. H. HAVERGAL, D. D.

1 E - ter - nal source of joys di - vine, To thee my soul as - pires; Oh, could I say "the Lord is mine!" "Tis all my soul de - sires.

2 My Hope, my Trust, my Life, my Lord, As - sure me of thy love; Oh, speak the kind trans-port-ing word, And bid my fears re - move.

3 Then shall my thankful powers re-joice, And tri - umph in my God, Till heavenly rap-ture tune my voice, To spread thy praise a-broad.

Metre 2.

SUFFIELD. C. M.

1 Teach me the mea-sure of my days, Thou maker of my frame; I would sur - vey life's nar - row space, And learn how frail I am.

2 A span is all that we can boast, An inch or two of time; Man is but van-i-ty and dust In all his flow'r and prime.

3 See the vain race of mor-tals move, Like shad-ows o'er the plain; They rage and strive, de-sire and love, But all their noise is vain.

4 Some walk in honor's gau - dy show, Some dig for gold - en ore; They toil for heirs they know not who, And straight are seen no more.

122

METRE 2.

FIDUCIA. C. M.

1 Fa-ther, I long, I faint to see The place of thine a-bode,
I'd leave these earth-ly courts and flee Up to thy seat, my God;
Here I be-hold thy dis-tant face, And 'tis a pleas-ing sight;

2 I'd part with all the joys of sense, To gaze up-on thy throne;
Pleas-ure springs fresh for ev - er thence, Un - speak-a - ble, un - know!
There all the heav'n-ly hosts are seen— In shi - ning ranks they move.

But to a-bide in thy embrace, Is in-fi-nite de-light.

And drink im-mor-tal vig-or in, With wonder and with love.

METRE 2.

CARR'S LANE. C. M.

1 Ye hum-ble souls that seek the Lord, Chase all your fears a - way;

2 Thus low the Lord of life was brought; Such won-ders love can do;

3 A moment give a - loose to grief, Let grate-ful sor - rows rise;

4 Then dry your tears and tune your songs, The Sa - vior lives a - gain;

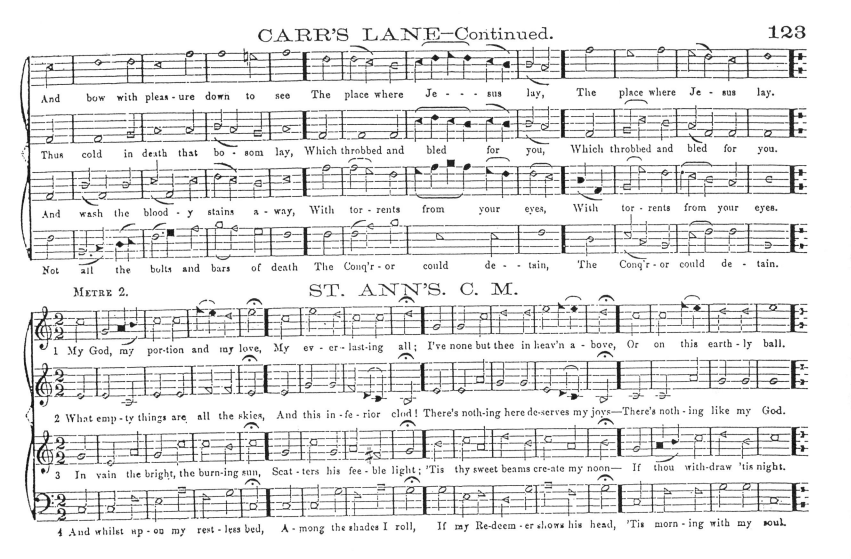

CARR'S LANE—Continued.

And bow with pleas-ure down to see The place where Je - - sus lay, The place where Je - sus lay.

Thus cold in death that bo - som lay, Which throbbed and bled for you, Which throbbed and bled for you.

And wash the blood-y stains a - way, With tor - rents from your eyes, With tor - rents from your eyes.

Not all the bolts and bars of death The Conq'r - or could de - tain, The Conq'r - or could de - tain.

METRE 2. **ST. ANN'S. C. M.**

1 My God, my por-tion and my love, My ev - er - last-ing all; I've none but thee in heav'n a - bove, Or on this earth - ly ball.

2 What emp - ty things are all the skies, And this in - fe - rior clod! There's noth-ing here de-serves my joys—There's noth - ing like my God.

3 In vain the bright, the burn-ing sun, Scat-ters his fee - ble light; 'Tis thy sweet beams cre-ate my noon— If thou with-draw 'tis night.

4 And whilst up - on my rest - less bed, A - mong the shades I roll, If my Re-deem - er shows his head, 'Tis morn - ing with my soul.

METRE 2.

BURFORD. C. M.

1. Lord, I ap-proach thy mer-cy seat, Where thou dost an-swer prayer; There hum-bly fall be-fore thy feet, For none can perish there.

2. Thy prom-ise is my on-ly plea; With this I ven-ture nigh; Thou call-est bur-dened souls to thee, And such, O Lord, am I.

3. Bowed down beneath a load of sin, By Sa-tan sore-ly press'd, By war with-out and fear with-in, I come to thee for rest.

4. Be thou my Shield, my hi-ding place; That, shel-tered near thy side, I may my fierce ac-cu-ser face; And tell him thou hast died.

METRE 2.

BEDFORD. C. M.

1. Ear-ly my God, with-out de-lay, I haste to seek thy face, My thirs-ty spir-it faints a-way, With-out thy cheer-ing grace.

2. So pil-grims on the scorching sand, Be-neath a burn-ing sky, Long for a cool-ing stream at hand, And they must drink or die.

3. I've seen thy glo-ry and thy power Through all thy tem-ple shine; My God, re-peat that heavenly hour, That vis-ion so di-vine.

4. Not all the bless-ings of a feast Can please my soul so well, As when thy rich-er grace I taste, And in thy pres-ence dwell.

SHIRLAND. S. M.

METRE 3.

1 My God, my life, my love, To thee, to thee I call; I can-not live if thou re-move, For thou art all in all.

2 Thy shining grace can cheer This dun-geon where I dwell; Tis par-a-dise when thou art here— If thou de-part 'tis hell.

3 The smilings of thy face, How a-mia-ble they are! 'Tis heav'n to rest in thine em-brace, And no where else but there.

4 To thee and thee a-lone, The an-gels owe their bliss; They sit a-round thy gra-cious throne, And dwell where Je-sus is.

BURBER. S. M.

METRE 3.

J. H. TENNEY.

1 Go to thy rest, my child! Go to thy dream-less bed, While yet so gen-tle, un-de-filed, With blessings on thy head.

2 Shall love with weak em-brace, Thy up-ward wing de-tain? No! gen-tle an-gel, seek thy place, A-mid the cher-ub train.

3 Thy heav'n-ly Fa-ther's voice Shall bid thee wel-come home; Shall soothe, and bid thee still re-joice! With kin-dred spir-its roam.

METRE 3.

WATCHMAN. S. M.

1 My God, per-mit my tongue, This joy to call thee mine, And let my ear-ly cries pre-vail, To taste thy love di-vine.

2 My thirst-y, faint-ing soul Thy mer-cy does im-plore; Not trav-el-ers in des-ert lands, Can pant for wa-ter more.

3 With-in thy churches, Lord, I long to find my place, Thy pow'r and glo-ry to be-hold, And feel thy quick'ning grace.

4 For life with-out thy love No rel-ish can af-ford; Nor joy can be com-pared with this, To serve and praise the Lord.

METRE 3.

BOYLESTON. S. M.

1 O bless the Lord, my soul! Let all with-in me join, And aid my tongue to bless his name, Whose favors are di-vine, Whose favors are di-vine.

2 O bless the Lord, my soul! Nor let his mer-cies, lie, For-got-ten in un-thank-ful-ness, And with-out prais-es die, And with-out prais-es die.

3 'Tis he for-gives thy sins, 'Tis he re-lieves thy pain, 'Tis he that heals thy sick-ness-es, And makes thee young again, And makes thee young again.

4 He crowns thy life with love, When ransom'd from the grave; He that redeem'd my soul from hell, Hath sov'reign pow'r to save, Hath sov'reign pow'r to save.

1 Bless'd are the sons of peace, Whose hearts and hopes are one; Whose kind de-signs to serve and please, Through all their ac-tions run.

2 Bless'd is the pi-ous house, Where zeal and friendship meet, Their songs of praise, their min-gled vows, Make their com-mun-ion sweet.

3 Thus when on Aa-ron's head They pour'd the rich per-fume, The oil through all his rai-ment spread, And pleas-ure filled the room.

4 Thus on the heav'n-ly hills The saints are bless'd a-bove, Where joy like morn-ing dew dis-tills, And all the air is love.

Metre 3.　　　　　　　　LITTLE MARLBOROUGH. S. M.

1 Lord, what a fee-ble piece Is this our mor-tal frame; Our life how poor a tri-fle 'tis, That scarce de-serves the name.

2 A-las, this brit-tle clay That built our bod-y first! And eve-ry month and eve-ry day, 'Tis mould'r-ing back to dust.

3 Our mo-ments fly a-pace, Our fee-ble pow'rs de-cay, Swift as a flood our has-ty days Are sweep-ing us a-way.

4 Yet if our days must fly, We'll keep their end in sight— We'll spend them all in wis-dom's ways, And let them speed their flight.

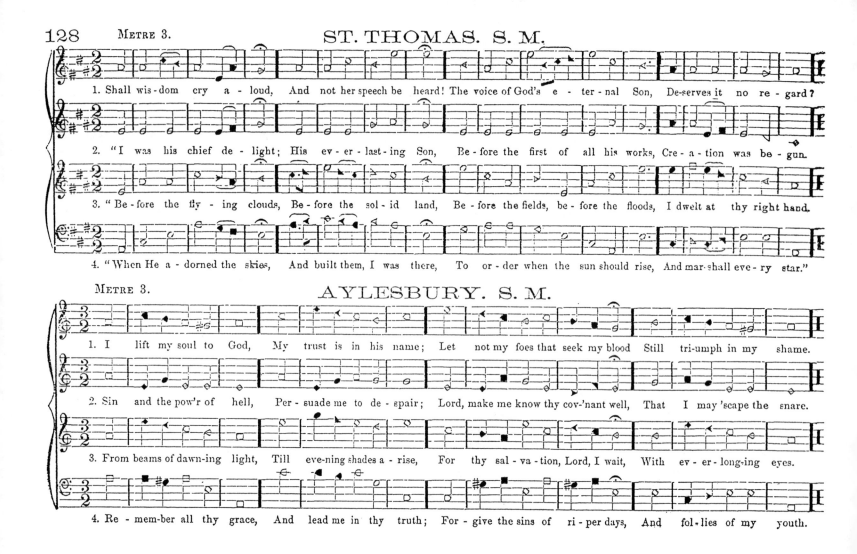

METRE 3.

ST. THOMAS. S. M.

1. Shall wis-dom cry a-loud, And not her speech be heard! The voice of God's e-ter-nal Son, De-serves it no re-gard?

2. "I was his chief de-light; His ev-er-last-ing Son, Be-fore the first of all his works, Cre-a-tion was be-gun.

3. "Be-fore the fly-ing clouds, Be-fore the sol-id land, Be-fore the fields, be-fore the floods, I dwelt at thy right hand.

4. "When He a-dorned the skies, And built them, I was there, To or-der when the sun should rise, And mar-shall eve-ry star."

METRE 3.

AYLESBURY. S. M.

1. I lift my soul to God, My trust is in his name; Let not my foes that seek my blood Still tri-umph in my shame.

2. Sin and the pow'r of hell, Per-suade me to de-spair; Lord, make me know thy cov-'nant well, That I may 'scape the snare.

3. From beams of dawn-ing light, Till eve-ning shades a-rise, For thy sal-va-tion, Lord, I wait, With ev-er-long-ing eyes.

4. Re-mem-ber all thy grace, And lead me in thy truth; For-give the sins of ri-per days, And fol-lies of my youth.

METRE 3.

BLOOMFIELD. S. M.

1 My sorrows like a flood, Impatient of restraint, Into thy bosom, O my God, Pour out a long complaint.

2 This impious heart of mine Could once defy the Lord—Could rush with violence into sin, In presence of thy sword.

3 How often have I stood A rebel to the skies! And yet, and yet, O matchless grace! Thy thunder silent lies.

4 Oh, shall I never feel The meltings of thy love? Am I of such hell-harden'd steel, That mercy cannot move!

METRE 3.

CHESTER. S. M.

1 Let every creature join, To praise th' Eternal God; Ye heav'nly hosts, begin the song, And sound his name abroad.

2 Thou sun, with golden beams, And moon with paler rays, Ye starry lights, ye twinkling flames, Shine to your Maker's praise.

3 He built the worlds above, And fixed their wond'rous frame; By his command they stand or move, And ever speak his name.

4 Ye vapors, when ye rise, Or fall in show'rs of snow—Ye thunders murm'ring round the skies, His pow'r and glory show.

METRE 3.

GORTON. S. M.

BEETHOVEN.

1 While my Re-deem-er's near, My Shepherd and my Guide, I bid fare-well to eve-ry fear; My wants are all sup-plied.

2 To ev-er-fragrant meads, Where rich a-bun-dance grows, His gra-cious hand in-dulg-nt leads, And guard my sweet re-pose.

3 Dear Shep-herd, if I stray, My wandering feet re-store; And guard me with thy watch-ful eye, And let me rove no more.

METRE 3.

LISBON. S. M.

1 Wel-come, sweet day of rest, That saw the Lord a-rise; Wel-come to this re-viv-ing breast, And these re-joic-ing eyes.

2 The King him-self comes near, And feasts his saints to-day; Here may we sit and see Him here, And love and praise and pray.

3 One day a-mid the place Where my dear God hath been, Is sweet-er than ten thousand days Of pleas-ur-a-ble sin.

4 My will-ing soul would stay In such a frame as this, And sit and sing her-self a-way To ev-er-last-ing bliss.

METRE 3.

NEW HOPE. S. M.

1 Come we that love the Lord, And let our joys be known; Join in a song with sweet ac-cord, And thus surround the throne.

2 The sorrows of the mind, Be ban-ished from the place! Re-li-gion nev-er was de-signed To make our pleasures less.

3 Let those re-fuse to sing Who nev-er knew our God; But fa-vorites of the heav'nly King May speak their joys a-broad.

4 This aw-ful God is ours, Our Fa-ther and our love; He will send down his heav'nly pow'rs To car-ry us a-bove.

METRE 3.

IDUMEA. S. M.

1 Is this the kind re-turn, And these the thanks we owe, Thus to a-buse e-ter-nal love, Whence all our bless-ings flow!

2 To what a stub-born frame, Hath sin re-duced our minds! What strange re-bel-lious wretch-es we, And God as strangely kind.

3 On us he bids the sun Shed his re-vi-ving rays; For us the skies the cir-cles run, To length-en out our days.

4 The brutes o-bey their God, And bow their necks to men; But we more base, more bru-tish things, Re-ject his ea-sy reign.

132

METRE 3.

REVIVING LIGHT. S. M.

1 How heavy is the night That hangs up-on our eyes, Till Christ with his re-vi-ving light, O-ver our souls a-rise, O-ver our souls a-rise.

2 Our guilty spirits dread To meet the wrath of heav'n; But in his Righteousness ar-ray'd, We see our sins for-giv'n, We see our sins for-giv'n.

3 Un-ho-ly and im-pure Are all our thoughts and ways; His hands infected na-ture cures, With sanc-ti-fy-ing, grace, With sanc-ti-fy-ing grace.

4 The pow'rs of hell agree To hold our souls in vain: He sets the sons of bon-dage free, And breaks th'accursed chain, And breaks th'accursed chain.

METRE 3.

STRAIT GATE. S. M.

1 De-stuc-tion's dangerous road, What mul-ti-tudes pur-sue! While that which leads the soul to God, Is known and sought by few!

2 Be-liev-ers find the way, Thro' Christ the liv-ing gate; But those who hate this ho-ly way, Com-plain it is too strait.

3 If self must be de-nied, And sin no more ca-ress'd, They rath-er choose the way that's wide, And strive to think it best.

4 En-com-pass'd by a throng, On num-bers they de-pend; They say so ma-ny can't be wrong, And miss a hap-py end.

METRE 3.

SUBLIMITY. S. M.

1. Be-hold the loft-y sky De-clares its Maker God, And all the starry works on high Proclaim his pow'r abroad, And all the star-ry works on high,

2. The darkness and the light, Still keep their course the same; While night to day, and day to night Divinely teach his name, While night to day, and day to night,

3. In eve-ry diff'rent land Their general voice is known; They show the wonders of his hand, And orders of his throne, They show the won-ders of his hand,

4. Ye Christian lands, rejoice! Here he reveals his word; We are not left to nature's voice To bid us know the Lord, We are not left to na-ture's voice,

pre-claim his pow'r a-broad.

Di-vine-ly teach his name.

And or-ders of his throne.

To bid us know the Lord.

METRE 3.

NEWTON. S. M.

1. Far as thy name is known The world de-clares thy praise; Thy saints, O Lord, be-fore thy throne,

2. With joy thy peo-ple stand On Zi-on's cho-sen hill; Pro-claim the won-ders of thy hand,

3. Let stran-gers walk around The ci-ty where we dwell; Com-pass and view the ho-ly ground,

4. The or-ders of thy house, The wor-ship of thy court, The cheer-ful songs, the sol-emn vows,

In time and to e-ter-ni-ty, 'Tis with the right-eous well; In time and to e-ter-ni-ty, 'Tis with the right-eous well.

'Tis well with them while life en-dures, And well when called to die; 'Tis well with them while life en-dures, And well when called to die.

'Tis well when dark-ness vails the skies, And strong temp-ta-tions blow; 'Tis well when darkness vails the skies, And strong temp-ta-tions blow.

And 'tis as well in God's ac-count, When they the fur-nace prove; And 'tis as well in God's account, When they the fur-nace prove.

METRE 3.

BADEA. S. M.

1 When gloom-y doubts and fears The trem-bling heart in-vade, And all the face of na-ture wears A u-ni-ver-sal shade:

2 Re-lig-ion can as-suage The temp-est of the soul; And eve-ry fear gives up its rage At her di-vine con-trol.

3 Through life's be-wil-dered way, Her hand un-err-ing leads, And o'er the path her heav'n-ly ray, A cheer-ing lus-tre sheds.

4 When rea-son, tired and blind, Sinks help-less and a-fraid: Thou blest sup-port-er of the mind! How pow'r-ful is thine aid.

METRE 3.

ASYLUM. S. M.

1. Great is the Lord our God, And let his praise be great: He makes his church-es his a - bode, His most de - light-ful seat.

2. In Zi - on God is known, A ref - uge in dis - tress: How bright has his sal - va-tion shone, How fair his heav'n-ly grace.

3. When kings a - gainst her join'd And saw the Lord was there, In wild con - fu-sion of the mind, They fled with hast - y fear.

4. When na-vies tall and proud, At - tempt to spoil our peace, He sends his tem-pest roar-ing loud, And sinks them in the seas.

METRE 3.

GLORIOUS WAR. S. M.

1. Hark, how the watchmen cry! At-tend the trumpet's sound, Stand to your arms, the foe is nigh, The Pow'rs of hell sur-round:

2. See on the moun-tain's top, The stan-dard of your God! In Je - sus' name I lift it up, All stained with hallow'd blood;

3. Go up with Christ your Head, Your Cap-tain's footsteps see; Fol - low your Cap - tain and be led To cer - tain vic - to - ry;

4. Our Cap - tain leads us on; He beck-ons from the skies, And reach - es out a star - ry crown, And bids us take the prize;

Who bow at Christ's command, Your arms and hearts prepare; The day of bat-tle is at hand, Go forth to glo-rious war, Go forth to glo-rious war.

His standard bearer I To all the na-tions call; Let all to Je-sus' cross draw nigh, He bore the cross for all, He bore the cross for all.

All power to him is giv'n, He ev-er lives the same; Sal-va-tion, hap-pi-ness and heav'n Are all in Je-sus' name, Are all in Je-sus' name.

Be faithful un-to death, Par-take my vic-to-ry, And thou shalt wear this glorious wreath, And thou shalt reign with me, And thou shalt reign with me.

METRE 3.

HANTS. S. M.

1 Give to the winds thy fears, Hope and be un-.......dis-may'd; God hears thy sighs and counts thy tears, God shall lift up thy head, God shall lift up thy head.

2 Thro' waves, and clouds and storms, He gently clears...... thy way; Wait thou his time, so shall this night Soon end in joyous day....... Soon end in joy-ous day.

3 What tho' thou ru-lest not, Yet heav'n and earth....... and hell Pro-claim God sitteth on the throne, And ruleth all things well,....... And ru-leth all things well.

4 Thine ev-er-last-ing truth, Fa-ther, thy cease-.....less love, Sees all thy children's wants, and knows What best for each will prove, What best for each will prove.

METRE 3.

OLMUTZ. S. M.

1 Blest be the tie that binds Our hearts in Christian love; The fel-low-ship of kindred minds, Is like to that a - bove, Is like to that a - bove.

2 Be-fore our Fa-ther's throne, We pour our ardent prayers! Our fears, our hopes, our aims are one—Our comforts and our cares, Our comforts and our cares.

3 We share our mu-tual woes, Our mu-tual bur-dens bear; And oft - en for each oth - er flows The sym-pa - thiz-ing tear, The sym - pa-thiz-ing tear.

4 When we are called to part, It gives us mu - tual pain; But we shall still be joined in heart, And hope to meet a - gain, And hope to meet a - gain.

METRE 3.

WORDS OF PEACE. S. M. (Double.)

1 How beau-teous are their feet, Who stand on Zi - on's hill! Who bring salvation on their tongues, And words of peace reveal! How charming is their voice!

2 How hap - py are our ears, That hear this joy-ful sound, Which kings and prophets waited for, And sought, but never found! How blessed are our eyes,

3 The watchmen join their voice, And tune-ful notes em-ploy; Je - ru-sa-lem breaks forth in songs, And deserts learn the joy, The Lord makes bare his arm

How sweet their ti-dings are! Zi - on, be - hold thy Sa - vior King, He reigns and tri-umphs here, He reigns and tri-umphs here."

That see this heav'n-ly light! Proph-ets and kings de-sired it long, But died with-out the sight! But died with-out the sight.

Through all the earth a - broad! Let eve - ry na-tion now be - hold Their Sa - vior and their God, Their Sa - vior and their God.

METRE 3.

TENDER MERCY. S. M.

1 My soul, repeat his praise Whose mercies are so great, Whose an-ger is so slow to rise, So rea-dy to a-bate, So rea-dy to a-bate.

2 God will not always chide; And when his strokes are felt, His strokes are fewer than our crimes, And lighter than our guilt, And lighter than our guilt.

3 High as the heav'ns are rais'd Above the ground we tread, So far the riches of his grace Our high-est thoughts exceed, Our highest thoughts exceed.

4 His pow'r subdues our sins, And his for - giv-ing love, Far as the east is from the west, Doth all our guilt re-move, Doth all our guilt re - move.

142

METRE 3.

HEAVENLY REST. S. M.

1 Oh where shall rest be found, Rest for.......... the wea-ry soul! 'Twere vain the ocean's depth to sound, Or pierce to either pole, Or pierce to ei-ther pole!

2 The world can nev - er give The bliss.......... for which we sigh; 'Tis not the whole of life to live, Nor all of death to die, Nor all of death to die.

3 Be-yond this vale of tears There is............ a life a-bove; Unmeasured by the flight of years, And all that life is love, And all that life is love.

4 There is a death whose pang Out-lasts.......... the fleet-ing breath; Oh what e-ter-nal horrors hang A-round the second death! A - round the second death.

METRE 3.

LABAN. S. M.

1 Dear Sa-vior, we are thine By ev - er-last-ing bonds; Our names, our hearts we would re - sign, Our souls are in thy hands.

2 To thee we still would cleave, With ev - er grow-ing zeal; If mil-lions tempt us Christ to leave, Oh let them ne'er pre - vail.

3 Thy Spir - it shall u - nite, Our souls to thee our Head; Shall form us to thy im - age bright, That we thy paths may tread.

4 Death may our souls di - vide From these a - bodes of clay; But love shall keep us near thy side Through all the gloom - y way.

1. Ye mes-sen-gers of Christ, His Sov'-reign voice o-bey; A-rise and fol-low where he leads, And peace at-tend your way.

2. The Mas-ter whom ye serve, Will need-ful strength be-stow; De-pend-ing on his prom-ised aid, With sa-cred cour-age go.

3. Moun-tains shall sink to plains, And hell in vain op-pose; The cause is God's and must prevail, In spite of all his foes.

4. Go, spread a Sa-vior's name, And tell his match-less grace, To the most guilty and de-praved Of Ad-am's num'rous race.

METRE 3.   ORANGE. S. M.

1. Blest Com-fort-er di-vine! Let rays of heav'n-ly love A-mid our gloom and darkness shine, And guide our souls a-bove.

2. Draw with thy still small voice, Us from each sin-ful way; And bid the mourning saints re-joice, Though earth-ly joys de-cay.

3. By thy in-spi-ring breath, Make eve-ry cloud of care, And e'en the gloom-y vale of death, A smile of glo-ry wear.

4. Oh, fill thou eve-ry heart With love to all our race! Great Com-fort-er, to us im-part These bless-ings of thy grace.

144

METRE 3.
SLOW—With Solemnity.

FLORIDA. S. M.

1 Let sinners take their course, And choose the road to death ; But in the worship of my God I'll spend my daily breath ; But in the worship of my God I'll spend my daily breath.

2 My thoughts address his throne When morning brings the light ; I seek his blessings every noon, And pay my vows at night ; I seek his blessings every noon, And pay my vows, &c.

3 Thou wilt re-gard my cries, O, my e-ter-nal God, While sinners perish in surprise Beneath thy angry rod, While sinners perish in surprise, Beneath thy angry rod.

4 Because they dwell at ease, And no sad changes feel ; They neither fear nor trust thy name, Nor learn to do thy will, They neither fear nor trust thy name, Nor learn to do thy will!

METRE 3.

SUBMISSION. S. M.

1 "My times are in thy hand," My God, I wish them there ; My life, my friends, my soul I leave To thy pa-ter-nal care.

2 "My times are in thy hand," What-ev-er they may be, Pleas-ing or pain-ful, dark or bright, As best may seem to thee.

3 "My times are in thy hand," Why should I doubt or fear? My Fa-ther's hand will nev-er cause His child a need-less tear.

4 "My times are in thy hand," Je-sus the cru-ci-fied ; The hand my cru-el sins have pierc'd, Is now my guard and guide.

RISING SUN. S. M.

1. See how the ri - sing sun Pur - sues his shi - ning way; And wide pro-claims his Ma-ker's praise, With eve - ry bright'ning ray.

2. Thus would my ri - sing soul Its heav'n-ly Pa-rent sing; And to its great O - rig - in - al The hum-ble trib-ute bring.

3. Se - rene I laid me down Be - neath his guard-ian care; I slept, and I a - woke and found My kind Pre-serv-er near!

4. O, how shall I re - pay The boun-ties of my God? This fee - ble spir - it pants be - neath The pleas - ing, pain-ful load.

LATHROP. S. M.

1. How gen-tle God's com-mands! How kind his pre-cepts are! Come, cast your burdens on the Lord, And trust his con-stant care.

2. His boun-ty will pro - vide, His saints se - cure - ly dwell; That hand which bears cre - a - tion up, Shall guard his children well

3. Why should this anxious load, Press down your wea - ry mind? Oh seek your heav'nly Fa - ther's throne, And peace and comfort find.

4. His good-ness stands approved, Un - changed from day to day; I'll drop my bur-den at his feet, And bear a song a - way.

Metre 4.

MELODY. 8,7,8,7.

1 Sinners, take the friendly warning—Soon that aw-ful day will break, And the trumpet with its dawn-ing, All the slumb'ring millions wake.

2 See as-sem-bled eve-ry na-tion! Loft-y cit-ies, temples, tow'rs, Wrapt in dreadful con-fla-gra-tion, Earth and sea the flames de-vour!

3 Ye who to the world dis-sem-ble, While you practice deeds of night; Sin-ners, now be-hold and trem-ble, All your crimes are brought to light.

4 Ye who now con-vic-tion sti-fling, Waste your time, the loss de-plore; Hear the an-gel—cease your tri-fling,—"Time," he cries, "shall be no more."

Metre 4.

CHARLESTON. 8,7,8,7.

1 Hail, my ev-er bless-ed Je-sus, On-ly thee I wish to sing; To my soul thy name is pre-cious, Thou my Prophet, Priest and King.

2 Oh, what mer-cy flows from heav-en, Oh, what joy and hap-pi-ness! Love I much?—I've much forgiven—I'm a mir-a-cle of grace.

3 Once with Adam's race in ru-in, Un-con-cerned in sin I lay; Swift de-struc-tion still pur-sue-ing, Till my Sa-vior pass'd that way.

4 Wit-ness, all ye hosts of heav-en, My Re-deem-er's ten-der-ness! Love I much?—I've much for-gin-en— I'm a mir-a-cle of grace.

148 METRE 4.

ADVOCATE. 8's & 7's.

1. Sa-vior, I do feel thy mer-it, Sprinkled with re-deem-ing blood; }
And my wea-ry troub-led spir-it, Now finds rest with thee my God! }
I am safe and I am hap-py, While in thy dear arms I lie,

2. Now I'll sing a Sa-vior's mer-it, Tell the world of his dear name; }
That if a-ny want his Spir-it, He is still the ver-y same; }
He that ask-eth soon re-ceiv-eth, He that seeks is sure to find;

Sin and Sa-tan can-not hurt me, While my Sa-vior is so nigh.

Whom-so-e'er on him be-liev-eth, He will nev-er cast be-hind.

METRE 4.

DIVINE COMPASSION. 8's & 7's.

1. Sweet the moments, rich in bless-ing, Which before the cross I spend: }
Life, and health, and peace possessing From the sinner's dy-ing Friend: }

2. Tru-ly bless-ed is the sta-tion, Low be-fore his cross to lie; }
While I see di-vine compas-sion, Floa-ting in his lan-guid eye; }

Here I'll sit, for - ev - er view-ing, Mer-cy's streams in streams of blood; Pre-cious drops my soul be-dew-ing, Plead and claim my peace with God.

Here it is I find my heav-en, While up - on the Lamb I gaze! Love I much?—I've much for-giv-en, I'm a mir - a - cle of grace.

3. Love and grief my heart dividing,
    With my tears his feet I'll bathe;
    Constant still in faith abiding,
    Life deriving from his death;

May I still enjoy this feeling,
    In all need to Jesus go;
    Prove his wounds each day more healing,
    And himself more deeply know,

METRE 4.

BETHLEHEM. 8,7,8,7.

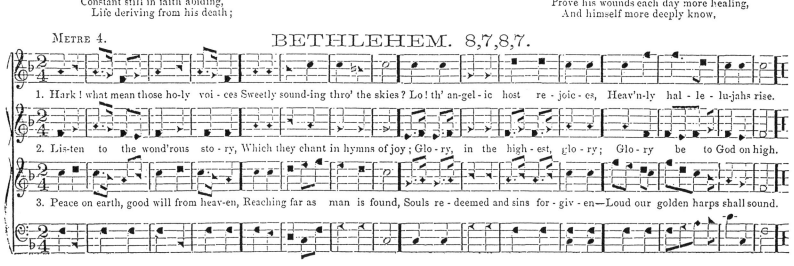

1. Hark! what mean those ho-ly voi - ces Sweetly sound-ing thro' the skies? Lo! th' an-gel-ic host re-joic-es, Heav'n-ly hal - le - lu-jahs rise.

2. Lis-ten to the wond'rous sto - ry, Which they chant in hymns of joy; Glo-ry, in the high-est, glo-ry; Glo-ry be to God on high.

3. Peace on earth, good will from heav-en, Reaching far as man is found, Souls re - deemed and sins for - giv - en—Loud our golden harps shall sound.

METRE 4.

PENITENCE. 8,7,8,7.

1 Je sus, full of all com - pas - sion, Hear thy hum - ble sup-pliant cry; Let me know thy great sal - va - tion—See! I lan-guish, faint and die.

2 Guilt-y, but with heart re - lent - ing, O-ver-whelm'd with helpless grief, Pros-trate at thy feet re - pent-ing, Send, O send me quick re - lief.

3 Whither should a wretch be fly-ing, But to Him who com-fort gives? Whither from the dread of dy - ing, But to Him who ev - er lives.

METRE 4.

DISCIPLE. 8,7,8,7,8,7,8,7.

1 Je - sus, I my cross have ta - ken, All to leave and fol-low thee; Na-ked, poor, de-spised, for - sa - ken, Thou from hence my all shalt be;

2 Let the world de-spise and leave me, They have left my Sa - vior too: Hu-man hearts and looks de-ceive me—Thou art not like them un-true;

3 Go, then earth-ly fame and treasure, Come, dis-as - ter, scorn and pain; In thy ser-vice pain is pleas-ure, With thy fa - vor loss is gain;

4. Man may trouble and dis-tress me, 'Twill but drive me to thy breast; Life with tri-als hard may press me, Heav'n will give me sweet-er rest;
5. Soul, then know thy full sal-va-tion— Rise o'er sin, and fear, and care; Joy to find in eve - ry sta-tion, Something still to do or bear;

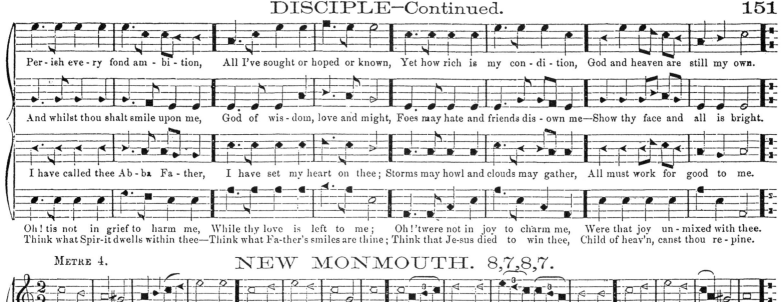

Per - ish eve - ry fond am - bi - tion, All I've sought or hoped or known, Yet how rich is my con - di - tion, God and heaven are still my own.

And whilst thou shalt smile upon me, God of wis - dom, love and might, Foes may hate and friends dis - own me—Show thy face and all is bright.

I have called thee Ab - ba Fa - ther, I have set my heart on thee; Storms may howl and clouds may gather, All must work for good to me.

Oh! tis not in grief to harm me, While thy love is left to me; Oh!'twere not in joy to charm me, Were that joy un - mixed with thee.
Think what Spir-it dwells within thee—Think what Fa-ther's smiles are thine; Think that Je-sus died to win thee, Child of heav'n, canst thou re - pine.

Metre 4.

NEW MONMOUTH. 8,7,8,7.

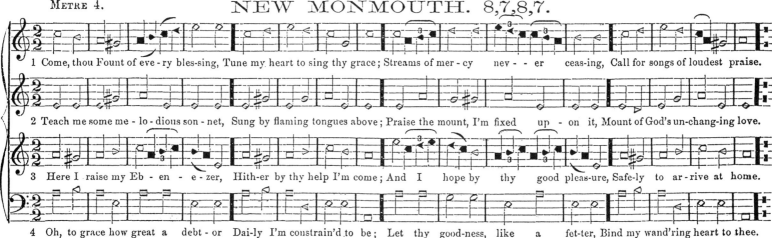

1 Come, thou Fount of eve - ry bles-sing, Tune my heart to sing thy grace; Streams of mer - cy nev - - er ceas-ing, Call for songs of loudest praise.

2 Teach me some me - lo - dious son - net, Sung by flaming tongues above; Praise the mount, I'm fixed up - on it, Mount of God's un-chang-ing love.

3 Here I raise my Eb - en - e - zer, Hith-er by thy help I'm come; And I hope by thy good pleas-ure, Safe-ly to ar - rive at home.

4 Oh, to grace how great a debt - or Dai-ly I'm constrain'd to be; Let thy good-ness, like a fet-ter, Bind my wand'ring heart to thee.

METRE 4. FEMALE PILGRIM. 8's & 7's.

1 Whith-er goest thou, pil-grim stran-ger, Pass-ing thro' this darksome vale?
Know'st thou not 'tis full of dan-ger, And will not thy cour-age fail?
"Pilgrim thou dost just-ly call me, Wand'ring o'er this waste so wide:

2 Such a Guide! no guide at-tends thee, Hence for thee my fears a - rise;
If some guardian Pow'r befriend thee, 'Tis un-seen by mor-tal eyes!
Yes, un-seen,—but still be-lieve me, Such a Guide my steps at - tends;

Yet no harm will e'er be-fall me While I'm blest with such a Guide.

He'll in eve-ry strait re-lieve me, He from eve-ry harm de-fends.

METRE 4. OLNEY. 8's & 7's.

1 Hail! thou once de-spis-ed Je - sus! Hail! thou Gal - i - lee - an King!
Thou didst suffer to re - lease us, Thou didst free sal - va - tion bring!

2 Pas-chal Lamb, by God ap-point-ed, All our sins on thee were laid;
By Al-might-y love a - noint - ed, Thou hast full a - tone-ment made;

Hail thou ag-o-niz-ing Sa-vior! Bear-er of our sin and shame! By thy mer-it we find fa-vor, Life is giv-en thro' thy name.

All thy people are for-giv-en Thro' the vir-tue of thy blood; Op-en'd is the gate of heav-en; Peace is made 'twixt man and God.

METRE 4.   RECONCILEMENT. 8's & 7's.

1 My Beloved, wilt thou own me. When my heart is all defiled? Tho' thy dy-ing love has won me, Tho' thy dying love has won me, Can I deem myself a child?

2 My Be-lov-ed, pass be-fore me; Nev-er from my sight re-move; Many   wa-ters flowing o'er me, Many waters flowing o'er me, Cannot quench my burning love.

3 My Be-lov-ed, now en-due me, with thine own attractive charms; May thy Spirit sweetly woo me; May thy Spirit sweetly woo me, Fold me in thy shel-tering arms.

4 My Be-lov-ed, safely hide me, In the drear and cloud-y day,   Ere the wind-y storm has tried me, Ere the windy storm has tried me, Hide my trembling soul, I pray.
5 My Beloved, kind-ly take me, To thy sympathizing breast; Nev-er, nev-er-more for-sake me, Never, nevermore forsake me, Guide me to the land of rest.

AUTUMN. 8's & 7's.

156

METRE 4.

CONQUEST. 8's & 7's.

1 Dark and thorn-y is the desert Thro' which pilgrims make their way;
But be-yond this vale of sor-rows, Lie the fields of end-less day;
Fiends loud howling thro' the desert Make them tremble as they go,

2 O young soldiers, are you wea-ry, Of the troubles of the way?
Does your strength begin to fail you, And your vig-or to de-cay?
Je-sus, Je-sus will go with you— He will lead you to his throne,

And the fie-ry darts of Sa-tan, Oft-en bring their courage low.

He who dyed his garments for you And the wine-press trod a-lone.

METRE 4.

RIPLEY. 8's & 7's.

1 Mighty God, while an-gels bless thee, May a mor-tal lisp thy name?
Lord of men as well as ' an-gels, Thou art eve-ry creature's theme:

2 For the grandeur of thy na-ture, Grand be-yond a seraph's thought,—
For the won-ders of creation,—Works with skill and kindness wrought,—

Lord of eve-ry land and na-tion, An-cient of e-ter-nal days, Sound-ed thro' the wide cre-a-tion Be thy just and law-ful praise.

For thy prov-i-dence that gov-erns Thro' thine em-pire's wide do-main, Wings an an-gel, guides a spar-row,—Bless-ed be thy gen-tle reign.

METRE 5. EBENEZER. 4 lines 7's.

1 I my Eb-en-e-zer raise To my kind Re-deem-er's praise; With a grate-ful heart I own Hith-er-to thy help I've known.

2 What may be my fu-ture lot, Well I know con-cerns me not; This should set my heart at rest, What thy will or-dains is best.

3 I my all to thee re-sign; Fa-ther, let thy will be mine; May but all my deal-ings prove Fruits of thy pa-ter-nal love.

4 Guard me, Sa-vior, by thy pow'r; Guard me in the try-ing hour; Let thy un-re-mit-ted care Save me from the lurk-ing snare.

158 Metre 5.

ENNIUS. 8 lines 7's.

1 Peo - ple of the liv - ing God, I have sought the world a-round, }
Paths of sin and sor - row trod, Peace and com-fort no-where found; } Now to you my spir-it turns— Turns a fu - gi - tive un - blest;

2 Lone - ly I no lon - ger roam, Like the cloud, the wind, the wave; }
Where you dwell, shall be my home, Where you die, shall be my grave; } Mine the God whom you a - dore, Your Re-deem-er shall be mine;

Breth-ren, where your al-tar burns, O re-ceive me in - to rest.

earth can fill my soul no more,— Eve-ry i - dol I re - sign.

Metre 5.

BOZRAH. 8 lines 7's.

1 Who is this that comes from far, Clad in gar-ments dipp'd in blood? }
Strong tri-umph-ant trav-el-er, Is he man or is he God? }

2 Wherefore are thy garments red, Dyed as in a crim - son sea? }
They that in the wine - vat tread, Are not stain'd so much as Thee. }

I that speak in right-eous-ness, Son of God and man I am, Might-y to re-deem your race, Je-sus is your Sa-vior's name.

"I, the Fa-ther's fav'r-ite Son Have the dread-ful wine-press trod; Borne the venge-ful wrath a-lone, All the fierc-est wrath of God."

METRE 5.   COOKHAM. 4 lines 7's.

1 Ho-ly Je-sus, love-ly Lamb, Thine and on-ly thine I am; Take my bod-y, spir-it, soul, On-ly thou pos-sess the whole.

2 Thou my dearest ob-ject be— Let me ev-er cleave to thee; Let me choose thee for my part— Let me give thee all my heart.

3 Whom have I on earth be-low? On-ly thee I wish to know; Whom have I in heav'n but thee? Thou art all in all to me.

4 All my treas-ure is a-bove— My best por-tion is thy love; Who the worth of love can tell, In-fi-nite un-search-a-ble!
5 Noth-ing else may I re-quire— Let me thee a-lone de-sire; Pleased with what thy love pro-vides, Weaned from all the world be-sides.

160 METRE 5.

ALETTA. 4 lines 7's.

WM. B. BRADBURY.

1 Depth of mer - cy, can there be Mer - cy still re-served for me; Can my God his wrath for-bear? Me, the chief of sin-ners, spare?

2 I have long with-stood his grace, Long pro-voked him to his face; Would not hearken to his calls—Griev'd him by a thous-and falls.

3 Kin - dled his re-lent-ings are,— Me he now de-lights to spare; Cries "how shall I give thee up?" Lets the lift-ed thun-der drop.

4 There for me the Sa - vior stands, Shows his wounds and spreads his hands; God is love! I know, I feel— Je - sus weeps and loves me still.

METRE 5.

EXAMINATION. 4 lines 7's.

1 'Tis a point I long to know, Oft it caus - es anx-ious thought, Do I love the Lord or no! Am I his, or am I not?

2 If I love, why am I thus? Why this dull, this life-less frame? Hardly, sure, can they be worse, Who have nev - er heard his name.

3 Could my heart so hard re-main? Pray'r a task and bur-den prove? Every tri - fle give me pain, If I knew a Sa-vior's love?

4 When I turn my eyes with-in, All is dark, and vain, and wild; Fill'd with un-be - lief and sin, Can I deem my-self a child?

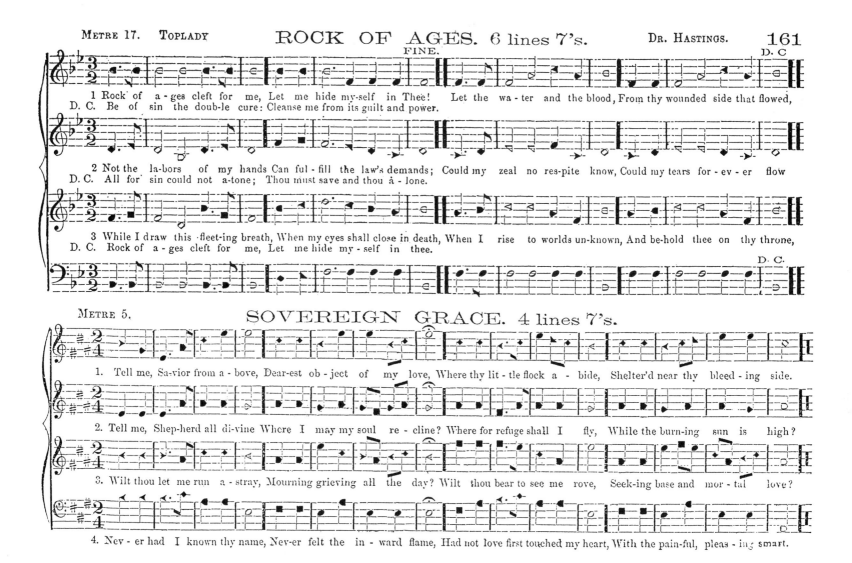

METRE 5.

ELTHAM. 8 lines 7's.

1 Hast-en, Lord, the glorious time, When be-neath Mes-si - ah's sway,
Eve-ry na - tion, eve-ry clime Shall the gos-pel call o - bey. } Might-iest kings his pow'r shall own, Hea-then tribes his name a - dore,

2 Then shall wars and tumults cease, Then be banished grief and pain;
Right-eous-ness, and joy and peace, Un-dis-turbed shall ev - er reign. { Bless we then our gracious Lord, Ev - er praise his glorious name;

Sa - tan and his host o'er-thrown, Bound in chains, shall hurt no more.

All his might-y acts re - cord; All his wondrous love pro - claim.

METRE 5. MARTYN. 8 lines 7's.

1 Ma - ry to the Sa-vior's tomb, Hast-ed at the ear - ly dawn;
Spice she brought and sweet perfume, But the Lord she loved had gone; }

2 But her sorrows quickly fled, When she heard his welcome voice;
Christ had risen from the dead; Now he bids her heart re - joice; }

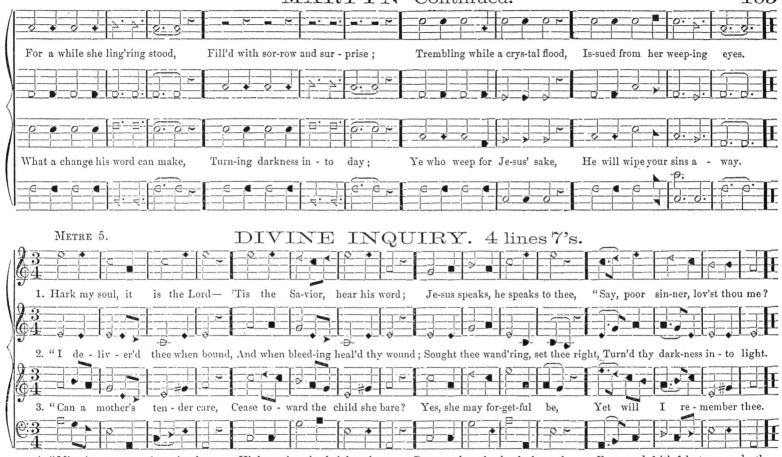

MARTYN—Continued.

For a while she ling'ring stood, Fill'd with sor-row and sur - prise; Trembling while a crys-tal flood, Is-sued from her weep-ing eyes.

What a change his word can make, Turn-ing darkness in - to day; Ye who weep for Je-sus' sake, He will wipe your sins a - way.

METRE 5. DIVINE INQUIRY. 4 lines 7's.

1. Hark my soul, it is the Lord— 'Tis the Sa-vior, hear his word; Je-sus speaks, he speaks to thee, "Say, poor sin-ner, lov'st thou me?

2. "I de - liv - er'd thee when bound, And when bleed-ing heal'd thy wound; Sought thee wand'ring, set thee right, Turn'd thy dark-ness in - to light.

3. "Can a mother's ten - der care, Cease to - ward the child she bare? Yes, she may for-get-ful be, Yet will I re - member thee.

4. "Mine is an un - chang-ing love, High-er than the heights above, Deep-er than the depths beneath, Free and faith-ful, strong as death.
5. "Thou shalt see my glo - ry soon, When the work of grace is done— Part-ner of my throne shalt be; Say, poor sin-ner, lov'st thou me?"

METRE 5. PLEYEL'S HYMN. 4 lines 7's.

1. Sin-ners, turn, why will you die? God your Ma-ker asks you why? God who did your be - ing give, Made you with himself to live.

2. He the fa - tal cause demands— Asks the work of his own hands: Why, ye thankless creatures, why, Will you cross his love and die?

3. Sin-ners, turn, why will you die? God your Sa - vior asks you why? God who did your spir - its give, Died him-self that you might live!

4. Will you let him die in vain?— Cru - ci - fy your Lord a - gain? Why, ye ran-som'd sin - ners, why, Will you slight his grace and die?

METRE 5. HENDON. 4 lines 7's.

1. To thy pastures fair and large, Heav'nly Shepherd, lead thy charge, And my couch with tend'rest care, 'Midst the springing grass prepare, 'Midst the springing grass prepare.

2. When I faint with summer's heat, Thou shalt guide my wea-ry feet, To the streams that still and slow, Thro' the verdant meadows flow, Thro' the verdant meadows flow.

3. Safe the drea-ry vales I tread, By the shades of death o'er-spread; With thy rod and staff supplied, This my guard and that my guide, This my guard and that my guide.

4. Constant to my la-test end, Thou my foot-steps shalt at - tend; And shalt bid thy hallowed dome Yield me an e - ter - nal home, Yield me an e - ter-nal home.

Metre 5.

VIOLA. 7's double.

1 Sin - ners! turn; why will ye die? God, your Ma-ker, asks you why?
God, who did your be - ing give, Made you with him-self to live—
D. C. Will ye not - in him be-lieve? He who died that you might live.

Sin - ners turn, why will ye die? God, your Sa-vior, asks you why?

D. C.

2 Sin - ners, turn; why will ye die? God, your Sa-vior, asks you why?
God, who did your spir - its give, Died him-self that you might live!
D. C. Why, ye thank-less crea-tures, why, Will you cross his love and die?

He the fa - tal cause de - mands, Asks the work of his own hands:

D. C.

Metre 5.

ALARMING VOICE. 4 lines 7's.

1 Sinner! art thou still secure! Wilt thou still refuse to pray? Can thy heart or hand endure, In the Lord's a-veng-ing day! In the Lord's a-veng-ing day!

2 See! his mighty arm is bared! Awful terrors clothe his brow! For his judgment stand prepar'd, Thou must either brake or bow, Thou must either brake or bow.

3 At his presence nature shakes, Earth affrighted hastes to flee: Solid mountains melt like wax; What will then become of thee! What will then become of thee?

4. Who his advent may abide? You that glory in your shame, Will you find a place to hide, When the world is wrapt in flame? When the world is wrapt in flame?

166

METRE 5.

RESURRECTION. 4 lines 7's.

1. An - gels roll the rock a - way; Death! yield up thy might - y prey; See! the Sa - vior leaves the tomb, Glow - ing with im - mor - tal bloom.

2. Hark! the wond'ring an-gels raise Loud - er notes of joy - ful praise; Let the earth's re - mo-test bound Ech - o with the bliss - ful sound.

3. Now, ye saints! lift up your eyes, See him high in glo - ry rise! Hosts of an - gels on the road, Hail him the in - car - nate God.

METRE 6.

GANGES. 8,8,6,8,8,6.

1. A-waked by Si - nai's aw - ful sound, My soul in bonds of guilt I found, And knew not where to go; E - ter-nal truth did loud proclaim,

2. When to the Law I trembling fled, It pour'd it curs-es on my head, I no re-lief could find; This fear-ful truth increased my pain,

3. A - gain did Si-nai's thun-ders roll, And guilt lay heav - y on my soul, A vast op-pres-sive load; A - las, I read and saw it plain,

4. The saints I heard with rap-ture tell, How Je-sus conquered Death and Hell, And broke the fowler's snare; Yet when I found this truth remain,
5. But while I thus in an-guish lay, The gra-cious Sa-vior pass'd that way, And felt his pit - y move; The sin - ner by his jus-tice slain,

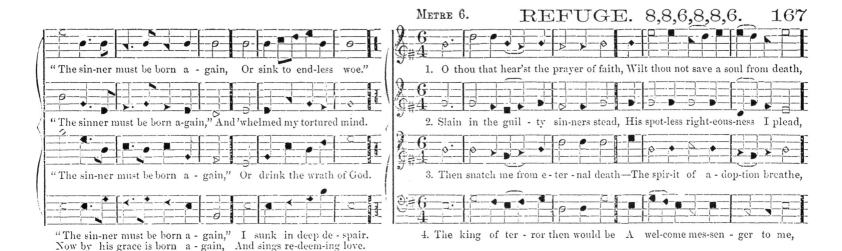

"The sin-ner must be born a - gain, Or sink to end-less woe."

"The sinner must be born a-gain," And 'whelmed my tortured mind.

"The sin-ner must be born a - gain," Or drink the wrath of God.

"The sin-ner must be born a - gain," I sunk in deep de - spair.
Now by his grace is born a - gain, And sings re-deem-ing love.

1. O thou that hear'st the prayer of faith, Wilt thou not save a soul from death,

2. Slain in the guil - ty sin-ners stead, His spot-less right-eous-ness I plead,

3. Then snatch me from e - ter - nal death—The spir-it of a - dop-tion breathe,

4. The king of ter - ror then would be A wel-come mes-sen - ger to me,

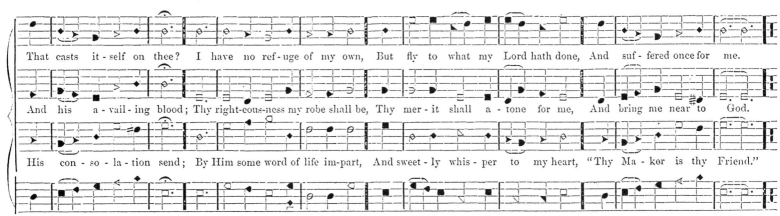

That casts it - self on thee? I have no ref-uge of my own, But fly to what my Lord hath done, And suf - fered once for me.

And his a - vail - ing blood; Thy right-eous-ness my robe shall be, Thy mer - it shall a - tone for me, And bring me near to God.

His con - so - la - tion send; By Him some word of life im-part, And sweet - ly whis - per to my heart, "Thy Ma - ker is thy Friend."

To bid me come a - way; Un - clogg'd by earth or earth-ly things, I'd mount, I'd fly with ea - ger wings, To ev - er - last-ing day.

METRE 6.

KINGWOOD. 8,8,6,8,8,6.

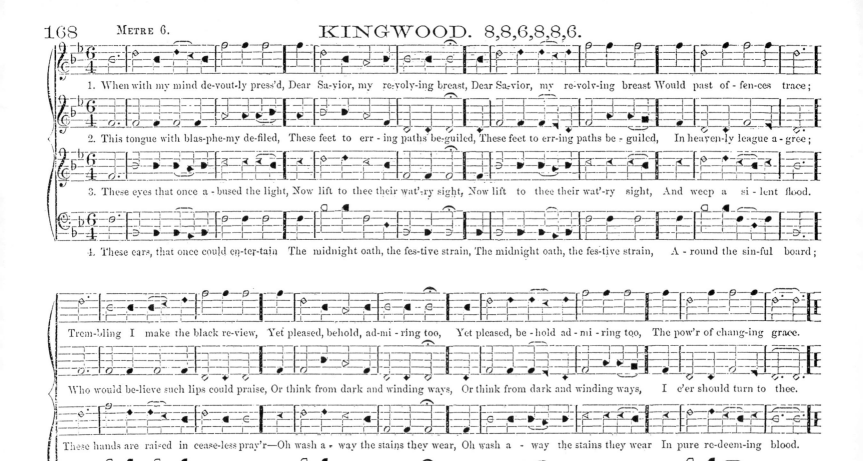

1. When with my mind de-vout-ly press'd, Dear Sa-vior, my re-volv-ing breast, Dear Sa-vior, my re-volv-ing breast Would past of-fen-ces trace;

2. This tongue with blas-phe-my de-filed, These feet to err - ing paths be-guiled, These feet to err-ing paths be - guiled, In heaven-ly league a-gree;

3. These eyes that once a-bused the light, Now lift to thee their wat'-ry sight, Now lift to thee their wat'-ry sight, And weep a si-lent flood.

4. These ears, that once could en-ter-tain The midnight oath, the fes-tive strain, The midnight oath, the fes-tive strain, A - round the sin-ful board;

Trem-bling I make the black re-view, Yet pleased, behold, ad-mi - ring too, Yet pleased, be-hold ad-mi-ring too, The pow'r of chang-ing grace.

Who would be-lieve such lips could praise, Or think from dark and winding ways, Or think from dark and winding ways, I e'er should turn to thee.

These hands are raised in cease-less pray'r—Oh wash a - way the stains they wear, Oh wash a - way the stains they wear In pure re-deem-ing blood.

Now deaf to all th' en-chant-ing noise, A - void the throng, detest their joys, A - void the throng, de-test their joys, And long to hear thy word.

ALDERTON. 8,8,6,8,8,6.

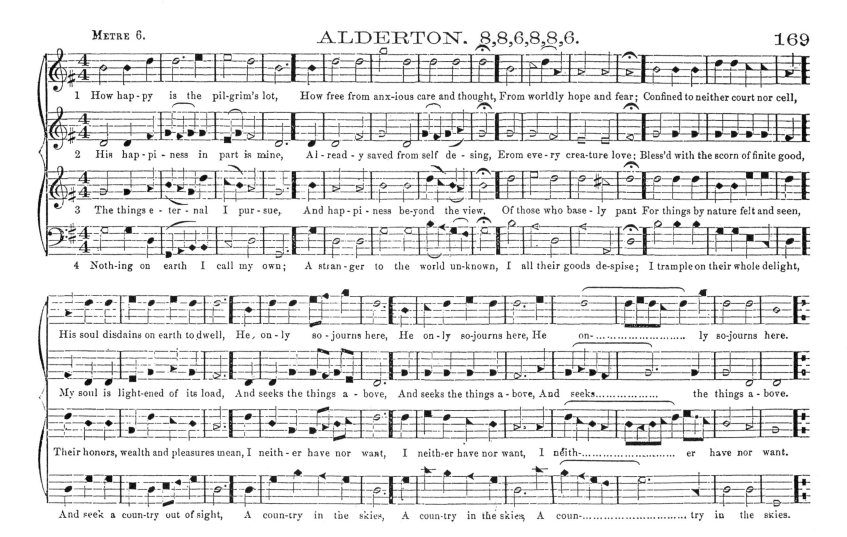

1 How hap-py is the pil-grim's lot, How free from anx-ious care and thought, From worldly hope and fear; Confined to neither court nor cell,

2 His hap-pi-ness in part is mine, Al-read-y saved from self de-sing, From eve-ry crea-ture love; Bless'd with the scorn of finite good,

3 The things e-ter-nal I pur-sue, And hap-pi-ness be-yond the view, Of those who base-ly pant For things by nature felt and seen,

4 Noth-ing on earth I call my own; A stran-ger to the world un-known, I all their goods de-spise; I trample on their whole delight,

His soul disdains on earth to dwell, He, on-ly so-journs here, He on-ly so-journs here, He on-................... ly so-journs here.

My soul is light-ened of its load, And seeks the things a-bove, And seeks the things a-bove, And seeks................ the things a-bove.

Their honors, wealth and pleasures mean, I neith-er have nor want, I neith-er have nor want, I neith-................... er have nor want.

And seek a coun-try out of sight, A coun-try in the skies, A coun-try in the skies, A coun-.................... try in the skies.

METRE 6.   HARMONIA. 8,8,6,8,8,6.

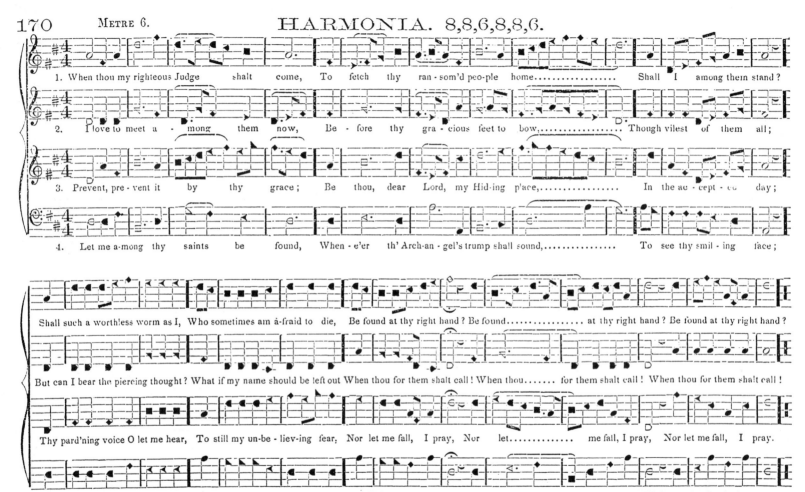

1. When thou my righteous Judge shalt come, To fetch thy ran-som'd peo-ple home................. Shall I among them stand?

2. I love to meet a-mong them now, Be-fore thy gra-cious feet to bow,................. Though vilest of them all;

3. Prevent, pre-vent it by thy grace; Be thou, dear Lord, my Hid-ing place,................. In the ac-cept-ed day;

4. Let me a-mong thy saints be found, When-e'er th' Arch-an-gel's trump shall sound,................. To see thy smil-ing face;

Shall such a worthless worm as I, Who sometimes am a-fraid to die, Be found at thy right hand? Be found................. at thy right hand? Be found at thy right hand?

But can I bear the piercing thought? What if my name should be left out When thou for them shalt call! When thou....... for them shalt call! When thou for them shalt call!

Thy pard'ning voice O let me hear, To still my un-be-liev-ing fear; Nor let me fall, I pray, Nor let................. me fall, I pray, Nor let me fall, I pray.

Then loudest of the crowd I'll sing, While heav'n's resounding mansions ring With sounds of sov'reign grace, With sounds...of sov'reign grace, With sounds of sov'reign grace.

Metre 6.

TRANSPORT. 8,8,6,8,8,6.

1 One spark, O God, of heav'n-ly fire A-wakes my soul with warm de-sire To reach the realms a - bove, To reach the realms a - bove;

2 O could I wing my way in haste, Soon with bright ser-aphs would I feast, And learn their sweet em-ploy! And learn their sweet em-ploy!

3 Too mean this lit-tle globe for me, Nor will I e'er con - tent-ed be To feast on things so vain; To feast on things so vain;

4 But, rest-ing in my Sa-vior's arms, My soul en-joys trans-port-ing charms Of ev-er-last-ing love! Of ev-er-last-ing love!

Im - mor - tal glo-ries round me shine, I drink the streams of life di - vine, And sing re-deem-ing love, And sing re-deem-ing love.

I'd glide a - long the heavenly stream, And join the most ex - alt - ed theme Of ev-er-last-ing joy, Of ev-er-last-ing joy.

Its great-est rich-es are but dross— Its gran-deur short, its pleas-ures cross— Its joys are mixed with pain, Its joys are mixed with pain.

Here's life, here's joy, here's solid peace—A friendship that will nev-er cease— A Rock that can-not move, A Rock that can-not move.

Metre 7. TAMWORTH. 8,7,8,7,4,7.

1 Oh thou God of my sal - va - tion, My Re - deem - er from all sin, }
Mov'd by thy di - vine com - pas - sion, Who hast died my heart to win; }
I will praise thee, I will praise thee, Where shall I thy praise be - gin.

2 While the an - gel choirs are cry - ing, Glo - ry to the great I AM, }
I with them would still be vie - ing, Glo - ry, glo - ry to the Lamb! }
Oh how pre - cious, Oh how pre - cious, Is the sound of Je - sus' name!

Metre 7. JUDGMENT. 8,7,8,7,4,7.

1 Day of Judg - ment! day of wonders! Hark! the trumpet's awful sound! }
Loud - er than a thousand thunders, Shakes the vast cre - a - tion round! }
How the summons! How the summons, Will the sin - ner's heart con - found!

2 See the Judge our na - ture wear - ing, Cloth'd in ma - jes - ty di - vine! }
You who long for his ap - pear - ing, Then shall say, "This God is mine!" }
Gra - cious Sa - vior, Gra - cious Sa - vior, Own me in that day for thine.

METRE 7. SABBATH MORNING. 8,7,8,7,4,7.

1 Hail, all hail! blest Sabbath morn-ing, Pre-lude to e - ter - nal rest; Heav'n de-scends to crown thy mem'-ry; Mil-lions rise to call thee bless'd;

2 Hail, all hail! bless'd courts of Zi - on, Hab - i - ta - tion of our King; May thy con-gre-ga - ted thou-sands Make thy domes with prais-es ring;

3 Hail, all hail! thrice bles-sed gos - pel, Cloth'd with en-er-gy di - vine; Word of life for - ev - er pre-cious—Treas-ure of th' e - ter - nal mind;

4 Hail, all hail! ye sac - red her - alds Of the cross, the cru - ci - fied; Lift the ban-ner, blow the trump-et, Tell the na - tions Je - sus died;

METRE 7. SERAPH'S HARP. 8,7,8,7,4,7.

Hal - le - lu - jah, Hal - le - lu - jah! Hail the day of sac-red rest.

Hal - le - lu - jah, Hal - le - lu - jah! Shout the praise of Zi-on's King.

Word e - ter-nal, Word e - ter - nal, Nerve the weak, illume the blind.

Hal - le - lu - jah, Hal - le - lu - jah! Je-sus' word is glo - ri - fied.

1 Hark! the voice of love and mer - cy! Sounds a-loud from Cal-va - ry!

2 "It is fin-ish'd!" Oh, what pleasure Do these precious words af-ford!

3 Fin-ish'd, all the types and sha-dows Of the cer - e - mo-nial law;

See it rends the rocks a-sun-der,—Shakes the earth and veils the sky! "It is fin-ish'd! It is fin-ished!" Hear the dy-ing Sa-vior cry.

Heavenly bless-ings with-out meas-ure, Flow to us from Christ the Lord; "It is fin-ished! It is fin-ished!" Saints the dy-ing words re-cord.

Fin-ished all that God has prom-ised, Death and hell no more shall awe; "It is fin-ished! It is fin-ished!"—Saints from hence your comfort draw.

Metre 7.

SACRED HERALD. 8,7,8,7,4,7.

1   On the mountain's top appearing, Lo! the sa-cred herald stands,) Mourning captive! God himself will loose thy bands,
Welcome news to Zi-on bear-ing, Zi-on long in hos-tile lands: }
                                                                 Mourning captive! God himself will loose thy bands.

2   Has thy night been long and mournful, All thy friends unfaithful proved?) Cease thy mourning, Zion still is well beloved,
Have thy foes been proud and scornful, By thy sighs and tears unmoved? }
                                                                         Cease thy mourning, Zion still is well beloved.

3   God, thy God, will now restore thee! He himself appears thy friend:) Great deliv'rance Zion's King vouchsafes to send,
All thy foes shall flee before thee, Here their boasted triumphs end. }
                                                                        Great deliv'rance Zion's King vouchsafes to send.

GREENWOOD. 8's, 7's, & 4.

Metre 7.

1 Sa-vior, vis-it thy plan-ta-tion— Grant us, Lord, a gra-cious rain!
All will come to des-o-la-tion,
Lord, re-vive us! Lord, re-vive us!

2 Keep no lon-ger at a dis-tance, Shine up-on us from on high,
Lest for want of thy as-sis-tance,

3 Once, O Lord, thy gar-den flour-ished, Eve-ry plant looked gay and green,
Then thy word our spir-its nour-ished,

Un-less thou re-turn a-gain.
All our help must come from thee.

Eve-ry plant should droop and die.

Hap-py sea-sons we have seen.

SWEET AFFLICTION. 8's, 7's, & 4.

Metre 7.

1 In the floods of trib-u-la-tion, While the bil-lows o'er me roll,

2 Thus the li-on yields me hon-ey, From the eat-er food is given;

3 'Mid the gloom, the viv-id light-nings With in-creas-ing bright-ness play;

4 So, in dark-est dis-pen-sa-tions Doth my faith-ful Lord ap-pear,

Je - sus whis - pers con - so - la - tion, And sup-ports my faint-ing soul; Hal - le - lu - jah, Hal - le - lu - jah, Hal - le - lu - jah, praise the Lord.

Strengthened thus I still press for - ward Sing - ing as   I wade to heaven, Sweet af - flic - tion, Sweet af - flic - tion, And my sins are all   for - given.

'Mid the thorn-brake beauteous flowrets Look more beau-ti - ful and gay; Hal - le - lu - jah, Hal - le - lu - jah,   Hal - le - lu - jah, praise the Lord.

With his rich - est con - so - la - tion, To re - an - i - mate and cheer; Sweet af - flic - tion, Sweet af - flic - tion, Thus to bring my   Sa - vior near.

GOSPEL VICTORY. 8,7,8,7,4,7.
Metre 7.

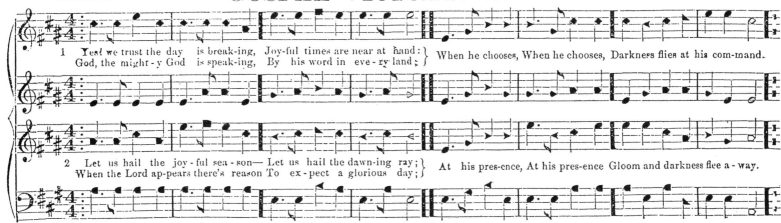

1 Yes! we trust the day   is break-ing, Joy-ful times are near at hand: } When he chooses, When he chooses, Darkness flies at his com-mand.
God, the might - y God is speak-ing, By his word in eve-ry land;

2   Let us hail the joy - ful sea - son— Let us hail the dawn-ing ray; } At his pres-ence, At his pres-ence Gloom and darkness flee a - way.
When the Lord ap-pears there's reason To ex-pect a glorious day;

178

METRE 7.

HANWELL. 8,7,8,7,4,7.

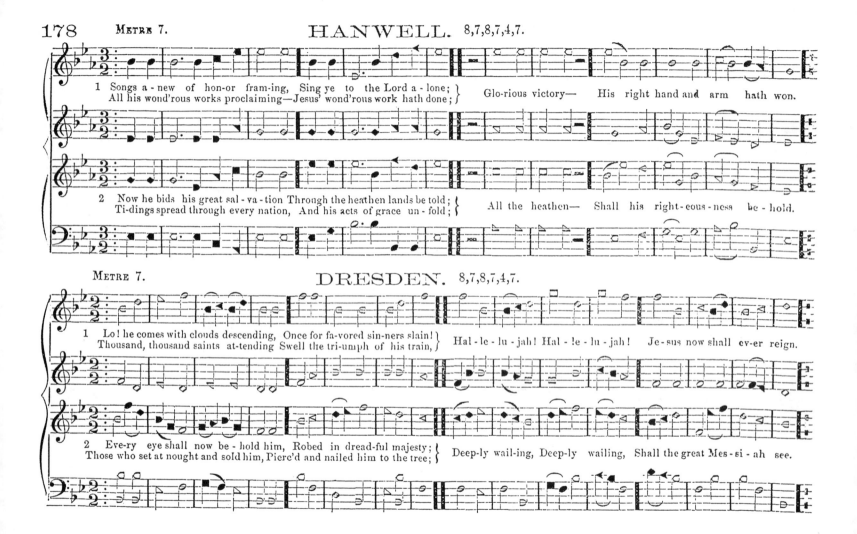

1 Songs a-new of hon-or fram-ing, Sing ye to the Lord a-lone; }
All his wond'rous works proclaiming—Jesus' wond'rous work hath done; }
Glo-rious victory— His right hand and arm hath won.

2 Now he bids his great sal-va-tion Through the heathen lands be told; {
Ti-dings spread through every nation, And his acts of grace un-fold; {
All the heathen— Shall his right-eous-ness be-hold.

METRE 7.

DRESDEN. 8,7,8,7,4,7.

1 Lo! he comes with clouds descending, Once for fa-vored sin-ners slain! }
Thousand, thousand saints at-tending Swell the tri-umph of his train, }
Hal-le-lu-jah! Hal-le-lu-jah! Je-sus now shall ev-er reign.

2 Eve-ry eye shall now be-hold him, Robed in dread-ful majesty; {
Those who set at nought and sold him, Pierc'd and nailed him to the tree; {
Deep-ly wail-ing, Deep-ly wailing, Shall the great Mes-si-ah see.

1. O my soul, what means this sad-ness? Where - fore art thou thus cast down? Let thy grief be turned to glad-ness,

2. What though Sa - tan's strong temp - ta-tions Vex and grieve thee day by day; And thy sin - ful in - cli - na-tions,

3. Though ten thousand ills be - set thee, From with - out and from with - in; Je - sus saith he'll ne'er for-get thee,

4. Though dis-tress - es now at - tend thee, And thou tread'st the thorn - y road; His right hand shall still de-fend thee,

Bid thy rest - less fears be-gone; Look to Je - sus, Look to Je - sus, And re - joice in his dear name.

Oft - en fill thee with dis - may; Thou shalt con - quer, Thou shalt con-quer, Through the Lamb's re-deem - ing blood.

But will save from hell and sin, He is faith - ful, He is faith - ful, To per - form his gra - cious word.

Soon he'll bring thee home to God: There-fore praise him—There-fore praise him— Praise the great Re-deem - er's name.

180 METRE 7. PILGRIM'S GUIDE. 8,7,8,7,4,7.

1. Guide me, O thou great Je - ho - vah, Pil-grim thro' this bar-ren land: I am weak, but thou art might-y Hold me with thy pow'rful hand;

2. O - pen now the crys-tal foun-tain Whence the healing streams do flow; Let the fie - ry, cloud - y pil-lar, Lead me all my journey through;

3. Feed me with the heav'nly man-na In the bar-ren wil-der - ness: Be my sword and shield and ban-ner, Be my robe of righ-teous-ness;

4. When I tread the verge of Jor - dan, Bid my anx-ious fears sub - side; Foe to death and hell's de - struc-tion, Land me safe on Canaan's side;

Bread of heav - en, Bread of heav - en, Feed me till I want no more, Feed me till I want no more.

Strong De - liv'r - er! Strong De-liv'r - er! Be thou still my Strength and Shield, Be thou still my Strength and Shield.

Fight and con - quer, Fight and con - quer All my foes by sov' - reign grace, All my foes by sov'-reign grace.

Songs of prais - es, Songs of prais - es, I will ev - er give to thee, I will ev - er give to thee.

Metre 8.

CONTEMPLATION. 6 lines 8's.

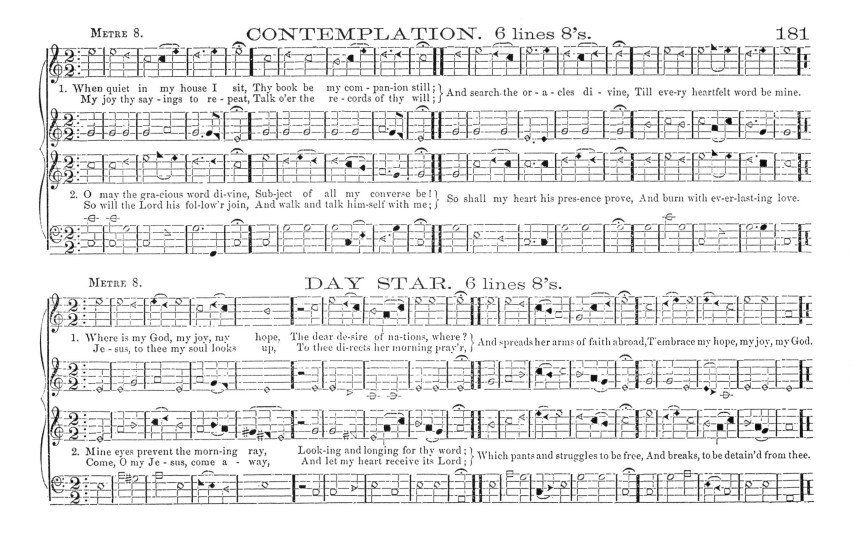

1. When quiet in my house I sit, Thy book be my com-pan-ion still; }
My joy thy say-ings to re-peat, Talk o'er the re-cords of thy will; } And search the or-a-cles di-vine, Till eve-ry heartfelt word be mine.

2. O may the gra-cious word di-vine, Sub-ject of all my converse be! }
So will the Lord his fol-low'r join, And walk and talk him-self with me; } So shall my heart his pres-ence prove, And burn with ev-er-last-ing love.

Metre 8.

DAY STAR. 6 lines 8's.

1. Where is my God, my joy, my hope, The dear de-sire of na-tions, where? }
Je-sus, to thee my soul looks up, To thee di-rects her morning pray'r, } And spreads her arms of faith abroad, T'embrace my hope, my joy, my God.

2. Mine eyes prevent the morn-ing ray, Look-ing and longing for thy word; }
Come, O my Je-sus, come a-way, And let my heart receive its Lord; } Which pants and struggles to be free, And breaks, to be detain'd from thee.

MYSTERIOUS LOVE. 6 lines 8's.

METRE 8.

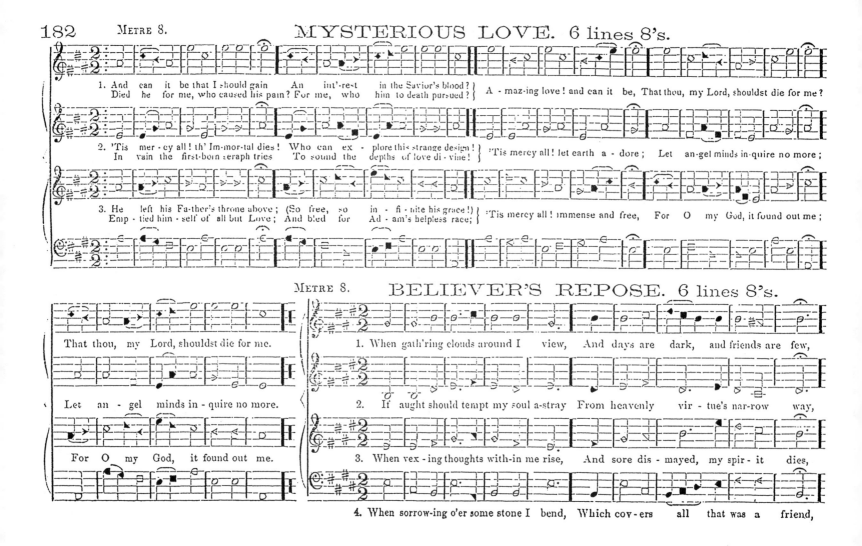

1. And can it be that I should gain An int'rest in the Savior's blood?
Died he for me, who caused his pain? For me, who him to death pursued?
A - maz-ing love! and can it be, That thou, my Lord, shouldst die for me?

2. 'Tis mer - cy all! th' Im-mor-tal dies! Who can ex - plore this strange design!
In vain the first-born seraph tries To sound the depths of love di - vine!
'Tis mercy all! let earth a - dore; Let an-gel minds in-quire no more;

3. He left his Fa-ther's throne above; (So free, so in - fi - nite his grace!)
Emp - tied him - self of all but Love; And bled for Ad - am's helpless race;
'Tis mercy all! immense and free, For O my God, it found out me;

That thou, my Lord, shouldst die for me.

Let an - gel minds in - quire no more.

For O my God, it found out me.

BELIEVER'S REPOSE. 6 lines 8's.

METRE 8.

1. When gath'ring clouds around I view, And days are dark, and friends are few,

2. If aught should tempt my soul a-stray From heavenly vir - tue's nar-row way,

3. When vex - ing thoughts with-in me rise, And sore dis - mayed, my spir - it dies,

4. When sorrow-ing o'er some stone I bend, Which cov - ers all that was a friend,

On him I lean, who not in vain, Ex-perienc'd eve-ry human pain; He sees my wants, al-lays my fears, And counts and treas-ures up my tears.

To fly the good I would pur-sue, Or do the sin I would not do; Still he that felt temp-ta-tion's pow'r, Shall guard me in that dang'rous hour.

Yet he who once vouchsafed to bear The sick'ning anguish of de-spair, Shall sweetly soothe, shall gently dry, The throb-bing heart, the streaming eye.

And from his voice, his hands his smile, Divides me for a lit-tle while,—Thou, Sa-vior, seest the tears I shed, For thou didst weep o'er Lazarus dead.

METRE 8.
VERNON. 6 lines 8's.

1 Come, O thou trav-el-er un-known, Whom still I hold but can-not see; My com-pa-ny be-fore is gone, And I am left a-lone with thee; With thee all night I mean to stay, And wres-tle till the break of day.

2 In vain thou strugglest to get free, I nev-er will unloose my hold; Art thou the man that died for me? The se-cret of thy love un-fold; Wrest-ling I will not let thee go, Till I thy name, thy nature know.

METRE 8.

LEAMING. 6 lines 8's.

ITALIAN MELODY.

1 The Lord my pas-ture shall pre-pare, And feed me with a shep-herd's care; His pres-ence shall my wants sup-ply, And guard me

2 When in the sul-try glebe I faint, Or on the thirs-ty moun-tain pant, To fer-tile vales and dew-y meads My wea-ry,

with a watch-ful eye. My noon-day walks he shall at-tend, And all my mid-night hours de-fend.

wand'-ring steps he leads. Where peace-fnl riv-ers, soft and slow, A-mid the ver-dant land-scape flow.

1 Lo! God is here! let us a-dore, And own how dreadful is the place! Let all with-in us feel his pow'r,

2 Lo! God is here! him day and night, Th'u-ni-ted choirs of an-gels sing; To him en-throned a-bove all height,

3 Glad-ly the toys of earth we leave, Wealth, pleasure, fame, for thee a-lone; To thee our will, soul, flesh we give,

4 Be-ing of be-ings! may our praise, Thy courts with grateful fragrance fill, Still may we stand be-fore thy face,

And si-lent bow be-fore his face! Who know his pow'r, his grace who prove, Serve him with awe, with rev'-rence love.

Heaven's host their no--blest prais-es bring; Dis-dain not, Lord, our mean-er song, Who praise thee with a stam'-ring tongue.

Oh take! oh seal them for thine own! Thou art the God, thou art the Lord— Be thou by all thy works a-dored.

Still hear and do thy sov'reign will; To thee may all our thoughts a-rise, A cease-less, pleas-ing sac-ri-fice.

METRE 9.

STOW. 6,6,6,6,8,8.

1. Yes, the Re - deem - er rose: The Sa - vior left the dead; And o'er our hell - ish foes, High raised his conquering head;

2. Lo the an - gel - ic bands, In full as - sem - bly meet, To wait his high com-mands, And wor - ship at his feet;

3. Then back to heav'n they fly, The joy - ful news to bear; Hark! as they soar on high, What mu - sic fills the air;

4. Ye mor-tals, catch the sound,— Re - deem'd by him from hell; And send the ech - o round The globe on which you dwell;

In wild dis-may the guards a-round Fall to the ground and sink a - way.

Joy - ful they come and wing their way, From realms of day to Jesus' tomb.

Their an-thems say,—"Jesus who bled, Hath left the dead:—He rose to - day."

'Trans-port-ed cry,—"Je-sus who bled, Hath left the dead, no more to die."

METRE 9. LENOX. 6's & 8's.

1. Hark! hark! the notes of joy Roll o'er the heav'nly plains,

2. Hark! hark! the sounds draw nigh, The joy - ful hosts de-scend;

3. Bear, bear the ti-dings round; Let eve - ry mor-tal know,

4. Strike, strike the harps a - gain To great Im-man-uel's name;

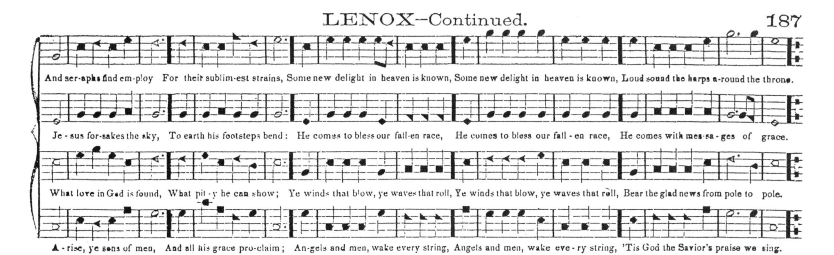

And ser-aphs find em-ploy For their sublim-est strains, Some new delight in heaven is known, Some new delight in heaven is known, Loud sound the harps a-round the throne.

Je - sus for-sakes the sky, To earth his footsteps bend: He comes to bless our fall-en race, He comes to bless our fall - en race, He comes with mes-sa-ges of grace.

What love in God is found, What pit-y he can show; Ye winds that blow, ye waves that roll, Ye winds that blow, ye waves that roll, Bear the glad news from pole to pole.

A - rise, ye sons of men, And all his grace pro-claim; An-gels and men, wake every string, Angels and men, wake eve-ry string, 'Tis God the Savior's praise we sing.

METRE 9.

GRATEFUL PRAISE. 6's & 8's.

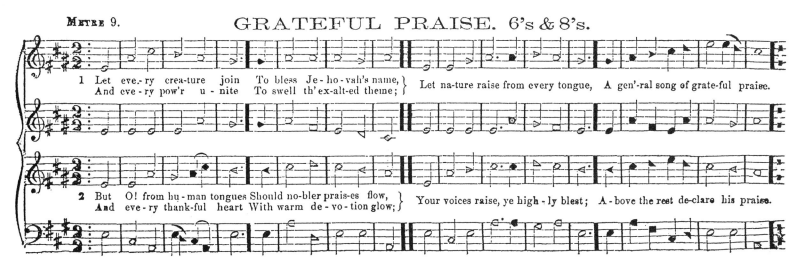

1 Let eve-ry crea-ture join To bless Je-ho-vah's name, } Let na-ture raise from every tongue, A gen'-ral song of grate-ful praise.
And eve-ry pow'r u - nite To swell th' ex-alt-ed theme; }

2 But O! from hu-man tongues Should no-bler prais-es flow, } Your voices raise, ye high-ly blest; A-bove the rest de-clare his praise.
And eve-ry thank-ful heart With warm de - vo-tion glow; }

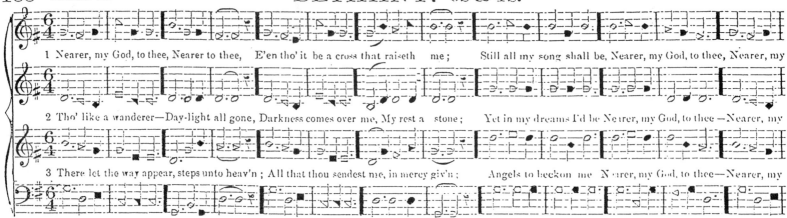

Be - fore the throne my Sure - ty stands, My name is writ - ten on his hands, My name is writ - ten on his hands.

His blood a - toned for all our race, And sprin-kles now the throne of grace, And sprin - kles now the throne of grace.

For - give him, Oh! for - give, they cry, Nor let that ran-som'd sin - ner die, Nor let that ran - som'd sin - ner die.

METRE 9.

CONFIDENCE. 6,6,6,6,8,8.

1 When Hannah, press'd with grief, Pour'd forth her soul in pray'r,
She quick - ly found re - lief, And left her bur-den there; } Like her in eve - ry try-ing case, Let us ap-proach the throne of grace.

2 When she be-gan to pray, Her heart was pain'd and sad—
But ere she went a - way, Was com-fort-ed and glad; } In trou-ble what a rest-ing place Have they who know the throne of grace.

3 Though men and dev-ils rage, And threaten to de - vour;
Thy saints from age to age, Are safe from all their pow'r. } Fresh strength they gain to run their race, By wait-ing at a throne of grace.

METRE 9.

ANTICIPATION. 6,6,6,6,8,8.

1 On earth the song be-gins, In heav'n more sweet, more loud, To him that drowns our sins In his a-ton-ing blood,

2 Ye saints on earth, re-peat What heav'n with rap-ture owns; And while be-fore his feet The eld-ers cast their crowns,

3 Sing as ye pass a-long, With joy and won-der sing, Till oth-ers learn the song, And own your Lord their King;

4 In-form the listen-ing world How Je-sus, when he fell, The pow'rs of darkness hurl'd Down to the depths of hell;

"To Him," they cry in rapt'-rous strains, "To Him," they cry in rapt'-rous strains, "Be hon-or, praise, and pow'r— A-men!"

Go, im-i-tate the choirs a-bove, Go, im-i-tate the choirs a-bove, And tell the world your Sa-vior's love.

Till con-verts join you as ye go, Till con-verts join you as ye go, And make a grow-ing heav'n be-low.

And ris-ing, bore the res-cued prize, And ris-ing, bore the res-cued prize, His church in tri-umph through the skies.

AUDLEY. 6,6,6,6,8,8.

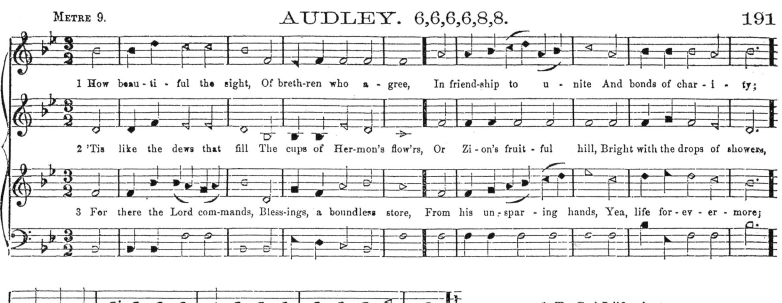

1 How beau - ti - ful the sight, Of breth-ren who a - gree, In friend-ship to u - nite And bonds of char - i - ty;

2 'Tis like the dews that fill The cups of Her-mon's flow'rs, Or Zi - on's fruit - ful hill, Bright with the drops of showers,

3 For there the Lord com-mands, Bless-ings, a boundless store, From his un - spar - ing hands, Yea, life for - ev - er - more;

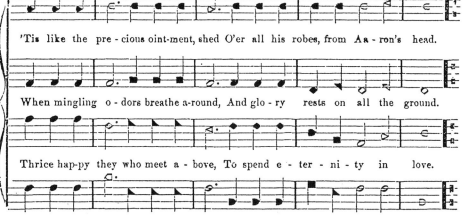

'Tis like the pre - cious oint-ment, shed O'er all his robes, from Aa - ron's head.

When mingling o - dors breathe a-round, And glo - ry rests on all the ground.

Thrice hap-py they who meet a - bove, To spend e - ter - ni - ty in love.

1 To God I lift mine eyes,
   From him is all my aid;
The God who built the skies,
   And earth and nature made;
God is the tower to which I fly;
His grace is nigh in every hour.

2 My feet shall never slide,
   And fall in fatal snares;
Since God, my guard and guide,
   Defends me from my fears:
Those wakeful eyes that never sleep,
Shall Israel keep, when dangers rise.

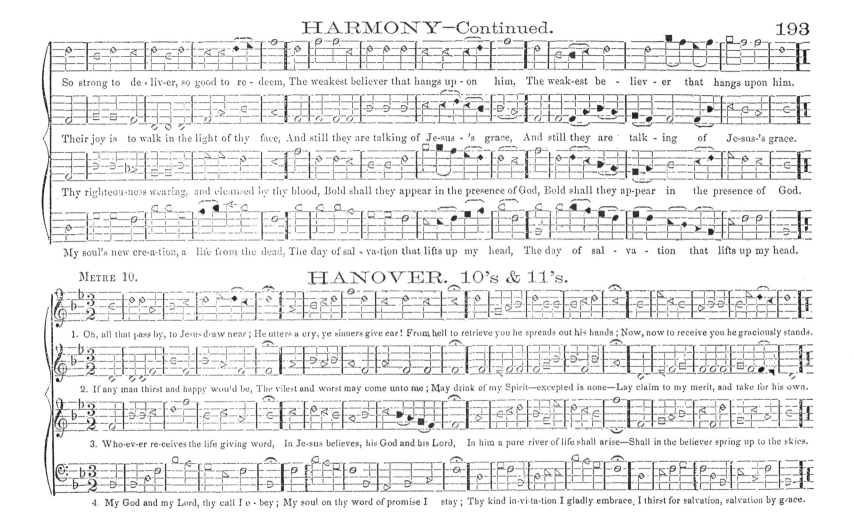

So strong to de-liv-er, so good to re-deem, The weakest believer that hangs up-on him, The weak-est be-liev-er that hangs upon him.

Their joy is to walk in the light of thy face, And still they are talking of Je-sus-'s grace, And still they are talk-ing of Je-sus-'s grace.

Thy righteousness wearing, and cleansed by thy blood, Bold shall they appear in the presence of God, Bold shall they ap-pear in the presence of God.

My soul's new cre-a-tion, a life from the dead, The day of sal-va-tion that lifts up my head, The day of sal-va-tion that lifts up my head.

METRE 10.

HANOVER. 10's & 11's.

1. Oh, all that pass by, to Jesus draw near; He utters a cry, ye sinners give ear! From hell to retrieve you he spreads out his hands; Now, now to receive you he graciously stands.

2. If any man thirst and happy wou'd be, The vilest and worst may come unto me; May drink of my Spirit—excepted is none—Lay claim to my merit, and take for his own.

3. Who-ev-er re-ceives the life giving word, In Je-sus believes, his God and his Lord, In him a pure river of life shall arise—Shall in the believer spring up to the skies.

4. My God and my Lord, thy call I o-bey; My soul on thy word of promise I stay; Thy kind in-vi-ta-tion I gladly embrace, I thirst for salvation, salvation by grace.

194

METRE 10.

STOCKBRIDGE. 10's & 11's.

1 Tho' trou-bles as-sail and dan-gers af-fright, Though friends should all fail and foes all u-nite, Yet one thing se-cures us, what-ev-er be-tide,

2 The birds with-out barn or storehouse are fed, From them let us learn to trust for our bread; His saints what is fit-ting shall ne'er be de-nied.

3 We all may, like ships, by tempests be toss'd On per-il-ous deeps, but need not be lost; Though Sa-tan en-ra-ges the wind and the tide,

4 His call we o-bey, like A-bra'm of old; We know not the way, but faith makes us bold; For though we are strangers, we have a sure Guide.

The prom-ise as-sures us the Lord will pro-vide.

So long as 'tis writ-ten the Lord will pro-vide.

Yet scrip-ture en-ga-ges the Lord will pro-vide.

And trust in all dan-gers the Lord will pro-vide.

METRE 10.

UNITIA. 10's & 11's.

1 Be-gone un-be-lief! my Sa-vior is near, And for my re-lief, will

2 Though dark be my way since he is my Guide, 'Tis mine to o-bey, 'tis

3 His love in time past for-bids me to think, He'll leave me at last in

4 Why should I com-plain, of want and dis-tress, Temp-ta-tion or pain? He

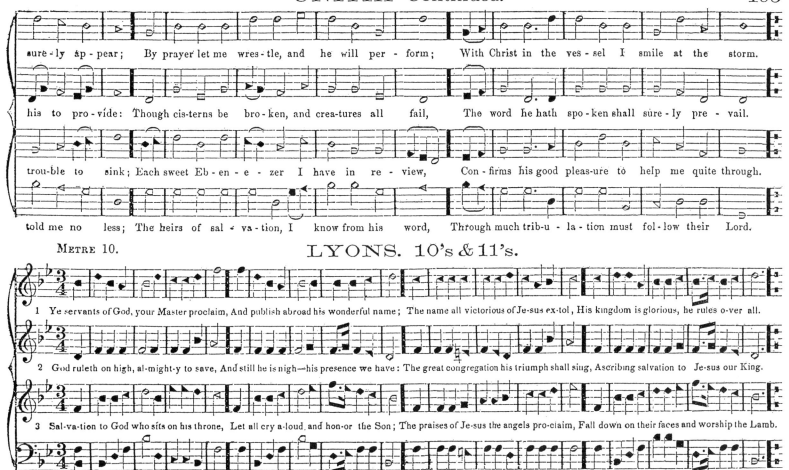

sure-ly ap-pear; By prayer let me wres-tle, and he will per-form; With Christ in the ves-sel I smile at the storm.

his to pro-vide: Though cis-terns be bro-ken, and crea-tures all fail, The word he hath spo-ken shall sure-ly pre-vail.

trou-ble to sink; Each sweet Eb-en-e-zer I have in re-view, Con-firms his good pleas-ure to help me quite through.

told me no less; The heirs of sal-va-tion, I know from his word, Through much trib-u-la-tion must fol-low their Lord.

METRE 10.

LYONS. 10's & 11's.

1 Ye servants of God, your Master proclaim, And publish abroad his wonderful name; The name all victorious of Je-sus ex-tol, His kingdom is glorious, he rules o-ver all.

2 God ruleth on high, al-might-y to save, And still he is nigh—his presence we have: The great congregation his triumph shall sing, Ascribing salvation to Je-sus our King.

3 Sal-va-tion to God who sits on his throne, Let all cry a-loud, and hon-or the Son; The praises of Je-sus the angels pro-claim, Fall down on their faces and worship the Lamb.

4 Then let us a-dore and give him his right, All glory and pow'r and wisdom and might! All honor and blessing, with angels above, And thanks never ceasing for infinite love,

Metre 11.

PROTECTION. 4 lines 11's.

1 How firm a foun-da-tion, ye saints of the Lord, Is laid for your faith in his ex-cel-lent word; What more can he say than to you he hath said,

2 "Fear not, I am with thee, O be not dis-may'd, For I am thy God and will still give thee aid; I'll strengthen thee, help thee and cause thee to stand,

3 "When thro' the deep wa-ters I call thee to go, The riv-ers of sor-row shall not o-ver-flow; For I will be with thee thy troubles to bless,

4 "When thro' fie-ry tri-als thy path-way shall lie, My grace all suf-fi-cient shall be thy sup-ply; The flames shall not hurt thee. I on-ly de-sign,

5 "E'en down to old age all my peo-ple shall prove My sov'reign, e-ter-nal, un-change-a-ble love; And then, when grey hairs shall their temples a-dorn,

Metre 11.

PRESCOTT. 4 lines 11's.

Who un-to the Sa-vior for ref-uge have fled.

Up-held by my righteous, om-nip-o-tent hand.

And sanc-ti-fy to thee thy deepest dis-tress.

Thy dross to con-sume and thy gold to re-fine.
Like lambs they shall still in my bo-som be borne."

1 I would not live al-ways, I ask not to stay, Where storm af-ter

2 I would not live al-ways thus fet-tered by sin; Temp-ta-tion with-

3 I would not live al-ways, no—wel-come the tomb—Since Je-sus has

4 Who, who would live al-ways; a-way from his God? A-way from yon

storm ri - ses dark o'er the way; The few lu - cid morn-ings that dawn on us here, Are fol - low'd by gloom or be - cloud - ed by care.

out and cor - rup - tion with - in; Where rap-ture of par-don is min-gled with fears; The cup of thanks-giv-ing with pen - i - tent tears.

lain there, I'll en - ter its gloom; There sweet be my rest till he bid me a - rise, To hail him in tri - umph de - scend - ing the skies.

heav - en, that bliss - ful a - bode; Where riv - ers of pleas-ure flow thro' the bright plains, And noon-tide of glo - ry e - ter - nal - ly reigns.

METRE 11. ## BAVARIA. 4 lines 11's.

1 Why shrinks my weak nature? ah! what can it mean? } Why ling'ring and trem-bling while glo-ry's so near? Or Whence the enchantment that fet-ters me here!
Why flut-ters my heart which till now was se rene? }

2 Thou world of il - lu-sion, for - ev - er a - dieu! } New worlds and new wonders my pas-sions in - vite, And glo-ries in - ef - fa - ble dawn on my sight.
Your phan-toms un - hal-low'd re-cede from my view! }

METRE 11. HINTON. 4 lines 11's.

1 O Zi-on, af-flict-ed with wave up-on wave; Whom no man can com-fort, whom no man can save; With darkness surrounded, by terror dis-may'd,

2 Loud roar-ing the bil-lows, now nigh o-ver-whelm, But skill-ful's the Pi-lot that sits at the helm; His wisdom conducts thee, his pow'r thee defends,

3 "O fear-ful! O faith-less!" in mer-cy he cries, "My prom-ise, my truth, are they light in thine eyes? Still, still I am with thee, my promise shall stand;

4 "Then trust me, and fear not, thy life is se-cure; My wis-dom is per-fect, su-preme is my pow'r; In love I cor-rect thee, thy soul to re-fine;

In toil-ing and row-ing thy strength is de-cay'd.

In safe-ty and qui-et the war-fare he ends.

Thro' tem-pest and toss-ing I'll bring thee to land.

To make thee at length in my like-ness to shine."

METRE 11. ST. DENNIS. 4 lines 11's.

1 Thou sweet gli-ding Kedron, by thy sil-ver stream, Our Sa-vior at midnight, when

2 How damp were the va-pors that fell on his head! How hard was his pillow, how

3 Oh gar-den of Ol-i-vet! dear hon-or'd spot, The theme of thy wonders shall

4 Come, saints, and adore him—come bow at his feet! Oh, give him the glo-ry, the

moon - light's pale beam Shone bright on the wa-ters, would fre-quent-ly stray, And lose in thy mur-murs the toils of the day.

hum - ble his bed! The an-gels as-ton-ish'd grew sad at the sight, And fol-low'd their Mas-ter with sol-emn de-light.

ne'er be for-got— The theme most trans-port-ing to ser-aphs a-bove; The tri-umph of sor-row, the tri-umph of love.

praise that is meet! Let joy-ful ho-san-nas un-ceas-ing a-rise, And join the full cho-rus that glad-dens the skies.

METRE 11. CHRISTIAN FAREWELL. 4 lines 11's.

1 Fare-well my dear breth-ren, the time is at hand, }
That we must be part-ed from this so-cial band; } Our sev'-ral engagements now call us a-way; Our part-ing is need-ful, and we must obey.

2 Fare-well my dear breth-ren, fare-well for a-while, }
We'll soon meet a-gain if kind Prov-i-dence smile; } And while we are parted and scatter'd abroad, We'll pray for each other, and trust in the Lord.

200   METRE 11.   WESLEY. 4 lines 11's.

1 Come children of Zion, & help us to sing Loud anthems of praise to our Savior and King, Whose life once was given our souls to redeem, And bring us to heaven to reign there with him.

2 In regions of darkness, and sorrow and pains, We all lay in ruin, in prison and chains; But Jesus has bought us with his precious blood, The ransom provided to bring us to God.

3 O come to the Savior and take up the cross, Seek treasure in heaven, count all else but loss; His mercy invites us, then let us comply—O why should we linger when he is so nigh.

4 We'll fear not the dangers that lie in our way—His arm will protect us by night & by day; All this we must suffer & patiently bear, Till Jesus shall take us where suff'rings are o'er.

METRE 12.   GREENFIELDS. 8 lines 8's.

1 How te-dious and tasteless the hours, When Je-sus no lon-ger I see; Sweet prospects, sweet birds and sweet flow'rs, Have all lost their sweetness to me; } The midsummer sun shines but dim, The fields strive in vain to look gay:

2 His name yields the rich-est per-fume; And sweet-er than mu-sic his voice: His pres-ence dis-pers-es my gloom, And makes all with-in me re-joice; } I should, were he always thus nigh, Have nothing to wish or to fear:

But when I am hap-py in him, De-cem-ber's as pleas-ant as May.

1. How blest is our broth-er bereft, Of all that can burden his mind; }
How easy the soul that has left This wea-ri-some bod-y be-hind; }

No mo-tal so hap-py as I, My sum-mer would last all the year.

2. This earth is af-fect-ed no more With sickness or shaken with pain, }
The war in the members is o'er, And nev-er shall vex him again; }

3. This languishing head is at rest; Its thinking and aching are o'er, }
This qui-et im-mo-va-ble breast, Is heaved by af-flic-tion no more; }

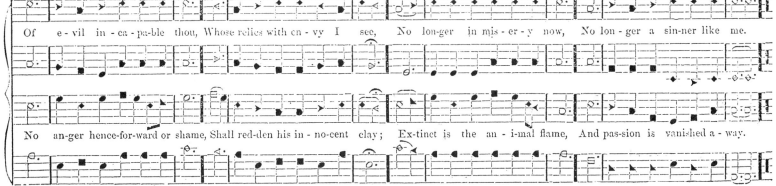

Of e-vil in-ca-pa-ble thou, Whose relics with en-vy I see, No lon-ger in mis-er-y now, No lon-ger a sin-ner like me.

No an-ger hence-for-ward or shame, Shall red-den his in-no-cent clay; Ex-tinct is the an-i-mal flame, And pas-sion is vanished a-way.

This heart is no lon-ger the seat Of trouble and tor-tur-ing pain; It ceas-es to flut-ter and beat,— It nev-er shall flut-ter a-gain,

202

METRE 12.

NEW JERUSALEM. 8 lines 8's.

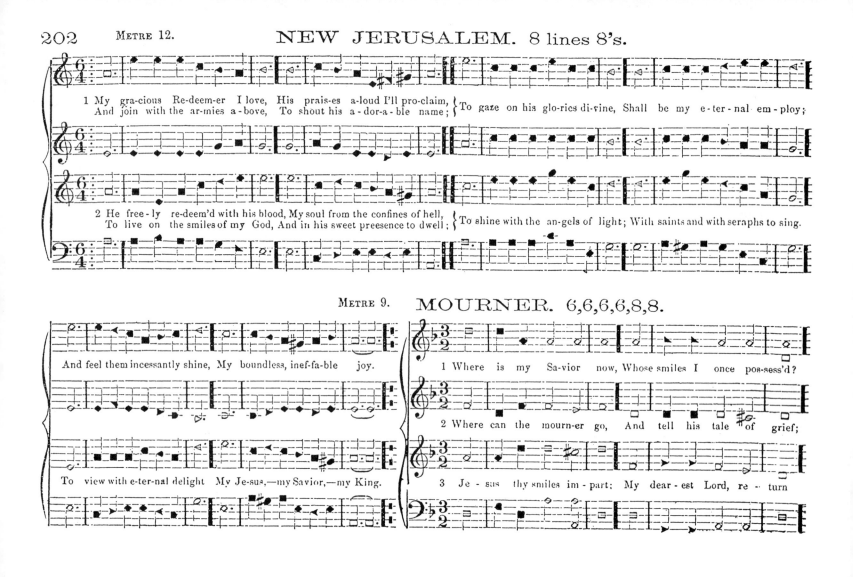

1 My gra-cious Re-deem-er I love, His prais-es a-loud I'll pro-claim,
And join with the ar-mies a-bove, To shout his a-dor-a-ble name; To gaze on his glo-ries di-vine, Shall be my e-ter-nal em-ploy;

2 He free-ly re-deem'd with his blood, My soul from the confines of hell,
To live on the smiles of my God, And in his sweet preesence to dwell; To shine with the an-gels of light; With saints and with seraphs to sing.

And feel them incessantly shine, My boundless, inef-fa-ble joy.

To view with e-ter-nal delight My Je-sus,—my Savior,—my King.

METRE 9. MOURNER. 6,6,6,6,8,8.

1 Where is my Sa-vior now, Whose smiles I once pos-sess'd?

2 Where can the mourn-er go, And tell his tale of grief;

3 Je-sus thy smiles im-part; My dear-est Lord, re-turn

Till he re-turn I bow By heav-iest grief op-press'd; My days of hap-pi-ness are gone, And I am left to weep a-lone.

Ah! who can soothe his woe, And give him sweet re-lief? Earth can-not heal the wound-ed breast, Or give the troubled sin-ner rest.

And ease my wound-ed heart, And bid me cease to mourn; Then shall this night of 'sor-row flee, And peace and heav'n be found in thee.

METRE 12.

UTICA. 4 lines 8's.

1 To Je-sus the crown of my hope, My soul is in haste to be gone; Oh! bear me ye cher-u-bim! up, And waft me a-way to his throne.

2 My Sa-vior! whom ab-sent I love; Whom not having seen I a-dore; Whose name is ex-alt-ed a-bove All glo-ry, do-minion and power;—

3 Dis-solve thou these bonds, that detain My soul from her por-tion in thee; Ah! strike off this ad-a-mant chain, And make me e-ter-nal-ly free.

4 When that hap-py e-ra be-gins, Ar-rayed in thy glo-ries I'll shine, Nor grieve a-ny more by my sins, The bo-som on which I re-cline.

Metre 13.

AMSTERDAM. 7,6,7,6,7,7,7,6.

1 Rise my soul, and stretch thy wings, Thy bet-ter por-tion trace; Rise from tran-si-to-ry things, T'wards heav'n thy na-tive place;

2 Riv-ers to the o-cean run, Nor stay in all their course; Fires as-cend-ing seek the sun, Both speed them to their source,

3 Cease, ye pil-grims, cease to mourn, Press on-ward to the prize; Soon the Sa-vior will re-turn, Tri-umph-ant to the skies.

4 Fly me rich-es! fly me cares! While I that coast ex-plore; Flattering world, with all your snares, So-lic-it me no more;

Sun, and moon, and stars de-cay, Time will soon this earth re-move; Rise my soul, make haste a-way, To seats pre-pared a-bove.

Thus a soul new born of God, Pants to view his glo-rious face, Up-wards tends to his a-bode, To rest in his em-brace.

Yet a sea-son, and you'll know Hap-py en-trance will be given, All your sor-rows left be-low, And earth ex-changed for heaven.

Pil-grims fix not here their home, Stran-gers tar-ry but a night, When the last dear morn is come, We'll rise to joy-ful light.

METRE 14. MISSIONARY HYMN. 7's and 6's.

1 From Green-land's i - cy moun-tains, From In-dia's cor - al strand, Where Af - ric's sun - ny foun-tains Roll down their gol-den sand;

2 What though the spi - cy bree - zes Blow soft o'er Cey-lon's isle: Though eve-ry pros-pect pleas-es, And on - ly man is vile;

3 Shall we whose souls are light-ed With wis-dom from on high— Shall we to men be-night-ed The lamp o life de - ny?

4 Waft, waft ye winds the sto - ry, And you, ye wa - ters, roll, Till, like a sea of glo - ry, It spreads from pole to pole;

From many an an-cient riv - er, From many a palm - y plain, They call us to de - liv - er Their land from er - ror's chain.

In vain with lav-ish kind-ness, The gifts of God are strown; The heath-en in his blind-ness, Bows down to wood and stone.

Sal - va - tion! O sal - va - tion! The joy-ful sound pro - claim, Till earth's re - mo-test na - tion Has learned Mes-si - ah's name.

Till o'er our ran-som'd na - ture, The Lamb for sin - ners slain, Re - deem - er, King, Cre - a - tor, In bliss re - turns to reign.

* This tune appears in some earlier editions under the title "Illumination," with the words, "Hail to the Lord's Anointed..." (see facing page).

SUMNER. 7s & 6s.

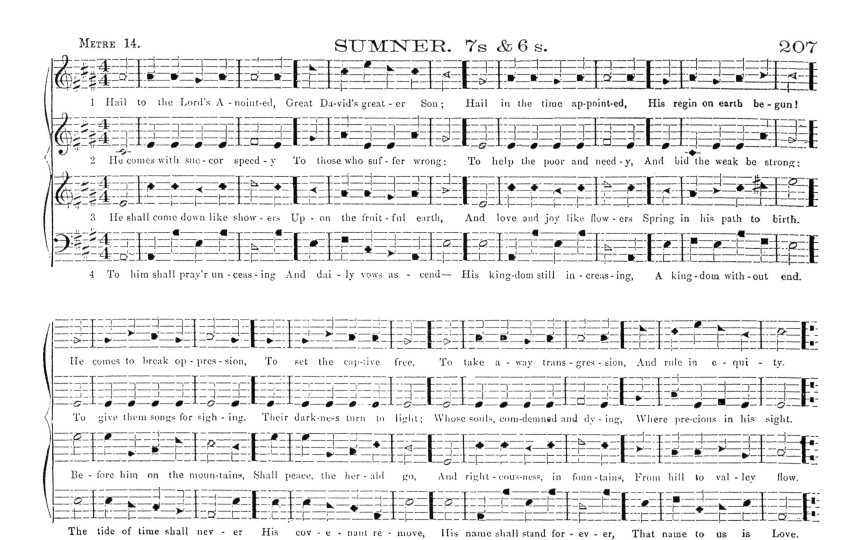

1 Hail to the Lord's A - noint-ed, Great Da-vid's great - er Son; Hail in the time ap-point-ed, His regin on earth be - gun!

2 He comes with suc-cor speed - y To those who suf - fer wrong: To help the poor and need - y, And bid the weak be strong:

3 He shall come down like show - ers Up - on the fruit - ful earth, And love and joy like flow - ers Spring in his path to birth.

4 To him shall pray'r un - ceas - ing And dai - ly vows as - cend— His king-dom still in - creas-ing, A king-dom with-out end.

He comes to break op - pres - sion, To set the cap-tive free, To take a - way trans - gres - sion, And rule in e - qui - ty.

To give them songs for sigh - ing. Their dark-ness turn to light; Whose souls, con-demned and dy - ing, Where pre-cious in his sight.

Be - fore him on the moun-tains, Shall peace, the her - ald go, And right - eous-ness, in foun-tains, From hill to val - ley flow.

The tide of time shall nev - er His cov - e - nant re - move, His name shall stand for - ev - er, That name to us is Love.

Metre 14.

ASPIRATION. 7's & 6's.

1 Go when the morn-ing shi - neth, Go when the noon is bright, Go when the eve de - cli - neth, Go in the hush of night;

2 Re-mem - ber all who love thee; All who are lov'd by thee! Pray, too, for those who hate thee If a - ny such there be;

3 Or if 'tis e'er de - nied thee In sol - i - tude to pray, Should ho - ly thoughts come o'er thee When friends are round thy way,

4 O not a joy or bless - ing With this can we com - pare— The grace our Fa - ther gave us To pour our souls in pray'r;

Go with pure mind and feel - ing, Fling earth - ly thought a - way, And in thy clos - et kneel - ing, Do thou in se - cret pray.

Then for thy - self in meek - ness A bles - sing hum-bly claim, And blend with each pe - ti - tion. The great Re-deem-er's name.

E'en then the si - lent breath-ing Thy spir - it rais'd a - bove, Will reach his throne of glo - ry, Where dwells e - ter - nal Love.

Whene'er thou pin'st in sad - ness, Be - fore his foot - stool fall; Re - mem - ber in thy glad - ness, His love, who gave thee all.

1. Some-times a light sur - pri - ses   The Chris-tian while he   sings;   It   is   the Lord who ri - ses,   With heal-ing   in   his wings:

2. In   ho - ly   com-tem-pla - tion,   We sweet - ly then pur - sue   The theme of God's sal - va - tion,   And   find it   ev - er   new;

3. It   can bring with it   noth - ing,   But   He will bear us   through;   Who gives the lil - ies cloth-ing,   Will clothe his   peo-ple   too;

4. Though vine nor fig-tree   nei-ther,   Their wont-ed   fruit should bear,   Though all the fields should wither,   Nor   flocks nor herds be   there;

When comforts   are de - clin - ing,   He grants the soul a - gain   A   sea - son of clear shin-ing,   To   cheer   it   af - ter   rain.

Set free from pres - ent sor - row,   We cheer-ful-ly can   say,   Let   the   un - known to-mor-row   Bring with   it   what it   may.

Be - neath the spread - ing heav - ens,   No creature but is   fed;   And He who feeds the ra - vens   Will   give his   chil - dren bread.

Yet God the   same a - bi - ding,   His praise shall tune my voice;   For while in   him con - fi - ding,   I   can - not but   re - joice.

MORNING. LIGHT 7's & 6's.

Metre 14.

1. The morning light is breaking, The dark-ness disappears, The sons of earth are wak-ing To pen - i - ten - tial tears, Each breeze that sweeps the ocean

2. Rich dews of grace come o'er us, In many a gen-tle show'r, And bright-er scenes be-fore us, Are ope-ning eve-ry hour; Each cry to heav-en go-ing

3. See heath-en na-tions bending Be - fore the God we love, And thousand hearts ascending In grat - i - tude a - bove; While sinners now confessing,

4. Blest riv - er of sal - va - tion, Pur-sue thy on-ward way: Flow thou to eve - ry na-tion, Nor in thy rich-ness stay; Stay not till all the low-ly

Metre 15.

ZION'S PILGRIM. 11's & 8's.

Brings tidings from a - far, Of na-tions in commotion, Prepared for Zion's war.

Abundant answers brings, And heavenly gales are blowing, With peace upon their wings.

The gos-pel call o - bey, And seek the Savior's blessing,—A nation in a day.

Triumphant reach their home; Stay not till all the holy Proclaim, "the Lord is come."

1. This is my Be-lov-ed, his form is di - vine His vestments shed odors around, The locks on his head are as grapes on the vine, When autumn with plenty is crown'd;

2. His voice as the sound of a dulci-mer sweet, Is heard thro' the shadows of death, The cedars of Leb-a-non bow at his feet, The air is perfumed with his breath;

3. Love sits in his eyelids and scatters delight, Thro' all the bright mansions on high, Their faces the Cherubim vail in his sight, And tremble with fulness of joy;

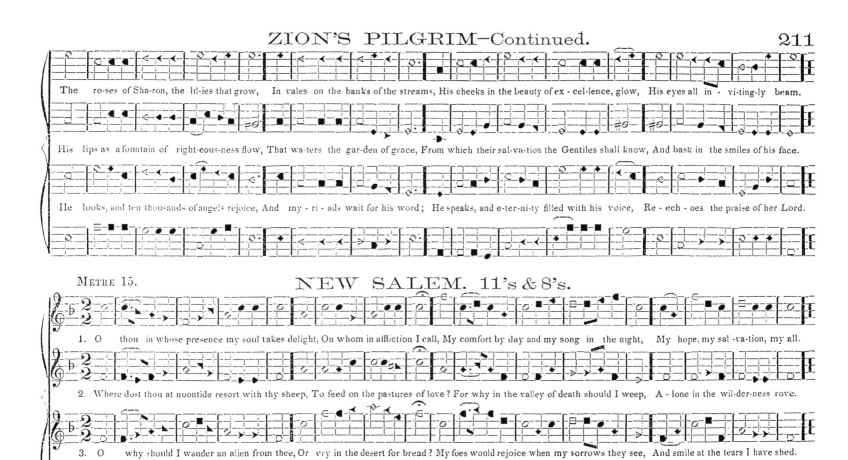

The ro-ses of Sha-ron, the lil-ies that grow, In vales on the banks of the streams, His cheeks in the beauty of ex - cel-lence, glow, His eyes all in - vi-ting-ly beam.

His lips as a fountain of right-eous-ness flow, That wa-ters the gar-den of grace, From which their sal-va-tion the Gentiles shall know, And bask in the smiles of his face.

He looks, and ten thousands of angels rejoice, And my - ri - ads wait for his word; He speaks, and e-ter-ni-ty filled with his voice, Re - ech - oes the praise of her Lord.

METRE 15.

NEW SALEM. 11's & 8's.

1. O thou in whose presence my soul takes delight, On whom in affliction I call, My comfort by day and my song in the night, My hope, my sal -va-tion, my all.

2. Where dost thou at noontide resort with thy sheep, To feed on the pastures of love? For why in the valley of death should I weep, A - lone in the wil-der-ness rove.

3. O why should I wander an alien from thee, Or cry in the desert for bread? My foes would rejoice when my sorrows they see, And smile at the tears I have shed.

4. Ye daughters of Zi-on, de-clare have you seen The Star that on Is-ra-el shone? Say if in your tents my Be-lov - ed hath been, And where with his flock he hath gone?

Metre 16.　MENDON. 7's & 6's.

1. Vain, de - lu - sive world, a - dieu, With all thy creature good; On - ly Je - sus I pur - sue, Who bought me with his blood.

2. Oth - er knowledge I dis - dain, 'Tis all but van - i - ty: Christ the Lamb of God was slain, He tast - ed death for me.

3. Here will I set up my rest; My fluc - tu - a - ting heart From the ha - ven of his breast, Shall nev - er - more de - part;

4. Him to know is life and peace, And pleas - ure with - out end; This is all my hap - pi - ness, On Je - sus to de - pend—

All thy pleas - ures I fore - go, I tram - ple on thy wealth and pride; On - ly Je - sus will I know, And Je - sus cru - ci - fied.

Me to save from end - less woe, The sin - a - ton - ing Vic - tim died; On - ly Je - sus will I know, And Je - sus cru - ci - fied.

Whith - er should a sin - ner go? His wounds for me stand o - pen wide; On - ly Je - sus will I know, And Je - sus cru - ci - fied.

Dai - ly in his grace to grow, And ev - er in his faith a - bide; On - ly Je - sus will I know, And Je - sus cru - ci - fied.

SALISBURY. 7,6,7,6,7,8,7,6.

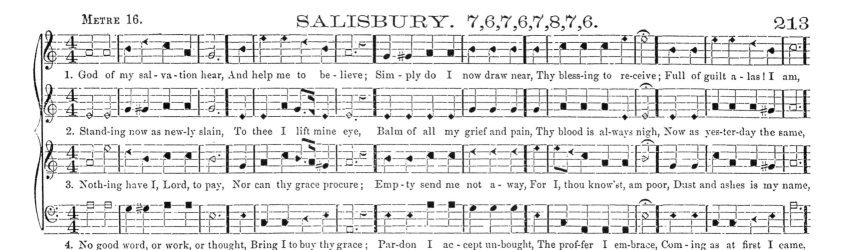

1. God of my sal-va-tion hear, And help me to be-lieve; Sim-ply do I now draw near, Thy bless-ing to re-ceive; Full of guilt a-las! I am,

2. Stand-ing now as new-ly slain, To thee I lift mine eye, Balm of all my grief and pain, Thy blood is al-ways nigh, Now as yes-ter-day the same,

3. Noth-ing have I, Lord, to pay, Nor can thy grace procure; Emp-ty send me not a-way, For I, thou know'st, am poor, Dust and ashes is my name,

4. No good word, or work, or thought, Bring I to buy thy grace; Par-don I ac-cept un-bought, The prof-fer I em-brace, Com-ing as at first I came,

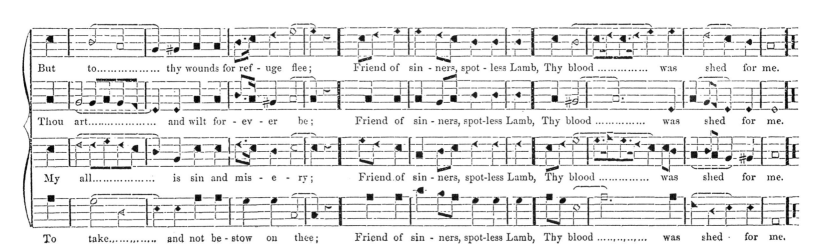

But to.............. thy wounds for ref-uge flee; Friend of sin-ners, spot-less Lamb, Thy blood .... was shed for me.

Thou art.................. and wilt for-ev-er be; Friend of sin-ners, spot-less Lamb, Thy blood .... was shed for me.

My all................. is sin and mis-e-ry; Friend of sin-ners, spot-less Lamb, Thy blood .... was shed for me.

To take............. and not be-stow on thee; Friend of sin-ners, spot-less Lamb, Thy blood .... was shed for me.

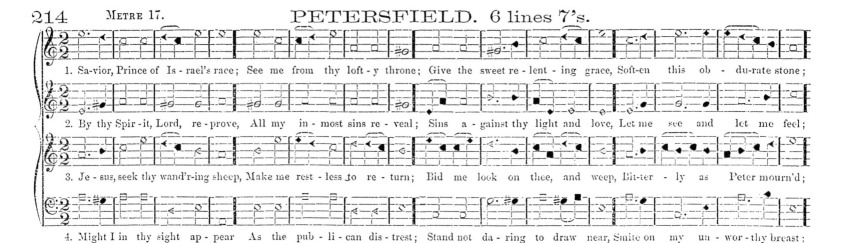

METRE 17.   PETERSFIELD. 6 lines 7's.

1. Sa-vior, Prince of Is-rael's race; See me from thy loft-y throne; Give the sweet re-lent-ing grace, Soft-en this ob-du-rate stone;

2. By thy Spir-it, Lord, re-prove, All my in-most sins re-veal; Sins a-gainst thy light and love, Let me see and let me feel;

3. Je-sus, seek thy wand'r-ing sheep, Make me rest-less to re-turn; Bid me look on thee, and weep, Bit-ter-ly as Peter mourn'd;

4. Might I in thy sight ap-pear As the pub-li-can dis-trest; Stand not da-ring to draw near, Smite on my un-wor-thy breast;

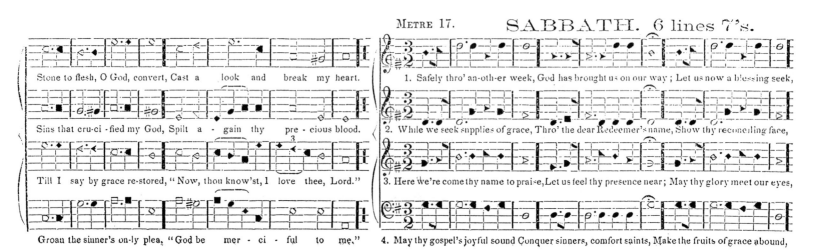

Stone to flesh, O God, convert, Cast a look and break my heart.

Sins that cru-ci-fied my God, Spilt a-gain thy pre-cious blood.

Till I say by grace re-stored, "Now, thou know'st, I love thee, Lord."

Groan the sinner's on-ly plea, "God be mer-ci-ful to me."

METRE 17.   SABBATH. 6 lines 7's.

1. Safely thro' an-oth-er week, God has brought us on our way; Let us now a blessing seek,

2. While we seek supplies of grace, Thro' the dear Redeemer's name, Show thy reconciling face,

3. Here we're come thy name to praise, Let us feel thy presence near; May thy glory meet our eyes,

4. May thy gospel's joyful sound Conquer sinners, comfort saints, Make the fruits of grace abound,

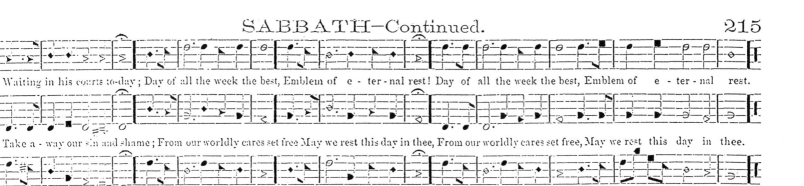

Waiting in his courts to-day; Day of all the week the best, Emblem of e-ter-nal rest! Day of all the week the best, Emblem of e-ter-nal rest.

Take a-way our sin and shame; From our worldly cares set free May we rest this day in thee, From our worldly cares set free, May we rest this day in thee.

While we in thy house appear: Here afford us, Lord, a taste Of our ev-er-last-ing feast, Here af-ford us, Lord, a taste Of our ev-er-last-ing feast.

Bring relief for all complaints,—Such let all our Sabbaths prove, Till we join the church above, Such let all our Sabbaths prove, Till we join the church a-bove.

METRE 17.

MOUNT CALVARY. 6 lines 7's.

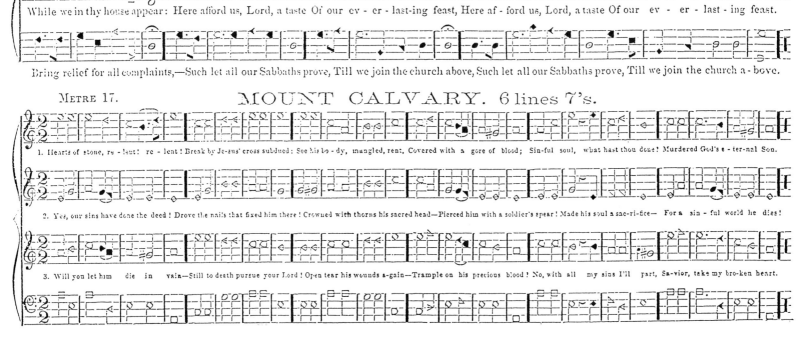

1. Hearts of stone, re-lent! re-lent! Break by Je-sus' cross subdued! See his bo-dy, mangled, rent, Covered with a gore of blood; Sin-ful soul, what hast thou done? Murdered God's e-ter-nal Son.

2. Yes, our sins have done the deed! Drove the nails that fixed him there! Crowned with thorns his sacred head—Pierced him with a soldier's spear! Made his soul a sac-ri-fice—For a sin-ful world he dies!

3. Will you let him die in vain—Still to death pursue your Lord! Open tear his wounds a-gain—Trample on his precious blood! No, with all my sins I'll part, Sa-vior, take my bro-ken heart.

METRE 18.

OLIVET. 6's & 4's.

1. My faith looks up to thee, Thou Lamb of Calvary! Savior divine! Now hear me while I pray, Take all my guilt a-way, Oh let me from this day, Be whol-ly thine.

2. May thy rich grace impart Strength to my fainting heart, My zeal inspire; As thou hast died for me, Oh! may my love to thee, Pure, warm and changeless be,—A living fire.

3. While life's dark maze I tread, And griefs around me spread, Be thou my guide; Bid darkness turn to day, Wipe sorrow's tears away, Nor let me ever stray From thee a - side.

4. When ends life's transient dream, When death's cold, sullen stream Shall o'er me roll, Blest Savior! then in love, Fear and distrust remove; O bear me safe above,—A ransom'd soul.

METRE 18.

SWANTON. 6's & 4's.

1. Come all ye saints of God! Wide thro' the earth abroad Spread Jesus' fame: Tell what his love has done; Trust in his name alone: Shout to his lofty throne, "Worthy the Lamb!"

2. Hence gloomy doubts and fears,   Swell the glad theme: Strike each melodious string,   "Worthy the Lamb!"
Dry up your mournful tears;   Praise ye our gracious King,   Join heart and voice to sing,

3 Hark—how the choirs above,   Dwell on his name!—   With light and glory crowned,   "Worthy the Lamb!"
Filled with the Savior's love,   There, too, may we be found,   While all the heavens resound,

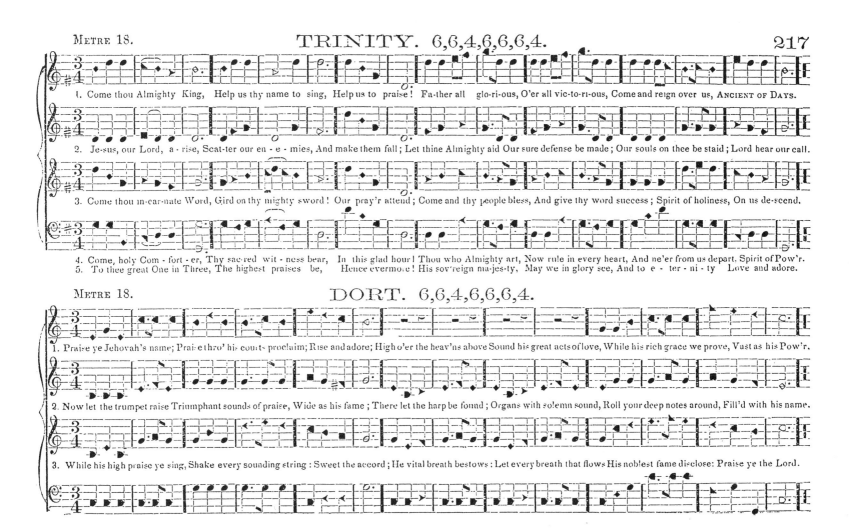

1. Come thou Almighty King, Help us thy name to sing, Help us to praise! Fa-ther all glo-ri-ous, O'er all vic-to-ri-ous, Come and reign over us, ANCIENT OF DAYS.

2. Je-sus, our Lord, a-rise, Scat-ter our en-e-mies, And make them fall; Let thine Almighty aid Our sure defense be made; Our souls on thee be staid; Lord hear our call.

3. Come thou in-car-nate Word, Gird on thy mighty sword! Our pray'r attend; Come and thy people bless, And give thy word success; Spirit of holiness, On us de-scend.

4. Come, holy Com-fort-er, Thy sac-red wit-ness bear,   In this glad hour! Thou who Almighty art, Now rule in every heart, And ne'er from us depart. Spirit of Pow'r.
5. To thee great One in Three, The highest praises be,   Hence evermore! His sov'reign ma-jes-ty, May we in glory see, And to e-ter-ni-ty Love and adore.

METRE 18.   DORT. 6,6,4,6,6,6,4.

1. Praise ye Jehovah's name; Praise thro' his courts proclaim; Rise and adore; High o'er the heav'ns above Sound his great acts of love, While his rich grace we prove, Vast as his Pow'r.

2. Now let the trumpet raise Triumphant sounds of praise, Wide as his fame; There let the harp be found; Organs with solemn sound, Roll your deep notes around, Fill'd with his name.

3. While his high praise ye sing, Shake every sounding string: Sweet the accord; He vital breath bestows: Let every breath that flows His noblest fame disclose: Praise ye the Lord.

218 METRE 19.

HARWELL. 8,7,8,7,7,7,8,6.

1 Hark, ten thou-sand harps and voices, Sound the notes of praise a-bove— { See, he sits on yon-der throne; Je-sus rules the world a-lone;
  Je-sus reigns, and heaven re-joices, Je-sus reigns the God of love;

2 Je-sus hail! whose glo-ry bright-ens, All a-bove, and gives it worth; { When we think of love like thine, Lord, we own it love di-vine:
  Lord of life—thy smile en-light-ens, Cheers and charms thy saints on earth;

CHORUS.

Hal-le-lu-jah! Hal-le-lu-jah! Hal-le-lu-jah, A-men.

Hal-le-lu-jah! Hal-le-lu-jah! Hal-le-lu-jah, A-men.

METRE 20. NEW CONCORD. 6,6,9,6,6,9.

1 Oh! how hap-py are they, Who their Sa-vior o-bey,

2 'Twas a heav-en be-low, My Re-deem-er to know;

3 Je-sus all the day long, Was my joy and my song;

4 Now my rem-nant of days Would I spend in his praise,

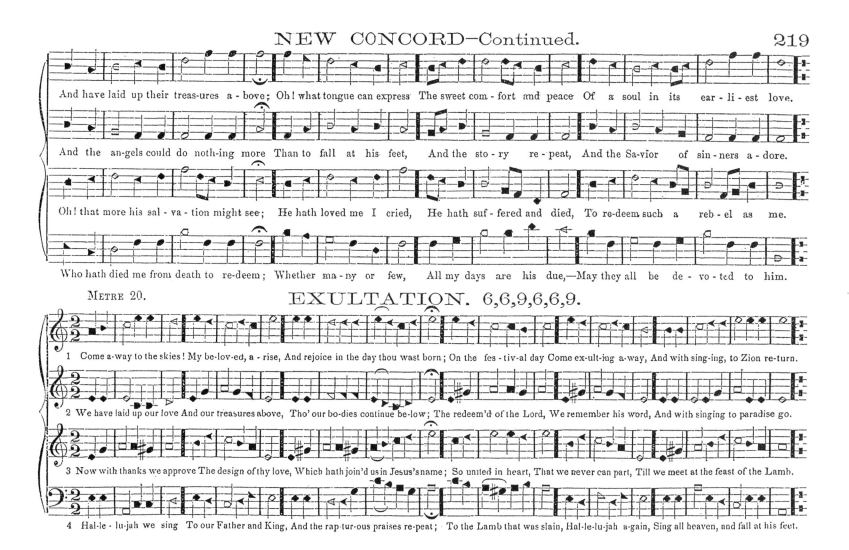

And have laid up their treas-ures a - bove; Oh! what tongue can express The sweet com - fort and peace Of a soul in its ear - li - est love.

And the an-gels could do noth-ing more Than to fall at his feet, And the sto - ry re - peat, And the Sa-vior of sin - ners a - dore.

Oh! that more his sal - va - tion might see; He hath loved me I cried, He hath suf - fered and died, To re-deem such a reb - el as me.

Who hath died me from death to re-deem; Whether ma - ny or few, All my days are his due,—May they all be de - vo - ted to him.

Metre 20.

EXULTATION. 6,6,9,6,6,9.

1 Come a-way to the skies! My be-lov-ed, a - rise, And rejoice in the day thou wast born; On the fes - tiv-al day Come ex-ult-ing a-way, And with sing-ing, to Zion re-turn.

2 We have laid up our love And our treasures above, Tho' our bo-dies continue be-low; The redeem'd of the Lord, We remember his word, And with singing to paradise go.

3 Now with thanks we approve The design of thy love, Which hath join'd us in Jesus's name; So united in heart, That we never can part, Till we meet at the feast of the Lamb.

4 Hal-le - lu-jah we sing To our Father and King, And the rap-tur-ous praises re-peat; To the Lamb that was slain, Hal-le-lu-jah a-gain, Sing all heaven, and fall at his feet.

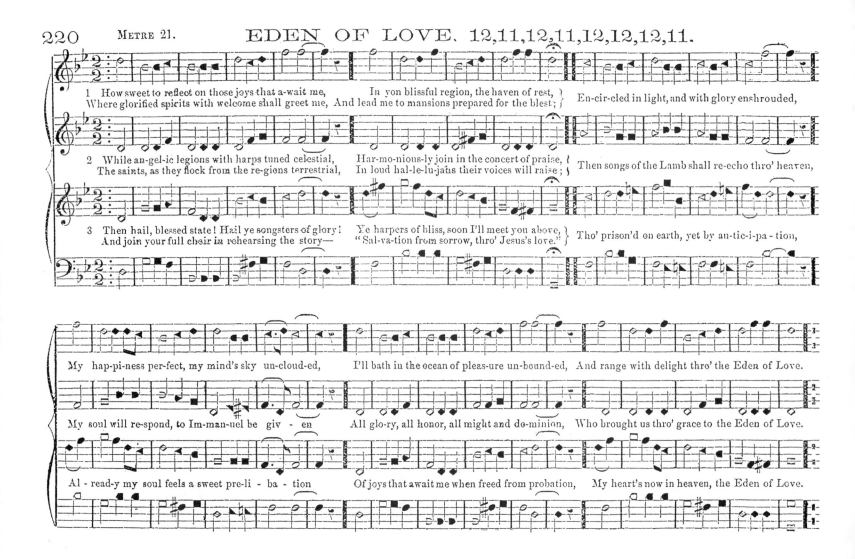

1 How sweet to reflect on those joys that a-wait me, In yon blissful region, the haven of rest,
Where glorified spirits with welcome shall greet me, And lead me to mansions prepared for the blest; }
En-cir-cled in light, and with glory enshrouded,

2 While an-gel-ic legions with harps tuned celestial, Har-mo-nious-ly join in the concert of praise,
The saints, as they flock from the re-gions terrestrial, In loud hal-le-lu-jahs their voices will raise; }
Then songs of the Lamb shall re-echo thro' heaven,

3 Then hail, blessed state! Hail ye songsters of glory! Ye harpers of bliss, soon I'll meet you above,
And join your full choir in rehearsing the story— "Sal-va-tion from sorrow, thro' Jesus's love." }
Tho' prison'd on earth, yet by an-tic-i-pa-tion,

My hap-pi-ness per-fect, my mind's sky un-cloud-ed, I'll bath in the ocean of pleas-ure un-bound-ed, And range with delight thro' the Eden of Love.

My soul will re-spond, to Im-man-uel be giv-en All glo-ry, all honor, all might and do-minion, Who brought us thro' grace to the Eden of Love.

Al-read-y my soul feels a sweet pre-li-ba-tion Of joys that await me when freed from probation, My heart's now in heaven, the Eden of Love.

DAUGHTER OF ZION. 4 lines 11's.

1 Daugh-ter of Zi - on, a-wake from thy sad-ness, A-wake, for thy foes shall oppress thee no more; Bright o'er thy hills dawns the Day-Star of gladness,

2 Strong were thy foes, but the arm that subdued them, And scat-tered their le-gions was mightier far; They fled like chaff from the scourge that pursued them—

3 Daugh-ter of Zi - on, the Power that saved thee, Extol'd with the harp and the timbrel should be; Shout! for the foe is destroy'd that en-slaved thee,

CHORUS

A - rise, for the night of thy sor - rows is o'er; Daugh-ter of Zi - on, a - wake from thy sad-ness, Awake, for thy foes shall op-press thee no more.

How vain were their steeds and their chariots of war. Daugh-ter of Zi - on, a-wake from thy sad-ness, A-wake, for thy foes shall oppress thee no more.

Th' op-pres-sor is vanquished and Zi-on is free. Daugh-ter of Zi - on, a-wake from thy sad-ness, A-wake, for thy foes shall oppress thee no more.

222   METRE 23.   MOUNT CARMEL. 10,10,10,11,11.

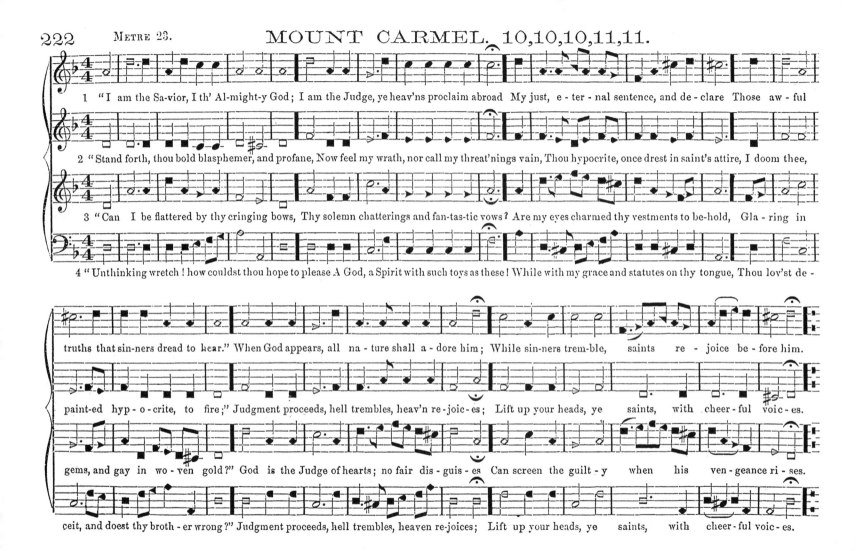

1 "I am the Sa-vior, I th' Al-might-y God; I am the Judge, ye heav'ns proclaim abroad My just, e - ter - nal sentence, and de - clare Those aw - ful

2 "Stand forth, thou bold blasphemer, and profane, Now feel my wrath, nor call my threat'nings vain, Thou hypocrite, once drest in saint's attire, I doom thee,

3 "Can I be flattered by thy cringing bows, Thy solemn chatterings and fan-tas-tic vows? Are my eyes charmed thy vestments to be-hold, Gla - ring in

4 "Unthinking wretch! how couldst thou hope to please A God, a Spirit with such toys as these! While with my grace and statutes on thy tongue, Thou lov'st de -

truths that sin-ners dread to hear." When God appears, all na - ture shall a - dore him; While sin-ners trem-ble, saints re - joice be - fore him.

paint-ed hyp - o - crite, to fire;" Judgment proceeds, hell trembles, heav'n re-joic-es; Lift up your heads, ye saints, with cheer-ful voic - es.

gems, and gay in wo - ven gold?" God is the Judge of hearts; no fair dis - guis - es Can screen the guilt - y when his ven - geance ri - ses.

ceit, and doest thy broth - er wrong?" Judgment proceeds, hell trembles, heaven re-joices; Lift up your heads, ye saints, with cheer-ful voic - es.

ZION. 10's & 11's.

1 House of our God, with cheer-ful an-thems ring, While all our lips and hearts his good-ness sing; With sa - cred joy his wondrous deeds pro-claim,

2 The heav'n of heav'ns he with his boun - ty fills; Ye ser-aphs bright, on ev - er bloom-ing hills, His hon-or sound; you to whom good a - lone,

3 Thou earth, en-light-ened by his rays di - vine, Pregnant with grass and corn, and oil and wine, Crowned with his goodness, let thy na-tions meet,

4 Zi - on, en-riched with his distinguished grace, Bless'd with the rays of thine Im - man - uel's face— Zi - on, Je - ho - vah's por-tion and de - light,

Let eve - ry tongue be vo-cal with his name; The Lord is good, his mer-cy nev - er end - ing, His goodness in per-pet - ual show'rs de-scend-ing.

Un-min - gled, ev - er-grow-ing, has been known; Thro' your immortal life with love in - creas-ing, Pro-claim your Maker's good-ness nev - er-ceas-ing.

And lay them-selves at his pa-ter-nal feet; With grate-ful love that lib'ral Hand con - fess-ing, Which thro' each heart dif-fu-seth eve - ry bless - ing.

Grav'n on his hand and hour-ly in his sight, In sac - red strains ex-alt that grace ex - cell - ing, Which makes thine humble hill his cho-sen dwell-ing.

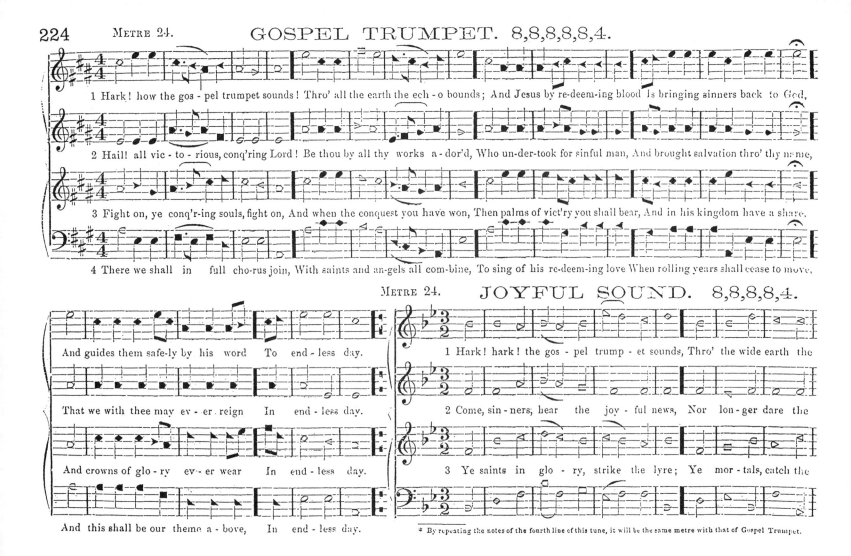

METRE 24. GOSPEL TRUMPET. 8,8,8,8,8,4.

1 Hark! how the gos-pel trumpet sounds! Thro' all the earth the ech-o bounds; And Jesus by re-deem-ing blood Is bringing sinners back to God,

2 Hail! all vic-to-rious, conq'ring Lord! Be thou by all thy works a-dor'd, Who un-der-took for sinful man, And brought salvation thro' thy name,

3 Fight on, ye conq'r-ing souls, fight on, And when the conquest you have won, Then palms of vict'ry you shall bear, And in his kingdom have a share.

4 There we shall in full cho-rus join, With saints and an-gels all com-bine, To sing of his re-deem-ing love When rolling years shall cease to move,

METRE 24. JOYFUL SOUND. 8,8,8,8,4.

And guides them safe-ly by his word To end-less day.

That we with thee may ev-er reign In end-less day.

And crowns of glo-ry ev-er wear In end-less day.

And this shall be our theme a-bove, In end-less day.

1 Hark! hark! the gos-pel trump-et sounds, Thro' the wide earth the

2 Come, sin-ners; hear the joy-ful news, Nor lon-ger dare the

3 Ye saints in glo-ry, strike the lyre; Ye mor-tals, catch the

* By repeating the notes of the fourth line of this tune, it will be the same metre with that of Gospel Trumpet.

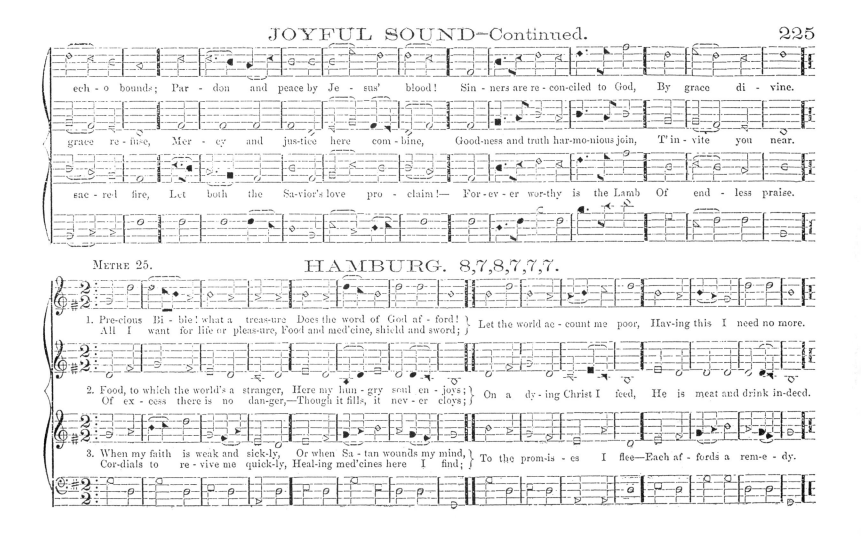

echo bounds; Pardon and peace by Jesus' blood! Sinners are reconciled to God, By grace divine.

grace refuse, Mercy and justice here combine, Goodness and truth harmonious join, T'invite you near.

sacred fire, Let both the Savior's love proclaim!— Forever worthy is the Lamb Of endless praise.

METRE 25.

HAMBURG. 8,7,8,7,7,7.

1. Precious Bible! what a treasure Does the word of God afford!
All I want for life or pleasure, Food and med'cine, shield and sword; } Let the world account me poor, Having this I need no more.

2. Food, to which the world's a stranger, Here my hungry soul enjoys;
Of excess there is no danger,—Though it fills, it never cloys; } On a dying Christ I feed, He is meat and drink indeed.

3. When my faith is weak and sickly, Or when Satan wounds my mind,
Cordials to revive me quickly, Healing med'cines here I find; } To the promises I flee—Each affords a remedy.

METRE 26.

MEDORA. 6,6,8,4,6,6,8,4.

1. Though nature's strength de-cay, And earth and hell with-stand, To Ca-naan's bounds I urge my way, At God's com-mand;

2. The good-ly land I see With peace and plen-ty bless'd; The land of sac-red lib-er-ty, And end-less rest;

3. There dwells the Lord our King, The Lord our right-eous-ness: Tri-umph-ant o'er the world and sin, The Prince of peace;

4. The ran-som'd na-tions bow, Be-fore the Sa-vior's face; Joy-ful their ra-diant crowns they throw, O'erwhelmed with grace;

The wat'-ry deep I pass, With Je-sus in my view, And thro' the howl-ing wil-der-ness My way pur-sue.

There milk and hon-ey flow, And oil and wine a-bound, And trees of life for-ev-er grow, With mercy crowned.

On Zi-on's sa-cred height His king-dom still main-tains; And glo-rious, with his saints in light, For-ev-er reigns.

He shows his scars of love; They kin-dle to a flame, And sound thro' all the worlds a-bove, "The slaughtered Lamb."

228   METRE 27.   COME YE DISCONSOLATE 11's & 10's.

1 Come ye dis-con-so-late, where e'er you lan-guish; Come at the mercy-seat fer-vent-ly kneel; Here bring your wounded hearts, here tell your anguish, Earth hath no sorrow that heav'n cannot heal.

2 Joy to the des-o-late, light of the stray-ing, Hope when all others die, fade-less and pure, Here speaks the Com-fort-er in mer-cy say-ing, "Earth hath no sorrow that heav'n cannot cure."

3 Here see the bread of life, see wa-ters flow-ing Forth from the throne of God, pure from above; Come to the feast pre-pared, come ev-er know-ing, Earth hath no sorrow but heav'n can re-move.

4 Go ask the in-fi-del what boon he brings us, What charms for aching hearts he can reveal, Sweet as that heav-en-ly promise hope brings us, Earth hath no sor-row that God can-not heal.

METRE 3.   SING TO ME OF HEAVEN. S. M.

1 O sing to me of heav'n When I am call'd to die; Sing songs of ho-ly ec-sta-cy, To waft my soul on high.

2 When cold and slug-gish drops Roll off my mar-ble brow, Burst forth in strains of joy-ful-ness,— Let heav'n be-gin be-low.

3 When the last mo-ment comes, O watch my dy-ing face, And catch the bright se-raph-ic gleam Which on each fea-ture plays.

4 Then to my rav-ish'd ear Let one sweet song be giv'n; Let mu-sic charm me last on earth, And greet me first in heav'n.

FRIENDSHIP. 6,6,6,6,8,6,8,6.

1 Ye sim - ple souls that stray Far from the path of peace, That un - fre - quent - ed way To life and hap - pi - ness—

2 Mad-ness and mis - er - y Ye count our lives be - neath, And noth - ing great can see, Or glo - rious in our death!

3 Poor pen-sive so - journ - ers, O'er-whelm'd with griefs and woes; Per-plexed with need-less fears, And pleas - ure's mor - tal foes,

4 So wretch-ed and ob - scure, The men whom ye de - spise; So fool-ish, weak and poor, A - bove your scorn we rise;

How long will ye your fol - ly love, And throng the downward road, And hate the wis - dom from a - bove, And mock the sons of God.

As born to suf - fer and to grieve Be-neath your feet we lie; And ut - ter - ly com - temned we live, And un - la - ment-ed die.

More irk-some than a ga-ping tomb, Our sight ye can - not bear, Wrapt in the mel - an - cho - ly gloom Of fan - ci - ful de - spair.

Our con-science in the Ho - ly Ghost, Can wit-ness bet - ter things; For He whose blood is all our boast, Hath made us priests and kings.

Metre 29.

OPORTO. 11,11,11,10.

1. Hither, ye faithful, haste with songs of triumph, To Bethlehem go your Lord of life to meet, To you this day is born a Prince and Sa-vior; O come and let us worship, O

2. O Jesus, for such wondrous condescension, Our praises and rev'rence are an off'ring meet; Now is the Word made flesh and dwells among us; O come and let us worship, O

PIA   CRES

3. Shout his Almighty name, ye choirs of angels, And let the celestial courts his praise repeat; Unto our God be glo-ry in the high-est; O come and let us worship, O

come, and let us worship, O come, and let us wor-ship at his feet.

come, and let us worship, O come, and let us wor-ship at his feet.

come, and let us worship, O come, and let us wor-ship at his feet.

Metre 30.

LENA. 8,8,7,8,8,7.

1. See the Lord of glory dy-ing! See him gasping, hear him crying!

2. See the rocks and mountains shaking, Earth unto her cen-tre quaking—

3. Heaven's bright melodious legions, Chanting thro' the tune - ful regions,

4. Hell, and all the pow'rs infernal, Vanquished by the King E-ter-nal,

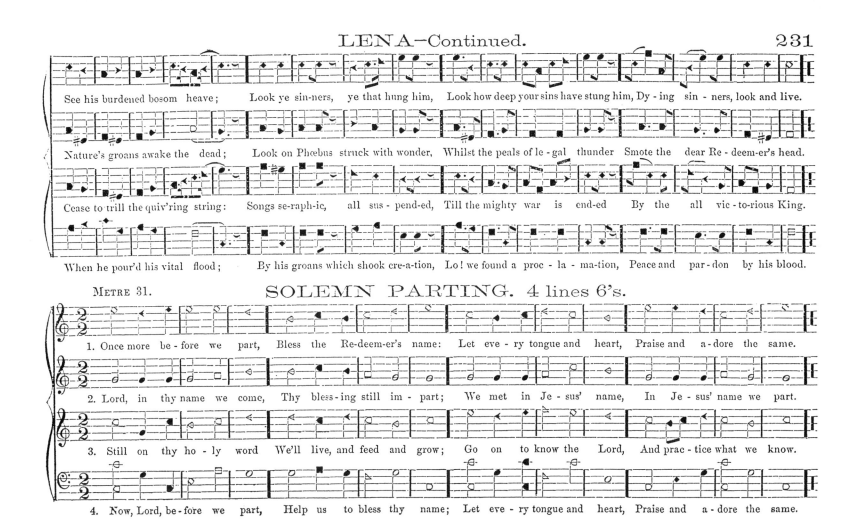

See his burdened bosom heave;　Look ye sin-ners,　ye that hung him,　Look how deep your sins have stung him, Dy - ing sin - ners, look and live.

Nature's groans awake the dead;　Look on Phœbus struck with wonder,　Whilst the peals of le - gal thunder Smote the dear Re - deem-er's head.

Cease to trill the quiv'ring string:　Songs se-raph-ic,　all sus - pend-ed,　Till the mighty war is end-ed By the all vic - to-rious King.

When he pour'd his vital flood;　By his groans which shook cre-a-tion, Lo! we found a proc - la - ma-tion, Peace and par - don by his blood.

METRE 31. SOLEMN PARTING. 4 lines 6's.

1. Once more be-fore we part, Bless the Re-deem-er's name: Let eve - ry tongue and heart, Praise and a-dore the same.

2. Lord, in thy name we come, Thy bless-ing still im - part; We met in Je - sus' name, In Je - sus' name we part.

3. Still on thy ho - ly word We'll live, and feed and grow; Go on to know the Lord, And prac - tice what we know.

4. Now, Lord, be - fore we part, Help us to bless thy name; Let eve - ry tongue and heart, Praise and a-dore the same.

METRE 32.

NEW YEAR. 5,5,5,11.

1 Come, let us a - new Our jour-ney pur-sue, Roll round with the year, Roll round with the year, And never stand still till the Master ap-pear,

2 Our life is a dream; Our time as a stream, Glides swift-ly a - way, Glides swift-ly a - way, The fu-gi-tive moment re - fu - ses to stay,

3 The ar-row is flown, The moment is gone, The mil-len - niel year, The mil-len-niel year, Rolls on to our view, and e-ter-ni-ty's near;

4 May each in the day Of his coming say, "I've fought my way thro' I've fought my way thro', And finish'd the work thou didst give me to do;

And nev-er stand still till the Mas-ter ap-pear.

The fu - gi-tive mo-ment re-fu - ses to stay.

Rolls on to our view, and e - ter - ni - ty's near.

And fin-ish'd the work thou didst give me to do."

METRE 34.

VOICE OF WARNING. 11,11,11,5,

1 Ah, guil-ty sin - ner, ruin - 'd by trans-gres-sion, What shall thy doom be,

2 Stop thoughtless sin - ner, stop a-while and pon-der Ere death ar - rest thee,

3 Oft has he call'd thee, but thou wouldst not hear him, Mer-cies and judg-ments

4 Come, then, poor sin-ner, come a - way this mo-ment, Just as you are, come,

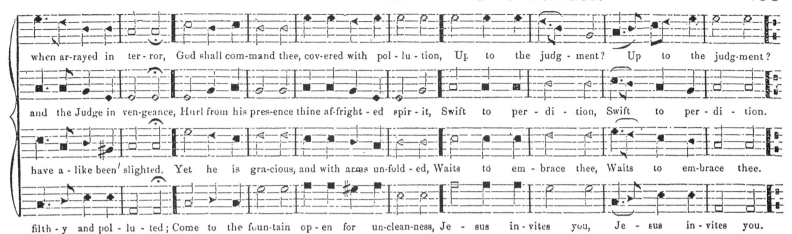

when ar-rayed in ter-ror, God shall com-mand thee, cov-ered with pol-lu-tion, Up to the judg-ment? Up to the judg-ment?

and the Judge in ven-geance, Hurl from his pres-ence thine af-fright-ed spir-it, Swift to per-di-tion, Swift to per-di-tion.

have a-like been slighted. Yet he is gra-cious, and with arms un-fold-ed, Waits to em-brace thee, Waits to em-brace thee.

filth-y and pol-lu-ted; Come to the foun-tain op-en for un-clean-ness, Je-sus in-vites you, Je-sus in-vites you.

Metre 37.

HOLY REST. 4 lines 10's.

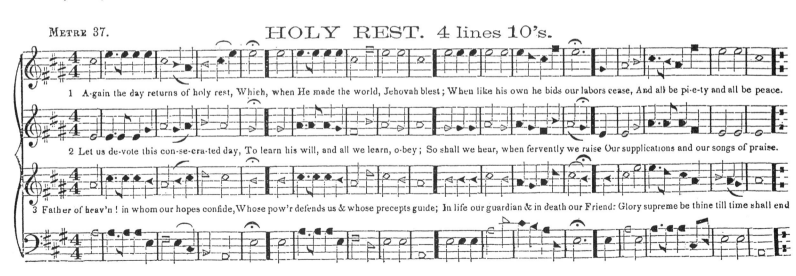

1 A-gain the day returns of holy rest, Which, when He made the world, Jehovah blest; When like his own he bids our labors cease, And all be pi-e-ty and all be peace.

2 Let us de-vote this con-se-cra-ted day, To learn his will, and all we learn, o-bey; So shall we hear, when fervently we raise Our supplications and our songs of praise.

3 Father of heav'n! in whom our hopes confide, Whose pow'r defends us & whose precepts guide; In life our guardian & in death our Friend: Glory supreme be thine till time shall end

METRE 35.

SWEET HARMONY. 10's & 11's.

1 O tell me no more of this world's vain store, The time for such trifles with me now is o'er; A coun-try I've found where true joys a - bound,

2 The souls that be-lieve, in glo - ry shall live, And me in that num-ber will Je - sus re - ceive; My soul don't de - lay, he calls thee a - way,

3 No mor - tal doth know what he can be-stow, What light, strength and comfort—go after him, go? Lo! onward I move t'a cit - ty a - bove,

4 Great spoils I shall win from death, hell and sin, 'Midst outward af-fliction shall feel Christ within; And when I'm to die, re - ceive me I'll cry,

METRE 36.

TRANSPORTING VISION. 7,6,7,6,7,7,7,7.

To dwell I'm de - ter-mined on that happy ground.

Rise, fol-low thy Sa-vior, and bless this glad day.

None guess-es how wondrous my jour-ney will prove.

For Je-sus hath loved me I can-not tell why.

1 Burst ye emeralds gates and bring To my raptur'd vis-ion, All th' estatic joys that spring,

2 Floods of ev-er-last-ing light Free - ly flash be - fore him; Myriads with supreme delight,

3 Four-and-twenty elders rise From their princely station, Shout his glorious vic-to-ries,

4 Hark! the thrilling symphonies, Seem methinks to seize us, Join we, too, the ho-ly lay—

Round the bright E-lys-ian; Lo we lift our long-ing eyes; Break ye in-ter-ven-ing skies, SUN OF RIGHTEOUSNESS arise! Ope the gates of Paradise.

In - stant-ly a - dore him; An - gels' trumps resound his fame, Lutes of lu-cid gold pro-claim All the music of his name, Heaven echoing the same.

Sing the great sal-va-tion; Cast their crowns be - fore his throne, Cry in rev-er - en - tial tone, "Glo-ry, be to God alone, Ho - ly! ho-ly! ho-ly One!"

Sing of Him who saves us; Sweet-est sounds in ser-aph's song—Sweetest sounds on mortal's tongue—Sweetest carol ever sung—Let its echoes flow along.

METRE 5. JONES. 7's. H. E. ENGLE.

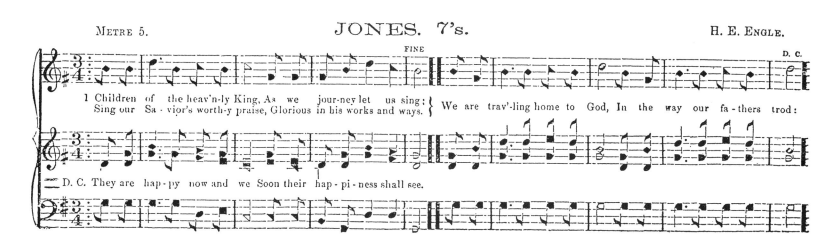

1 Children of the heav'n-ly King, As we jour-ney let us sing; We are trav'-ling home to God, In the way our fa - thers trod:
Sing our Sa - vior's worth-y praise, Glorious in his works and ways.

D. C. They are hap-py now and we Soon their hap-pi-ness shall see.

Metre 38.

BELIEVER'S DEPARTURE. 10,6,10,6,8,8,8,6.

1 What's this that steals, that steals upon my frame? Is it death? Is it death? }
That soon will quench, will quench this vital flame? Is it death? Is it death? }   If this be death I soon shall be   From every pain and sorrow free;

2 Weep not, my friends—my friends, weep not for me; All is well—all is well! }
My sins are pardoned, pardoned—I am free;   All is well—All is well! }   There's not a cloud that doth a - rise   To hide my Jesus from my eyes—

I shall the King of glory see; All is well—all is well!

I soon shall mount the upper skies, All is well—all is well!

Metre 39.

PRAISE VICTORIOUS. 7,7,8,7,7,7,8,7.

1 Head of the Church triumphant,   We joy-ful-ly a - dore Thee; Till thou appear, thy

2 While in af-flic-tion's fur-nace,   And passing thro' the fire, Thy love we praise, that

3 Thou dost conduct thy peo - ple   Thro' torrents of temptation ; Nor will we fear, while

4 By faith we see the   glo - ry   To which thou wilt restore us ; The cross despise for

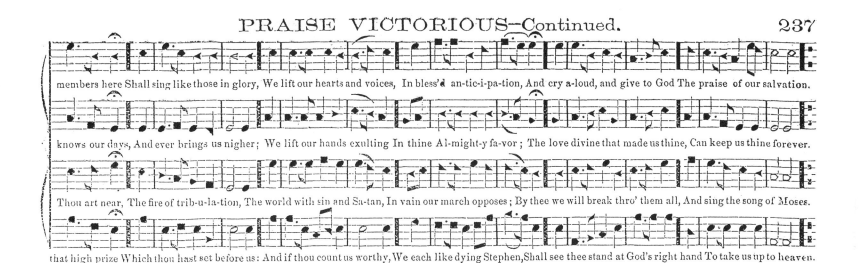

members here Shall sing like those in glory, We lift our hearts and voices, In bless'd an-tic-i-pa-tion, And cry a-loud, and give to God The praise of our salvation.

knows our days, And ever brings us nigher; We lift our hands exulting In thine Al-might-y fa-vor; The love divine that made us thine, Can keep us thine forever.

Thou art near, The fire of trib-u-la-tion, The world with sin and Sa-tan, In vain our march opposes; By thee we will break thro' them all, And sing the song of Moses.

that high prize Which thou hast set before us: And if thou count us worthy, We each like dying Stephen, Shall see thee stand at God's right hand To take us up to heaven.

METRE 5.   JESSUP. 7's.   C. E. POLLOCK.

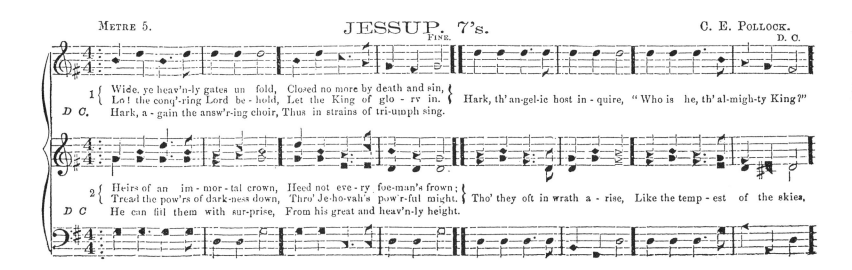

1 { Wide, ye heav'n-ly gates un-fold, Closed no more by death and sin, }
{ Lo! the conq'ring Lord be-hold, Let the King of glo-ry in. }   Hark, th'an-gel-ic host in-quire, "Who is he, th'al-migh-ty King?"

D C.   Hark, a-gain the answ'r-ing choir, Thus in strains of tri-umph sing.

2 { Heirs of an im-mor-tal crown, Heed not eve-ry foe-man's frown; }
{ Tread the pow'rs of dark-ness down, Thro' Je-ho-vah's pow'r-ful might. }   Tho' they oft in wrath a-rise, Like the temp-est of the skies,

D C   He can fill them with sur-prise, From his great and heav'n-ly height.

METRE 5.

WELCOME. 7's. Double.

G. T. LINTON.

1 {
Wel - come, welcome day of rest, To the world in kind - ness given;
Wel - come to this care-worn breast, As the beam-ing light from heaven;
}

Day of soft and sweet re - pose, Gent - ly now thy mo-ments run,

D. C. As the peace - ful stream-let flows, Ra - diant with a sum - mer's sun.

2 {
Day of tid - ings from the skies, Day of sol - emn praise and prayer,
Day to make the sim - ple wise, O how great thy bless - ings are!
}

Wel-come, wel-come, day of rest, With thy in-fluence all di - vine:

D. C. May thy hal-low'd hours be blest, To this fee - ble heart of mine.

METRE 42.

SOVEREIGN SUMMONS. 6 lines 10's.

1 The Lord, the Sov' - reign, sends his sum - mons forth, Calls the South na - tions and a - wakes the North; From East to West the

2 Be - hold! the Judge de-scends; his guards are nigh, Tem - pest and fire at - tend him down the sky: Heav'n, earth and hell draw

3 Be - hold! my cov - 'nant stands for - ev - er good, Seal'd by th'E - ter - nal sac - ri - fice in blood, And signed with all the

4 I, their al - might - y Sa - vior and their God, I am their Judge, ye heav'ns pro-claim a - broad My just, e - ter - nal

sounding order spread, Thro' distant worlds and regions of the dead; No more shall atheists mock his long delay; His vengeance sleeps........ no more, be-hold the day.

near; let all things come To hear his justice and the sinner's doom; But gather first my saints, (the Judge commands,) Bring them, ye an - - - gels, from their dis-tant lands.

names; the Greek, the Jew, That paid the ancient worship or the new; There's no distinction here; come spread their thrones, And near me seat my fav'r - ites and my sons.

sentence, and declare Those awful truths that sinners dread to hear; Sinner in Zi-on, tremble and retire, I doom thee, paint................ ed hyp - - o - crite, to fire.

METRE 43.

BOUNDLESS MERCY. 7's & 6's.

1 Drooping souls, no longer grieve, Heaven is pro-pi - tious;
If in Christ you do believe, You will find him precious; } Jesus now is passing by, Calls the mourners to him, Brings salvation from on high, Now look up and view him.

2 From his hands, his feet, his side, Runs the healing lotion;
See the con-so-la-ting tide, Bound-less as the o - cean; } See the healing waters move For the sick and dying; Now resolve to gain his love, Or to per-ish try-ing.

3 Grace's store is al-ways free, Drooping souls to glad-den;
Jesus calls, "Come unto me," Ye weary, heavy laden; } Tho' your sins like mountains high, Rise and reach to heaven, Soon as you on me rely, All shall be forgiven.

METRE 44.

FINAL DECISION. 9's & 8's.

1. That great, tremendous day's ap - proach-ing, That aw - ful scene is draw-ing nigh,
Which was foretold by an - cient proph - ets, De-creed from all e - ter - ni - ty; Prepare, my soul, re - flect and won - der,

2. See na-ture stand-ing in a - maze - ment, To hear the last loud trumpet sound:
A-rise, ye dead, and come to judg - ment, Ye na-tions of this world a-round: The orb - ed lamps all vailed in sack - cloth,

3. Green graveyards, and the tombs of mar - ble, Give up their dead, both small and great;
And the whole world, both saint and sin - ner, Are com - ing to the judg-ment seat; See Je - sus on the throne of jus - tice,

That aw - ful scene is draw - ing near, When you shall see the great trans - ac - tion, When Christ in judg-ment shall ap-pear.

No more their shi - ning cir - cuit run, The wheel of time now stopp'd for - ev - er, E - ter - nal things are now be - gun.

In clouds de-scend - ing from the sky, With count-less hosts of shi - ning an - gels, With hal - le - lu - jah's shout for joy.

1 High in yon-der realms of light Dwell the raptured saints a-bove, Far be-yond our fee-ble sight, Hap-py in Immanuel's love;

2 Oft the big un-bid-den tear, Steal-ing down the fur-row'd cheek, Told, in el-o-quence sin-cere, Tales of woe they could not speak;

3 'Mid the cho-rus of the skies, 'Mid th'an-gel-ic lyres a-bove, Hark, their songs me-lo-dious rise, Songs of praise to Je-sus love;

4 All is tran-quil and se-rene, Calm and un-dis-turb'd re-pose; There no cloud can in-ter-vene, There no an-gry tem-pest blows;

Once they knew, like us be-low Pil-grims in this vale of tears, Tort'ring pain, and heav-y woe, Gloom-y doubts, dis-tress-ing fears.

But these days of weep-ing o'er, Pass'd this scene of toil and pain, They shall feel dis-tress no more— Nev-er, nev-er weep a-gain.

Hap-py spir-its, ye are fled Where no grief can en-trance find; Lull'd to rest the ach-ing head, Soothed the anguish of the mind.

Eve-ry tear is wiped a-way, Sighs no more shall heave the breast, Night is lost in end-less day, Sor-row—in e-ter-nal rest.

242 METRE 44. REDEEMING GRACE. 9's & 8's.

1. Come all who love my Lord and Master, And like old Dá - vid I will tell,
Though chief of sinners, I've found favor, By grace redeemed from death and hell;
Far as the east from west is part - ed, So far my sins by dy - ing love,

2. I late estranged from Jesus wander'd And thought each dangerous poison good:
But he in mer-cy long pursued me With cries of his re-deem-ing blood;
Though like Bar-ti-meus I was blind - ed, In na-ture's dark-est night conceal'd,

3. Now I will serve him while He spares me, And with his peo-ple sing a - loud,
Tho' hell oppose and sinners mock me, In rapt'rous strains I'll praise my God.
By faith I view the heavenly con-cert, They sing high strains of Je - sus' love,

METRE 45. CHRISTIAN WARFARE. 7,7,7,5,7,7,7,5.

From me by faith are sep - a - ra - ted, Blest an - te - past of joys a - bove.

1. Sol-diers of the cross, a-rise! Lo! your Captain from the skies,

But Je - sus' love remov'd my blindness, And he his pard'ning grace revealed.

2. Who the cause of Christ would yield? Who would leave the battle field?

3. By the mer-cies of our God, By Emanuel's streaming blood,

Oh! with de-sire my soul is long-ing, And fain would be with Christ above.

4. By the woes which rebels prove, By the bliss of ho-ly love,

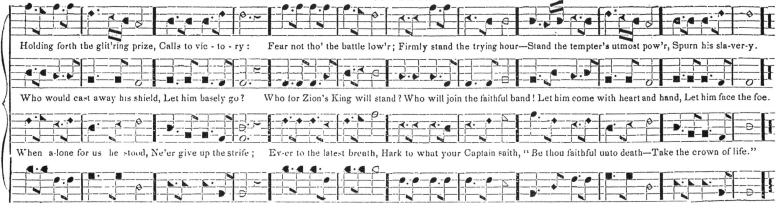

Holding forth the glit'ring prize, Calls to vic - to - ry: Fear not tho' the battle low'r; Firmly stand the trying hour—Stand the tempter's utmost pow'r, Spurn his sla-ver-y.

Who would cast away his shield, Let him basely go? Who for Zion's King will stand? Who will join the faithful band! Let him come with heart and hand, Let him face the foe.

When a-lone for us he stood, Ne'er give up the strife; Ev-er to the latest breath, Hark to what your Captain saith, "Be thou faithful unto death—Take the crown of life."

Sinners, seek the joys a-bove, Sinners, turn and live! Here is freedom worth the name—Tyrant sin is put to shame—Grace inspires the hallow'd flame—God the crown will give.

METRE 46. EVENING THOUGHT. 8,3,3,6.

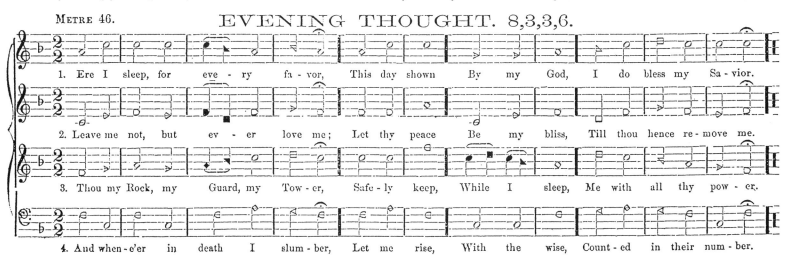

1. Ere I sleep, for eve - ry fa - vor, This day shown By my God, I do bless my Sa - vior.

2. Leave me not, but ev - er love me; Let thy peace Be my bliss, Till thou hence re - move me.

3. Thou my Rock, my Guard, my Tow - er, Safe - ly keep, While I sleep, Me with all thy pow - er.

4. And when-e'er in death I slum - ber, Let me rise, With the wise, Count - ed in their num - ber.

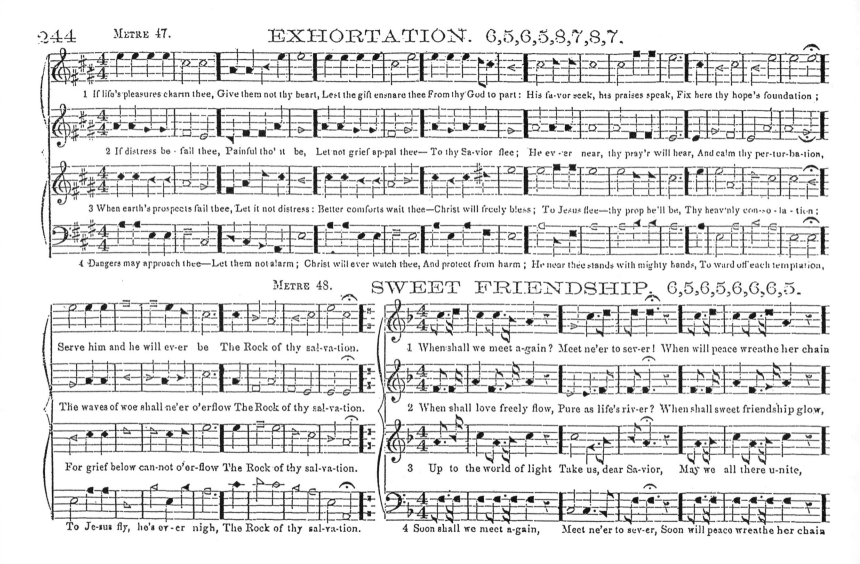

244   METRE 47.   EXHORTATION. 6,5,6,5,8,7,8,7.

1 If life's pleasures charm thee, Give them not thy heart, Lest the gift ensnare thee From thy God to part: His fa-vor seek, his praises speak, Fix here thy hope's foundation;

2 If distress be-fall thee, Painful tho' it be, Let not grief ap-pal thee— To thy Sa-vior flee; He ev-er near, thy pray'r will hear, And calm thy per-tur-ba-tion,

3 When earth's prospects fail thee, Let it not distress: Better comforts wait thee—Christ will freely bless; To Jesus flee—thy prop he'll be, Thy heav'nly con-so-la-tion;

4 Dangers may approach thee—Let them not alarm; Christ will ever watch thee, And protect from harm; He near thee stands with mighty hands, To ward off each temptation,

METRE 48.   SWEET FRIENDSHIP. 6,5,6,5,6,6,6,5.

Serve him and he will ev-er be The Rock of thy sal-va-tion.

The waves of woe shall ne'er o'erflow The Rock of thy sal-va-tion.

For grief below can-not o'er-flow The Rock of thy sal-va-tion.

To Je-sus fly, he's ev-er nigh, The Rock of thy sal-va-tion.

1 When shall we meet a-gain? Meet ne'er to sev-er! When will peace wreathe her chain

2 When shall love freely flow, Pure as life's riv-er? When shall sweet friendship glow,

3 Up to the world of light Take us, dear Sa-vior, May we all there u-nite,

4 Soon shall we meet a-gain, Meet ne'er to sev-er, Soon will peace wreathe her chain

Round us for ev-er? Our hearts will ne'er re - pose Safe from each blast that blows, In this dark vale of woes, Nev-er, no, nev-er.

Changeless for-ev-er? Where joys ce-les-tial thrill, Where bliss each heart shall fill: And fears of part-ing chill, Nev-er, no, nev-er.

Hap-py for-ev - er? Where kindred spir-its dwell, There may our mu-sic swell, And time our joys dis - pel, Nev-er, no, nev-er.

Round us for-ev-er! Our hearts will then re - pose, Se - cure from world-ly woes; Our songs of praise shall close, Nev-er, no, nev-er.

METRE 49.

PEACEFUL REST. 8,6,8,8,6.

1 There is an hour of peaceful rest To mourning wand'rers giv'n; There is a tear for souls distress'd, A balm for eve-ry wound - ed breast—'Tis found a-lone in heav'n.

2 There is a home for weary souls, By sins and sorrows driv'n; When toss'd on life's tempestuous shoals, When storms a-rise and o - cean rolls, And all is drear but heav'n.

3 There faith lifts up the tearless eye, The heart with anguish riv'n; It views the tempest passing by, Sees eve - ning shadows quick - ly fly, And all se-rene in heav'n.

4 There fragrant flow'rs immortal bloom, And joys supreme are giv'n; There rays divine disperse the gloom,—Beyond the dark and nar-row tomb, Appears the dawn of heav'n.

METRE 50.

TO-DAY. 6,4,6,4.

1. To - day the Sa - vior calls: Ye wand'-rers, come; O ye be - night - ed souls, Why lon - ger roam.

2. To - day the Sa - vior calls: O hear him now; With - in these sa - cred walls To Je - sus bow.

3. To - day the Sa - vior calls: For ref - uge fly; The storm of jus - tice falls, And death is nigh.

4. The Spir - it calls to - day: Yield to his pow'r; Oh, grieve him not a - way; 'Tis mer - cy's hour.

METRE 52.

LOVELY MORNING. 11,11,10,4,11.

1. The last love-ly morn-ing all blooming and fair,
   Is fast on-ward fleeting, and soon will ap-pear; } While the mighty, mighty, mighty trump sounds, "Come, come away," O let us be read-y, and hail the bright day.

2. And when that bright morning in splendor shall dawn,
   Our tears will be end - ed, our sorrows all gone; } While the mighty, mighty, mighty trump sounds, "Come, come away," O let us be read-y, and hail the bright day.

3. The graves will be o - pen'd, the dead will arise,
   And with the Re - deem-er mount up to the skies, } While the mighy, mighty, mighty trump sounds, "Come, come away," O let us be read-y, and hail the bright day.

HEALING FOUNTAIN. 7,7,7,7,6,6,7,7.

1 See the foun-tain o-pen'd wide That from pol - lu - tion frees us, Flow-ing from the wound-ed side Of our Im-man-uel Je-sus!

2 Sin-ners, hear the Sa - vior's call, Con - sid - er what you're do - ing; Jesus Christ can cleanse you all, Will you not come un - to him!

3 Dy-ing sin-ners, come and try; These wa-ters will re - lieve you! With-out mon-ey, come and buy, For Christ will free-ly give you.

4 He who drinks shall never die; These wa-ters fail him nev-er; Sin-ners come, and now ap-ply, And drink and live for - ev - er.
5 Weep-ing Ma-ry, full of grief, Came beg-ging for these wa-ters; Je-sus gave her full re-lief, With Zi-on's sons and daughters.

CHORUS

Ho! eve-ry one that thirsts, Come ye to the wa-ters; Free-ly drink and quench your thirst With Zi-on's sons and daugh-ters.

Ho! eve-ry one that thirsts, Come ye to the wa-ters; Free-ly drink and quench your thirst With Zi-on's sons and daughters.

METRE 53.* HEAVENLY TREASURE. 9,8,9,8,9,8,10,8.

1 Re - lig - ion! 'tis a glo - rious treas - ure, The pur - chase of a Sa - vior's blood;
It fills the soul with con - so - la - tion, It lifts the thoughts to things a - bove; } It calms our fears, it soothes our sor - rows,

2 While journeying here thro' trib - u - la - tion, In Chris - tian love we'll march a - long;
And while strife severs the am - bi - tious, In Je - sus Christ we'll all be one: } Re - lig - ion pure u - nites to - geth - er,

3 How fleet - ing — vain, — how trans - i - to - ry, This world with all its pomp and show;
Its vain de - lights and short-lived pleas - ures, I'll glad - ly leave them all be - low; }
4 This earth - ly house must be dis - solv - ed, And mor - tal life will soon be o'er;
All earth - ly love and earth - ly sor - row, Shall pain my eyes and heart no more; } But love and grace shall be my sto - ry,
Re - lig - ion pure will stand for ev - er,

It smoothes our way o'er life's rough sea; 'Tis mixed with goodness, meek humble pa - tience: This heav'n - ly por - tion mine shall be.

In bonds of love and makes us free; While end - less a - ges are on - ward roll - ing, This heav'n - ly por - tion mine shall be.

While I in Christ such beau - ties see; While end - less a - ges are on - ward roll - ing, This heav'n - ly por - tion mine shall be.
And my glad heart shall strength - en'd be, While end - less a - ges are on - ward roll - ing, This heav'n - ly por - tion mine shall be.

* A greater variety of Metres will be continued throughout the Second Part of this work.

PART II.

CONTAINING THE LONGER TUNES OE DIFFERENT METRES, SET PIECES, AND ANTHEMS.

" Nor now among the choral harps, in this
The native clime of song are those unknown,
With higher notes ascending, who below,
In holy ardor aimed at lofty strains.
True fame is never lost : many whose names

Were honored much on earth, are famous here
For poetry, and with archangel harps
Hold no unequal rivalry in song !
Leading the choirs of heaven, in numbers high.
In numbers ever sweet and ever new."—POLLOK.

METRE 1. **MISSIONARY CHANT. L. M.** CH. ZEUNER.

1 "Go preach my gos-pel," saith the Lord; "Bid the whole earth my grace receive ; He shall be saved that trusts my word, And he condemned who'll not be-lieve.

2 "I'll make your great commission known; And ye shall prove my gos-pel true, By all the works that I have done, By all the wonders ye shall do.

3 "Teach all the na-tions my com-mands; I'm with you till the world shall end ; All power is trust-ed in my hands; I can de-stroy, and I de-fend.

4 He spake, and light shone round his head; On a bright cloud to heaven he rode: They to the farthest na-tions spread The grace of their ascended God.

METRE 1. WESTFORD. L. M.

1 Descend from heaven, in-mor-tal Dove, Stoop down and take us on thy wings, And mount and bear us far above The reach of these inferior things; And mount and bear us

2 Adoring saints around him stand, And thrones and pow'rs before him fall; The God shines gracious thro' the Man, And sheds sweet glories on them all, The God shines gracious

far a-bove The reach of these in-fe-rior things; Beyond, beyond this lower sky, Up where e-ter-nal a-ges roll, Where sol-id pleas-ures nev-er die, And fruits im-

thro' the Man, And sheds sweet glories on them all, Oh, what amazing joys they feel While to their gold-en harps they sing, And sit on eve-ry heaven-ly hill, And spread the

Metre 2.

SILOAM. C. M.

mor-tal feast the soul, Oh, for a sight, a pleasant sight, Of our al-might-y Fa-ther's throne; There sits our Savior crown'd with light, Clothed in a body like our own.

tri-umphs of their King, When shall the day, dear Lord, appear, That I shall mount to dwell above, And stand and bow among them there, And view thy face and sing thy love!

1 By cool Si-lo-am's sha-dy rill How fair the lil-y grows! How sweet the breath beneath the hill, Of Sharon's dew-y rose.

2 Lo! such the child whose ear-ly-feet The paths of peace have trod, Whose se-cret heart with in-fluence sweet Is Up-ward drawn to God.

3 By cool Si-lo-am's sha-dy rill The lil-y must de-cay, The rose that blooms beneath the hill, Must short-ly fade a-way.

4 And soon, too soon, the wint'-ry hour Of man's ma-tu-rer age Will shake the soul with sor-row's pow'r And storm-y pas-sion's rage.

5 O thou who giv-est life and breath, We seek thy grace a-lone, In child-hood, man-hood, age, and death, To keep us still thine own.

METRE 1.

WETHERSFIELD L. M.

1. Far from my thoughts, vain world, be gone, Let my religious hours alone: Fain would my eyes my Savior see—I wait a vis-it, Lord, from thee!

2. Haste then, but with a smiling face, And spread the table of thy grace; Bring down a taste of truth di-vine, and cheer my heart with sac-red wine.

My heart grows warm with ho-ly fire, And kin-dles with a pure de-sire; Come my dear Je-sus from a-bove, And feed my soul with heaven-ly love.

Bless'd Jesus, what de-li-cious fare! How sweet thy en-ter-tain-ments are! Nev-er did an-gels taste a-bove Re-deem-ing grace and dy-ing love.

The trees of life im-mor-tal stand, In bloom-ing rows at thy righ hand, And in sweet mur-murs by thy side Riv-ers of bliss per-pet-ual glide.

Hail great Im-man-uel, all di-vine! In thee thy Fa-ther's glories shine, Thou brightest, sweetest, fairest One, That eyes have seen or an-gels known.

1. They have gone to the land where the patriarchs rest, Where the bones of the prophets are laid, Where the chosen of Israel the promise possess'd, And Jehovah his mandates display'd,

2. They have gone to the land where the gospel's glad sound Sweetly tuned by the angels above, Was re-echoed on earth through the regions around, In the accents of heav-en-ly love.

3. They have gone—the glad heralds of mercy have gone   Where the beast and false prophet have since trodden down
           To the land where the martyrs once bled ;   The fair fabric that Zion had reared,

4. They have gone—O thou Shepherd of Israel! have gone, The glad mission in love to restore; Thou wilt never forsake them nor leave them alone, Thy rich blessings we humbly implore.

DIM   FOR

To the land where the Savior of sinners once trod : Where he labor'd, and languished and bled ; Where he triumphed o'er death and ascended to God. As He captive cap-tiv-i-ty led.

Where the Spirit descended in tokens of flame, The rich gifts of his grace to reveal; Where apostles wrought signs in Immanuel's name, For the truth of their mission to seal.

Where the churches once planted, and watered, and bless'd   Have been smitten, despoil'd! and by heathen possess'd,
           With the dews which the Spirit distilled,   And the places that knew them defiled ;

Let thy blessings go with them—O be thou their shield From the shafts of the fowler that fly; O thou Savior of sinners! thine arm be revealed, In thy mercy and might from on high.

METRE 55.

SPRING. 8,8,8,8,7,7.

1 The voice of my be-lov-ed sounds, While o'er the moun-tain top he bounds; He flies ex-ult-ing

2 The scat-tered clouds are fled at last— The rain is gone, the win-ter's past, The love-ly ver-nal

o'er the hills, And all my soul with trans-port fills. Gent-ly doth he chide my stay, "Rise, my love, and come a-way;"

flow'rs ap-pear,— The warb-ling choir en-chants our ear; Now with sweet-ly pen-sive moan, Coos the tur-tle-dove a-lone,

SLOW AND SOFT.

Gent-ly doth he chide my stay, "Rise, my love, and come a-way, Rise— Rise, my love, and come a---way."

Now with sweet-ly pen-sive moan, Coos the tur-tle--dove a-lone, Coos— Coos the tur-tle-dove a---lone.

PILGRIM'S FAREWELL. 8,8,8,8,6,6,6,6,4,8.

1 Farewell, Farewell, Farewell, my friends, I must be gone, I have no home nor stay with you; I'll take my staff and trav-el on Till I a bet-ter world can view.

2 Fare-well, Fare-well, Fare-well, my breth-ren in the Lord, To you I'm bound in chords of love; Yet we believe his gracious word, And soon we all shall meet above.

3 Farewell, Farewell, Farewell old soldiers of the cross, You've struggled long and hard for heav'n; You've counted all things else but loss, Fight on, the crown will soon be giv'n!

4 Fare-well, Fare-well, Fare-well, ye bloom-ing sons of God, Sore conflicts yet await for you; Yet dauntless keep the heavenly road, Till Canaan's happy land we view.

CHORUS

I'll march to Canaan's land, I'll land on Canaan's shore, Where pleasures never end. And troubles come no more: Farewell, farewell, farewell, my lov-ing friends, fare-well.

I'll march to Canaan's land, I'll land on Canaan's shore, Where pleasures never end, And troubles come no more; Farewell, farewell, farewell, my faithful friends, farewell.

I'll march to Canaan's land, I'll land on Canaan's shore, Where pleasures never end, And troubles come no more; Fight on, fight on, fight on, the crown will soon be given.

I'll march to Canaan's land, I'll land on Canaan's shore, Where pleasures never end, And troubles come no more, Farewell, farewell, farewell, my faithful friends, farewell.

256   METRE 57.   UNITED PRAISES. 8,6,8,6,8,8,8,6.

1 Sing hal-le - lu - jah, praise the Lord! Sing with a cheer-ful voice; Ex - alt our God with one ac-cord, And in his name re - joice;

2 There we to all e - ter-ni - ty Shall join th' an-gel-ic lays, And sing in per-fect har-mo - ny To God our Sa-vior's praise:

Ne'er cease to sing, thou ran-som'd host, To Father, Son, and Ho - ly Ghost, Till in the realms of end - less light, Your praises shall u - nite.

"He hath re-deemed us by his blood, And made us kings and priests to God; For us, for us the Lamb was slain," Praise ye the Lord! A - men.

Metre 58.
SLOW AND SOFT.

PASSIVENESS. 10,8,10,7,10,10,10,7.

1 Shed not a tear o'er your friend's early bier, When I am gone, When I am gone; Smile if the slow tolling bell you should hear, When I am gone, I am gone.

2 Plant ye a tree which may wave over me, When I am gone, When I am gone; Sing ye a song if my grave you should see, When I am gone, I am gone.

3 Plant ye a rose that may bloom o'er my bed, When I am gone, When I am gone; Breathe not a sigh for the blest early dead, When I am gone, I am gone.

Weep not for me when you stand round my grave; Think who has died his beloved to save; Think of the crown all the ransom'd shall have, When I am gone, I am gone.

Come at the close of a bright sum-mer day, Come when the sun sheds his last ling'ring ray, Come and re-joice that I thus pass'd away, When I am gone, I am gone.

Praise ye the Lord that I'm freed from all care, Serve ye the Lord that my bliss you may share, Look ye on high and believe I am there, When I am gone, I am gone.

We'll praise him a - gain when we pass o - ver Jor-dan, We'll praise him a - gain when we pass o - ver Jor - dan.

We'll praise him a - gain when we pass o - ver Jor - dan, We'll praise him a - gain when we pass o - ver Jor - dan.

We'll praise him a - gain when we pass o - ver Jor-dan, We'll praise him a - gain when we pass o - ver Jor - dan.

METRE 2. AZMON. C. M.

CODA—To be sung after the last two verses.

1 Plung'd in a gulf of dark despair, We wretched sinners lay, Without one cheerful beam of hope, Or spark of glimm'ring day. Hal-le-lu-jah! Hal-le-lu-jah! Hal-le-lu- jah!

2 With pitying eyes the Prince of Grace Beheld our help'ess grief; He saw, and O, amazing love, He flew to our relief.

3 Down from the shining seats above, With joyful haste he fled, Entered the grave in mortal flesh, And dwelt among the dead. Hal-le- lu-jah! Hal-le-lu-jah! Hal-le-lu-jah!
4 O for this love! let rocks and hills, Their lasting silence break, And all harmonious human tongues The Savior's praises speak.

5 Angels, assist our mighty joys, Strike all your harps of gold: But when you raise your highest notes, His love can ne'er be told.

METRE 2.   PARTING HYMN.   C. M. and Chorus.

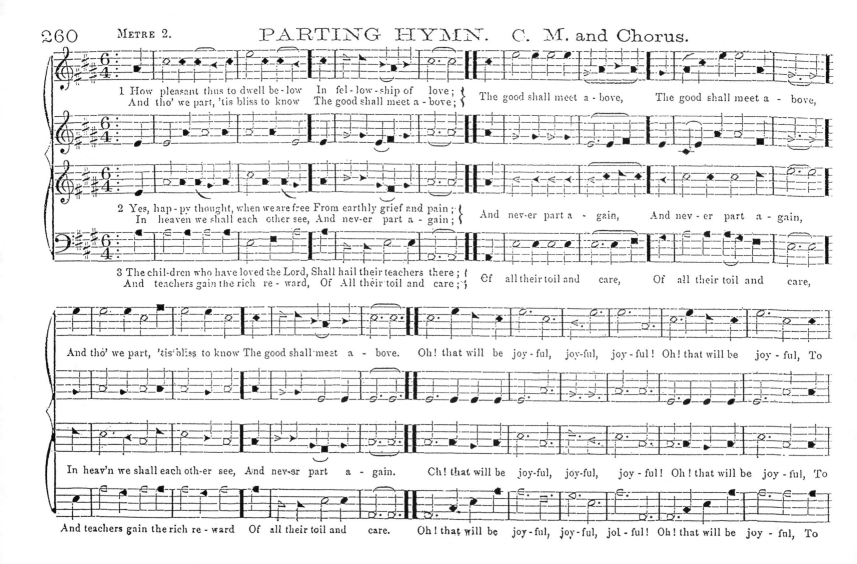

1 How pleasant thus to dwell be-low   In fel-low-ship of love;
And tho' we part, 'tis bliss to know   The good shall meet a-bove;   The good shall meet a - bove,   The good shall meet a - bove,

2 Yes, hap-py thought, when we are free From earthly grief and pain;
In heaven we shall each other see, And nev-er part a - gain;   And nev-er part a - gain,   And nev-er part a - gain,

3 The chil-dren who have loved the Lord, Shall hail their teachers there;
And teachers gain the rich re - ward, Of All their toil and care;   Of all their toil and care,   Of all their toil and care,

And tho' we part, 'tis bliss to know The good shall meet a - bove.   Oh! that will be joy-ful, joy-ful, joy-ful! Oh! that will be joy-ful, To

In heav'n we shall each oth-er see, And nev-er part a - gain.   Oh! that will be joy-ful, joy-ful, joy - ful! Oh! that will be joy-ful, To

And teachers gain the rich re - ward Of all their toil and care.   Oh! that will be joy-ful, joy-ful, jol-ful! Oh! that will be joy - ful, To

meet to part no more, To meet to part no more,...... On Ca-naan's hap-py shore, And sing the ev-er-last-ing song With those who've gone before.

meet to part no more, To meet to part no more...... On Ca-naan's hap-py shore, And sing the ev-er-last-ing song With those who've gone before.

meet to part no more, To meet to part no more...... On Ca-naan's happy shore, And sing the ev-er-last-ing song With those who've gone before.

METRE 2.

MANOAH. C. M.

1 Fa - ther I long, I faint to see The place of thine a - bode: I'd leave thine earthly courts, and flee up to thy seat my God!

2 There all the heavenly hosts are seen In shi-ning ranks they move, And drink im-mor-tal vig-or in, With won - der and with love.

3 Fa-ther! I long, I faint to see the place of thine a - bode; I'd leave thine earthly courts, and be For ev - er with my God.

METRE 59. HOME. 11,11,11,11,5,11.

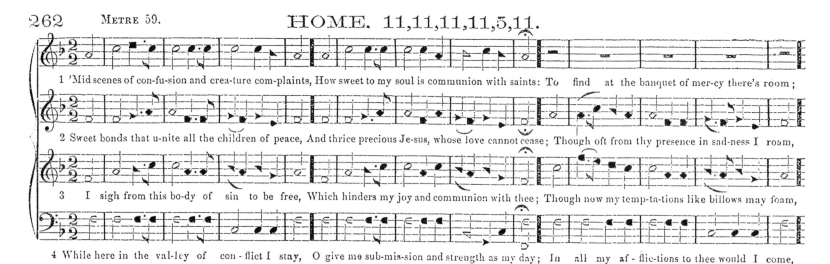

1 'Mid scenes of con-fu-sion and crea-ture com-plaints, How sweet to my soul is communion with saints: To find at the banquet of mer-cy there's room;

2 Sweet bonds that u-nite all the children of peace, And thrice precious Je-sus, whose love cannot cease; Though oft from thy presence in sad-ness I roam,

3 I sigh from this bo-dy of sin to be free, Which hinders my joy and communion with thee; Though now my temp-ta-tions like billows may foam,

4 While here in the val-ley of con-flict I stay, O give me sub-mis-sion and strength as my day; In all my af-flic-tions to thee would I come,

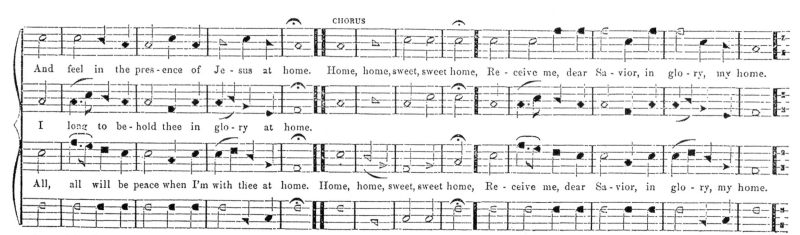

And feel in the pres-ence of Je-sus at home. Home, home, sweet, sweet home, Re-ceive me, dear Sa-vior, in glo-ry, my home.

I long to be-hold thee in glo-ry at home.

All, all will be peace when I'm with thee at home. Home, home, sweet, sweet home, Re-ceive me, dear Sa-vior, in glo-ry, my home.

Re-joic-ing in hope of my glo-ri-ous home.

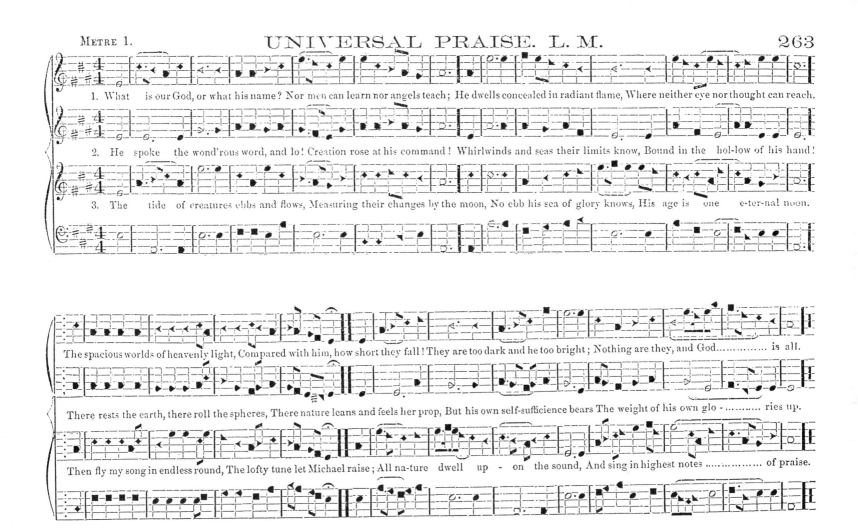

1. What is our God, or what his name? Nor men can learn nor angels teach; He dwells concealed in radiant flame, Where neither eye nor thought can reach.

2. He spoke the wond'rous word, and lo! Creation rose at his command! Whirlwinds and seas their limits know, Bound in the hol-low of his hand!

3. The tide of creatures ebbs and flows, Measuring their changes by the moon, No ebb his sea of glory knows, His age is one e-ter-nal noon.

The spacious worlds of heavenly light, Compared with him, how short they fall! They are too dark and he too bright; Nothing are they, and God.............. is all.

There rests the earth, there roll the spheres, There nature leans and feels her prop, But his own self-sufficience bears The weight of his own glo - .... ries up.

Then fly my song in endless round, The lofty tune let Michael raise; All na-ture dwell up - on the sound, And sing in highest notes .... of praise.

METRE 1.

GRACIOUS REWARD. L. M.

1 A poor way-fa-ring Man of grief Has oft-en cross'd me on my way, Who sued so hum-bly for re-lief, That I could nev-er an-swer nay.

2 Once when my scanty meal was spread He en-ter'd; not a word He spake; Just per-ish-ing for want of bread; I gave Him all,—He bless'd it, brake,

3 I spied Him where a fountain burst Clear from the Rock, His strength was gone; The heedless waters mock'd His thirst, He heard it, saw it hurrying on;

4 'Twas night; the floods were out; it blew A win-ter hur-ri-cane a-loof— I heard His voice a-broad, and flew To bid Him welcome to my roof;

I had not pow'r to ask His name, Whith-er He went or whence He came, Yet was there something in his eye, That won my love, I knew not why.

And ate, and gave me part a-gain: Mine was an an-gel's portion then, For while I fed with ea-ger haste, That crust was man-na to my taste.

I ran and rais'd the Suff'-rer up, Thrice from the stream He drained my cup, Dipt and re-turn'd it run-ning o'er; I drank, and nev-er thirst-ed more.

I warm'd—I clothed—I cheer'd my Guest, I laid him on my couch to rest, Then made the hearth my bed, and seemed In E-den's gar-den while I dreamed.

ITALY. L. M.

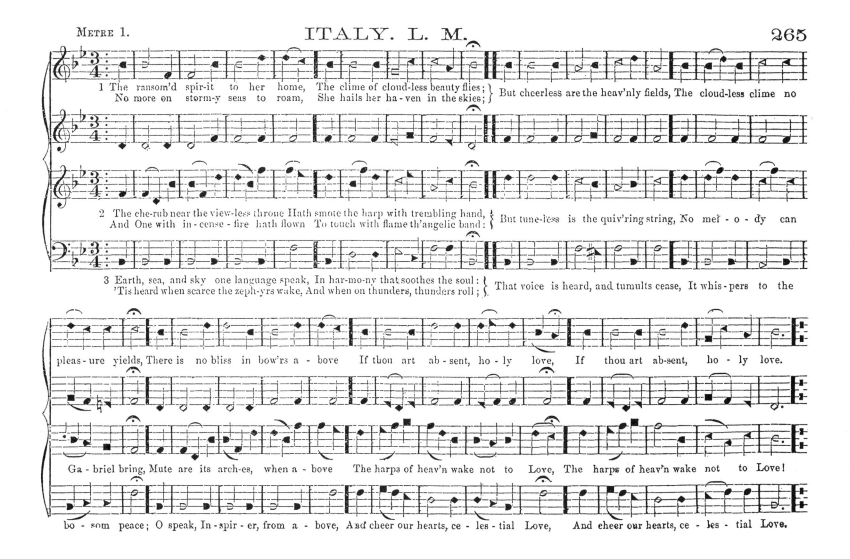

1 The ransom'd spir-it to her home, The clime of cloud-less beauty flies; No more on storm-y seas to roam, She hails her ha-ven in the skies; } But cheerless are the heav'nly fields, The cloud-less clime no

2 The che-rub near the view-less throne Hath smote the harp with trembling hand, And One with in-cense-fire hath flown To touch with flame th'angelic band: } But tune-less is the quiv'ring string, No mel-o-dy can

3 Earth, sea, and sky one language speak, In har-mo-ny that soothes the soul: 'Tis heard when scarce the zeph-yrs wake, And when on thunders, thunders roll; } That voice is heard, and tumults cease, It whis-pers to the

pleas-ure yields, There is no bliss in bow'rs a-bove If thou art ab-sent, ho-ly love, If thou art ab-sent, ho-ly love.

Ga-briel bring, Mute are its arch-es, when a-bove The harps of heav'n wake not to Love, The harps of heav'n wake not to Love!

bo-som peace; O speak, In-spir-er, from a-bove, And cheer our hearts, ce-les-tial Love, And cheer our hearts, ce-les-tial Love.

METRE 1.   GOLGOTHA. L. M.

1 Now let our mournful songs record the dying sorrows of our Lord: When he com-plained in tears and blood, As one for-saken of his God.

2 They wound his head, his hands, his feet Till streams of blood each other meet, By lot his gar-ments they divide, And mock the pangs in which he died.

The Jews beheld him thus forlorn,   He rescued others from the grave,   Now let him try him-self to save.
And shaked their heads and laughed in scorn—   Now let him try himself to save,

But God, his Father, heard his cry,   The nations learn his righteousness,   And humble sinners taste his grace.
Raised from the dead, he reigns on high;   And humble sinners taste his grace,

DOVER. L. M.

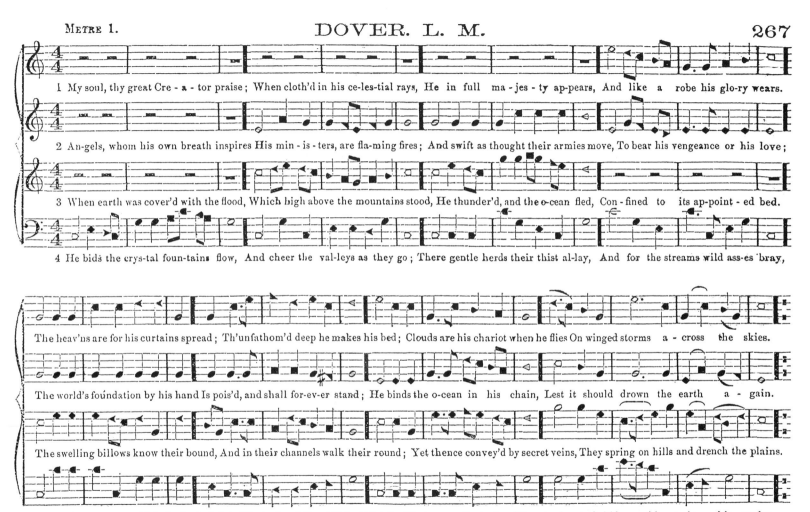

1 My soul, thy great Cre - a - tor praise; When cloth'd in his ce-les-tial rays, He in full ma - jes - ty ap-pears, And like a robe his glo-ry wears.

2 An-gels, whom his own breath inspires His min - is - ters, are fla-ming fires; And swift as thought their armies move, To bear his vengeance or his love;

3 When earth was cover'd with the flood, Which high above the mountains stood, He thunder'd, and the o-cean fled, Con - fined to its ap-point - ed bed.

4 He bids the crys-tal foun-tains flow, And cheer the val-leys as they go; There gentle herds their thist al-lay, And for the streams wild ass-es bray,

The heav'ns are for his curtains spread; Th'unfathom'd deep he makes his bed; Clouds are his chariot when he flies On winged storms a - cross the skies.

The world's foundation by his hand Is pois'd, and shall for-ev-er stand; He binds the o-cean in his chain, Lest it should drown the earth a - gain.

The swelling billows know their bound, And in their channels walk their round; Yet thence convey'd by secret veins, They spring on hills and drench the plains.

From pleasant trees which shade the brink, The lark and linnet light to drink; Their songs the lark and linnet raise, And chide our si-lence in his praise.

Metre 1.

SOCIAL BAND. L. M.

1 Say now, ye love-ly, so-cial band, Who walk the way to Canaan's land,
Ye who have fled from Sodom's plain, Say, do you wish to turn a-gain? } Have you just ventured to the field, Well armed with helmet, sword and shield,

2 Be-ware of pleas-ure's sy-ren song, A - las ! it cannot soothe thee long;
It can-not qui - et Jor-dan's wave, Nor cheer the dark and silent grave ! } Oh let your thoughts delight to soar Where earth and time shall be no more,

And shall the world with dread alarms Compel you now to ground your arms!

Explore by faith the heav'nly fields, And pluck the fruit that Canaan yields.

Metre 1.

LOVING KINDNESS. L. M.

1 A-wake, my soul, in joy-ful lays, And sing thy great Redeemer's praise ;

2 He saw me ru-in'd in the fall, Yet loved me not-with-stand-ing all ;

3 Tho' num'rous hosts of mighty foes, Tho' earth and hell my way oppose,

4 When trouble, like a gloom-y cloud, Hath gather'd thick and thunder'd loud,

He just-ly claims a song from thee, His lov-ing kind-ness, oh how free, His lov-ing kind-ness, lov-ing kindness, His lov-ing kind-ness, oh how free!

He saved me from my lost es-tate, His lov-ing kind-ness, oh how great! His lov-ing kind-ness, lov-ing kindness, His lov-ing kind-ness, oh how great!

He safe-ly leads my soul a - long, His lov-ing kind-ness, oh how strong! His lov-ing kindness, loving kindness, His lov-ing kind-ness, oh how strong!

He near my soul has al-ways stood, His lov-ing kind-ness, oh how good! His lov-ing kindness, loving kindness, His lov-ing kind-ness, oh how good!

LOUD HALLELUJAH. L. M.

METRE 1.

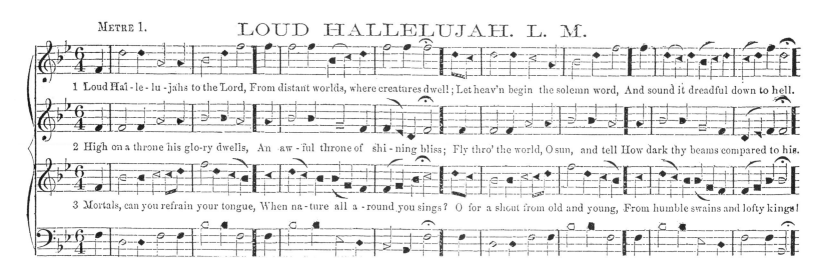

1 Loud Hal - le - lu - jahs to the Lord, From distant worlds, where creatures dwell! ; Let heav'n begin the solemn word, And sound it dreadful down to hell.

2 High on a throne his glo-ry dwells, An aw - ful throne of shi - ning bliss; Fly thro' the world, O sun, and tell How dark thy beams compared to his.

3 Mortals, can you refrain your tongue, When na - ture all a - round you sings? O for a shout from old and young, From humble swains and lofty kings!

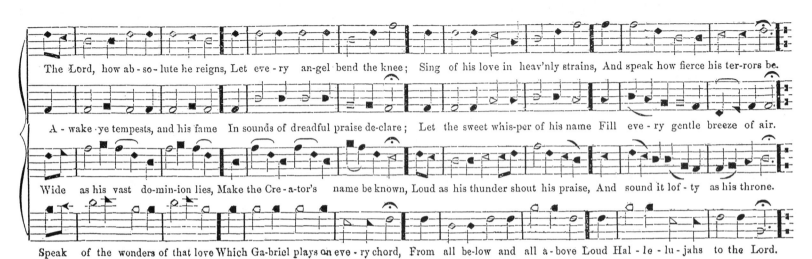

The Lord, how ab-so-lute he reigns, Let eve-ry an-gel bend the knee; Sing of his love in heav'nly strains, And speak how fierce his ter-rors be.

A-wake ye tempests, and his fame In sounds of dreadful praise de-clare; Let the sweet whis-per of his name Fill eve-ry gentle breeze of air.

Wide as his vast do-min-ion lies, Make the Cre-a-tor's name be known, Loud as his thunder shout his praise, And sound it lof-ty as his throne.

Speak of the wonders of that love Which Ga-briel plays on eve-ry chord, From all be-low and all a-bove Loud Hal-le-lu-jahs to the Lord.

METRE VARIOUS. ANTHEM. "Blessed be the Lord God, the God of Israel."

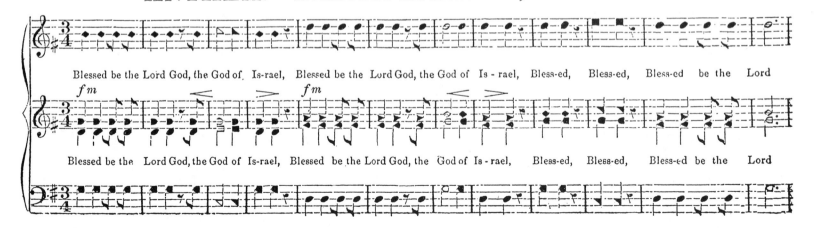

Blessed be the Lord God, the God of Is-rael, Blessed be the Lord God, the God of Is-rael, Bless-ed, Bless-ed, Bless-ed be the Lord

Blessed be the Lord God, the God of Is-rael, Blessed be the Lord God, the God of Is-rael, Bless-ed, Bless-ed, Bless-ed be the Lord

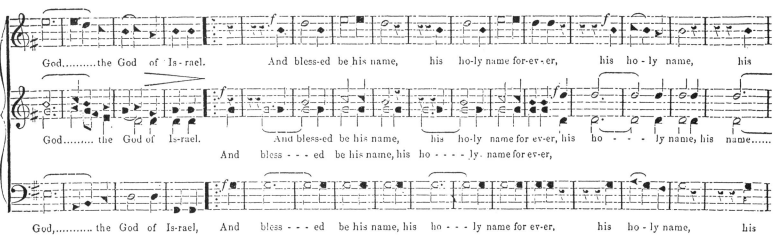

God,........the God of Is-rael. And bless-ed be his name, his ho-ly name for-ev-er, his ho-ly name, his

God,........ the God of Is-rael. And bless-ed be his name, his ho-ly name for ev-er, his ho - - - ly name, his name......

And bless - - - ed be his name, his ho - - - - ly name for ev-er,

God,.......... the God of Is-rael, And bless - - - ed be his name, his ho - - ly name for ev-er, his ho-ly name, his

name for-ev-er, And let the whole earth, and let the whole earth be fill-ed with his glo-ry. A-men, and A-men. A - - men......

name for-ev-er, And let the whole earth, and let the whole earth be fill-ed with his glo-ry. A-men, and A-men. A - - men......

METRE VARIOUS.

THE SABBATH DAY.

A. N. JOHNSON.

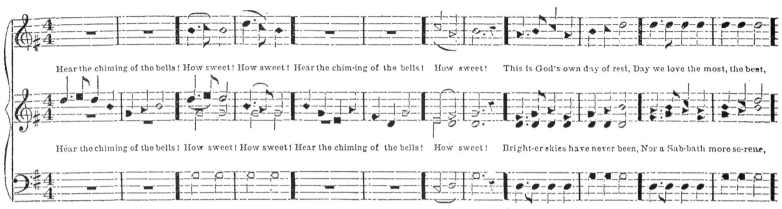

Hear the chiming of the bells! How sweet! How sweet! Hear the chim-ing of the bells!   How sweet!   This is God's own day of rest, Day we love the most, the best,

Hear the chiming of the bells! How sweet! How sweet! Hear the chiming of the bells!   How sweet!   Bright-er skies have never been, Nor a Sab-bath more so-rene,

God has made this Sabbath fair! Heavenly music fills the air;
To God's tem-ple we repair, To the place of praise and prayer,

Oh, what glad-ness fills the breast,   As the bells chime on!   Sweet chimes! Chim-ing of   the bells!   Chime on! Chime on! Chime on!   Chime   on!

Let   us praise the great un - seen While the bells chime on!   Sweet chime! Chim-ing of   the bells!   Chime on! Chime   on! Chime on!   Chime   on!

Hearts are hap - py eve - ry where   As the bells chime on!   Sweet chimes! Chim-ing of   the bells!   Chime on! Chime on! Chime on! Chime   on!
And we'll hum-bly wor - ship there,   As the bells chime on!   Sweet chimes! Chim-ing of   the bells!   Chime on! Chime on! Chime on! Chime   on!

MIDDLETON. 8 lines 7's.

PIA

1 Hail the day that saw him rise Rav-ish'd from our wish-ful eyes: Christ awhile to mortals giv'n, Re-as-cends his na-tive heav'n,

2 Him though high-est heav'n re-ceives, Still he loves the earth he leaves; Tho're-turn-ing to his throne, Still he calls mankind his own;

3 Mas-ter, (may we ev-er say,) Ta-ken from our Head to-day, See, thy faithful servants, see, Ev-er ga-zing up to thee;

4 Ev-er up-ward let us move, Waft-ed on the wings of love, Looking when our Lord shall come, Longing for our blessed home.

CRES

FOR

There the pompous triumph waits; Lift your heads, e-ter-nal gates, Wide unfold the ra-diant scene, Take the King of glo-ry in.

Still for us he in-ter-cedes; Prev-a-lent his death he pleads; Next him-self pre-pares our place, Har-bin-ger of hu-man race.

Grant, tho' part-ed from our sight, High a-bove yon a-zure height, Grant our hearts may thither rise, Fol-lowing thee be-yond the skies.

There we shall with thee re-main, Partners of thine end-less reign; There thy face un-cloud-ed see, Find our heav'n a heav'n in thee.

METRE VARIOUS. # HOLY! LORD GOD OF SABAOTH!

Ho - ly!   Ho - ly!   Ho - ly! Lord God of Sa - ba - oth! Heav'n and earth are full of the maj - es - ty of thy glo - ry!

Ho - ly!   Ho - ly!   Ho - ly! Lord God of Sa - ba - oth! Heav'n and earth are full of the ma - jes - ty of thy glo - ry!

Ho - ly!   Ho - ly!   Ho - ly! Lord God of Sa - ba - oth! Heav'n and earth are full of th ma - jes - ty of thy glo - ry!

Glo - ry be to thee—   Glo - ry be to thee—   Glo - ry be to thee— to thee, O Lord most high.

Glo - ry be to thee—   Glo - ry be to thee— to thee, to thee, O Lord most high.

Glo - ry be to thee—   Glo - ry be to thee— to thee, to thee, O Lord, most high.

REST. S. M.

1 Like No - ah's wea - ry dove, That soar'd the earth a - round, But not a rest - ing place a - bove The cheer-less wa - ters found.

2 O cease, my wander-ing soul, On rest - less wing to roam; All the wide world, to ei - ther pole, Has not for thee a home.

3 Be - hold the ark of God, Be - hold the o - pen door; Has - ten to gain that dear a - bode, And rove, my soul, no more.

4 There safe shalt thou a - bide, There, sweet shall be thy rest, And eve - ry long-ing sat - is - fied, With full sal - va - tion blest.
5 And when the waves of ire, A - gain the earth shall fill, The ark shall ride the sea of fire: Then rest on Si - on's hill.

WOODLAND. 8,6,8,8,6.

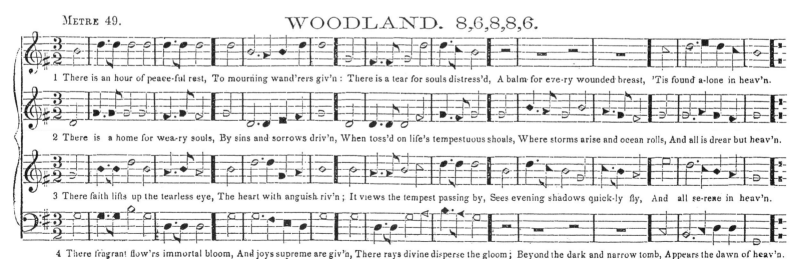

1 There is an hour of peace-ful rest, To mourning wand'rers giv'n: There is a tear for souls distress'd, A balm for eve-ry wounded breast, 'Tis found a-lone in heav'n.

2 There is a home for wea-ry souls, By sins and sorrows driv'n, When toss'd on life's tempestuous shoals, Where storms arise and ocean rolls, And all is drear but heav'n.

3 There faith lifts up the tearless eye, The heart with anguish riv'n; It views the tempest passing by, Sees evening shadows quick-ly fly, And all se-rene in heav'n.

4 There fragrant flow'rs immortal bloom, And joys supreme are giv'n, There rays divine disperse the gloom; Beyond the dark and narrow tomb, Appears the dawn of heav'n.

Metre 63. STREAM OF DEATH. 8,8,4,8,8,4.

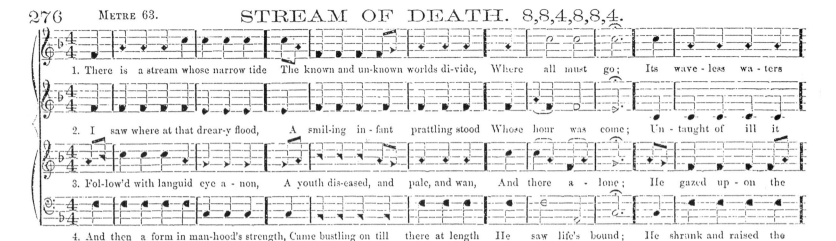

1. There is a stream whose narrow tide The known and un-known worlds di-vide, Where all must go; Its wave-less wa-ters

2. I saw where at that drear-y flood, A smil-ing in-fant prattling stood Whose hour was come; Un-taught of ill it

3. Fol-low'd with languid eye a - non, A youth dis-eased, and pale, and wan, And there a - lone; He gazed up-on the

4. And then a form in man-hood's strength, Came bustling on till there at length He saw life's bound; He shrank and raised the

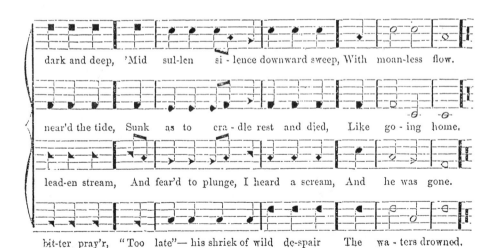

dark and deep, 'Mid sul-len si - lence downward sweep, With moan-less flow.

near'd the tide, Sunk as to cra - dle rest and died, Like go - ing home.

lead-en stream, And fear'd to plunge, I heard a scream, And he was gone.

bit-ter pray'r, "Too late"— his shriek of wild de-spair The wa - ters drowned.

5. Next stood upon the surgeless shore
   A being bowed by many a score
   Of toilsome years;
   Earth-bound and sad he left the bank,
   Back turned his dimming eyes, and sank,
   Ah, full of fears.

6. How bitter must thy waters be,
   O death! how hard a thing, ah me!
   It is to die;
   I mused, when to that stream again,
   Another form of mortal men,
   With smiles drew nigh.

7. "'Tis the last pang," he camly said,
   "To me, O death! thou hast no dread;
   Savior I come!
   Spread but thine arms on yonder shore,
   I see, ye waters, bear me o'er,
   There is my home."

1 Let me go where saints are go-ing To the man-sions of the blest; Let me go where my Re-deem-er Has pre-pared his peo-ple's rest.

2 Let me go where none are wea-ry, Where is raised no wail of woe; Let me go and bathe my spir-it In the rap-tures an-gels know.

3 Let me go, why should I tar-ry What has earth to bind me here? What but cares, and toils, and sorrows? What but death, and pain, and fear?

4 Let me go where tears and sighing are for-ev-er-more un-known, Where the joy-ous songs of glo-ry, Call me to a hap-pier home.

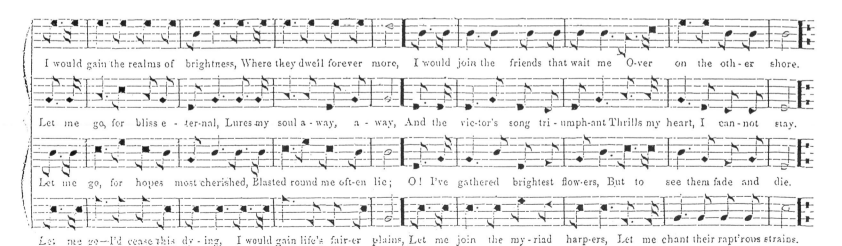

I would gain the realms of brightness, Where they dwell forever more, I would join the friends that wait me O-ver on the oth-er shore.

Let me go, for bliss e-ter-nal, Lures my soul a-way, a-way, And the vic-tor's song tri-umph-ant Thrills my heart, I can-not stay.

Let me go, for hopes most cherished, Blasted round me oft-en lie; O! I've gathered brightest flow-ers, But to see them fade and die.

Let me go—I'd cease this dy-ing, I would gain life's fair-er plains, Let me join the my-riad harp-ers, Let me chant their rapt'rous strains.

METRE 70.

ALBEN. 8's & 5.

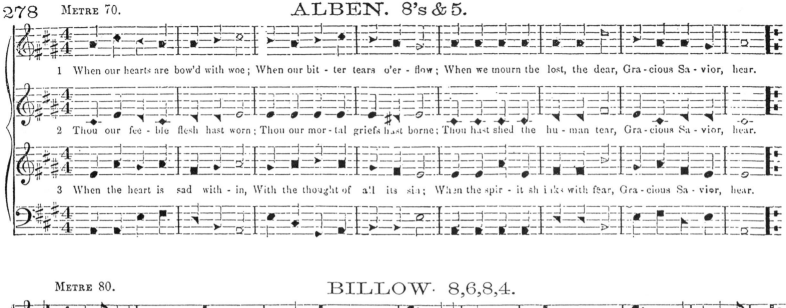

1 When our hearts are bow'd with woe; When our bit - ter tears o'er - flow; When we mourn the lost, the dear, Gra - cious Sa - vior, hear.

2 Thou our fee - ble flesh hast worn; Thou our mor - tal griefs hast borne; Thou hast shed the hu - man tear, Gra - cious Sa - vior, hear.

3 When the heart is sad with - in, With the thought of all its sin; When the spir - it shrinks with fear, Gra - cious Sa - vior, hear.

METRE 80.

BILLOW. 8,6,8,4.

1 Star of peace, to wand'rers weary, Bright the beams that smile on me; Cheer the pilot's vision dreary, Far, far at sea, Cheer the pilot's vis-ion drea-ry, Far, far at sea.

2 Star of hope, gleam on the billow, Bless the soul that sighs for thee; Bless the sailor's lonely pillow, Far, far at sea, Bless the sailors's lonely pil-low, Far, far at sea.

3 Star of faith, when winds are mocking All his toil, he flies to thee; Save him on the billows rocking, Far, far at sea, Save him on the bil-lows rocking, Far, far at sea.

4 Star divine, O safely guide him, Bring the wand'rer home to thee; Sore temptations long have tried him, Far, far at sea, Sore temptations long have tried him, Far, far at sea.

1 Sweet as the shepherd's tune-ful reed, From Zi-.........-on's mount I heard the sound; Gay sprang the flow'rets of the mead,

2 Peace, troubled soul, whose plaintive moan, Hath taught...... these rocks the notes...... of woe; Cease thy complaint, suppress thy groan,

3 Come, free-ly come, by sin op-press'd, Un - bur -.......... den here the weight - y load, Here find thy ref-uge and thy rest,

4 As spring the winter, day the night, Peace, sor -......... row, gloom hath chased a - way, And smiling joy, a ser -aph bright,

And glad-.........den'd na - ture smil'd a - round; The voice of peace sa - lutes mine ear, Christ's love-.........-ly voice per-fumes the air.

And let........... thy tears for-get to flow; Be - hold the pre-cious balm is found, To lull thy pain, to heal thy wound.

Safe on........ the bo - som of thy God! Thy God's thy Sa - vior, glo - rious word, That sheathes...... th' A-veng-er's glitt'ring sword.

Shall tend thy steps and near thee stay; While glo - ry weaves th' im-mor-tal crown, And waits to claim thee for her own.

Metre 2.

ARCHDALE. C. M.

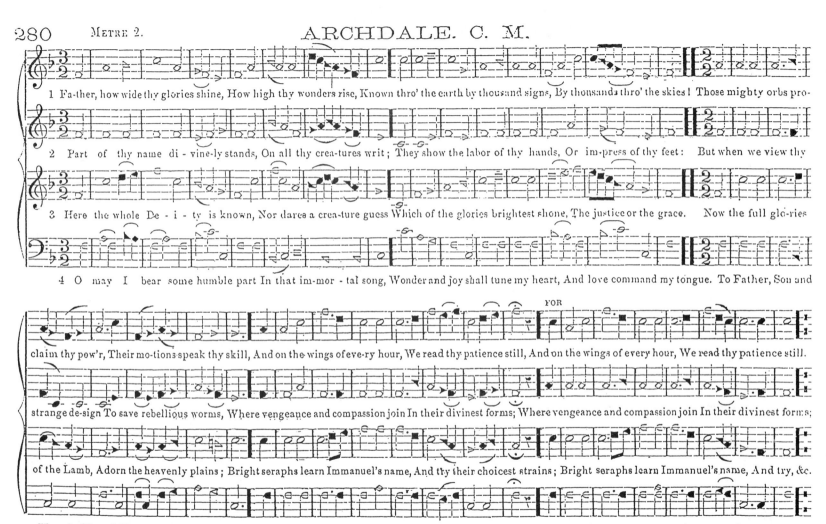

1 Fa-ther, how wide thy glories shine, How high thy wonders rise, Known thro' the earth by thousand signs, By thousands thro' the skies ! Those mighty orbs pro-

2 Part of thy name di-vine-ly stands, On all thy crea-tures writ ; They show the labor of thy hands, Or im-press of thy feet: But when we view thy

3 Here the whole De-i-ty is known, Nor dares a crea-ture guess Which of the glories brightest shone, The justice or the grace. Now the full glo-ries

4 O may I bear some humble part In that im-mor-tal song, Wonder and joy shall tune my heart, And love command my tongue. To Father, Son and

claim thy pow'r, Their mo-tions-speak thy skill, And on the-wings of eve-ry hour, We read thy patience still, And on the wings of every hour, We read thy patience still.

strange de-sign To save rebellious worms, Where vengeance and compassion join In their divinest forms; Where vengeance and compassion join In their divinest forms;

of the Lamb, Adorn the heavenly plains ; Bright seraphs learn Immanuel's name, And try their choicest strains ; Bright seraphs learn Immanuel's name, And try, &c.

Ho-ly Ghost, Who sweet-ly all a-gree To save a world of sin-ners lost, E-ter-nal glo-ry be; To save a world of sinners lost, E-ter-nal glo-ry be.

1 Watchman! tell us of the night, What its sings of promise are? Trav'ler! o'er yon mountain's height, See the glory-beaming Star! Watchman! does its beauteous ray

2 Watchman! tell us of the night? High - er yet that star ascends; Trav'ler! blessedness and light, Peace and truth its course portends; Watchman, will its beams alone

3 Watchman! tell us of the night? For the morning seems to dawn; Trav'ler! darkness takes its flight, Doubt and terror are withdrawn; Watchman! let thy wand'rings cease,

CHORUS

Aught of hope or joy fore-tell? Trav'ler! yes, it brings the day, Prom-ise'd day of Is - ra - el!   Trav'ler! yes, it brings the day, Prom-is'd day of Is - ra - el.

Gild the spot that gave them birth? Trav'ler! a-ges are its own, See! it bursts o'er all the earth!   Trav'ler! a-ges are its own, See! it bursts o'er all the earth.

Hie thee to thy qui-et home; Trav'ler! lo! the Prince of Peace, Lo! the Son of God is come.   Trav'ler! Lo! the Prince of Peace, Lo! the Son of God is come.

METRE 65.

THE CHARIOT. 11,12,12 12.

1 The cha-riot! The cha-riot! its wheels roll in fire, As the Lord com-eth down in the pomp of his ire; Lo! self-mov-ing it drives on its path-way of cloud,

2 The glo-ry! The glo-ry! a-round him are pour'd Mighty hosts of the an-gels that wait on the Lord; And the glo-ri-fied saints and the mar-tyrs are there,

3 The trump-et! The trump-et! the dead have all heard: Lo! the depths of the stone-cover'd charnel are stirr'd; From the sea, from the earth, from the south, from the north,

4 The judgment! The judgment! the thrones are all set, Where the Lamb and the white-vested elders are met; There all flesh is at once in the sight of the Lord,

METRE 66.

THE ROYAL PROCLAMATION. 8,8,8,8,8,8,3.

And the heav'ns with the burden of Godhead are bow'd.

And there all who the palm-wreaths of vic-to-ry wear.

All the vast gen-e-ra-tions of man-are come forth.

And the doom of e-ter-ni-ty hangs on his word.

1 Hear the roy-al proc-la-ma-tion, The glad ti-dings of sal-va-tion,

2 See the roy-al ban-ner fly-ing, Hear the her-alds loud-ly cry-ing,

3 Turn un-to the Lord most ho-ly, Shun the paths of vice and fol-ly,

4 Here is wine, and milk, and hon-ey, Come and pur-chase with-out mon-ey,

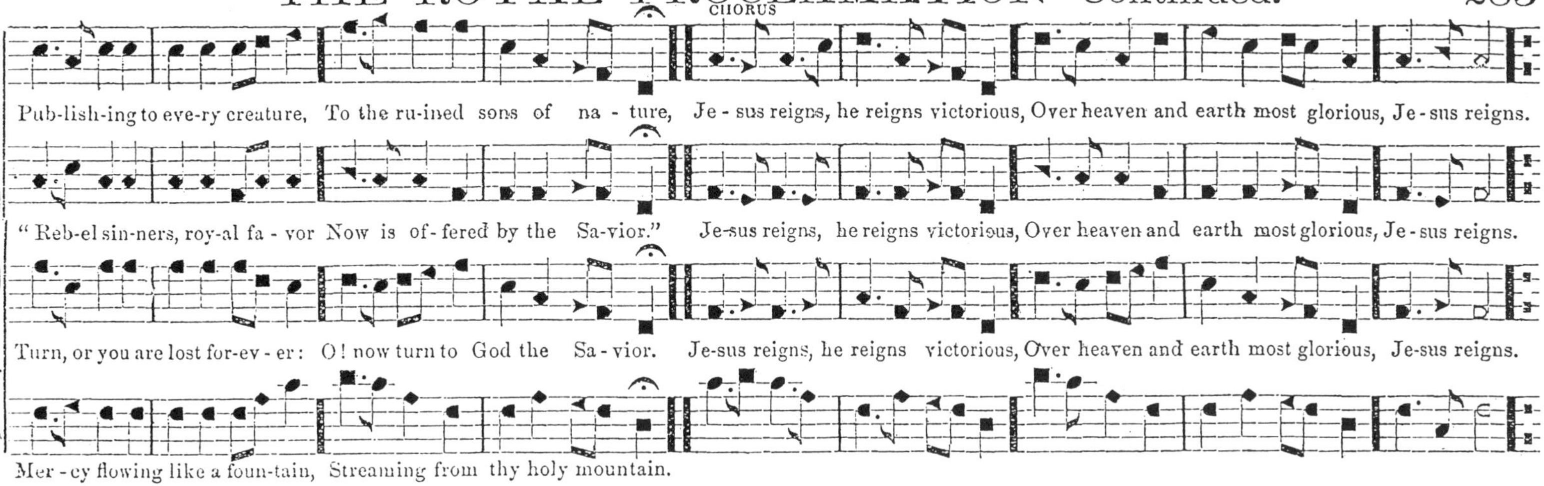

Metre 2.

WOODSTOCK. C. M.

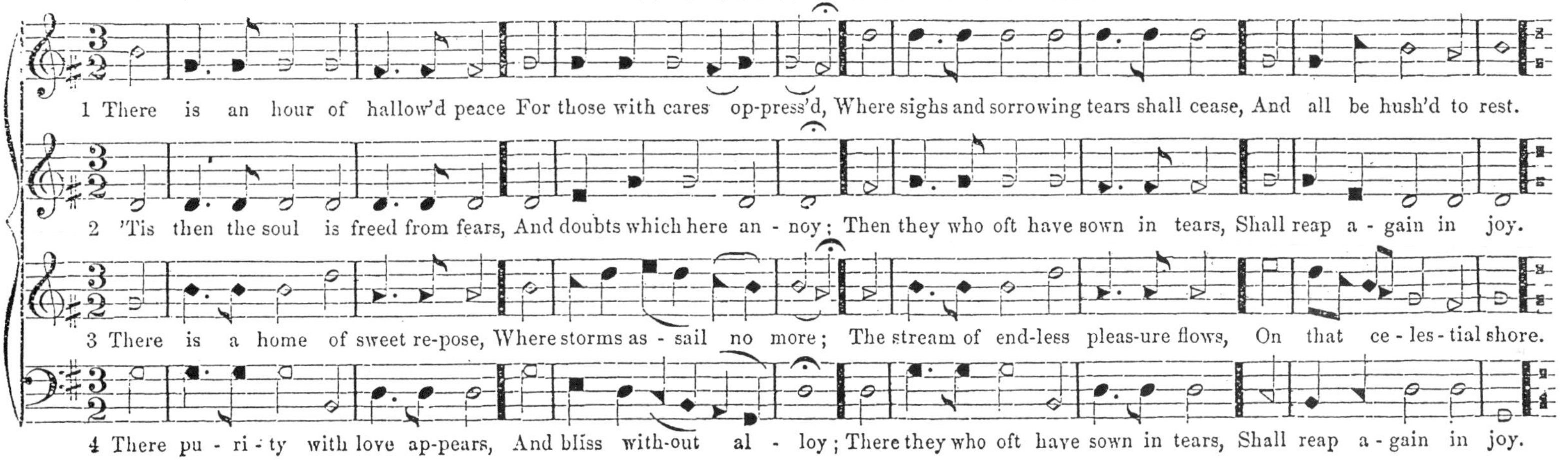

Metre 2.

COMMUNION. C. M.

1 How sweet and aw-ful   is the place, With Christ with-in the doors, } Here eve-ry bow-el of our God, With soft com-pas-sion rolls,......
While ev-er-last-ing   love dis-plays The choic-est of her stores;

2 While all our hearts and all our songs Join to ad-mire the feast, } Why was I made to hear thy voice, And enter while there's room,
Each of us cry   with thank-ful tongues, Lord, why was I   a guest?

3 'Twas the same love that spread the feast, That sweet-ly forced us in, }
Else we had still   re-fused to taste, And per-ish'd in   our sin. } Pit-y the na-tions, O our God! Constrain the earth to come,

Here peace and pardon bought with blood, Is food for dy-ing souls.

When thousands make a wretched choice, And rath-er starve than come.

Send thy vic-to-rious word a-broad, And bring the strangers home.

Metre 2.

FELICITY. C. M.

1 Earth has engross'd my love too long, 'Tis time I lift mine eyes Upward, dear Father,

2 Ser-aphs with el-e-va-ted strains, Circle the throne around! And move and charm the

3 Hark! how beyond the narrow bounds Of time and space they run; And ech-o in ma-

4 O sac-red beau-ties of the man, (The God re-sides with-in:) His flesh all pure with-
5 Then all at once to living strains, They summon eve-ry chord; Tell how he triumph'd

to thy throne, And to my native skies; There the blest Man, my Savior, sits, The God how bright he shines, And scatters in-fin-ite delight On all the happy minds.

starry plains, With an immortal sound, Jesus the Lord their harps employs; Jesus my love, they sing; Jesus the life of both our joys, Sounds sweet from every string.

jes-tic sounds, The God-head of the Son! And now they sink the lofty tune, And gentler notes they play; And bring the Father's Equal down, To dwell in humble clay.

out a stain; His soul without a sin: But when to Calvary they turn, Silent their harps a-bide; Suspended songs a moment mourn The God that lov'd and died.
o'er his pains, And chant the rising Lord. Now let me mount and join their song, And be an angel too: My heart, my hand, my ear, my tongue, Here's joyful work for you.

Metre 67.

GOD IS LOVE. 6,5,6,5,3.

1 Lo, the heav'ns are break-ing, Pure and bright a-bove; Life and light a - - wak - - ing, Mur-mur, God is Love, God is Love.

2 Round yon pine-clad mountain, Flows a gold - en flood; Hear the spark-ling foun - - tain, Whis-pers, God is good, God is good.

3 See the stream-let bound-ing Through the vale and wood, Hear its rip - ples sound - - ing, Mur-mur, God is good, God is good.

4 Mu - sic now is ring - ing Through the sha-dy grove, Feath-ered songs-ters sing - - ing, War - ble, God is Love, God is Love.
5 Wake, my heart, and springing, Spread thy wings a-broad; Soar - ing still and sing - - ing, God is ev - er good, Ev - er good.

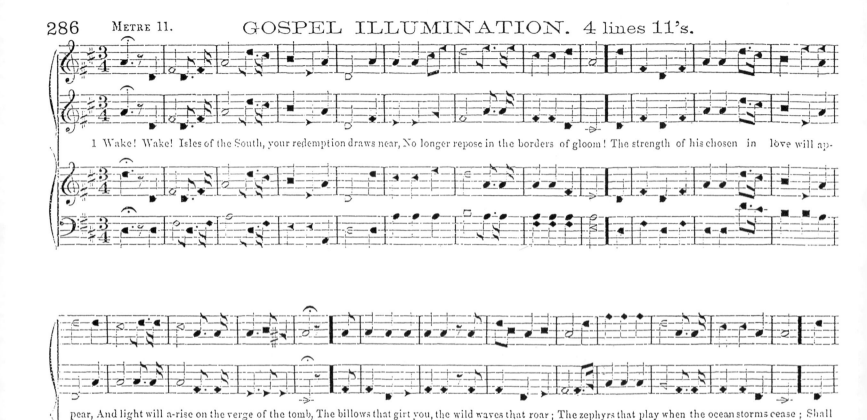

1 Wake! Wake! Isles of the South, your redemption draws near, No longer repose in the borders of gloom! The strength of his chosen in love will ap-

pear, And light will a-rise on the verge of the tomb, The billows that girt you, the wild waves that roar; The zephyrs that play when the ocean storms cease; Shall

waft the glad sound to your des - o - late shore, Shall waft the glad tidings of pardon and peace—Shall waft the glad tidings of pardon and peace. The heathen will hasten to

welcome the time: The day-spring the prophet in vis - ion once saw; When the beams of Mes-si - ah will il - lu - mine each clime, And the isles of the o-cean will

wait for his law, And the isles of the o-cean will wait for his law. On the regions that sit in the darkness of night, The land of de-spair to ob-liv-ion a prey;

The morn-ing will o-pen with heal-ing and light, The glad Star of Beth-le-hem will bright-en to-day, The glad Star of Beth-le-hem will bright-en to-day.

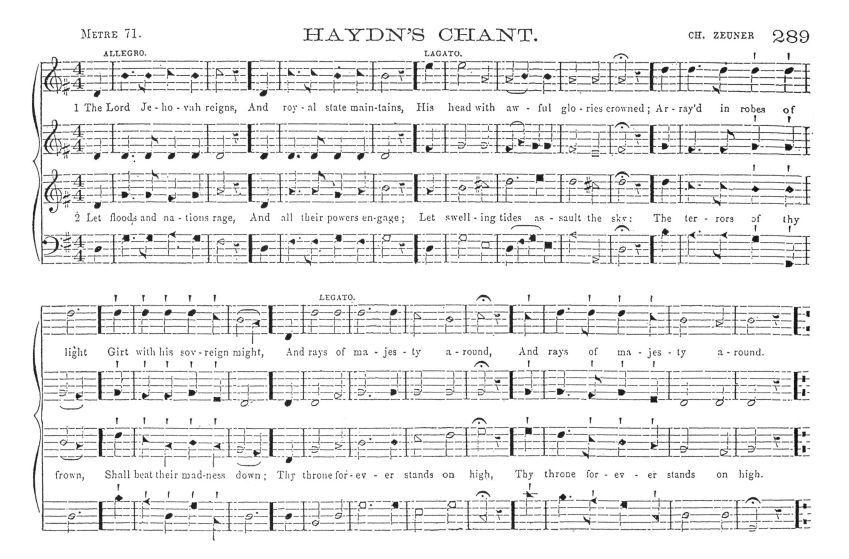

1 The Lord Je-ho-vah reigns, And roy-al state main-tains, His head with aw-ful glo-ries crowned; Ar-ray'd in robes of

2 Let floods and na-tions rage, And all their powers en-gage; Let swell-ing tides as-sault the sky: The ter-rors of thy

light Girt with his sov-reign might, And rays of ma-jes-ty a-round, And rays of ma-jes-ty a-round.

frown, Shall beat their mad-ness down; Thy throne for-ev-er stands on high, Thy throne for-ev-er stands on high.

DEDICATION ANTHEM.

Praise God from whom all bless - ings flow, Praise him, all crea - tures here be - low, Praise him, all crea - tures here be - low;

Praise God, from whom all blessings flow, Praise him all creatures here be-low, Praise him, all crea - tures here be - low;

Praise God, from whom all bless - ings flow, Praise him, all crea - tures here be - low, Praise him, all crea - tures here be - low;

Praise God, from whom all blessings flow, Praise him, all creatures here be - low, Praise him, all crea - tures here be - low.

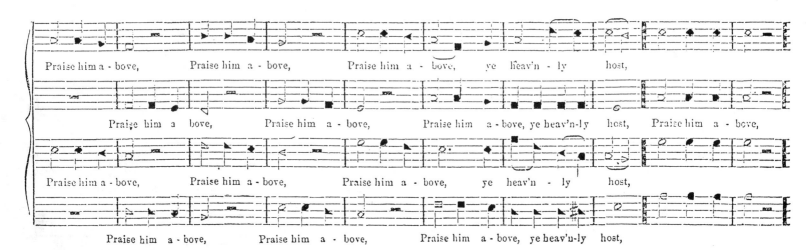

Praise him a - bove, Praise him a - bove, Praise him a - bove, ye heav'n - ly host,

Praise him a - bove, Praise him a - bove, Praise him a - bove, ye heav'n-ly host, Praise him a - bove,

Praise him a - bove, Praise him a - bove, Praise him a - bove, ye heav'n - ly host,

Praise him a - bove, Praise him a - bove, Praise him a - bove, ye heav'n-ly host,

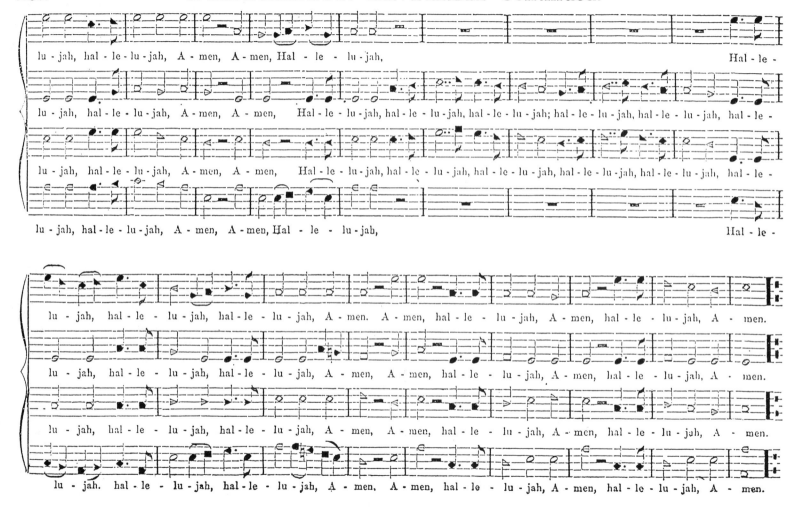

What shall I ren-der un-to the Lord, For all his ben-e-fits toward me? I will take the cup, the cup of sal-va-tion,

What shall I ren-der un-to the Lord, For all his ben-e-fits toward me? I will take the cup, the cup of sal-va-tion,

What shall I ren-der un-to the Lord, For all his ben-e-fits to-ward me? I will take the cup, the cup of sal-va-tion,

And call up-on the name of the Lord. I will pay my vows, will pay my vows unto the Lord, Now in the pres-ence of all his people,

And call up-on the name of the Lord. I will pay my vows, will pay my vows unto the Lord, Now in the pres-ence of all his people,

And call up-on the name of the Lord. I will pay my vows, will pay my vows unto the Lord, Now in the pres-ence of all his people,

In the courts of the Lord's house, In the courts of the Lord's house, In the midst of thee, O Je-ru-sa-lem. Praise ye the Lord.

In the courts of the Lord's house, In the courts of the Lord's house, In the midst of thee, O Je-ru-sa-lem. Praise ye the Lord.

METRE VARIOUS. CHORUS-ANTHEM: "Praise the God of Israel."

Praise the God of Israel, glo-ri-fy his name; of his sal-va-tion, of his sal-va-tion, of his sal-va-tion from day to day,

Praise the God of Israel, glo-ri-fy his name, of his sal-va-tion, of his sal-va-tion, of his sal-va-tion from day to day,

Praise the God of Israel, glo-ri-fy his name, Be telling of his sal-va-tion, Be telling of his sal-va-tion, Be telling of his sal-va-tion from day to day,

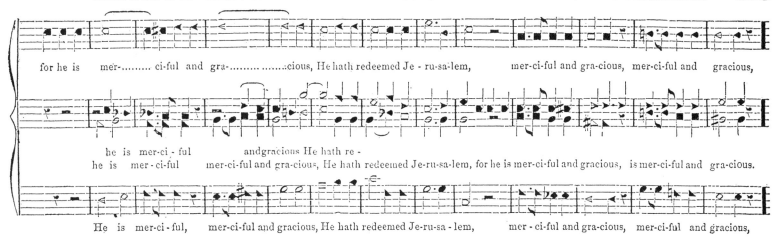

for he is mer-......... ci-ful and gra-............:cious, He hath redeemed Je - ru-sa-lem, mer-ci-ful and gra-cious, mer-ci-ful and gracious,

he is mer-ci - ful andgracious He hath re -

he is mer-ci-ful mer-ci-ful and gra-cious, He hath redeemed Je-ru-sa-lem, for he is mer-ci-ful and gracious, is mer-ci-ful and gra-cious.

He is mer-ci - ful, mer-ci-ful and gracious, He hath redeemed Je-ru-sa - lem, mer - ci-ful and gra-cious, mer-ci-ful and gracious,

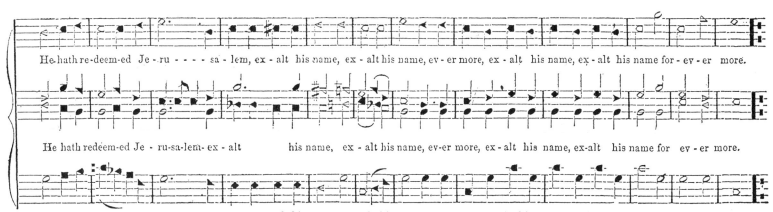

He hath re-deem-ed Je - ru - - - - sa - lem, ex - alt his name, ex - alt his name, ev - er more, ex - alt his name, ex - alt his name for - ev - er more.

He hath redeem-ed Je - ru-sa-lem- ex - alt his name, ex - alt his name, ev-er more, ex-alt his name, ex-alt his name for ev - er more.

He hath re-deem-ed Je - ru - - - sa - lem, ex - alt his name, ex - alt his name ev-er more, ex-alt his name, ex-alt his name for - ev - er more.

METRE VARIOUS.

HEAVENLY VISION.

I be – held and lo! a great mul-ti-tude which no man could num-ber, Thous-ands of thousands, and ten thousand times ten thousand, Thousands of chousands, and ten thousand times ten

thous – and, Stood be – fore the Lamb, And they had palms in their hands ; And they rest not day nor night, say-ing, ho – ly, ho – ly, ho – ly, Lord God Al – might – y, Which

was, and is, and is to come, Which was and is, and is to come. And I heard a might-y an-gel fly - - - - - - - ing through the midst of heav'n,

Say-ing with a loud voice, woe, woe, woe, woe - - - - - - be un-to the earth by reas-on of the trump-et which is yet to sound,

And when the last trump-et sound-ed, The great men and no-bles, rich men and poor, Bond and free, gath - ered themselves to-geth - er, and cri - ed to the rocks and mountains to fall up-

on them and hide them from the face of him that sit-teth on the throne, For the great day of his wrath is come, And who shall be a-ble to stand? And who shall be a - ble to stand?

METRE 2.

PISGAH. C. M.

1. When I can read my ti-tle clear To man-sions in the skies, I'll bid farewell to eve-ry fear, And wipe my weeping eyes,

2. Should earth a-gainst my soul en-gage, And hell-ish darts be hurled, Then I can smile at Sa-tan's rage, And face a frowning world;

3. Let cares like a wild del-uge come, And storms of sor-row fall, May I but safe-ly reach my home, My God, my heav'n, my all,

4. There shall I bathe my wea-ry soul In seas of heav'n-ly rest, And not a wave of trou-ble roll, Across my peaceful breast;

And wipe my weep-ing eyes, And wipe my weep-ing eyes; I'll bid fare-well to eve-ry fear, And wipe my weep-ing eyes.

And face a frown-ing world, And face a frown-ing world, Then I can smile at Sa-tan's rage, And face a frown-ing world.

My God, my heav'n, my all, My God, my heav'n, my all, May I but safe-ly reach my home, My God, my heav'n, my all.

A-cross my peace-ful breast; A-cross my peace-ful breast; And not a wave of trou-ble roll A-cross my peace-ful breast.

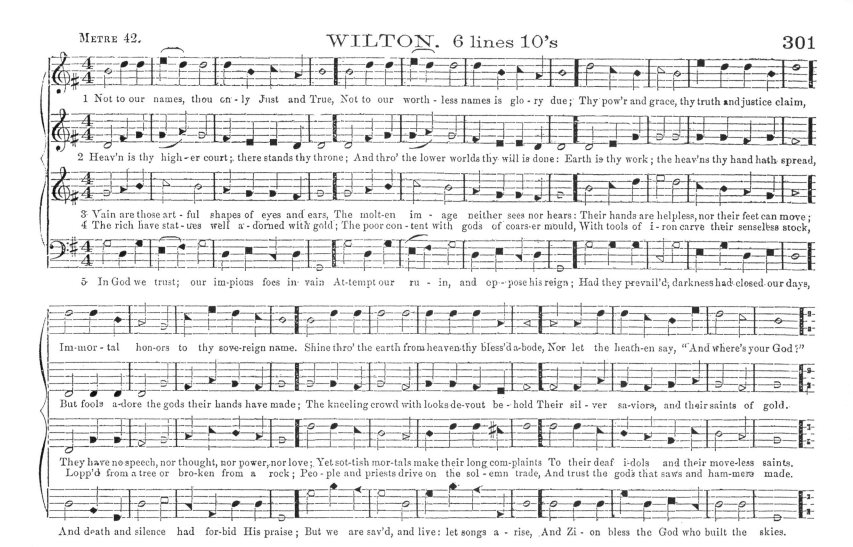

1 Not to our names, thou on-ly Just and True, Not to our worth-less names is glo-ry due; Thy pow'r and grace, thy truth and justice claim,

2 Heav'n is thy high-er court; there stands thy throne; And thro' the lower worlds thy will is done: Earth is thy work; the heav'ns thy hand hath spread,

3 Vain are those art-ful shapes of eyes and ears, The molt-en im-age neither sees nor hears: Their hands are helpless, nor their feet can move;
4 The rich have stat-ues well a-dorned with gold; The poor con-tent with gods of coars-er mould, With tools of i-ron carve their senseless stock,

5 In God we trust; our im-pious foes in vain At-tempt our ru-in, and op-pose his reign; Had they prevail'd, darkness had closed our days,

Im-mor-tal hon-ors to thy sove-reign name. Shine thro' the earth from heaven thy bless'd a-bode, Nor let the heath-en say, "And where's your God?"

But fools a-dore the gods their hands have made; The kneeling crowd with looks de-vout be-hold Their sil-ver sa-viors, and their saints of gold.

They have no speech, nor thought, nor power, nor love; Yet sot-tish mor-tals make their long com-plaints To their deaf i-dols and their move-less saints.
Lopp'd from a tree or bro-ken from a rock; Peo-ple and priests drive on the sol-emn trade, And trust the gods that saws and ham-mers made.

And death and silence had for-bid His praise; But we are sav'd, and live: let songs a-rise, And Zi-on bless the God who built the skies.

302

METRE 2.

RESIGNATION. C. M.

1 And let this fee-ble bo-dy fail, And let it faint or die; Shall join the dis-em-bo-died saints, And find its long-sought rest,
My soul shall quit this mournful vale, And soar to worlds on high;

2 In hope of that im-mor-tal crown, I now the cross sus-tain; I'll suf-fer on my three-score years, Till my de-liv'r-er come,
And glad-ly wan-der up and down; And smile at toil and pain;

3 Oh! what hath Je-sus bought for me! Be-fore my ravish'd eyes I see a world of spir-its bright, Who taste the pleasures there—
Riv-ers of life di-vine I see, And trees of Par-a-dise;

(That on-ly bliss for which it pants,) In the Redeemer's breast.

And wipe a-way his ser-vant's tears, And take his ex-ile home.

They all are robed in spot-less white, And conq'ring palms they bear.

METRE 2.

LINGHAM. C. M.

1 O for a thou-sand tongues to sing, My great Redeemer's praise,

2 My gra-cious Mas-ter and my God, As-sist me to pro-claim,

3 Je-sus the name that calms our fears, That bids our sorrows cease,

4 He breaks the pow'r of can-cell'd sin, He sets the pris'ner free;

My great Redeemer's praise; The glories of my God and King, The triumphs of, The triumphs of his grace, The triumphs of his grace, The triumphs of his grace.

As-sist me to pro-claim, To spread thro' all the earth a-broad, The honors of, the honors of thy name, The honors of thy name, The hon - ors of thy name.

That bids our sorrows cease; 'Tis mu-sic in the sin-ner's ears, 'Tis life, and health, 'Tis life, and health and peace, 'Tis life, and health and peace, 'Tis life, and health and peace.

He sets the pris'ner free; His blood can make the foul - est clean— His blood avails, His blood avails for me, His blood avails for me, His blood a - vails for me.

Metre 2.

ZERAH. C. M.

1 To us a Child of hope is born, To us a Son is giv'n; Him shall the tribes of earth obey, Him all the hosts of heav'n, Him shall the tribes of earth obey, Him all the hosts of heav'n.

2 His name shall be the Prince of Peace, For evermore adored, The Wonderful, the Counsellor, The great and mighty Lord, The Wonderful, the Counsellor, The great, &c.

3 His pow'r increasing, still shall spread; His reign no end shall know, Justice shall guard his throne above, And peace abound below. Justice shall guard, &c., And peace, &c.

4 To us a Child of hope is born, To us a Son is giv'n—The Wonderful the Counsellor, Thy mighty Lord of heav'n, The Wonderful, the Counsellor, The mighty Lord of heav'n.

METRE VARIOUS.

EASTER ANTHEM.

The Lord is ris'n in-deed! Hal - - le - lu -jah! The Lord is ris'n in-deed! Hal - le - lu -jah! Now is Christ

risen from the dead, and become the first fruits of them that slept, Now is Christ risen from the dead and become the first fruits of them that slept. Hal-le-lu-jah! Hal-le-lu-jah!

And did he rise? And did he rise?

He rose, he rose,

Hal - le - lu - jah! And did he rise? And did he rise? Did he rise? Hear it, ye nations, hear it, O ye dead!

He

And did he rise?......... And did he rise?........

He rose, He rose,

rose, He rose: He burst the bars of death, He burst the bars of death, He burst the bars of death, And triumph'd o'er the grave. Then, Then, Then I rose, Then I rose,

Then I rose, Then I rose; Then first hu-man-i-ty tri-umph-ant pass'd the crystal ports of light, And seized e - ter - nal youth. Man, all immortal,

hail! hail! heav-en all lav-ish of strange gifts to man, Thine all the glory, Man's the boundless bliss, Thine all the glo - ry, Man's the boundless bliss.

JORDAN. C. M.

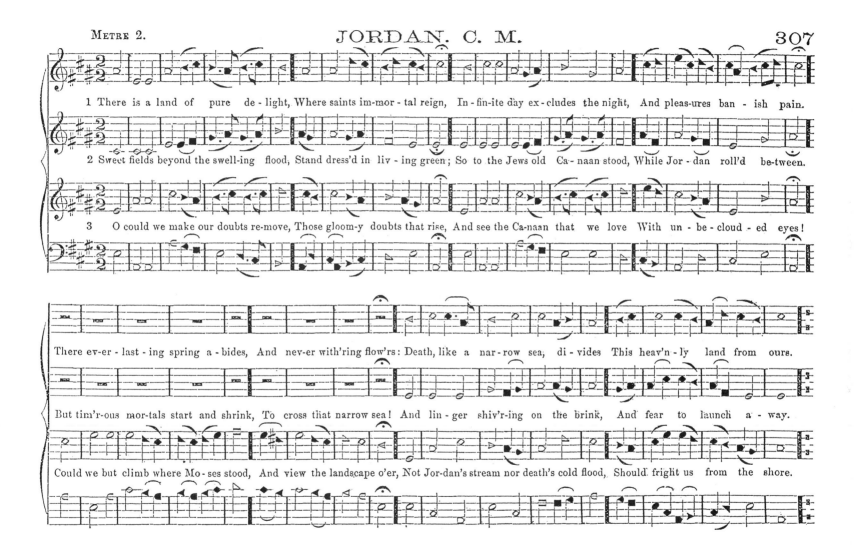

1 There is a land of pure de-light, Where saints im-mor-tal reign, In-fin-ite day ex-cludes the night, And pleas-ures ban-ish pain.

2 Sweet fields beyond the swell-ing flood, Stand dress'd in liv-ing green; So to the Jews old Ca-naan stood, While Jor-dan roll'd be-tween.

3 O could we make our doubts re-move, Those gloom-y doubts that rise, And see the Ca-naan that we love With un-be-cloud-ed eyes!

There ev-er-last-ing spring a-bides, And nev-er with'r-ing flow'rs: Death, like a nar-row sea, di-vides This heav'n-ly land from ours.

But tim'r-ous mor-tals start and shrink, To cross that narrow sea! And lin-ger shiv'r-ing on the brink, And fear to launch a-way.

Could we but climb where Mo-ses stood, And view the landscape o'er, Not Jor-dan's stream nor death's cold flood, Should fright us from the shore.

308   METRE 1.   PARTING HAND. L. M.   D. C.

1 My Christian friends, in bonds of love, Whose hearts in sweetest union join, }
  Your friendship's like a drawing band, Yet we must take the parting hand. }   Your company's sweet, your union dear, Your words de-light-ful to my ear;
  D. C. Yet when I see that we must part, You draw like chords around my heart.

2 How sweet the hours have passed away Since we have met to sing and pray; }
  How loathe we are to leave the place Where Jesus shows his smiling face. }   O could I stay with friends so kind, How would it cheer my drooping mind,
  D. C. But du-ty makes me understand, That we must take the parting hand.

3 And since it is God's holy will,   My youthful friends, in Christian ties, 4 How oft I've seen your flowing tears,   And now, my friends, both old and young,
  We must be parted for a while,   Who seek for mansions in the skies,   And heard you tell your hopes and fears,   I hope in Christ you'll still go on ;
  In sweet submission all as one,   Fight on, we'll gain the happy shore,   Your hearts with love were seen to flame,   And if on earth we meet no more,
  We'll say, our Father's will be done.   Where parting will be known no more.   Which makes me hope we'll meet again.   O may we meet on Canaan's shore.

METRE 10.   WURTEMBURG. 10,10,11,11.

1 O praise ye the Lord, prepare a new song,   And let all his saints In full concert join: With voic-es u-ni-ted, the anthem prolong,

3 Be joyful, ye saints, sus-tain'd by his might, And let your glad songs a-wake with each morn,   For those who o-bey him are still his de-light;

And show forth his praises in music divine. Let praise to the Lord who made us, as-cend; Let each grate-ful heart be glad in its King, Let each grateful

His hand with salvation the meek will adorn. Then praise ye the Lord, prepare a new song, And let all his saints in full concert join, And let all his

heart be glad in its King; The God whom we worship our songs will attend, And view with complacence the off'rings we bring, And view with complacence, &c.

saints in full concert join; With voices u-ni-ted the anthem prolong, And show forth his praises in music divine. And show forth his praises in music divine.

METRE 2.

SALVATION. C. M.

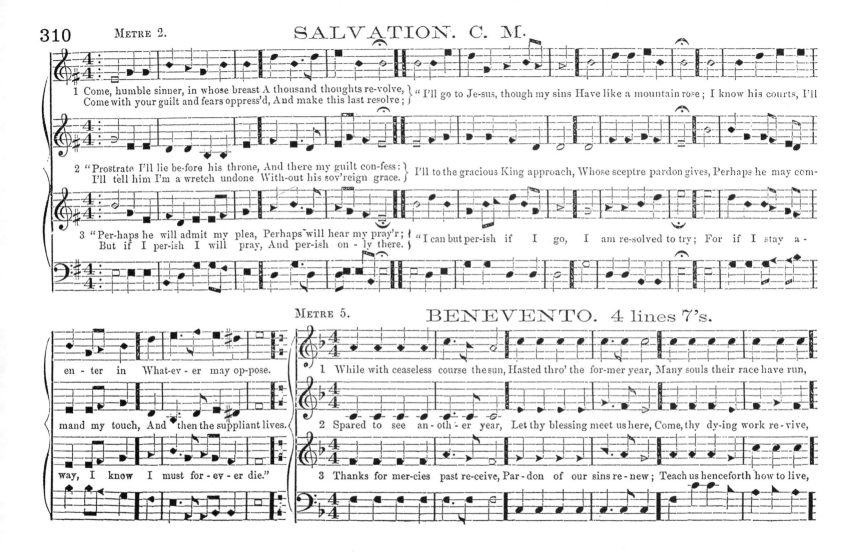

1 Come, humble sinner, in whose breast A thousand thoughts re-volve,
Come with your guilt and fears oppress'd, And make this last resolve; } "I'll go to Je-sus, though my sins Have like a mountain rose; I know his courts, I'll

2 "Prostrate I'll lie be-fore his throne, And there my guilt con-fess:
I'll tell him I'm a wretch undone With-out his sov'reign grace. } I'll to the gracious King approach, Whose sceptre pardon gives, Perhaps he may com-

3 "Per-haps he will admit my plea, Perhaps will hear my pray'r;
But if I per-ish I will pray, And per-ish on-ly there. } "I can but per-ish if I go, I am re-solved to try; For if I stay a-

METRE 5.

BENEVENTO. 4 lines 7's.

en - ter in What-ev - er may op-pose.

mand my touch, And then the suppliant lives.

way, I know I must for-ev-er die."

1 While with ceaseless course the sun, Hasted thro' the for-mer year, Many souls their race have run,

2 Spared to see an-oth-er year, Let thy blessing meet us here, Come, thy dy-ing work re-vive,

3 Thanks for mer-cies past re-ceive, Par-don of our sins re-new; Teach us henceforth how to live,

Nev - er more to meet us here; Fix'd in an e-ter-nal state, They have done with all below; We a lit - tle lon - ger wait; But how lit - tle none can know.

Bid thy drooping garden thrive; Sun of Righteousness, arise! Warm our hearts and bless our eyes; Let our prayer thy pity move; Make this year a time of love.

With e - ter - ni - ty in view; Bless thy word to old and young, Fill us with a Savior's love; When our life's short race is run, May we dwell with thee a-bove.

METRE 2.

BROWN. C. M.

1 Come, let us join our friends a-bove, Who have ob-tain'd the prize, And on the ea-gle wings of love, To joys ce - les - tial rise.

2 Let saints be - low in con-cert sing With those to glo-ry gone, For all the ser-vants of our King In heav'n and earth are one.

3 One fam - i - ly,—we dwell in him; One Church a-bove, be-neath, Though now di - vi - ded by the stream, The nar-row stream of death.

4 One ar - my of the liv - ing God, To his commands we bow; Part of the host have cross'd the flood, And part are cross-ing- now.
5 Dear Sa-vior! be our constant Guide, Then, when the word is giv'n, Bid Jordan's nar-row stream di - vide, And land us safe in heaven.

METRE 5.

THE THREE MOUNTAINS. 4 lines 7's.

1 When on Si-nai's top I see, God de-scend in ma-jes-ty To pro-claim his ho-ly law, All my spir-it sinks with awe.

2 When in ec-sta-cy sub-lime, Ta-bor's glo-rious steep I climb, At the too trans-port-ing light, Dark-ness rush-es o'er my sight.

3 When on Cal-va-ry I rest, God in flesh made man-i-fest, Shines in my Re-deem-er's face, Full of beau-ty, truth and grace.

4 Here I would for-ev-er stay, Weep and gaze my soul a-way; Thou art heav'n on earth to me, Love-ly, mourn-ful Cal-va-ry.

METRE 4.

MOUNT VERNON. 8,7,8,7.

1 Sis-ter, thou wast mild and love-ly, Gen-tle as the sum-mer breeze, Pleas-ant as the air of eve-ning When it floats a-mong the trees.

2 Peace-ful be thy si-lent slum-ber, Peace-ful in the grave so low; Thou no more wilt join our num-ber, Thou no more our songs shalt know.

3 Dear-est sis-ter, thou hast left us, Here thy loss we deep-ly feel, But 'tis God that hath be-reft us, He can all our sor-rows heal.

4 Yet a-gain we hope to meet thee, When the day of life is fled; Then in heav'n with joy to greet thee, Where no farewell tear is shed.

Metre 2.

ZION'S LIGHT. C. M.

1 That glo-rious day is draw-ing nigh, When Zi-on's light shall come;
She shall a - rise and shine on high, Bright as the morn-ing sun: } The north and south their sons re-sign, And earth's foun-da-tions bend;

2 The King who wears the splen-did crown, The a-zure's fla-ming bow;
The ho - ly cit - y shall bring down, To bless his church be-low; } When Zi-on's bleed-ing, conq'ring King, Shall sin and death de-stroy,

Metre 2.

Cloth'd as a bride, Je - ru - sa - lem All glo-rious shall de-scend.

The morn-ing stars shall join to sing, And Zi - on shout for joy.

CALVARY. C. M.

1 My thoughts that oft - en mount the skies, Go search the world be-neath,

2 The ty-rant, how he tri-umphs here, His tro-phies spread a-round!

3 These skulls, what ghast-ly fig - ures now! How loathe-some to the eyes!

4 But where the souls, those deathless things That left that dy-ing clay!

Where na-ture all in ru-in lies, Where na-ture all in ru-in lies, And owns,......... And owns,............ And owns................ her sov'reign, Death.

And heaps of dust and bones appear, And heaps of dust and bones appear, Thro' all,.......... Thro' all,............ Thro' all................ the hol-low ground.

These are the heads we lately knew, These are the heads we lately knew, So beau-........... So beau-........... So beau-................ -teous and so wise.

My thoughts, now stretch out all your wings, My thoughts, now stretch out all your wings, And trace, And trace, And trace.................. e - ter-ni-ty.

METRE VARIOUS.   DISMISSION ANTHEM.

1 Lord, dis-miss us with thy bless-ing, Bid us all de-part in peace; Still on gos-pel man-na feed-ing, Pure se-raph-ic love increase; Fill each breast with

con - so - la tion, Up to thee our voic-es raise, When we reach that blissful station, Then we'll give thee nobler praise, Then we'll, &c., And we'll sing hallelujah! Amen, halle-

lu-jah! And we'll sing hal-le-lu-jah, A-men, hallelujah, to God and the Lamb, Hal-le-lu-jah for-ev - er, Hal-le-lu-jah for - ev - er, Hal-le-lu-jah for - ev - er and ev-er, A - men.

316   METRE 4.

FAREWELL. 8,7,8,7,8,7,8,7.

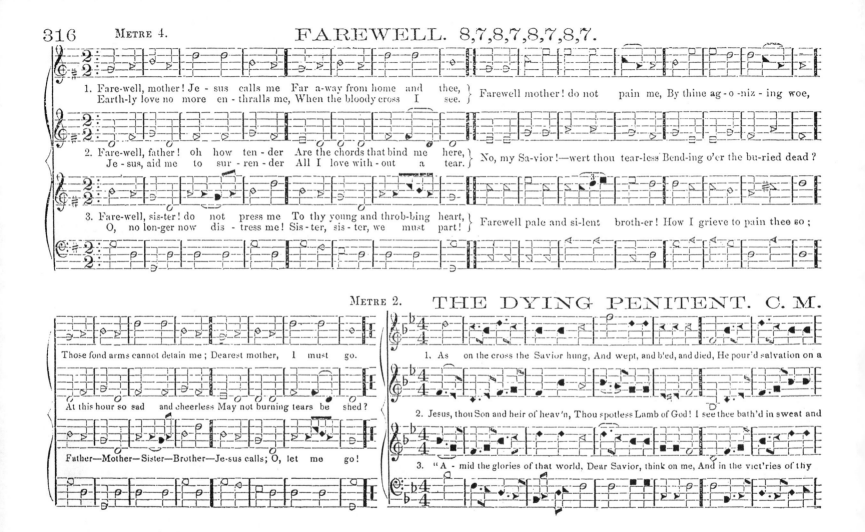

1. Fare-well, mother! Je - sus calls me Far a-way from home and thee,
Earth-ly love no more en - thralls me, When the bloody cross I see. } Farewell mother! do not pain me, By thine ag-o-niz-ing woe,

2. Fare-well, father! oh how ten - der Are the chords that bind me here,
Je - sus, aid me to sur - ren - der All I love with - out a tear. } No, my Sa-vior!—wert thou tear-less Bend-ing o'er the bu-ried dead?

3. Fare-well, sis-ter! do not press me To thy young and throb-bing heart,
O, no lon-ger now dis - tress me! Sis-ter, sis-ter, we must part! } Farewell pale and si-lent broth-er! How I grieve to pain thee so;

Those fond arms cannot detain me; Dearest mother, I must go.

At this hour so sad and cheerless May not burning tears be shed?

Father—Mother—Sister—Brother—Je-sus calls; O, let me go!

METRE 2.

THE DYING PENITENT. C. M.

1. As on the cross the Savior hung, And wept, and b'ed, and died, He pour'd salvation on a

2. Jesus, thou Son and heir of heav'n, Thou spotless Lamb of God! I see thee bath'd in sweat and

3. "A - mid the glories of that world, Dear Savior, think on me, And in the vict'ries of thy

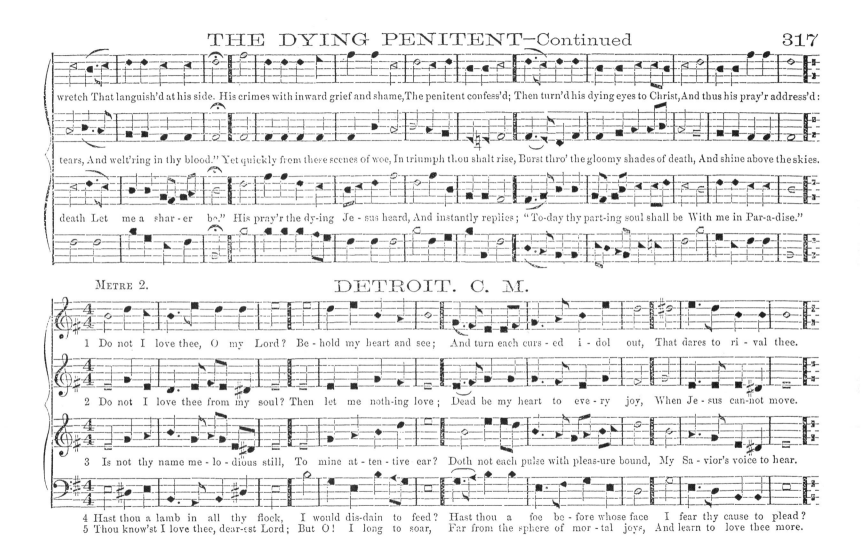

wretch That languish'd at his side. His crimes with inward grief and shame, The penitent confess'd; Then turn'd his dying eyes to Christ, And thus his pray'r address'd:

tears, And welt'ring in thy blood." Yet quickly from these scenes of woe, In triumph thou shalt rise, Burst thro' the gloomy shades of death, And shine above the skies.

death Let me a shar-er be." His pray'r the dy-ing Je-sus heard, And instantly replies; "To-day thy part-ing soul shall be With me in Par-a-dise."

METRE 2.

DETROIT. C. M.

1 Do not I love thee, O my Lord? Be-hold my heart and see; And turn each curs-ed i-dol out, That dares to ri-val thee.

2 Do not I love thee from my soul? Then let me noth-ing love; Dead be my heart to eve-ry joy, When Je-sus can-not move.

3 Is not thy name me-lo-dious still, To mine at-ten-tive ear? Doth not each pulse with pleas-ure bound, My Sa-vior's voice to hear.

4 Hast thou a lamb in all thy flock, I would dis-dain to feed? Hast thou a foe be-fore whose face I fear thy cause to plead?
5 Thou know'st I love thee, dear-est Lord; But O! I long to soar, Far from the sphere of mor-tal joys, And learn to love thee more.

METRE VARIOUS.

ANTHEM. The Earth is the Lord's. 24th Psalm.

1 The earth is the Lord's and the fulness there-of; the world, and they that dwell there-in,   2 For he hath found-ed it up - on the seas, and es-tab-lished it up-

on the flood; 3 Who shall ascend into the hill of the Lord? And who shall stand in his ho - ly place? 4 He that hath clean hands and a pure heart; Who hath not lifted

up his soul un-to van-i-ty, nor sworn de-ceit-ful-ly. 5 He shall receive the blessing from the Lord, And righteousness from the God of his sal - va - tion.

He shall receive the blessing from the Lord, And righteousness from the God of his sal-va-tion. 6 This is the gen - e - ra - tion of them that seek him, that seek thy face, O

God of Ja-cob. 7 Lift up your heads,   O ye gates, And be ye lift-ed up, ye ev-er-last-ing doors, and the King of glo-ry shall come in, The King of glo-ry

shall come in, The King of glo-ry shall come in, 8 Who is this King of glo-ry? who is this King of glo-ry? The LORD,   The   LORD,   strong and

might-y, The LORD, the LORD, might-y in bat - tle. 9 Lift up your heads, O ye gates; E - ven lift them up ye ev-er-last-ing doors, And the King of

glo-ry shall come in, the King of glo-ry shall come in, The King of glo-ry shall come in. Who is this King of glo-ry? Who is this King of glo - ry? The Lord of

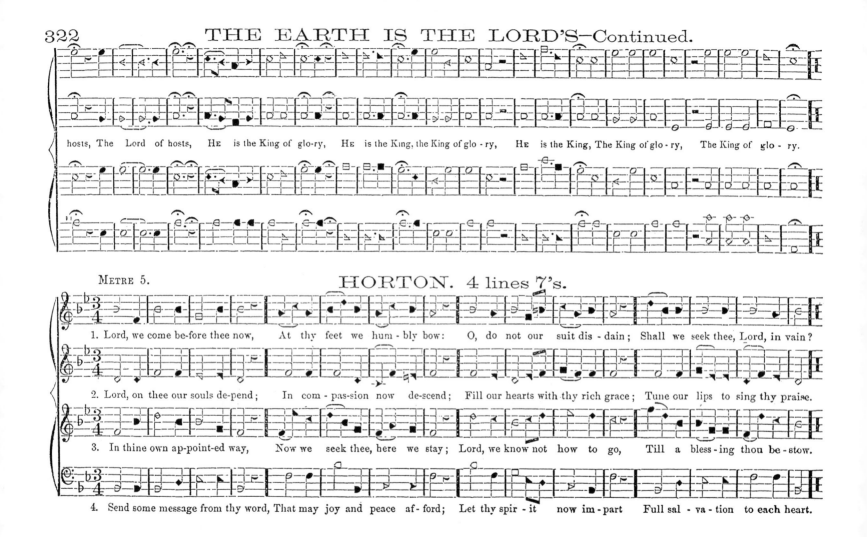

hosts, The Lord of hosts, HE is the King of glo-ry, HE is the King, the King of glo-ry, HE is the King, The King of glo-ry, The King of glo-ry.

METRE 5. HORTON. 4 lines 7's.

1. Lord, we come be-fore thee now, At thy feet we hum-bly bow: O, do not our suit dis-dain; Shall we seek thee, Lord, in vain?

2. Lord, on thee our souls de-pend; In com-pas-sion now de-scend; Fill our hearts with thy rich grace; Tune our lips to sing thy praise.

3. In thine own ap-point-ed way, Now we seek thee, here we stay; Lord, we know not how to go, Till a bless-ing thou be-stow.

4. Send some message from thy word, That may joy and peace af-ford; Let thy spir-it now im-part Full sal-va-tion to each heart.

1. When marshall'd on the night-ly plain, The glitt'-ring host be-stud the sky,
One Star a-lone of all the train, Can fix the sin-ner's wand'ring eye. } Hark! hark! to God, the cho-rus breaks,

2. Once on the ra-ging seas I rode, The storm was loud, the night was dark;
The o-cean yawn'd and rude-ly blow'd The wind that toss'd my found'ring bark; } Deep hor-ror then my vi-tals froze,

3. It was my guide, my light, my all, It bade my dark fore-bo-dings cease;
And thro' the storm and dan-ger's thrall, It led me to the port of peace; } Now safe-ly moored, my per-ils o'er,

From eve-ry host, from eve-ry gem: But one a-lone the Sa-vior speaks, It is the Star of Beth-le-hem.

Death-struck, I ceased the tide to stem; When sud-den-ly a Star a-rose— It was the Star of Beth-le-hem.

I'll sing first in night's di-a-dem, For-ev-er and for-ev-er more, The Star— the Star of Beth-le-hem.

324

Metre 69.

THE FATHERLAND. 9,8,9,8,9,8,9,8.

1 There is a place where my hopes are staid; My heart and my treasure are there; Where verdure and blossoms never fade, And fields are eternally fair;

2 There is a place where the angels dwell, A pure and a peaceful abode; The joys of that place no tongue can tell, For there is the palace of God:

3 There is a place where my friends are gone, Who worshipp'd and suffer'd with me; Exalted with Christ high on his throne, The King in his beauty they see:

4 There is a place where I hope to live, When life and its troubles are o'er; A place which the Lord to me will give, And then I shall sorrow no more:

That blissful place is my Fatherland, By faith its delights I explore; Come, Favor my flight, angelic bands, And waft me in peace to the shore.

That blissful place is my Fatherland, By faith its delights I explore; Come, favor my flight, angelic bands, And waft me in peace to the shore.

That blissful place is my Fatherland, By faith its delights I explore; Come, favor my flight, angelic bands, And waft me in peace to the shore.

1 We plough the fertile meadows, and sow the furrow'd land; But yet the waving harvest depends on God's own hand; It is his mercy gives us the sunshine and the rain,

2 By him were all things fashioned around us and afar, He made the earth and ocean, and every shining star; He made the pleasant spring time, the summer bright and warm,

3 He makes the glorious sunset, the moon to sail on high, He bids the breezes fan us, and thundering clouds to fly ; He gives us every blessing,— to him our lives we owe ;

CHORUS

That paints the verdant beauty, the mountain and the plain. Every blessing we enjoy, comes to us from God; Then praise his name, then praise his name, For he is ever good, For he, &c.

The golden days of autumn, the winter and the storm. Every blessing we enjoy, comes to us from God; Then praise his name, then praise his name, For he is ever good, For he is, &c.

He sent his Son to save us from sin, and death and woe. Every blessing we enjoy, comes to us from God ; Then praise his name, then praise his name, For he is ever good, &c.

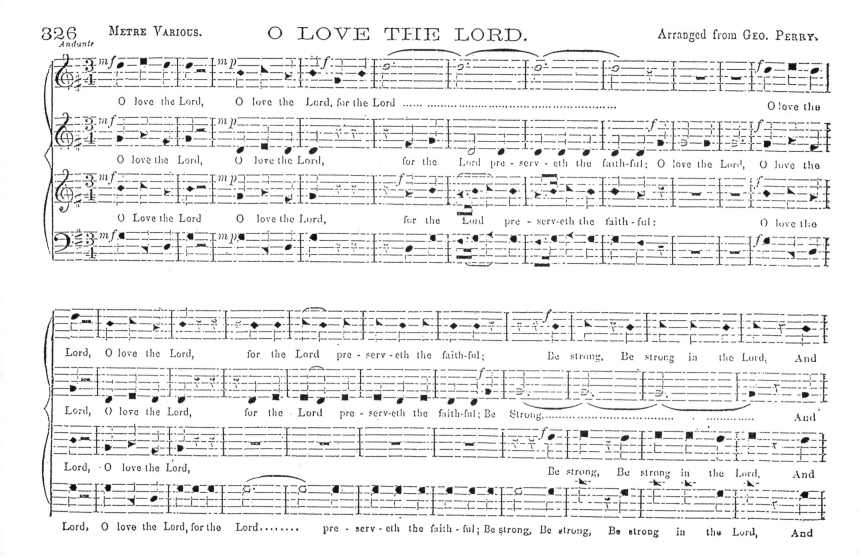

O LOVE THE LORD.

326 *Andante* — Metre Various. — Arranged from Geo. Perry.

1 On Jor-dan's storm-y banks I stand, And cast a wish-ful eye, To Ca-naan's fair and hap-py land, Where my pos-ses-sions lie;

2 There gen-'rous fruits that nev-er fail, On trees im-mor-tal grow; There rocks and hills, and brooks and vales, With milk and hon-ey flow.

3 No chill-ing winds nor poisonous breath, Can reach that healthful shore; Sick-ness and sor-row, pain and death, Are felt and feared no more.

O the trans-port-ing rapt-'rous scene, That ri-ses to my sight; Sweet fields ar-ray'd in liv-ing green, And riv-ers of de-light.

All o'er those wide, ex-tend-ed plains, Shines one e-ter-nal day; There God, the Son, for-ev-er reigns, And scat-ters night a-way.

When shall I reach that hap-py place, And be for-ev-er blest? When shall I see my Fa-ther's face, And in his bo-som rest.

1. Zion! awake, thy strength renew, Put on thy robes of beauteous hue; And let th' admiring world behold The King's fair daughter cloth'd in gold, Church of our God, arise and shine,

2 Gentiles and kings thy light shall view, All shall admire and love thee too; Shall come like clouds across the sky, Or doves that to their windows fly. Zion awake, thy strength renew,

Bright with the beams of truth divine; Then shall thy radiance stream a - far, Wide as the heath-en na-tions are;

Wide as the　　hea-.......then na-tions are.
The King's fair　daugh-.......ter cloth'd in gold.

Put on thy robes of beau teous hue; And let th' ad-mi-ring world be - hold The King's fair daughter cloth'd in gold.

Wide as the hea - then na-tions are.
The King's fair daughter clothed in gold.

Wide as the　hea -..................then na-tions are.
The King's fair daugh -.................ter cloth'd in gold.

METRE 5. MARY AT THE SAVIOR'S TOMB. 8 lines 7's.

1 Ma - ry to the Sa-vior's tomb Hast-ed at the ear-ly dawn, Spice she brought and rich per-fume, But the Lord she loved was gone;

2 Je-sus who is al-ways near, Though too oft-en un-per-ceived, Came her drooping heart to cheer, Kind-ly ask-ing why she griev'd;

3 Grief and sigh-ing quick-ly fled, When she heard his wel-come voice, Just be-fore she thought him dead, Now he bids her heart re-joice;

4 He who came to com-fort her, When she thought her all was lost, Will for your re-lief ap-pear, Though you now are tem-pest-toss'd;

For a while she ling'r - ing stood, Fill'd with sor - row and sur - prise, Trem - bling while a crys - tal flood Is-sued from her weep-ing eyes.

Though at first she knew him not, When he called her by her name, She her heav-y grief for - got, For she found him still the same.

What a change his word can make, Turn - ing dark-ness in - to day, You who weep for Je-sus' sake, He will wipe your tears a-way.

On his word your bur - den cast, On his love your thoughts employ, Weep-ing for a night may last, But with morn-ing comes the joy.

ARIEL. 8,8,6,8,8,6.

1 Oh, could I speak the match-less worth, Oh, could I sound the glo-ries forth, Which in my Sa-vior shine! I'd soar and touch the

2 I'd sing the pre-cious blood he spilt, My ran-som from the dreadful guilt, Of sin and wrath di-vine: I'd sing his glo-rious

3 I'd sing the char-ac-ters he bears, And all the forms of love he wears, Ex-alt-ed on his throne; In loft-iest songs of

4 Well the de-light-ful day will come, When my dear Lord will bring me home, And I shall see his face; Then, with my Sa-vior,

heav'n-ly strings, And vie with Ga-briel while he sings In notes al-most di-vine, In notes al-most.............. di-vine.

right-eous-ness, In which all per-fect heav'n-ly dress, My soul shall ev-er shine, My soul shall ev-............. er shine.

sweet-est praise, I would to ev-er-last-ing days, Make all his glo-ries known, Make all his glo............. ries known.

Broth-er, Friend, A blest e-ter-ni-ty I'll spend, Tri-umph-ant in his grace, Tri-umph-ant in............. his grace.

METRE 15.

BE JOYFUL IN GOD. 11,8.11,8.

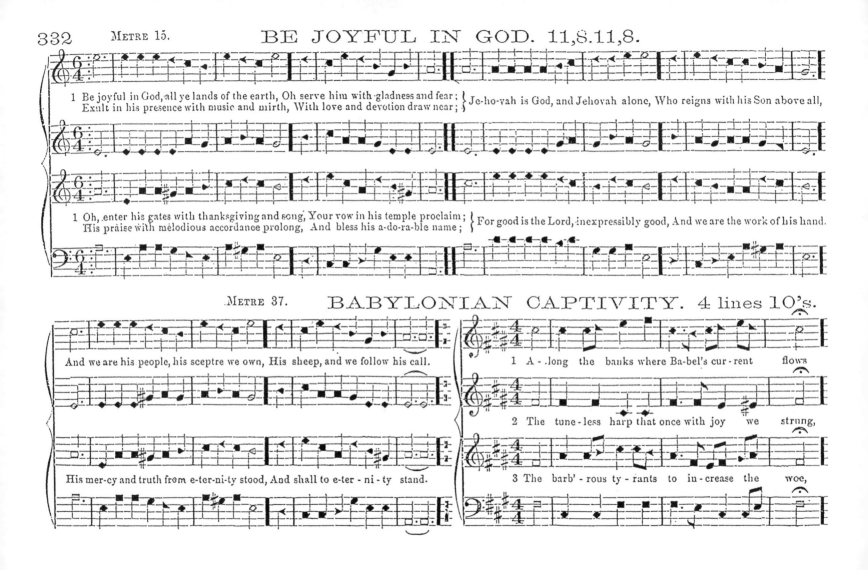

1 Be joyful in God, all ye lands of the earth, Oh serve him with gladness and fear ; } Je-ho-vah is God, and Jehovah alone, Who reigns with his Son above all,
Exult in his presence with music and mirth, With love and devotion draw near ; }

1 Oh, enter his gates with thanksgiving and song, Your vow in his temple proclaim ; } For good is the Lord, inexpressibly good, And we are the work of his hand.
His praise with melodious accordance prolong, And bless his a-do-ra-ble name ; }

METRE 37.

BABYLONIAN CAPTIVITY. 4 lines 10's.

And we are his people, his sceptre we own, His sheep, and we follow his call.

His mer-cy and truth from e-ter-ni-ty stood, And shall to e-ter-ni-ty stand.

1 A-long the banks where Ba-bel's cur-rent flows

2 The tune-less harp that once with joy we strung,

3 The barb'-rous ty-rants to in-crease the woe,

Our cap-tive bands in deep despondence stay'd, While Zi - on's fall in sad re-mem-brance rose, Her friends, her children mingled with the dead.

Where praise employed and mirth in-spired the lay, In mournful si - lence on the wil-lows hung, And growing grief prolonged the tedious day.

With taunt-ing smiles a song of Zi - on claim, Bid sa - cred praise in strains melodious flow, While they blaspheme the great Jehovah's name.

While Zion's fall in sad remembrance rose,..... ....
In mournful si - lence on the willows hung,..... .....
Bid sacred praise in strains melodious flow,..... .....

METRE 2.

JERUSALEM! My Glorious Home. C. M.

Je - ru-sa-lem, my glorious home! Name ever dear to me! When, When shall my labors have an end, In joy,......... In joy,.........

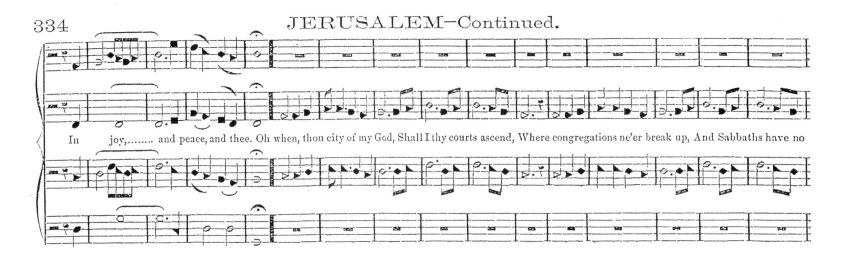

In joy,........ and peace, and thee. Oh when, thou city of my God, Shall I thy courts ascend, Where congregations ne'er break up, And Sabbaths have no

end? There hap-pier bow'rs than E - den's bloom, No sin nor sor-row know: Blest seats! blest seats! thro' rude and stormy scenes, I onward press to you, I

on-ward press to you, to you, to you, Je-ru-sa-lem! Je-ru-sa-lem! Name ever dear to me! Why should I shrink at pain and woe? Or

feel at death dis-may? I've Ca-naan's good-ly land......... in view, And realms of end......-less day. Je-ru-sa-lem, my glorious home! my

soul still pants for thee; Then, then shall my la - bors have an end, When I.........,... thy joys,............., When

I................ thy joys shall see, When I thy joys shall see! Je - ru - sa - lem! Je - ru - sa - lem! Name ev - er dear to me.

CRANBROOK. S. M.

Heav'n with the echo shall resound,   Heav'n with the echo shall resound,

1. Grace, 'tis a pleas - ing sound, Har - mo - nious to the ear;   Heav'n with the echo shall resound, with the echo shall resound,

Heav'n with the echo shall re-sound ......   Heav'n with the echo shall resound,

Heav'n with the echo shall resound, with the echo shall resound,

And all the earth shall hear,

And all the earth shall hear, And   all the earth shall hear,   And all   the earth shall   hear.

And all the earth shall hear, And all the earth, And all the earth shall   hear.

2. Grace first contrived a way
    To save rebellious man;
And all the steps that grace displays,
    Which drew the wondrous plan.

3. Grace led my roving feet
    To tread the heavenly road;
And new supplies each hour I meet,
    While passing on to God.

4. Grace all the work shall crown,
    Through everlasting days;
It lays in heaven the topmost stone,
    And well deserves the praise.

Metre 25.

PARTING WORDS. 8,7,8,7,7,7.

1 Let me go, the day is breaking; Dear companions, let me go !
We have spent a night of waking, In the wilderness be-low: } Upward now I bend my way, Part we here at break of day, Part we here at break of day.

2 Let me go, I must not tarry,
  Wrestling thus with doubts and fears;
Angels wait my soul to carry
  Where my risen Lord appears.
Friends and kindreds, weep not so—
If ye love me let me go.

3 We have traveled long together,
  Hand in hand and heart in heart;
Both thro' fair and stormy weather,
  And 'tis hard ! 'tis hard to part.
While I sigh farewell to you,
Answer, one and all, Adieu.

4 'Tis not darkness gathering round me,
  That withdraws me from your sight,
Walls of flesh no more can bound me,
  But translated into light,
Like the lark on mounting wing,
Though unseen, ye hear me sing.

5 Heav'n's broad day hath o'er me broken,
  Far beyond earth's span of sky;
Am I dead!—nay, by this token,
  Know that I have ceased to die.
Would you solve the mystery,
Come up hither,—Come and see.

Metre 9.

LISCHER. 6,6,6,6,8,8.

1 Welcome, delightful morn, Thou day of sacred rest !
I hail thy kind return ; Lord, make these moments blest ; } From the low train of mor-tal toys, I soar to reach im-mor-tal joys, I   soar   to reach im-mor-tal joys.

AIN. S. M.

1 How charming is the place, Where my Re - deem - er God, Un - veils the beauties of his face, and sheds his love a - broad !

3 Here, on the mer - cy seat, With ra - diant glo - ry crown'd Our joy-ful eyes be - hold him sit, And smile on all a - round.

5 To them his sove - reign will, He gra - cious - ly im - parts; And in re-turn ac - cepts, with smiles, The trib - ute 'of their hearts.

2 Not the fair pal - a - ces, To which the great re - sort, Are once to be com-pared with this, Where Je - sus holds his court.

4 To him their prayers and cries, Each hum - ble soul pre-sents; He list - ens to their bro-ken sighs, And grants them all their wants.

6 Give me, O Lord, a place With - in thy blest a - bode, A - mong the chil - dren of thy grace, The ser - vants of my God.

Metre 4.

HUMILITY. 8,7,8,7.

1 Let thy grace, Lord, make me lowly, Humble all my swelling pride; { I'll for-bid my vain as-pi-ring, Nor at earth-ly hon-ors aim,
Fall-en, guilt-y and un-ho-ly, Great-ness from mine eyes I'll hide.

2 Wean'd from earth's delusive pleasures, In thy love I'll seek for mine; { Thus the tran-sient world de-spis-ing, On the Lord my hopes re-ly;
Placed in heav'n my no-bler treas-ures, Earth I qui-et-ly re-sign.

No am-bi-tious heights de-si-ring Far a-bove my humble claim.

Thus my joys from him a-ris-ing Like him-self shall nev-er die.

Metre 11.

CANA. 4 lines 11's.

1 "Do this" and re-mem-ber the blood that was shed, {
Ere Cal-va-ry's Vic-tim to slaugh-ter was led,

2 Re-mem-ber that Vic-tor o'er death and the grave; {
He liv-eth for-ev-er His peo-ple to save.

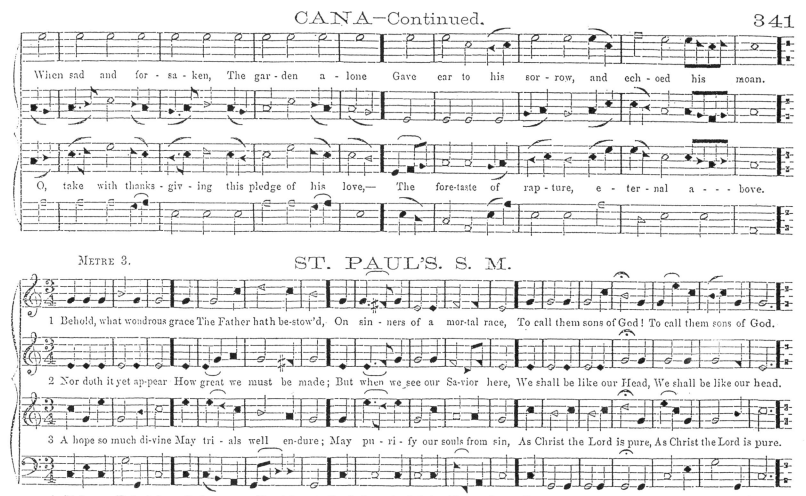

When sad and for-sa-ken, The gar-den a-lone Gave ear to his sor-row, and ech-oed his moan.

O, take with thanks-giv-ing this pledge of his love,— The fore-taste of rap-ture, e-ter-nal a---bove.

METRE 3.

ST. PAUL'S. S. M.

1 Behold, what wondrous grace The Father hath be-stow'd, On sin-ners of a mor-tal race, To call them sons of God! To call them sons of God.

2 Nor doth it yet ap-pear How great we must be made; But when we see our Sa-vior here, We shall be like our Head, We shall be like our head.

3 A hope so much di-vine May tri-als well en-dure; May pu-ri-fy our souls from sin, As Christ the Lord is pure, As Christ the Lord is pure.

4 If in my Father's love I share a fil-ial part, Send down thy Spir-it like a dove, To rest up-on my heart, To rest up-on my heart.
5 We would no longer lie Like slaves be-neath the throne; Our faith shall Ab-ba, Fa-ther cry, And thou the kindred own, And thou the kindred own.

METRE 11. GARDEN. 11's.

1 While na-ture was sink-ing iu stil-ness to rest, The last beams of day-light shone dim in the west, O'er fields by the moonlight, my wandering feet Then led me to muse in some lone- ly re-treat.

2 While pass-ing a gar-den I paus'd then to hear A voice faint and plaintive from one that was there: The voice of the Suff'rer af-fect-ed my heart, In ag-o-ny pleading the poor sinner's part.

3 I listened a moment, then turned me to see
What Man of compassion this Stranger could be !
I saw Him low kneeling upon the cold ground,
Alone on a spot in the garden He found.
4 His mantle was wet with the dews of the night ;
His locks by pale moonbeams were glist'ning and bright ;
His eyes, bright as diamonds, to heaven were raised,
While angels in wonder stood round him amazed !

5 So deep were his sorrows, so fervent his prayers,
That down o'er his bosom rolled sweat, blood, and tears !
I wept to behold Him ! I asked Him his name !
He answered, " 'Tis JESUS ! from heaven I came ! "
6 " I am thy Redeemer, for thee I must die !
The cup is most bitter, but cannot pass by !
Thy sins like a mountain were laid upon Me,
And all this deep anguish I suffer for thee ! "

7 I trembled with horror, and loudly did cry,
" Lord, save a poor sinner ! O save, or I die ! "
He smiled when He saw me, and said to me, " Live !
Thy sins which are many, I freely forgive."
8 How sweet was the moment He bade me rejoice !
His smile, oh how pleasant ! how cheering His voice !
I flew from the garden to spread it abroad,
And shouted " Salvation" and " Glory to God ! "

1 I love to stay where my mo-ther sleeps, And gaze on each star as it twink-ling peeps, Thro' that bend-ing wil-low which lone-ly

2 I love to kneel on the green turf there, A-far from the scene of my dai-ly care, And breathe to my Sa-vior my eve-ning

3 I still re-mem-ber how oft she led, And knelt me by her as with God she plead, That I might be his when the clod was

4 I love to think how be-neath the ground, She slumbers in death as a cap-tive bound, She'll slumber no more when the trump shall

weeps, O'er my mo-ther's grave, O'er my mo-ther's grave, Through that bend-ing wil-low, O'er my mo-ther's grave.

pray'r, O'er my mo-ther's grave, O'er my mo-ther's grave, Through that bend-ing wil-low, O'er my mo-ther's grave.

spread, O'er my mo-ther's grave, O'er my mo-ther's grave, Through that bend-ing wil-low, O'er my mo-ther's grave.

sound.

METRE 73.

THE HAPPY LAND. 6,4,6,4,6,7,6,4.

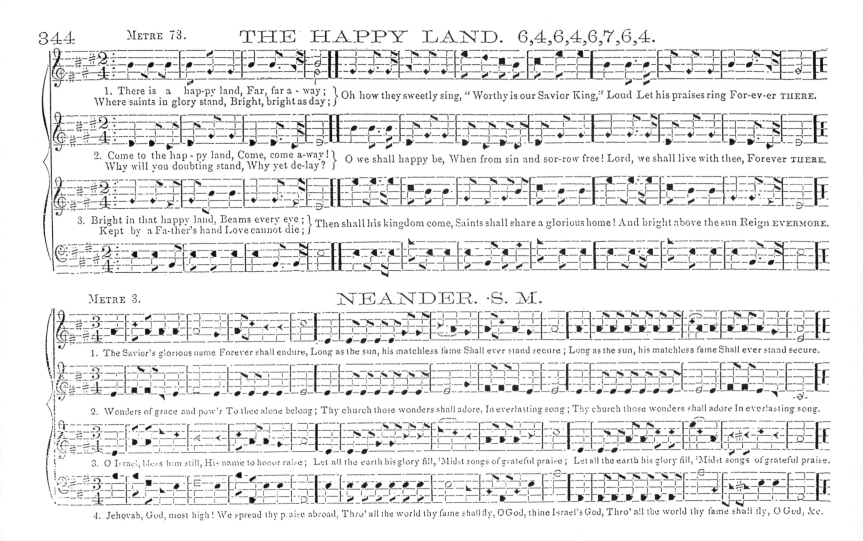

1. There is a hap-py land, Far, far a - way;
Where saints in glory stand, Bright, bright as day; } Oh how they sweetly sing, "Worthy is our Savior King," Loud Let his praises ring For-ev-er THERE.

2. Come to the hap - py land, Come, come a-way!
Why will you doubting stand, Why yet de-lay? } O we shall happy be, When from sin and sor-row free! Lord, we shall live with thee, Forever THERE.

3. Bright in that happy land, Beams every eye;
Kept by a Fa-ther's hand Love cannot die; } Then shall his kingdom come, Saints shall share a glorious home! And bright above the sun Reign EVERMORE.

METRE 3.

NEANDER. S. M.

1. The Savior's glorious name Forever shall endure, Long as the sun, his matchless fame Shall ever stand secure; Long as the sun, his matchless fame Shall ever stand secure.

2. Wonders of grace and pow'r To thee alone belong; Thy church those wonders shall adore, In everlasting song; Thy church those wonders shall adore In everlasting song.

3. O Israel, bless him still, His name to honor raise; Let all the earth his glory fill, 'Midst songs of grateful praise; Let all the earth his glory fill, 'Midst songs of grateful praise.

4. Jehovah, God, most high! We spread thy praise abroad, Thro' all the world thy fame shall fly; O God, thine Israel's God, Thro' all the world thy fame shall fly, O God, &c.

NEWKIRK. 8 lines 10's.

1. Joy - ful - ly, joy-ful - ly, on-ward I move, Bound for the land of bright spir-its a - bove:
An - gel - ic chor-is - ters sing as I come, "Joy-ful - ly, Joy-ful - ly haste to thy home;" } Soon with my pil-grim-age end-ed be - low,

2. Friends fondly cherished have passed on before, Waiting they watch me approaching the shore;
Sing-ing to cheer me thro' death's chilling gloom, "Joy-ful - ly, Joy-ful - ly haste to thy home:" } Sounds of sweet mel-o - dy fall on my ear;

3. Death, with thy weapons of war, lay me low; Strike, king of ter-rors, I fear not the blow;
Je - sus hath bro-ken the bars of the tomb, Joy-ful - ly, Joy-ful - ly will I go home. } Bright will the morn of e - ter - ni - ty dawn,

Home to the land of bright spir - its I go; Pil - grim and stran-ger no more shall I roam, Joy-ful - ly, Joy - ful - ly rest - ing at home.

Harps of the bless - ed, your voic - es I hear! Rings with the har - mo - ny heav-ens high dome, Joy-ful - ly, Joy - ful - ly haste to thy home.

Death shall be ban-ished, his scep - tre be gone; Joy-ful - ly then shall I wit-ness his doom; Joy-ful - ly, Joy - ful - ly, safe-ly at home.

METRE 76.

ROCKVALE. 7,5,7,5,7,5,7,5.

1 Onward speed thy conq'ring flight; An-gel, onward speed; Cast a-broad thy radiant light, Bid the shades re-cede; Tread the i-dols in the dust, Heathen fanes de-stroy;

2 Onward speed thy conq'ring flight; An-gel, onward haste: Quickly on each mountain's height, Be thy standard placed: Let the blissful ti-dings float Far o'er vale and hill,

3 Onward speed thy conq'ring flight; An-gel, on-ward fly; Long has been the reign of night; Bring the morning nigh; 'Tis to thee the heathen lift, Their im-plor-ing wail:

4 Onward speed thy conq'ring flight; An-gel, onward speed; Morning bursts upon the sight; 'Tis the time de-creed: Je-sus now his kingdom takes, Thrones and empires fall,

Spread the Gos-pel's holy trust, Spread the Gos-pel's joy.

Till the sweetly echo-ing note, Eve-ry bo--som thrill.

Bear them heaven's ho-ly gift, Ere their cour-age fail.

And the joy-ous song a-wakes, "God is all in all."

METRE 75.

LANGDON. 8,7,8,7,6,6,6,6.

1 Watchmen! on-ward to your sta - tions, Blow the trump-et long and loud; }
Preach the Gos-pel to the na-tions, Speak to eve-ry gath-'ring crowd; }

2 Watchmen! hail the ri-sing glo-ry Of the great Mes-si--ah's reign; }
Tell the Sa-vior's bleed-ing sto-ry, Tell it to the list'-ning train: }

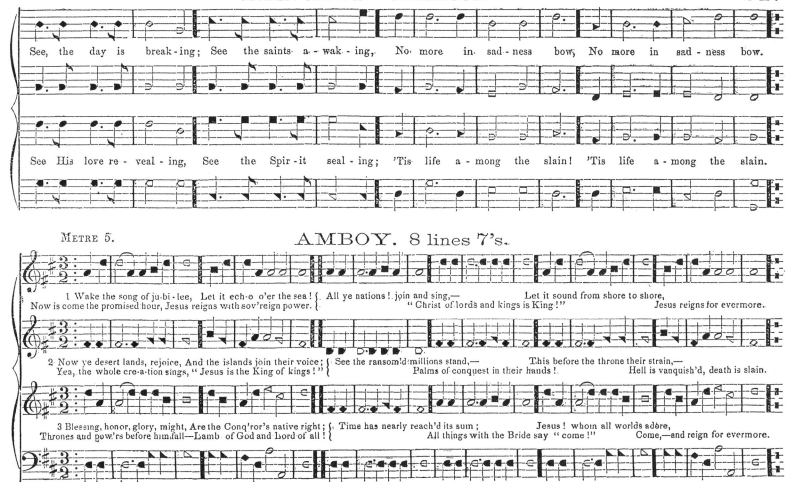

See, the day is break-ing; See the saints a - wak - ing, No more in sad - ness bow; No more in sad - ness bow.

See His love re - veal - ing, See the Spir - it seal - ing; 'Tis life a - mong the slain! 'Tis life a - mong the slain.

METRE 5. AMBOY. 8 lines 7's.

1 Wake the song of ju-bi-lee, Let it ech-o o'er the sea! { All ye nations! join and sing,— Let it sound from shore to shore,
Now is come the promised hour, Jesus reigns with sov'reign power. { "Christ of lords and kings is King!" Jesus reigns for evermore.

2 Now ye desert lands, rejoice, And the islands join their voice; { See the ransom'd millions stand,— This before the throne their strain,—
Yea, the whole cre-a-tion sings, "Jesus is the King of kings!" { Palms of conquest in their hands! Hell is vanquish'd, death is slain.

3 Blessing, honor, glory, might, Are the Conq'ror's native right; { Time has nearly reach'd its sum; Jesus! whom all worlds adore,
Thrones and pow'rs before him fall—Lamb of God and Lord of all! { All things with the Bride say "come!" Come,—and reign for evermore.

METRE 3.

BEALOTH. S. M.

1 I love thy king-dom, Lord, The house of thine a - bode, The church our bless'd Re-deem-er saved With his own precious blood,

3 For her my tears shall fall, For her my prayers as - cend; To her my toils and cares be given, Till toils and cares shall end.

5 Je - sus, thou Friend di - vine, Our Sa - vior and our King, Thy hand from ev' - ry snare and foe Shall great de-liv-rance bring.

2 I love thy church, O God; Her walls be - fore thee stand, Dear as the ap - ple of thine eye, And gra-ven on thine hand.

4 Be - yond my high - est joy, I prize her heav'n-ly ways, Her sweet com-mun - ion, sol-emn vows, Her hymns of love and praise.

6 Sure as thy truth shall last, To Zi - on shall be giv'n The brightest glo-ries earth can yield, And bright-er bliss of heav'n.

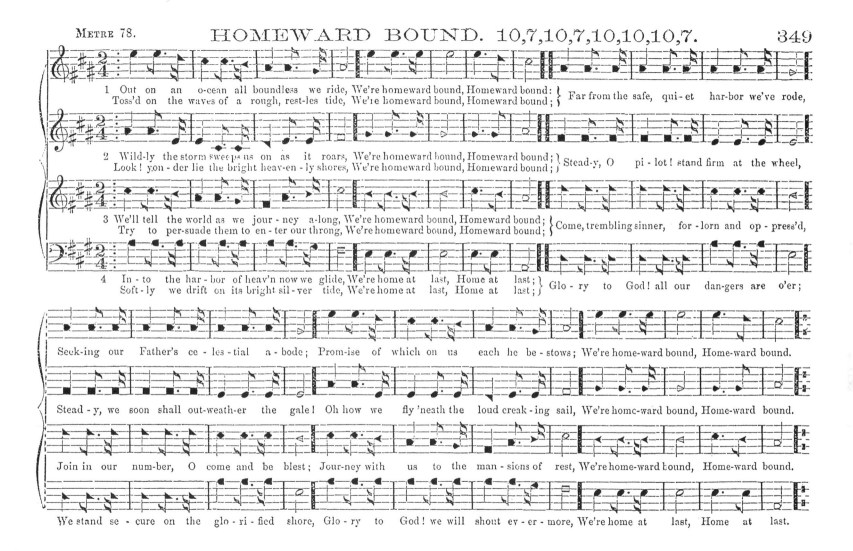

METRE 79. THE ROCK. 11,12,12,11.

1 In sea-sons of grief to my God I'll re-pair, When my heart is o'er whelm-ed in sorrow and care; From the ends of the earth unto thee will I cry—

2 When sa-tan, my foe comes in like a flood To di-vert my poor soul from the fountain of good, I will pray to my Savior who kindly did die—

3 And when I have end-ed my pil-grim-age here, In my Savior's pure right-eousness let me appear:— From the swellings of Jordan to thee will I cry,

4 And when the last trumpet shall sound thro' the skies, And the dead from the dust of the earth shall a-rise, With the millions I'll join, far above yonder sky,

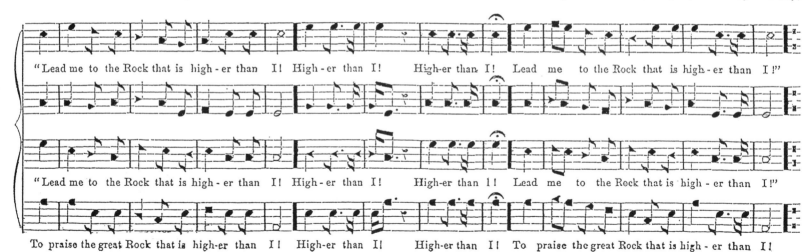

"Lead me to the Rock that is high-er than I! High-er than I! High-er than I! Lead me to the Rock that is high-er than I!"

"Lead me to the Rock that is high-er than I! High-er than I! High-er than I! Lead me to the Rock that is high-er than I!"

To praise the great Rock that is high-er than I! High-er than I! High-er than I! To praise the great Rock that is high-er than I!

1 He's gone, the spotless soul is gone, Triumphant to his place a-bove;
The prison walls are broken down, The angels speed his swift remove;
And shouting on their wings he flies, And gains his rest in Par - a-dise.

2 Saved by the mer-its of his Lord, Glo-ry and praise to Christ he gives;
Yet still his mer-ci - ful re-ward Ac-cord-ing to his works re-ceives,
And with the bliss he sow'd below, His bliss e - ter - nal - ly shall grow,

3 Fa-ther, to us vouchsafe the grace Which brought our friend victorious thro';
Let us his shining footsteps trace; Let us his stead-fast faith pur-sue;
Fol-low this fol-lower of the Lamb, And conquer all thro' Je-sus' name.

4 Oh may we all like him be-lieve, And keep the faith and win the prize!
Fa-ther, prepare, and then receive Our hal-low'd spir-its to the skies,
To chant with all our friends above, Thy glorious, ev-er - last-ing love.

CHORUS

Ho-san-na! ho-san-na! ho-san-na to the Lamb of God! Glory, glory, let us sing! Grateful honors to our King! Hosanna! hosanna! hosanna to the Lamb of God!

Ho-san-na! ho-san-na! ho-san-na to the Lamb of God! Glory, glory, let us sing! Grateful honors to our King! Hosanna! hosanna! hosanna to the Lamb of God!

Metre 13.

REMEMBER CALVARY. 7's & 6's.

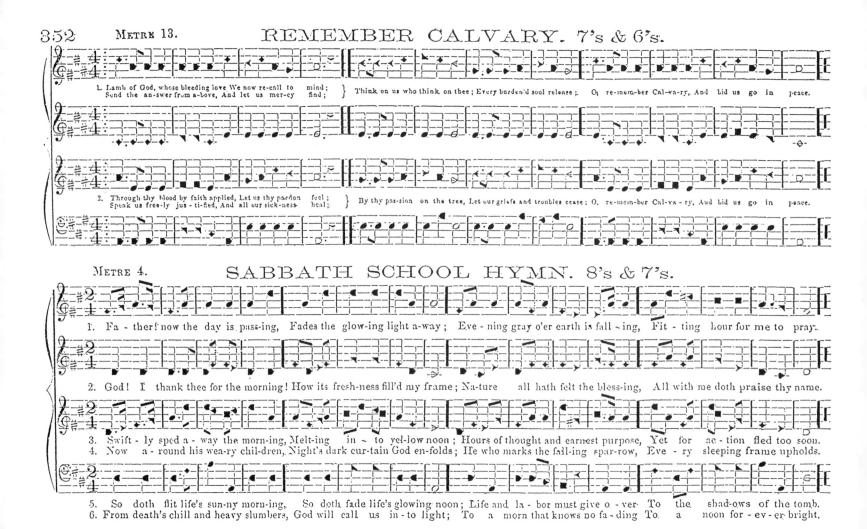

1. Lamb of God, whose bleeding love We now re-call to mind;
Send the an-swer from a-bove, And let us mer-cy find;
} Think on us who think on thee; Every burden'd soul release; O, re-mem-ber Cal-va-ry, And bid us go in peace.

2. Through thy blood by faith applied, Let us thy pardon feel;
Speak us free-ly jus-ti-fied, And all our sick-ness heal;
} By thy pas-sion on the tree, Let our griefs and troubles cease; O, re-mem-ber Cal-va-ry, And bid us go in peace.

Metre 4.

SABBATH SCHOOL HYMN. 8's & 7's.

1. Fa-ther! now the day is pass-ing, Fades the glow-ing light a-way; Eve-ning gray o'er earth is fall-ing, Fit-ting hour for me to pray.

2. God! I thank thee for the morning! How its fresh-ness fill'd my frame; Na-ture all hath felt the bless-ing, All with me doth praise thy name.

3. Swift-ly sped a-way the morn-ing, Melt-ing in-to yel-low noon; Hours of thought and earnest purpose, Yet for ac-tion fled too soon.
4. Now a-round his wea-ry chil-dren, Night's dark cur-tain God en-folds; He who marks the fall-ing spar-row, Eve-ry sleeping frame upholds.

5. So doth flit life's sun-ny morn-ing, So doth fade life's glowing noon; Life and la-bor must give o-ver To the shad-ows of the tomb.
6. From death's chill and heavy slumbers, God will call us in-to light; To a morn that knows no fa-ding To a noon for-ev-er bright.

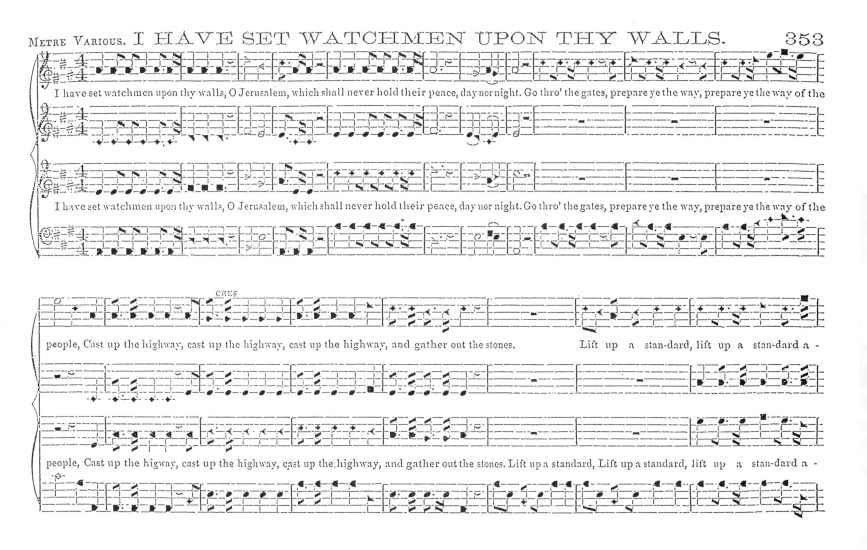

I have set watchmen upon thy walls, O Jerusalem, which shall never hold their peace, day nor night. Go thro' the gates, prepare ye the way, prepare ye the way of the

I have set watchmen upon thy walls, O Jerusalem, which shall never hold their peace, day nor night. Go thro' the gates, prepare ye the way, prepare ye the way of the

CRES

people, Cast up the highway, cast up the highway, cast up the highway, and gather out the stones. Lift up a stan-dard, lift up a stan-dard a-

people, Cast up the higway, cast up the highway, cast up the.highway, and gather out the stones. Lift up a standard, Lift up a standard, lift up a stan-dard a-

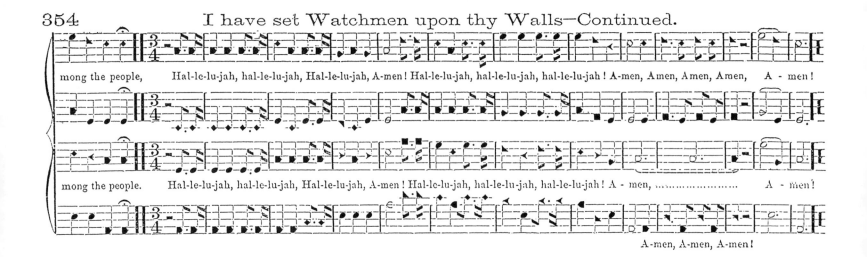

mong the people,   Hal-le-lu-jah, hal-le-lu-jah, Hal-le-lu-jah, A-men! Hal-le-lu-jah, hal-le-lu-jah, hal-le-lu-jah! A-men, Amen, Amen, Amen,   A - men!

mong the people.   Hal-le-lu-jah, hal-le-lu-jah, Hal-le-lu-jah, A-men! Hal-le-lu-jah, hal-le-lu-jah, hal-le-lu-jah! A - men, ...   A - men!

A-men, A-men, A-men!

METRE 37.   EVENING HYMN. (CHANT.)   4 lines 10's.

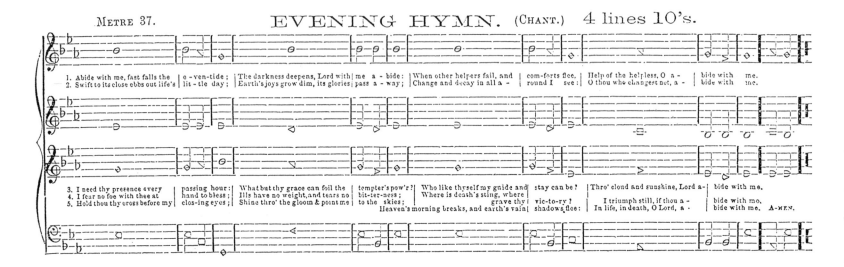

1. Abide with me, fast falls the | e-ven-tide; | The darkness deepens, Lord with| me a - bide; | When other helpers fail, and | com-forts flee. | Help of the helpless, O a - | bide with me.
2. Swift to its close ebbs out life's | lit-tle day; | Earth's joys grow dim, its glories| pass a - way; | Change and decay in all a - | round I see! | O thou who changest not, a - | bide with me.

3. I need thy presence every | passing hour; | What but thy grace can foil the | tempter's pow'r? | Who like thyself my guide and | stay can be? | Thro' cloud and sunshine, Lord a-| bide with me.
4. I fear no foe with thee at | hand to bless; | Ills have no weight, and tears no | bit-ter-ness; | Where is death's sting, where | | I triumph still, if thou a - | bide with me.
5. Hold thou thy cross before my | clos-ing eyes; | Shine thro' the gloom & point me | to the skies; | Heaven's morning breaks, and earth's vain| grave thy | vic-to-ry? shadows flee; | In life, in death, O Lord, a - | bide with me. A-MEN.

METRE VARIOUS.

THE ROSE OF SHARON.

I am the Rose of Sharon and the Lily of the valley;

I am the rose of Sharon and the Lily of the valley,

As the li - ly a-mong the thorns, so is my

So is my Be-lov-ed among the sons,

Love a - mong the daughters. As the apple tree, the apple tree a - mong the trees of the wood, So is my Be-loved a-mong the sons, So is my Be-lov-ed a-

mong the sons.   I sat down, un-der his shadow, With great delight, And his fruit...... was sweet to my taste, And his fruit   was   sweet to my taste.

I sat   down

Stay me with flagons,

He brought me to the banqueting house, His banner over me was love.

He brought me to the banqueting house, His banner over me was love, He brought me to the banqueting house, His banner over me was love.   Comfort me with

For I am sick,

By the roes and by the hinds of the field,

For I am sick of love. I charge you, O ye daughters of Jerusalem,

apples, For I am sick; For I am sick of love. I charge you, Oh ye daughters of Jerusalem, By the roes & by the hinds of the field, That ye stir not

The voice of my Beloved,

That ye stir not up nor a - - - wake, a - wake, a-wake, a - wake, my love till he please.

up, That ye stir not up, That ye stir not up nor a - - - wake, a - wake, a-wake, a - wake, my love till he please, Be - hold he

And said un-to me,

Leaping upon the mountains, Skipping upon the hills.

cometh, Leaping upon the mountains, Skipping upon the hills,   Leaping upon the mountains, Skipping upon the hills.   My Be-lov-ed spake,   Rise

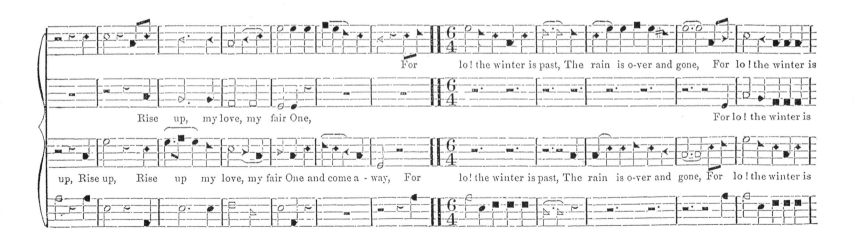

For   lo! the winter is past, The rain is o-ver and gone,   For lo! the winter is

Rise   up,   my love, my fair One,   For lo! the winter is

up, Rise up,   Rise   up   my love, my fair One and come a - way,   For   lo! the winter is past, The rain is o-ver and gone, For   lo! the winter is

past, The rain is o-ver and gone, The rain is over, The rain is over, The rain is over and gone, For lo! the winter is past, The rain is o-ver and gone.

METRE 2. BLESSED INFANCY. C. M.

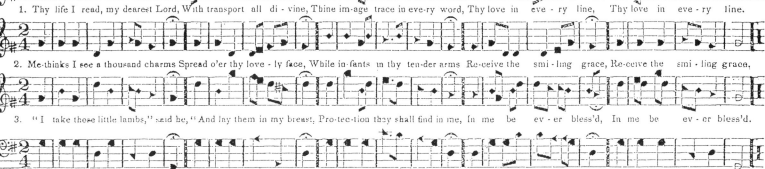

1. Thy life I read, my dearest Lord, With transport all di - vine, Thine im-age trace in eve-ry word, Thy love in eve-ry line, Thy love in eve-ry line.

2. Me-thinks I see a thousand charms Spread o'er thy love-ly face, While in-fants in thy ten-der arms Re-ceive the smi-ling grace, Re-ceive the smi-ling grace.

3. "I take these little lambs," said he, "And lay them in my breast, Pro-tec-tion they shall find in me, In me be ev - er bless'd, In me be ev - er bless'd.

4. "Death may the bands of life unloose, But can't dissolve my love; Mil-lions of in-fant souls compose The fam - i - ly a - bove, The fam - i - ly a - bove."

HYMN CHANT.

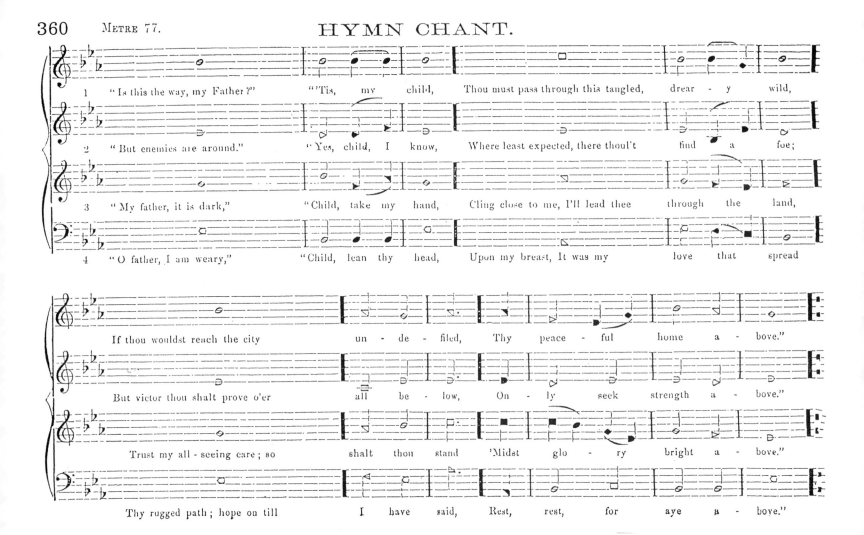

1. And must this bod - y die? This mor-tal frame de - cay? And must these ac-tive limbs of mine, Lie mould'-ring..... in the clay?

2. Cor - rup-tion, earth and worms, Shall but re-fine this flesh, Till my tri - umph-ant spir-it comes, To put it......... on a - fresh.

3. God my Re - deem - er lives, And oft - en from the skies Looks down and watch-es all my dust, 'Till he shall...... bid it rise.

4. Ar - ray'd in glo - rious grace Shall these vile bo-dies shine, And eve - ry shape and eve - ry face, Look heav'n - ly...... and di - vine.

METRE 3. MOUNT EPHRAIM. S. M.

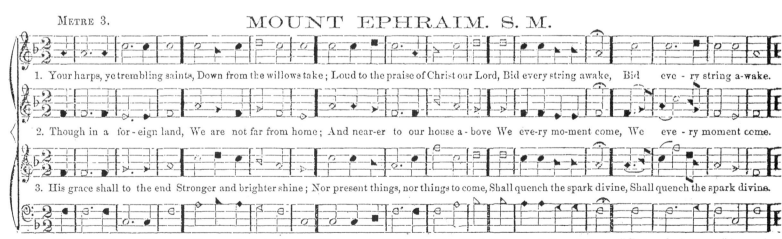

1. Your harps, ye trembling saints, Down from the willows take; Loud to the praise of Christ our Lord, Bid every string awake, Bid eve - ry string a-wake.

2. Though in a for-eign land, We are not far from home; And near-er to our house a-bove We eve-ry mo-ment come, We eve - ry moment come.

3. His grace shall to the end Stronger and brighter shine; Nor present things, nor things to come, Shall quench the spark divine, Shall quench the spark divine.

4. The time of love will come, When we shall clearly see, Not on - ly that he shed his blood, But each shall say "for me," But each shall say "for me."

FAREWELL ANTHEM.

Metre Various.

My friends, I am going a long and te-dious jour-ney, nev-er to re-turn; I am go-ing a

My friends, I am go-ing a long and te-dious jour - ney, never to re-turn; I am go-ing, I am go-ing a

My friends, I am go-ing a long and te - dious jour - ney, nev-er to re-turn; I am go-ing, I am go-ing a long and

My friends, I am go-ing a long and te - dious jour - ney............ nev-er to re-turn; I am going a long journey, never to re-turn; I am

long and tedious journey, never to re-turn, I am go-ing, I am go-ing a long journey, never to re-turn, nev-er to re-turn,....

long and tedious journey, nev-er to re-turn, I am go-ing a long journey, never to re-turn, nev-er, nev-er, nev-er to re-turn, ...

te - dious journey, nev-er to re-turn; I am going a long journey, never to re - - turn, nev-er to re - - turn, nev-er to re - - turn,

going a long journey, nev-er to re-turn; I am go-ing a long journey, never to re-turn, nev-er to re - - turn, nev-er to re-

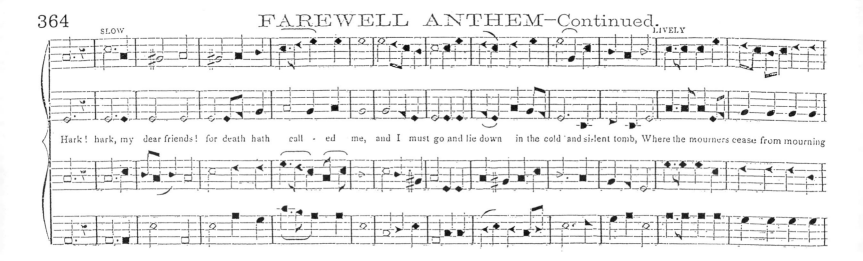

Hark! hark, my dear friends! for death hath call - ed me, and I must go and lie down in the cold and silent tomb, Where the mourners cease from mourning

and the pris'ner is set free, Where the rich and the poor are both alike: Fare you well! Fare you well! Fare you well! Fare you well! Fare you well, my friends!

ORRINGTON. S. M.

1 When gloomy doubts and fears The trembling heart invade, And all the face of nature wears A universal shade;

2 Religion can assuage The tempest of the soul; And every fear gives up its rage At her divine control.

3 Through life's bewildered way, Her hand unerring leads, And o'er the path her heav'nly ray, A cheering lustre sheds.

4 When reason, tired and blind, Sinks helpless and afraid; Thou blest supporter of the mind! How pow'rful is thine aid.

Metre 5. DEPTH OF MERCY. 4 lines 7's.

1. Depth of mercy! can there be Mercy still reserved for me; Can my God his wrath forbear? Me, the chief of sinners, spare?

2. I have long withstood his grace, Long provoked him to his face; Would not hearken to his calls—Grieved him by a thousand falls.

3. Kindled his relentings are,—Me he now delights to spare; Cries, "How shall I give thee up?" Lets the lifted thunder drop.

4. There for me the Savior stands, Shows his wounds and spreads his hands; God is Love! I know—I feel—Jesus weeps and loves me still.

METRE 4. CARLISLE. 8's & 7's.

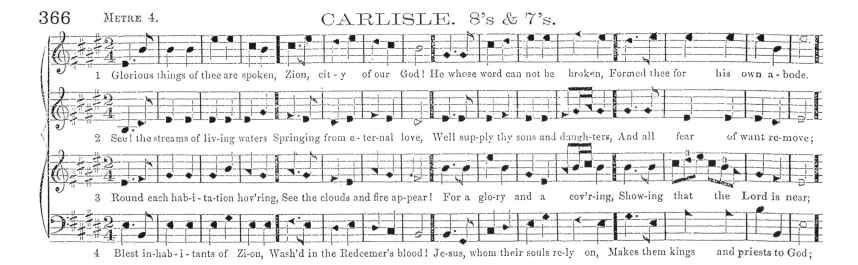

1 Glorious things of thee are spoken, Zion, cit - y of our God! He whose word can not be broken, Formed thee for his own a - bode.

2 See! the streams of liv-ing waters Springing from e-ter-nal love, Well sup-ply thy sons and daugh-ters, And all fear of want re-move;

3 Round each hab-i - ta-tion hov'ring, See the clouds and fire ap-pear! For a glo-ry and a cov'r-ing, Show-ing that the Lord is near;

4 Blest in-hab - i - tants of Zi-on, Wash'd in the Redeemer's blood! Je-sus, whom their souls re-ly on, Makes them kings and priests to God;

On the Rock of a - ges found - ed, What can shake thy sure re - pose? With sal-va-tion's wall sur-round-ed, Thou may'st smile at all thy foes.

Who can faint while such a riv - er, Ev-er flows their thirst t'as-suage? Grace which like the Lord the Giv-er, Nev-er fails from age to age.

Thus de - riv - ing from their ban-ner, Light by night and shade by day; Safe they feed up-on the man-na Which he gives them when they pray.

'Tis his love his peo-ple rais-es, O - ver self to reign as kings, And as priests his sol-emn praises, Each for a thank-off'ring brings.

Metre 5.

EARNEST CALL. 4 lines 7's.

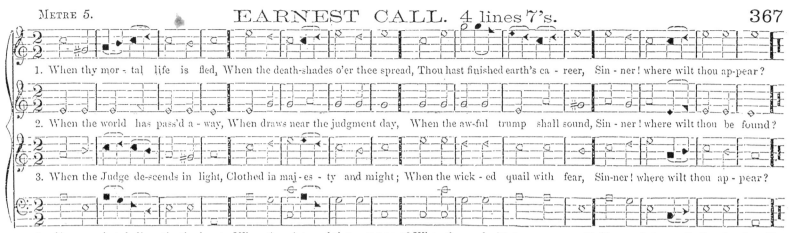

1. When thy mor-tal life is fled, When the death-shades o'er thee spread, Thou hast finished earth's ca - reer, Sin-ner! where wilt thou ap-pear?

2. When the world has pass'd a - way, When draws near the judgment day, When the aw-ful trump shall sound, Sin - ner! where wilt thou be found?

3. When the Judge de-scends in light, Clothed in maj-es - ty and might; When the wick - ed quail with fear, Sin-ner! where wilt thou ap - pear?

4. Sin-ner, what shall soothe thy heart, When the saints and thou must part? When the good with joy are crown'd, Sin - ner! where wilt thou be found?

Metre 5.

SINCERITY. 4 lines 7's.

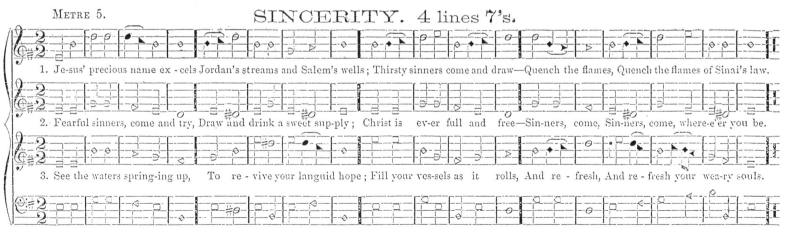

1. Je-sus' precious name ex - cels Jordan's streams and Salem's wells; Thirsty sinners come and draw—Quench the flames, Quench the flames of Sinai's law.

2. Fearful sinners, come and try, Draw and drink a sweet sup-ply; Christ is ev-er full and free—Sin-ners, come, Sin-ners, come, where-e'er you be.

3. See the waters spring-ing up, To re - vive your languid hope; Fill your ves-sels as it rolls, And re - fresh, And re - fresh your wea-ry souls.

4. Lo the Spir-it now in - vites; Lo! the cheerful Bride u - nites; Je - sus calls, be not a - fraid, Lo! for you! Lo! for you! the well is made.

METRE 8.

PLYMOUTH DOCK. 6 lines 8's.

1 Je - sus, thy bound-less love to me, No thought can reach nor tongue de-clare; O knit my thank-ful heart to thee,

2 O grant that noth-ing in my soul, May dwell but thy pure love a-lone! O may thy love pos-sess me whole;

3 O love, how cheer-ing is thy ray! All pain be-fore thy pres-ence flies; Care, an-guish, sor-row, melt a-way,

4 Un - wea - ried may I this pur-sue, Daunt-less to the high prize as-pire; Hour-ly with-in my soul re-new,

And reign with-out a ri-val there; Thine, whol-ly thine a-lone I am, Be thou a--lone my con-stant flame.

My joy, my treas-ure and my crown! Strange flames far from my heart re-move, My eve-ry act, word, thought be love.

Wher-e'er thy heal-ing beams a-rise: O Je-sus, noth-ing may I see; Noth-ing de-sire or seek but thee.

This ho-ly flame, this heaven-ly fire; And day and night be all my care To guard that sac--red treas-ure there.

1 From Greenland's icy mountains, From India's coral strand, Where Afric's sunny fountains Roll down their golden sand; From many an ancient river,

2 What though the spicy breezes Blow soft o'er Ceylon's isle; Though eve-ry prospect pleases, And on - ly man is vile; In vaid with lavish kindness,

3 Shall we, whose souls are lighted With wisdom from on high— Shall we to men be-night-ed, The lamp of life de-ny? Sal-va-tion, O sal-va-tion,

4 Waft, waft, ye winds, his story, And you, ye waters, roll, Till like a sea of glo-ry, It spreads from pole to pole; Till o'er our ransom'd nature,

From many a palm - y plain, They call us to de-liv-er Their land from error's chain, They call us to de-liv-er, Their land from er-ror's chain.

The gifts of God are strown; The heathen in his blindness, Bows down to wood and stone, The heathen in his blindness, Bows down to wood and stone.

The joy-ful sound pro-claim, Till earth's remotest nation, Has learn'd Messiah's name, Till earth's remotest na-tion, Has learn'd Mes-si-ah's name.

The Lamb for sin-ners slain, Re-deem-er, King, Cre-a-tor, In bliss returns to reign, Re-deem-er, King, Cre-a-tor, In bliss re-turns to reign.

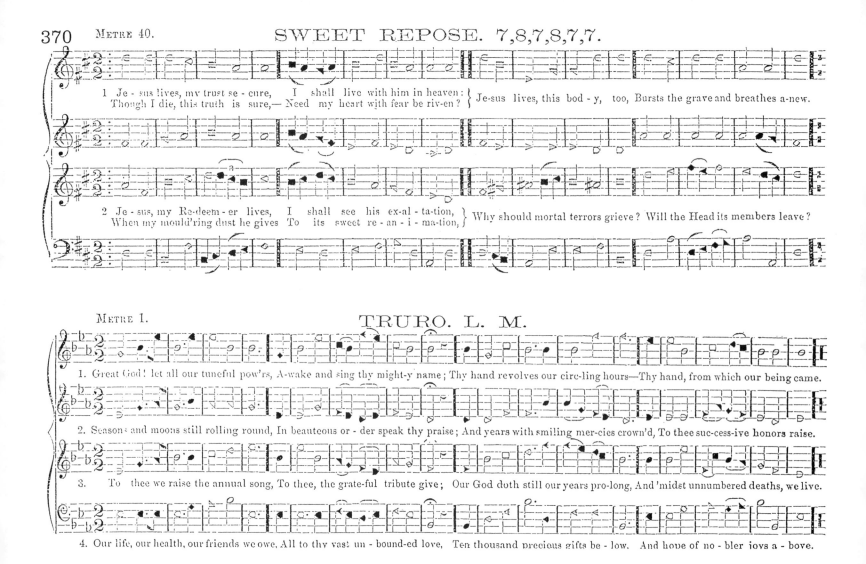

METRE 40.

SWEET REPOSE. 7,8,7,8,7,7.

1 Je - sus lives, my trust se - cure, I shall live with him in heaven: } Je-sus lives, this bod - y, too, Bursts the grave and breathes a-new.
Though I die, this truth is sure,— Need my heart with fear be riv-en?

2 Je - sus, my Re-deem - er lives, I shall see his ex-al - ta-tion, } Why should mortal terrors grieve? Will the Head its members leave?
When my mould'ring dust he gives To its sweet re - an - i - ma-tion,

METRE 1.

TRURO. L. M.

1. Great God! let all our tuneful pow'rs, A-wake and sing thy might-y name; Thy hand revolves our circ-ling hours—Thy hand, from which our being came.

2. Seasons and moons still rolling round, In beauteous or - der speak thy praise; And years with smiling mer-cies crown'd, To thee suc-cess-ive honors raise.

3. To thee we raise the annual song, To thee, the grate-ful tribute give; Our God doth still our years pro-long, And 'midst unnumbered deaths, we live.

4. Our life, our health, our friends we owe, All to thy vast un - bound-ed love, Ten thousand precious gifts be - low. And hope of no - bler joys a - bove.

GERMANY. 8,7,8,7,7,7,8,7.

1 Did Je - ho - vah but de - sign me For a mo - ment's dream of time?
To these perishing joys con - fine me, Barr'd from yon e - - ter - nal clime?

2 Soon this frame will be a plun - der, Crumbling for the worms be - low,
Must I, as it sinks a - sun - der, All to mould'ring dark - ness go?

3 Is not life a path allowed me,
Up to life beyond the sky?
Why has God with thought endowed me,
If the pow'rs of thought must die?
Happy were I made to be,
Like the brute from reason free;
Playful midst the sweets before me,
Thoughtless of the doom that's o'er me.

4 No,—reviler, scorn and error
Ne'er shall steal my trust away;
Rescued raised from mortal terror
I shall triumph o'er decay;
No; my soul is not a breath,
Not the passive prey of death;
From my Maker I enjoy it,
Storms of fate can ne'er destroy it.

Is this mu-sing mind a breath, Lost in all vic - to - rious death?—Frail as dust and va - por fly - - ing, When these mor-tal pow'rs are dy-ing.

All of con-scious life be - reft, At my ut - most lim - it left, Born to quench each warm sen - sa - tion Deep in drear an - ni - hi - la - tion.

372 METRE 41.

GLORIOUS TRIUMPH. 12,11,12,8.

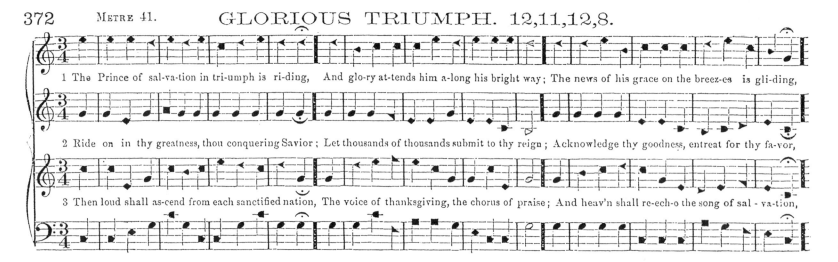

1 The Prince of sal-va-tion in tri-umph is ri-ding, And glo-ry at-tends him a-long his bright way; The news of his grace on the breez-es is gli-ding,

2 Ride on in thy greatness, thou conquering Savior; Let thousands of thousands submit to thy reign; Acknowledge thy goodness, entreat for thy fa-vor,

3 Then loud shall as-cend from each sanctified nation, The voice of thanksgiving, the chorus of praise; And heav'n shall re-ech-o the song of sal - va-tion,

And na-tions are own-ing his sway.

And fol-low thy glo-ri-ous train.

In rich and me-lo-di-ous lays.

METRE 12.

CONFLICT 8 lines 8's.

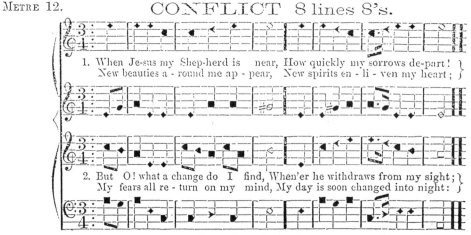

1. When Je-sus my Shep-herd is near, How quickly my sorrows de-part! New beauties a-round me ap-pear, New spirits en-li-ven my heart;

2. But O! what a change do I find, When'er he withdraws from my sight; My fears all re-turn on my mind, My day is soon changed into night:

3. Such changes as oft I pass through, Teach me my own weakness to know, I learn what my Shepherd can do— That all to his mer-cy I owe;

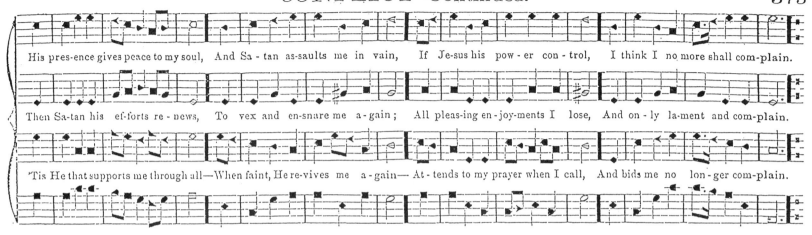

His pres-ence gives peace to my soul, And Sa-tan as-saults me in vain, If Je-sus his pow-er con-trol, I think I no more shall com-plain.

Then Sa-tan his ef-forts re-news, To vex and en-snare me a-gain; All pleas-ing en-joy-ments I lose, And on-ly la-ment and com-plain.

'Tis He that supports me through all—When faint, He re-vives me a-gain—At-tends to my prayer when I call, And bids me no lon-ger com-plain.

Metre 62.

ADORATION. 11,8,11,8.

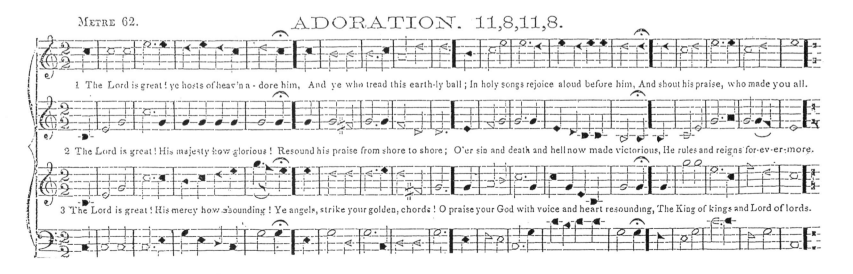

1 The Lord is great! ye hosts of heav'n a-dore him, And ye who tread this earth-ly ball; In holy songs rejoice aloud before him, And shout his praise, who made you all.

2 The Lord is great! His majesty how glorious! Resound his praise from shore to shore; O'er sin and death and hell now made victorious, He rules and reigns for-ev-er-more.

3 The Lord is great! His mercy how abounding! Ye angels, strike your golden, chords! O praise your God with voice and heart resounding, The King of kings and Lord of lords.

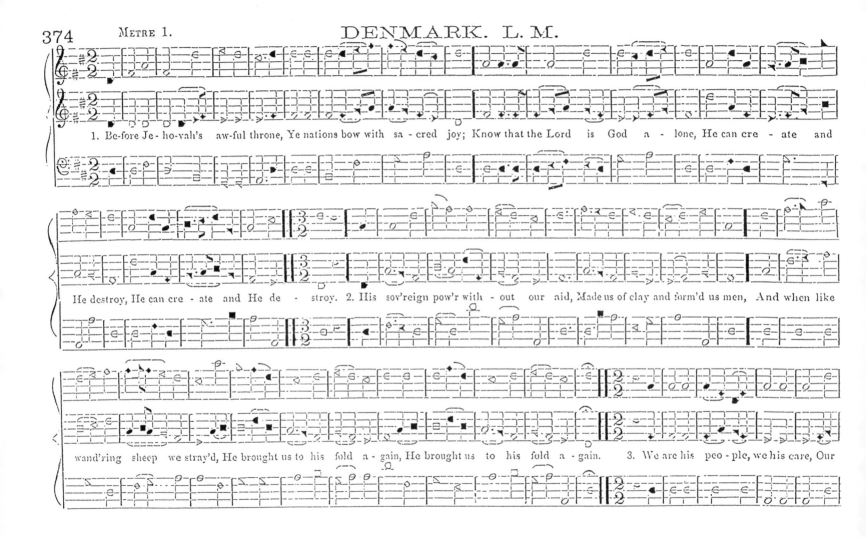

374 METRE 1.

DENMARK. L. M.

1. Be-fore Je-ho-vah's aw-ful throne, Ye nations bow with sa-cred joy; Know that the Lord is God a-lone, He can cre-ate and

He destroy, He can cre-ate and He de-stroy. 2. His sov'reign pow'r with-out our aid, Made us of clay and form'd us men, And when like

wand'ring sheep we stray'd, He brought us to his fold a-gain, He brought us to his fold a-gain. 3. We are his peo-ple, we his care, Our

souls and all our mor-tal frame: What lasting honors shall we rear, Al-might-y Ma-ker, to thy name? 4 We'll crowd thy gates with thank. - ful songs, High as the

heav'ns our voic - - - es raise, And earth, And earth with her ten thou-sand, thou-sand tongues, Shall fill thy courts with sounding praise, Shall fill thy courts with sound-ing

praise, Shall fill, Shall fill thy courts with sounding praise. 5 Wide, Wide as the world is thy command, Vast as e-ter - ni - ty, e - ter - ni-ty thy love, Firm as a rock thy

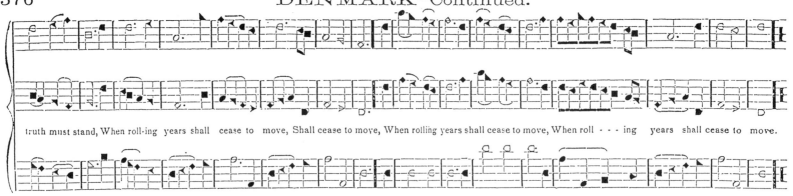

truth must stand, When roll-ing years shall cease to move, Shall cease to move, When rolling years shall cease to move, When roll - - - ing years shall cease to move.

METRE 64.

GETHSEMANE. 8,8,6,8,8.

1 Beyond where Cedron's waters flow, Behold the suff'ring Savior go To sad Geth-sem-a-ne; His countenance is all di-vine, Yet grief appears in eve-ry line.

2 He bows beneath the sins of men; He cries to God, and cries again, In sad Geth-sem-a-ne; He lifts his mournful eyes a-bove—" My Father, can this cup remove?"

3 With gentle res-ig-na-tion still, He yielded to his Father's will, In sad Geth-sem-a-ne; " Behold me here, thine on-ly Son And, Fa-ther, let thy will be done."

4 The Father heard; and angels there, Sustain'd the Son of God in pray'r, In sad Gethsemane; He drank the dreadful cup of pain—Then rose to life and joy a-gain.
5 When storms of sorrow round us sweep, And scenes of anguish make us weep, To sad Gethsemane We'll look, and see the Savior there, And humbly bow, like him, in pray'r.

1. God is a name my soul a-dores, Th' Almighty Three, th' Eternal one; Nature and grace with all their pow'rs Confess the In-fi-nite, Unknown.

2. Thy voice pro-duced the seas and spheres, Bid the waves roar and planets shine; But noth-ing like thyself appears, Thro' all the spacious works of thine.

3. A glance of thine runs thro' the globes, Rules the bright worlds, & moves their frame; Bright sheets of light compose thy robes; Thy guards are form'd of living flame.

4. How shall af-fright-ed mor-tals dare, To sing thy glo-ry or thy grace! Be-neath thy feet we lie so far, And see but shad-ows of thy face;

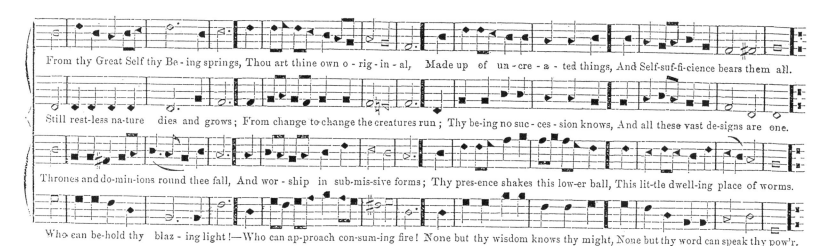

From thy Great Self thy Be-ing springs, Thou art thine own o-rig-in-al, Made up of un-cre-a-ted things, And Self-suf-fi-cience bears them all.

Still rest-less na-ture dies and grows; From change to change the creatures run; Thy be-ing no suc-ces-sion knows, And all these vast de-signs are one.

Thrones and do-min-ions round thee fall, And wor-ship in sub-mis-sive forms; Thy pres-ence shakes this low-er ball, This lit-tle dwell-ing place of worms.

Who can be-hold thy blaz-ing light!—Who can ap-proach con-sum-ing fire! None but thy wisdom knows thy might, None but thy word can speak thy pow'r.

PENITENT MOURNER. C. M.

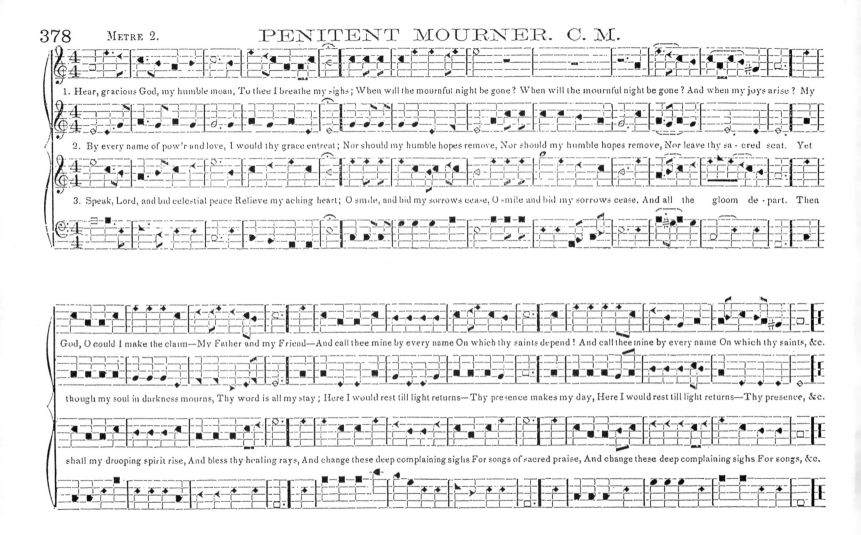

1. Hear, gracious God, my humble moan, To thee I breathe my sighs; When will the mournful night be gone? When will the mournful night be gone? And when my joys arise? My

2. By every name of pow'r and love, I would thy grace entreat; Nor should my humble hopes remove, Nor should my humble hopes remove, Nor leave thy sa - cred seat. Yet

3. Speak, Lord, and bid celestial peace Relieve my aching heart; O smile, and bid my sorrows cease, O smile and bid my sorrows cease, And all the gloom de - part. Then

God, O could I make the claim—My Father and my Friend—And call thee mine by every name On which thy saints depend! And call thee mine by every name On which thy saints, &c.

though my soul in darkness mourns, Thy word is all my stay; Here I would rest till light returns— Thy presence makes my day, Here I would rest till light returns—Thy presence, &c.

shall my drooping spirit rise, And bless thy healing rays, And change these deep complaining sighs For songs of sacred praise, And change these deep complaining sighs For songs, &c.

Metre 2. LAND OF REST. C. M.

1 O land of rest, for thee I sigh, When will the moment come, When I shall lay my
2 No tranquil joys on earth I know, No peaceful shelt'ring dome; This world's a wilder-
3 To Je-sus Christ I sought for rest, He bid me cease to roam, And fly for ref-uge

4 I would at once have quit the field
  Where foes with fury roam
  But O, my passport was not sealed,
  I could not yet go home.
  O this is not my home, etc.

5 When by affliction sharply tried,
  I view the gaping tomb;
  Altho' I dread death's chilling tide,
  Yet still I sigh for home.
  O this is not my home, etc.

6 Weary of wand'ring round and round,
  This vale of sin and gloom,
  I long to quit th' unhallow'd ground
  And dwell with Christ at home.
  O this is not my home, etc.

CHORUS

ar-mor by, And dwell in peace at home! O this is not my home—No, this is not my home; This world's a wilderness of woe,—This world is not my home.
ness of woe,—This world is not my home! O this is not my home—No, this is not my home; This world's a wilderness of woe,—This world is not my home.
to his breast, And he'd conduct me home! O this is not my home—No, this is not my home: This world's a wilderness of woe,—This world is not my home.

METRE 1.

RADNOR. L. M. HYMN 117.—RIPPON.

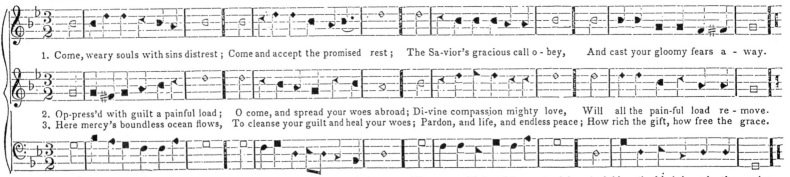

1. Come, weary souls with sins distrest ; Come and accept the promised rest ; The Sa-vior's gracious call o - bey, And cast your gloomy fears a - way.

2. Op-press'd with guilt a painful load ; O come, and spread your woes abroad ; Di-vine compassion mighty love, Will all the pain-ful load re - move.
3. Here mercy's boundless ocean flows, To cleanse your guilt and heal your woes ; Pardon, and life, and endless peace ; How rich the gift, how free the grace.

4. Lord, we accept, with thankful heart, The hope thy gracious words impart ; We come with trembling, yet rejoice, And bless the kind, in - vi - ting voice.
5. Dear Savior, let thy pow'rful love, Confirm our faith, our fears re - move! And sweetly influence every breast, And guide us to e - ter - nal rest.

METRE 1.

TALLIS' EVENING HYMN. L. M. HYMN 496.—RIPPON.

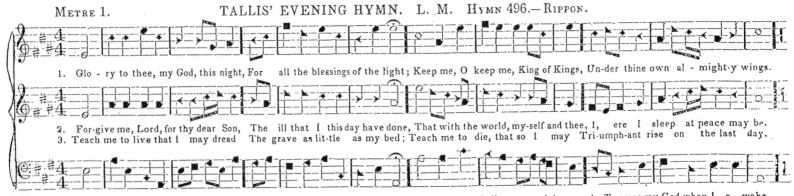

1. Glo - ry to thee, my God, this night, For all the blessings of the light ; Keep me, O keep me, King of Kings, Un-der thine own al - might-y wings.

2. For-give me, Lord, for thy dear Son, The ill that I this day have done, That with the world, my-self and thee, I, ere I sleep at peace may be.
3. Teach me to live that I may dread The grave as lit-tle as my bed ; Teach me to die, that so I may Tri-umph-ant rise on the last day.

4. O let my soul on thee re - pose, And may sweet sleep my eyelids close ; Sleep that shall me more vig'rous make To serve my God when I a - wake.
5. If in the night I sleep - less lie, My soul with heav'ly thoughts supply ; Let no ill dreams disturb my rest, No pow'rs of dark - ness me mo - lest.

PART III.

CONTAINING A SELECTION OF THREE-PART TUNES FROM THE FIRST AND SECOND EDITIONS OF
A COMPILATION OF GENUINE CHURCH MUSIC

Presented in a four-shape, four-syllable system. The natural major and minor scales are:

C major scale

Fa Sol La Fa Sol La Mi Fa

A minor scale

La Mi Fa Sol La Fa Sol La

INFINITE DELIGHT. C. M.   Hymn 555.—Dr. Rippon.

Metre 2.

Lord, 'tis an in-fi-nite de-light To see thy love-ly face; To dwell whole a-ges in thy sight, And feel thy vi-tal

rays.   And feel thy vi-tal rays.

2. This Gabriel knows, and sings thy name,
   With rapture on his tongue;
Moses, the saint, enjoys the same,
   And Heaven repeat the song.

3. While the bright nation sound thy praise,
   From each eternal hill;
Sweet odours exhaling grace
   The happy regions fill.

4. Thy love!—a sea without a shore,
   Spreads life and joy abroad,
Oh, 'tis a heaven worth dying for,
   To see a smiling God!

5. Sweet was the journey to the sky,
   The wondrous prophet tried;
"Climb up the mount" says God "and die,"
   The prophet climbed—and died.

6. Softly his fainting head he lay
   Upon his Maker's breast;
His Maker kiss'd his soul away,
   And laid his flesh to rest.

7. Show me thy face, and I'll away
   From all inferior things;
Speak. Lord, and here I quit my clay,
   And stretch my airy wings.

MOUNT EPHRAIM. S. M. Hymn 224.—Dr. Rippon.

Your harps, ye trembling saints,   Down from the willows take;   Loud to the praise of Christ our Lord,   Bid ev'ry string awake.

Though in a foreign land,   His grace shall to the end   The time of love will come,   Tarry his leisure, then,
We are not far from home;   Stronger and brighter shine;   When we shall clearly see,   Wait the appointed hour;
And nearer to our house above   Nor present things, nor things to come,   Not only that he shed his blood,   Wait till the Bridegroom of your souls
We ev'ry moment come.   Shall quench the spark divine.   But each shall say "for me."   Reveals his love with pow'r.

ST. BRIDE'S. S. M. Hymn 176.—Village Hymns.

Bless'd comforter divine,   Whose rays of heavenly love   Amid our gloom and darkness shine,   And point our souls above:

Thou, who with "still small voice,"   Thou, whose inspiring breath   Thou, who dost fill the heart
Dost stop the sinner's way,   Can make the cloud of care,   With love to all our race—
And bid the mourning saint rejoice,   And e'en the gloomy vale of death   Bless'd comforter! to us impart
Though earthly joys decay:—   A smile of glory wear:—   The blessings of thy grace.

Metre 2

BURSTALL. C. M. Hymn 245, Part I.—M. H.

383

Oh for a closer walk with God,   A calm and heav'nly frame;   A light to shine upon the road   That leads me to the Lamb.

Where is the blessedness I knew
When first I saw the Lord?
Where is the soul-refreshing view
Of Jesus and his word?

What peaceful hours I once enjoyed,
How sweet their memory still!
But they have left an aching void
The world can never fill.

Return, O holy dove, return!
Sweet messenger of rest!
I hate the sins that made thee mourn,
And drove thee from my breast.

The dearest idol I have known,
Whate'er that idol be,
Help me to tear it from thy throne,
And worship only thee.

Metre 2.

MILAN. C. M. Hymn 2.—Assem. Coll.

Awake, awake the sacred song   To our incarnate Lord;   Let ev'ry heart and ev'ry tongue   Adore th' eternal word.

That awful word, that sov'reign pow'r,
By whom the worlds were made,
(O happy morn! illustrious hour!)
Was once in flesh arrayed.

Then shone Almighty pow'r and love,
In all their glorious forms,
When Jesus left his throne above
To dwell with sinful worms.

To dwell with misery below
The Saviour left the skies,
And sunk to wretchedness and wo,
That worthless man might rise.

Adoring angels tuned their songs
To hail the joyful day;
With rapture, then, let mortal tongues
Their grateful worship pay.

Metre 1.   TRIUMPH. L. M.   Hymn 16, Book II.—Dr. Watts.

Lord, what a heaven of saving grace   Shines through the beauties of thy face,   And lights our passions to a flame—   Lord,

When I can say, my God is mine,	While such a scene of sacred joys	Well, we shall quickly pass the night,	There shall we drink full draughts of bliss,
When I can feel thy glories shine,	Our raptur'd eyes and souls employs,	To the fair coasts of perfect light:	And pluck new life from heav'nly trees;
I tread the world beneath my feet,	Here we could sit and gaze away	Then shall our joyful senses rove	Yet now and then, dear Lord, bestow
And all that earth calls good or great.	A long and everlasting day.	O'er the dear objects of our love.	A drop of heav'n on worms below.

Metre 4.   RAPTURE. 8's & 7's.   Hymn 76, Part I.—M. H.

how   we   love   thy   charm - ing   name.

Love divine, all loves excelling,   Joy of heav'n, to earth come down,
Fix on us thy humble dwelling;   All thy faithful mercies crown:

Send comforts down from thy right hand,	Breathe, O breathe thy loving spirit	Take away our bent of sinning
While we pass through this barren land,	Into every troubled breast!	Alpha and Omega be,
And in thy temple let us see	Let us all in thee inherit,	End of faith as its beginning,
A glimpse of love, a glimpse of thee.	Let us find that second rest.	Set our hearts at liberty.

Jesus, thou art all compassion,   Pure, unbounded love thou art;   Visit us with thy salvation,   Enter ev'ry trembling heart.

Come, Almighty to deliver,
Let us all thy grace receive,
Suddenly return, and never,
Never more thy temples leave:

Thee we would be always blessing,
Serve thee as thy hosts above,
Pray, and praise thee without ceasing,
Glory in thy perfect love.

Finish then thy new creation,
Pure and spotless let us be;
Let us see thy great salvation,
Perfectly restor'd in thee!

Chang'd from glory into glory,
Till in heaven we take our place,
Till we cast our crowns before thee,
Lost in wonder, love, and praise!

BATH. L. M.   Hymn 10, Book III.—DR. WATTS.

Metre 1.

Nature with open volume stands,   To spread her Maker's praise abroad,   And ev'ry labor of his hands   Shows something worthy of a God.

But in the grace that rescu'd man,
His brightest form of glory shines;
Here on the cross 'tis fairest drawn
In precious blood and crimson lines.

Here his whole name appears complete,
Nor wit can guess, nor reason prove,
Which of the letters best is writ,
The power, the wisdom, or the love.

Here I hold his inmost heart,
Where grace and vengeance strangely join,
Piercing his Son with sharpest smart,
To make the purchas'd pleasures mine:

O! the sweet wonders of that cross,
Where God the Saviour lov'd and died!
Her noblest life my spirit draws
From his dear wounds and bleeding side.

386

Metre 3.

HADDAM. S. M.   Psalm 61.—Dr. Watts.

When overwhelm'd with grief,   My heart within me dies;   Helpless, and far from all relief,   To heav'n I lift mine eyes.

Oh lead me to the rock
That's high above my head,
And make the covert of thy wings
My shelter and my shade.

Within thy presence, Lord,
For ever I'll abide;
Thou art the tower of my defence,
The refuge where I hide.

Thou givest me the lot
Of those that fear thy name;
If endless life be their reward,
I shall possess the same.

Metre 1.

FARMINGTON. L. M.   Hymn 166.—Dr. Rippon.

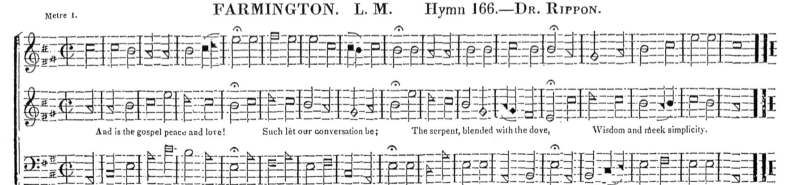

And is the gospel peace and love!   Such let our conversation be;   The serpent, blended with the dove,   Wisdom and meek simplicity.

Whene'er the angry passions rise,
And tempt our thoughts or tongues to strife,
To Jesus let us lift our eyes,
Bright pattern of the christian life!

O how benevolent and kind;
How mild! how ready to forgive!
Be this the temper of our mind,
And these the rules by which we live.

To do his heavenly Father's will,
Was his employment and delight;
Humility and holy zeal
Shone thro' his life, divinely bright!

Dispensing good where'er he came,
The labors of his life were love;
O, if we love the Saviour's name,
Let his divine example move.

Blow ye the trumpets, blow   The gladly solemn sound;   Let all the nations know,   Let all the nations know,   To earth's remotest bound,   To earth's remotest bound,   The year of Jubilee is come,   Return, ye ransom'd sinners, home;   The year of ju-bi-lee is come,   Re-turn, ye ran-som'd sinners, home.

Jesus, our great High Priest,
  Hath full atonement made:
Ye weary spirits, rest,
  Ye mournful souls, be glad,
The year of Jubilee is come;
Return, ye ransom'd sinners, home.

Extol the Lamb of God,
  The all-atoning Lamb;
Redemption in his blood
  Throughout the world proclaim:
The year of Jubilee is come;
Return, ye ransom'd sinners, home.

Ye slaves of sin and hell,
  Your liberty receive,
And safe in Jesus dwell,
  And blest in Jesus live:
The year of Jubilee is come;
Return, ye ransom'd sinners, home.

Ye who have sold for nought
  Your heritage above,
Shall have it back unbought,
  The gift of Jesus's love:
The year of Jubilee is come;
Return, ye ransom'd sinners, home.

Metre 2. **BROOMSGROVE. C. M.** Psalm 71, Part II.—Dr. Watts.

My Saviour, my Almighty friend,   When I begin thy praise,   Where will the growing numbers end, The numbers of thy grace?   The numbers of thy grace?

Thou art my everlasting trust,	My feet shall travel all the length	When I am fill'd with sore distress,	How will my lips rejoice to tell
Thy goodness I adore;	Of the celestial road,	For some surprising sin,	The vict'ries of my King!
And since I knew thy graces first,	And march, with courage in thy strength	I'll plead thy perfect righteousness,	My soul redeem'd from sin and hell,
I speak thy glories more.	To see my Father, God.	And mention none but thine.	Shall thy salvation sing.

Metre 1. **ORRAMOOR. L. M.** Hymn 166.—Assem. Coll.

My God, permit me not to be   A stranger to myself and thee;   Amidst a thousand thoughts I rove,   Forgetful of my highest love.

Why should my passions mix with earth,	Call me away from flesh and sense;	Be earth, with all her scenes, withdrawn;
And thus debase my heavenly birth?	One sovereign word can draw me thence:	Let noise and vanity be gone;
Why should I cleave to things below,	I would obey the voice divine,	In secret silence of the mind,
And let my God, my Saviour go!	And all inferior joys resign.	My heaven, and there my God, I find:

Oh thou that hear'st when sinners cry, Though all my crimes before thee lie, Be - hold them not with an - gry look, But blot their mem'ry

from   thy   book.

2 Create my nature pure within,
  And form my soul averse to sin:
  Let thy good spirit ne'er depart,
  Nor hide thy presence from my heart.

3 I cannot live without thy light,
  Cast out and banish'd from thy sight;
  Thine holy joys, my God, restore,
  And guard me that I fall no more.

4 Though I have griev'd thy spirit, Lord,
  Thy help and comfort still afford,
  And let a wretch come near thy throne,
  To plead the merits of thy Son.

5 A broken heart, my God, my king,
  Is all the sacrifice I bring;
  The God of grace will ne'er despise
  A broken heart for sacrifice

390 METRE 7. **KERSHAW.** 8, 7, 8, 7, 4, 7. Hymn 2, Part I.—M. H.

Come, ye sinners, poor and needy,
Jesus ready stands to save you,
Weak and wounded, sick and sore,
Full of pity, love and pow'r:
He is a-ble, He is a-ble, He is a-ble,

Now, ye needy, come and welcome,
God's free bounty glorify;
True belief and true repentance,
Every grace that brings you nigh,
Without money, Come to Jesus Christ and buy.

Let not conscience make you linger,
Nor of fitness fondly dream:
All the fitness he requireth
Is to feel the need of him:
This he gives you, 'Tis the Spirit's glimm'ring beam.

Come, ye weary, heavy-laden,
Bruis'd and mangled by the fall,
If you tarry till you're better
You will never come at all;
Not the righteous, Sinners Jesus came to call.

METRE 8. **BROADMEAD.** 6 lines, 8's. Hymn 70, Part I.—M. H.

He is will-ing, doubt no more.

Agonizing in the garden,
Lo! your Maker prostrate lies!
On the bloody tree behold him!
Hear him cry before he dies,
"It is finish'd!" Sinners, will not this suffice?

Thou hidden love of God, whose height, Whose depth, unfathom'd, no man knows,

Thy secret voice invites me still
The sweetness of thy yoke to prove;
And fain I would, but though my will
Seems fix'd, yet wide my passions rove:
Yet hindrances strew all the way—
I aim at thee, yet from thee stray.

I see from far thy beauteous light,   I only sigh for thy repose: My heart is pain'd, nor can it be   At rest till it finds rest in thee.

'Tis mercy all, that thou hast brought
  My mind to seek her peace in thee;
Yet while I seek and find thee not,
  No peace my wand'ring soul shall see:
O, when shall all my wand'rings end,
And all my steps to theeward tend?

Is there a thing beneath the sun
  That strives with thee my heart to share?
Ah! tear it thence, and reign alone,
  The Lord of every motion there;
Then shall my heart from earth be free,
When it has found repose in thee.

Each moment draw from earth away
  · My heart, that lowly waits thy call;
Speak to my inmost soul, and say;
  " I am thy love, thy God, thy all!"
To feel thy power, to hear thy voice,
To taste thy love, be all my choice.

VIRGINIA. C. M.   Psalm 5.—Dr. Watts.

Metre 2.

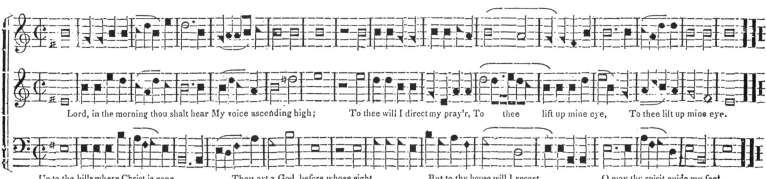

Lord, in the morning thou shalt hear My voice ascending high;   To thee will I direct my pray'r, To   thee   lift up mine eye,   To thee lift up mine eye.

Up to the hills where Christ is gone
To plead for all his saints,
Presenting at his Father's throne
Our songs and our complaints.

Thou art a God, before whose sight
The wicked shall not stand:
Sinners shall ne'er be thy delight,
Nor dwell at thy right hand.

But to thy house will I resort,
To taste thy mercies there;
I will frequent thy holy court,
And worship in thy fear.

O may thy spirit guide my feet
In ways of righteousness,
Make every path of duty straight.
And plain before my face.

Metre 3.

STAFFORD. S. M. Hymn 104, Book II.—Dr. Watts.

Raise your triumphant songs   To an immortal tune;   Let the wide earth resound,   Let the wide earth resound the deeds   Ce-

Sing how eternal love
Its chief beloved chose,
And bid him raise our wretched race
From their abyss of woes.

His hand no thunder bears,
Nor terror clothes his brow,
No bolts to drive our guilty souls
To fiercer flames below.

'Twas mercy fill'd the throne,
And wrath stood silent by,
When Christ was sent with pardon down
To rebels doom'd to die.

Now sinners dry your tears,
Let hopeless sorrow cease;
Bow to the sceptre of his love,
And take the offer'd peace.

CONVERSION. 4 lines, 11's. Hymn 15—Dr. Rip'n.

Metre 11.

les - - tial grace hath done.

Lord, we obey thy call;
We lay an humble claim
To the salvation thou hast brought,
And love and praise thy name.

Thy mercy, my God, is the theme of my song,   The

Without thy sweet mercy I could not live here—
Sin soon would reduce me to utter despair;
But through thy free goodness my spirits revive,
And he that first made me still keeps me alive.

Thy mercy is more than a match for my heart,
Which wonders to feel its own hardness depart:
Dissolved by thy goodness, I fall to the ground,
And weep to the praise of the mercy I found.

joy of my heart, and the boast of my tongue; Thy free grace alone, from the first to the last, Hath won my affections, and bound my soul fast.

The door of thy mercy stands open all day,
To the poor and needy, who knock by the way;
No sinner shall ever be empty sent back,
Who comes seeking mercy for Jesus's sake.

Thy mercy in Jesus exempts me from hell—
Its glories I'll sing, and its wonders I'll tell:
'Twas Jesus, my friend, when he hung on the tree.
Who opened the channel of mercy for me.

Great Father of mercies, thy goodness I own,
And covenant love of thy crucified Son;
All praise to the spirit, whose whisper divine
Seals mercy and pardon and righteousness mine.

METRE 5.   FRANKFORT.   4 lines, 7's.   Hymn 354.—DR. RIPPON.

Lord, I cannot let thee go Till a blessing thou bestow; Do not turn away thy face— Mine's an urgent, pressing case.

Dost thou ask me who I am?
Ah, my Lord, thou know'st my name;
Yet the question gives a plea
To support my suit with thee.

Thou didst once a wretch behold,
In rebellion blindly bold,
Scorn thy grace, thy pow'r defy—
That poor rebel, Lord, was I.

Once a sinner, near despair,
Sought thy mercy-seat by pray'r;
Mercy heard, and set him free—
Lord, that mercy came to me.

Many days have pass'd since then,
Many changes I have seen,
Yet have been upheld till now—
Who could hold me up but thou?

Metre 1.   SUFFOLK. L. M.   Hymn 484.—Assem. Coll.

Where is my God? does he retire Beyond the reach of hum - ble sighs? Are these weak breath - ings of de - sire Too

No, Lord, my breathings of desire,
  My weak petitions, if sincere,
Are not forbidden to aspire,
  But reach to thy all-gracious ear.

Look up, my soul, with cheerful eye,
  See where the great Redeemer stands—
The glorious Advocate on high,
  With precious incense in his hands.

He smiles on ev'ry humble groan,
  He recommends each broken pray'r;
Recline thy hope on him alone,
  Whose pow'r and love forbid despair.

Metre 3.   MATTHIAS. S. M.   Hymn 345.—Dr. Rippon.

lan - guid to as - cend the skies?

Teach my weak heart, O gracious Lord,
  With stronger faith to call thee mine;
Bid me pronounce the blissful word
  My Father, God, with joy divine:

Almighty Maker, God!   How wondrous is thy name!

Nature in every dress
  Her humble homage pays,
And finds a thousand ways t' express
  Thine undissembled praise.

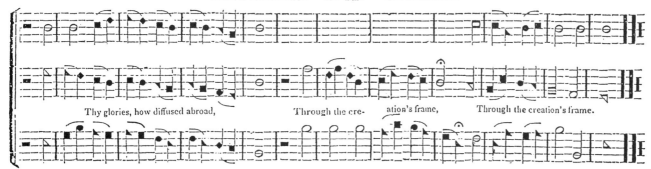

Thy glories, how diffused abroad, Through the cre- ation's frame, Through the creation's frame.

My soul would rise and sing
  To her Creator too,
Fain would my tongue adore my King,
  And pay the worship due.

But pride, that busy sin,
  Spoils all that I perform,
Curs'd pride, that creeps securely in,
  And swells a haughty worm.

Create my soul anew,
  Else all my worship's vain;
This wretched heart will ne'er be true,
  Until 'tis form'd again.

BRUSSELS. L. M.   Hymn 574.—DR. RIPPON.

Metre 1.

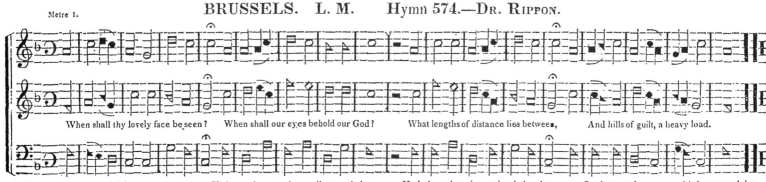

When shall thy lovely face be seen? When shall our eyes behold our God? What lengths of distance lies between, And hills of guilt, a heavy load.

Our months are ages of delay,
  And slowly every moment wears:
Fly, winged time, and roll away
  These tedious rounds of sluggish years.

Ye heavenly gates, loose all your chains,
  Let the eternal pillars bow:
Blest Saviour, cleave the starry plains,
  And make the chrystal mountains flow.

Hark, how thy saints unite their cries,
  And pray and wait the general doom:
Come, thou, the soul of all our joys,
  Thou, the desire of nations, come.

Our heart-strings groan with deep complaint,
  Our flesh lies panting, Lord, for thee;
And ev'ry limb and ev'ry joint
  Stretches for immortality.

Metre 61. INVOCATION. 7, 6, 7, 7, 6.

Draw nigh to us, Jehovah, Draw nigh to us, Jehovah, Draw nigh to us, Jehovah. In our social meeting; In this propitious hour. O may we feel thy

Draw nigh to us, bless'd Jesus,
In our social meeting;
O may we feel thy favor,
Thou ever blessed Saviour!
In this social meeting.

Draw nigh to us, bless'd Spirit,
In our social meeting;
Convince and renovate us,
And new in Christ create us,
In this social meeting.

ANXIETY. L. M. Hymn 71, Book I.—Dr. Watts.

Metre 1.

power, O may we feel thy power, In this social meeting.

Often I seek my Lord by night,

Jesus, my love, my soul's delight!   With warm desires and restless thought,   I seek him oft, but find him not.

Then I arise, and search the street,
Till I my Lord, my Saviour meet:
I ask the watchman of the night,
Where did you see my soul's delight?

Sometimes I find him in my way,
Directed by a heavenly ray;
I leap for joy to see his face,
And hold him fast in mine embrace.

I bring him to my mother's home,
Nor does my Lord refuse to come
To Zion's sacred chambers, where
My soul first drew the vital air.

He gives me there his bleeding heart,
Pierc'd for my sake with deadly smart,
I give my soul to him, and there
Our loves their mutual tokens share.

KENT. L. M.   Hymn 316.—Village Hymns.

Metre 1.

Come, gracious Spirit, heav'nly Dove,   With light and comfort from above;   Be thou our guardian, thou our guide, O'er ev'ry thought and step preside.

Conduct us safe, conduct us far
From ev'ry sin and hurtful snare;
Lead to thy word that rules must give,
And teach us lessons how to live.

The light of truth to us display,
And make us know and choose thy way;
Plant holy fear in ev'ry heart,
That we from God may ne'er depart.

Lead us to holiness, the road
That we must take to dwell with God;
Lead us to Christ, the living way,
Nor let us from his pastures stray.

Lead us to God, our final rest,
In his enjoyment to be bless'd;
Lead us to heav'n, the seat of bliss,
Where pleasure in perfection is.

METRE 18.   BERMONDSEY.   6, 6, 4, 6, 6, 6, 4.   HYMN 387.—DR. RIPPON.

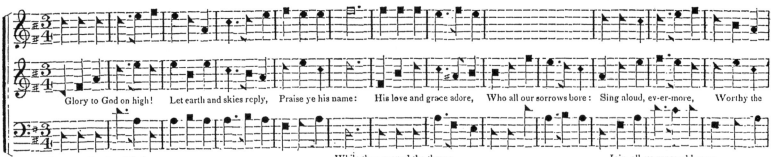

Glory to God on high!   Let earth and skies reply,   Praise ye his name: His love and grace adore,   Who all our sorrows bore: Sing aloud, ev-er-more,   Worthy the

Jesus, our Lord and God,
Bore sin's tremendous load,
    Praise ye his name:
Tell what his arm hath done,
What spoils from death he won—
Sing his great name alone!
    Worthy the Lamb.

While they around the throne
Cheerfully join in one,
    Praising his name:
Those who have felt his blood
Sealing their peace with God,
Sound his dear fame abroad,
    Worthy the Lamb.

Join, all ye ransom'd race,
Our holy Lord to bless!
    Praise ye his name:
In him we will rejoice,
And make a joyful noise,
Shouting with heart and voice,
    Worthy the Lamb.

Lamb!   Worthy the Lamb!   Worthy the Lamb!   Sing aloud ev - er-more, Worthy the Lamb!

What tho' we change our place,
Yet we shall never cease
    Praising his name:
To him our songs we bring,
Hail him our gracious king,
And without ceasing, sing
    Worthy the Lamb.

Then let the hosts above,
In realms of endless love,
    Praise his dear name:
To him ascribed be
Honor and majesty,
Thro' all eternity!
    Worthy the Lamb.

INDEX OF TUNES

INDEX OF TUNES

INDEX OF TUNES

METRICAL INDEX

METRICAL INDEX

METRICAL INDEX

INDEX OF FIRST LINES

INDEX OF FIRST LINES

INDEX OF FIRST LINES